BEING
WRONG

ADVENTURES IN
THE MARGIN OF ERROR

KATHRYN SCHULZ

An Imprint of HarperCollinsPublishers

Designed by Suet Yee Chong

Library of Congress Cataloging-in-Publication Data has been applied for.

ISBN 978-0-06-117604-3

10   11   12   13   14   ID/RRD   10   9   8   7   6   5   4

For my family,
given and chosen

And for Michael and Amanda,
at whose expense
I wrote about what I knew

CONTENTS

PART IV EMBRACING ERROR

Perhaps the history of the errors of mankind, all things considered, is more valuable and interesting than that of their discoveries. Truth is uniform and narrow; it constantly exists, and does not seem to require so much an active energy, as a passive aptitude of soul in order to encounter it. But error is endlessly diversified; it has no reality, but is the pure and simple creation of the mind that invents it. In this field, the soul has room enough to expand herself, to display all her boundless faculties, and all her beautiful and interesting extravagancies and absurdities.

—*Benjamin Franklin, Report of Dr. Benjamin Franklin, and Other Commissioners, Charged by the King of France, with the Examination of the Animal Magnetism, as Now Practiced in Paris (1784)*

MAN: You said pound cake.

WOMAN: I didn't say pound cake, I said crumb cake.

MAN: You said pound cake.

WOMAN: Don't tell me what I said.

MAN: You said pound cake.

WOMAN: I said crumb cake.

MAN: I actually saw the crumb cake but I didn't get it because you said pound cake.

WOMAN: I said crumb cake.

MAN: Well, I heard pound cake.

WOMAN: Then you obviously weren't listening. Crumb cake doesn't even sound like pound cake.

MAN: Well, maybe you accidentally said pound cake.

WOMAN: I said crumb cake.

—*overheard in Grand Central Station, November 13, 2008*

PART I

THE IDEA OF ERROR

1.

Wrongology

It infuriates me to be wrong when I know I'm right.
—Molière

Why is it so fun to be right? As pleasures go, it is, after all, a second-order one at best. Unlike many of life's other delights—chocolate, surfing, kissing—it does not enjoy any mainline access to our biochemistry: to our appetites, our adrenal glands, our limbic systems, our swoony hearts. And yet, the thrill of being right is undeniable, universal, and (perhaps most oddly) almost entirely undiscriminating. We can't enjoy kissing just anyone, but we can relish being right about almost anything. The stakes don't seem to matter much; it's more important to bet on the right foreign policy than the right racehorse, but we are perfectly capable of gloating over either one. Nor does subject matter; we can be equally pleased about correctly identifying an orange-crowned warbler or the sexual orientation of our coworker. Stranger still, we can enjoy being right even about disagreeable things: the downturn in the stock market, say, or the demise of a friend's relationship, or the fact that, at our spouse's insistence, we just spent fifteen minutes schlepping our suitcase in exactly the opposite direction from our hotel.

Like most pleasurable experiences, rightness is not ours to enjoy all the time. Sometimes we are the one who loses the bet (or the hotel). And sometimes, too, we are plagued by doubt about the correct answer or course of action—an anxiety that, itself, reflects the urgency of our desire to be right. Still, on the whole, our indiscriminate enjoyment of being right is matched by an almost equally indiscriminate feeling that we *are* right. Occasionally, this feeling spills into the foreground, as when we argue or evangelize, make predictions or place bets. Most often, though, it is just psychological backdrop. A whole lot of us go through life assuming that we are basically right, basically all the time, about basically everything: about our political and intellectual convictions, our religious and moral beliefs, our assessment of other people, our memories, our grasp of facts. As absurd as it sounds when we stop to think about it, our steady state seems to be one of unconsciously assuming that we are very close to omniscient.

To be fair, this serene faith in our own rightness is often warranted. Most of us navigate day-to-day life fairly well, after all, which suggests that we are routinely right about a great many things. And sometimes we are not just routinely right but spectacularly right: right about the existence of atoms (postulated by ancient thinkers thousands of years before the emergence of modern chemistry); right about the healing properties of aspirin (recognized since at least 3000 BC); right to track down that woman who smiled at you in the café (now your wife of twenty years). Taken together, these moments of rightness represent both the high-water marks of human endeavor and the source of countless small joys. They affirm our sense of being smart, competent, trustworthy, and in tune with our environment. More important, they keep us alive. Individually and collectively, our very existence depends on our ability to reach accurate conclusions about the world around us. In short, the experience of being right is imperative for our survival, gratifying for our ego, and, overall, one of life's cheapest and keenest satisfactions.

This book is about the opposite of all that. It is about being wrong: about how we as a culture think about error, and how we as individuals cope when our convictions collapse out from under us. If we relish being right and regard it as our natural state, you can imagine how we feel about being wrong. For one thing, we tend to view it as rare and bizarre—an inexplicable aberration in the normal order of things. For another, it leaves us feeling idiotic and ashamed. Like the term paper returned to us covered in red ink, being wrong makes us cringe and slouch down in our seat; it makes our heart sink and our dander rise. At best we regard it as a nuisance, at worst a nightmare, but in either case—and quite unlike the gleeful little rush of being right—we experience our errors as deflating and embarrassing.

And that's just for starters. In our collective imagination, error is associated not just with shame and stupidity but also with ignorance, indolence, psychopathology, and moral degeneracy. This set of associations was nicely summed up by the Italian cognitive scientist Massimo Piattelli-Palmarini, who noted that we err because of (among other things) "inattention, distraction, lack of interest, poor preparation, genuine stupidity, timidity, braggadocio, emotional imbalance, . . . ideological, racial, social or chauvinistic prejudices, as well as aggressive or prevaricatory instincts." In this rather despairing view—and it is the common one—our errors are evidence of our gravest social, intellectual, and moral failings.

Of all the things we are wrong about, this idea of error might well top the list. It is our meta-mistake: we are wrong about what it means to be wrong. Far from being a sign of intellectual inferiority, the capacity to err is crucial to human cognition. Far from being a moral flaw, it is inextricable from some of our most humane and honorable qualities: empathy, optimism, imagination, conviction, and courage. And far from being a mark of indifference or intolerance, wrongness is a vital part of how we learn and change. Thanks to error, we can revise our understanding of ourselves and amend our ideas about the world.

Given this centrality to our intellectual and emotional development, error shouldn't be an embarrassment, and cannot be an aberration. On the contrary. As Benjamin Franklin observed in the quote that heads this book, wrongness is a window into normal human nature—into our imaginative minds, our boundless faculties, our extravagant souls. This book is staked on the soundness of that observation: that however disorienting, difficult, or humbling our mistakes might be, it is ultimately wrongness, not rightness, that can teach us who we are.

This idea is not new. Paradoxically, we live in a culture that simultaneously despises error and insists that it is central to our lives. We acknowledge that centrality in the very way we talk about ourselves—which is why, when we make mistakes, we shrug and say that we are human. As bats are batty and slugs are sluggish, our own species is synonymous with screwing up. This built-in propensity to err is also recognized within virtually every religious, philosophical, and scientific account of personhood. Nor are errors, in these accounts, just surface features or passing oddities, like hiccups or fingernails or déjà vu. Twelve hundred years before René Descartes penned his famous "I think, therefore I am," the philosopher and theologian (and eventual saint) Augustine wrote *"fallor ergo sum"*: I err, therefore I am. In this formulation, the capacity to get things wrong is not only part of being alive, but in some sense proof of it. For Augustine as for Franklin, being wrong is not just what we do. In some deep sense, it is who we are.

And yet, if fallibility is built into our very name and nature, it is in much the same way the puppet is built into the jack-in-the-box: in theory wholly predictable, in practice always a jarring surprise. In this respect, fallibility is something like mortality, another trait that is implicit in the word "human." As with dying, we recognize erring as something that happens to everyone, without feeling that it is either plausible or desirable that it will happen to us. Accordingly, when mistakes happen anyway, we typically respond as if they hadn't, or as if they shouldn't have: we deny them, wax defensive about them, ignore them, downplay them, or blame them on somebody else.

Our reluctance to admit that we are wrong is not just an individual failing. With the exception of those error-prevention initiatives employed in high-risk fields like aviation and medicine, our culture has developed remarkably few tools for addressing our propensity to err. If you commit a moral transgression, you can turn to at least a handful of established options to help you cope with it. Virtually every religious tradition includes a ritual for penitence and purification, along the lines of confession in Catholicism and Yom Kippur in Judaism. Twelve-step programs advise their participants to admit "to God, to ourselves, and to another human being the exact nature of our wrongs." Even the criminal justice system, although far from reform-minded these days, has one foot rooted in a tradition of repentance and transformation. By contrast, if you commit an error—whether a minor one, such as realizing halfway through an argument that you are mistaken, or a major one, such as realizing halfway through a lifetime that you were wrong about your faith, your politics, yourself, your loved one, or your life's work—you will not find any obvious, ready-to-hand resources to help you deal with it.

How could you? As a culture, we haven't even mastered the basic skill of saying "I was wrong." This is a startling deficiency, given the simplicity of the phrase, the ubiquity of error, and the tremendous public service that acknowledging it can provide. Instead, what we have mastered are two alternatives to admitting our mistakes that serve to highlight exactly how bad we are at doing so. The first involves a small but strategic addendum: "I was wrong, *but* . . ."—a blank we then fill in with wonderfully imaginative explanations for why we weren't so wrong after all. (More on this in Part Three.) The second (infamously deployed by, among others, Richard Nixon regarding Watergate and Ronald Reagan regarding the Iran-Contra affair) is even more telling: we say, "mistakes were made." As that evergreen locution so concisely demonstrates, all we really know how to do with our errors is *not* acknowledge them as our own.*

---

* Western culture has another mechanism for admitting mistakes, but its extreme obscurity only underscores the point that such devices are woefully rare. In poetry, there is an entire form, the palinode, dedicated to retracting the sentiments of an earlier poem. (In Greek, *palin* means "again," and *ōdē* means "song," making a palinode linguistically identical to a recantation: to "recant" means to sing again. We invoke this same idea when we say that someone who has shifted positions on an issue is "singing a different tune.") The most famous palinode—which isn't saying much—was written by the seventh-century poet Stesichorus, and serves to retract his earlier claim that Helen

By contrast, we positively excel at acknowledging other people's errors. In fact, if it is sweet to be right, then—let's not deny it—it is downright savory to point out that someone else is wrong. As any food scientist can tell you, this combination of savory and sweet is the most addictive of flavors: we can never really get enough of reveling in other people's mistakes. Witness, for instance, the difficulty with which even the well-mannered among us stifle the urge to say "I told you so." The brilliance of this phrase (or its odiousness, depending on whether you get to say it or must endure hearing it) derives from its admirably compact way of making the point that not only was I right, I was also right about being right. In the instant of uttering it, I become right squared, maybe even right factorial, logarithmically right—at any rate, really, extremely right, and really, extremely delighted about it. It is possible to refrain from this sort of gloating (and consistently choosing to do so might be the final milestone of maturity), but the feeling itself, that triumphant *ha!*, can seldom be fully banished.

Of course, parading our own brilliance and exulting in other people's errors is not very nice. For that matter, even *wanting* to parade our own brilliance and exult in other people's errors is not very nice, although it is certainly very human. This is where our relationship to wrongness begins to show its stakes. Of all the strife in the world—strife of every imaginable variety, from conflict over crumb cake to conflict in the Middle East—a staggering amount of it arises from the clash of mutually incompatible, entirely unshakable feelings of rightness. Granted, we find plenty of other reasons to fight with one another as well, ranging from serious and painful breaches in trust to resource scarcity to the fact that we haven't had our coffee yet. Still, an impressive number of disputes amount to a tug-of-war over who possesses the truth: we fight over the right to be right. Likewise, it is surprisingly difficult to get angry unless you are either convinced that you are correct, or humiliated and defensive about being wrong.

---

of Troy was solely responsible for the carnage of the Trojan War. My personal favorite example, however, comes from Ogden Nash. Having famously observed that "Candy / Is dandy / But liquor / Is quicker," and apparently living to regret it, Nash followed up with this: "Nothing makes me sicker / Than liquor / And candy / Is too expandy."

Our default attitude toward wrongness, then—our distaste for error and our appetite for being right—tends to be rough on relationships. This applies equally to relationships among nations, communities, colleagues, friends, and (as will not be lost on most readers) relatives. Indeed, an old adage of therapists is that you can either be right or be in a relationship: you can remain attached to Team You winning every confrontation, or you can remain attached to your friends and family, but good luck trying to do both.

If insisting on our rightness tends to compromise our relationships, it also reflects poorly on our grasp of probability. I've already suggested that error isn't rare, yet it often seems remarkably scarce in our own lives—enough so that we should take a moment to establish exactly how un-rare it really is. By way of example, consider the domain of science. The history of that field is littered with discarded theories, some of which are among humanity's most dramatic mistakes: the flat earth, the geocentric universe, the existence of ether, the cosmological constant, cold fusion. Science proceeds by perceiving and correcting these errors, but over time, the corrections themselves often prove wrong as well. As a consequence, some philosophers of science have reached a conclusion that is known, in clumsy but funny fashion, as the Pessimistic Meta-Induction from the History of Science. The gist is this: because even the most seemingly bulletproof scientific theories of times past eventually proved wrong, we must assume that today's theories will someday prove wrong as well. And what goes for science goes in general—for politics, economics, technology, law, religion, medicine, child-rearing, education. No matter the domain of life, one generation's verities so often become the next generation's falsehoods that we might as well have a Pessimistic Meta-Induction from the History of Everything.

What is true of our collective human pursuits is also true of our individual lives. All of us outgrow some of our beliefs. All of us hatch theories in one moment only to find that we must abandon them in the next. Our tricky senses, our limited intellects, our fickle memories, the veil of emotions, the tug of allegiances, the complexity of the world around us: all of this conspires to ensure that we get things wrong again and again. You might never have given a thought to what I'm calling wrongology; you might be the farthest thing in the world from a wrongologist; but, like it or not, you are already a wrongitioner. We all are.

A book about being wrong can't get very far without first making its way across a definitional quagmire: *Wrong? About what? Says who?* We can be wrong about the integrity of our money manager, the identity of the murder suspect, or the name of the shortstop for the '62 Mets; about the structure of a hydrogen molecule or the date of the Second Coming; about the location of our car keys or the location of weapons of mass destruction. And that's just the straightforward stuff. There are also all those things about which we can never be proved wrong, but about which we tend to believe that people who disagree with us *are* wrong: the author of the Bible, the ethics of abortion, the merits of anchovies, whether it was you or your girlfriend who left the laptop in front of the window before the storm.

As arbitrary as this list is, it raises some important questions about any project that proposes to treat error as a coherent category of human experience. The first question concerns the stakes of our mistakes. The difference between being wrong about your car keys and being wrong about weapons of mass destruction is the difference between "oops" and a global military crisis—consequences so dramatically dissimilar that we might reasonably wonder if the errors that led to them can have anything in common. The second question is whether we can be wrong, in any meaningful sense, about personal beliefs. It's a long way from the Mets to the moral status of abortion, and some readers will suspect that the conceptual distance between being wrong about facts and being "wrong" about convictions is unbridgeable. Other readers, meanwhile, will raise a different objection: that we can never be completely sure of the truth, and therefore can't legitimately describe *anything* as "right" or "wrong."

In short, trying to forge a unified theory out of our ideas about error is akin to herding cats. Nor is the opposite approach, divvying up wrongness into categories, much easier. Still both tactics have been attempted. The former is a pet project of Western philosophy, which has been attempting to define the essential nature of error from the get-go. For at least the first two thousand years of its existence, philosophy understood itself as the pursuit of knowledge and truth—a job description that obliged its practitioners to be almost equally obsessed with error and falsity. (You can't define error, Socrates observes in Plato's *Theaetetus*, without also defining knowledge; your theory of one hinges entirely on your theory of the other.) As philosophy diversified and formalized its areas of inquiry— into ethics, metaphysics, logic, and so forth—the branch concerned with the study of knowledge became known as epistemology. Epistemologists disagree among themselves about many aspects of error, but from Plato onward they have shared a rough consensus on how to define it: to be wrong is to believe something is true when it is false—or, conversely, to believe it is false when it is true. This admirably straightforward definition will be useful to us, partly because it will help us eavesdrop on philosophical conversations about error, and partly because it captures what we typically mean by wrongness in everyday life. Still, as we'll soon see, this definition is bedeviled by a problem so significant that I will choose not to rely on it.

If philosophy has traditionally sought to unify and define wrongness, a far newer field—the multidisciplinary effort known sometimes as human factors research and sometimes as decision studies—has sought to subdivide and classify it. "Decision studies" is something of a euphemism; the field focuses primarily on *bad* decisions, without which it wouldn't need to exist. Likewise, the "human factors" in question—stress, distraction, disorganization, inadequate training, lack of information, and so forth—are those that contribute to inefficiencies, hazards, and mistakes. For these reasons, the field is also (although less often) referred to as error studies, which, for clarity's sake, is the name I'll use here.

Error-studies practitioners are a motley crew, ranging from psychologists and economists to engineers and business consultants, and the work they do is similarly diverse. Some seek to reduce financial losses for corporations by eliminating mistakes in manufacturing processes. Others try to improve safety procedures in situations, ranging from angioplasties to air traffic control, where human error poses a major threat to life and health. As that suggests, error studies, unlike epistemology, is an applied science.

Although its researchers look at the psychological as well as the structural reasons we get things wrong, their overall objective is practical: they seek to limit the likelihood and impact of future mistakes.

In service of this goal, these researchers have become remarkable taxonomists of error. A brief survey of their literature reveals a dizzying proliferation of categories of wrongness. There are slips and lapses and mistakes, errors of planning and errors of execution, errors of commission and errors of omission, design errors and operator errors, endogenous errors and exogenous errors. I could go on, but only at the expense of plunging you into obscure jargon and precise but—it must be said—painful explication. (A sample: "Mistakes may be defined as deficiencies or failures in the judgmental and/or inferential processes involved in the selection of an objective or in the specification of the means to achieve it, irrespective of whether or not the actions directed by this decision-scheme run according to plan.")

Mistakes *may* be defined this way, but not by me. Don't misunderstand: I'm grateful to the error-studies folks, as we all should be. At a moment in history when human error could easily unleash disaster on a global scale, they are trying to make our lives safer and easier. And, because they are among the few people who think long and hard about error, I count them as my colleagues in wrongology. The same goes for epistemologists, whose project has somewhat more in common with my own. Still, I depart from both groups of thinkers in important ways. My own interest lies neither in totalizing nor in atomizing error; and my aim is neither to eliminate mistakes nor to illuminate a single, capital-T Truth. Instead, I'm interested in error as an idea and as an experience: in how we think about being wrong, and how we feel about it.

This attention to how we think and feel about error casts a different light on some of the difficulties with defining it. Take the matter of stakes. The question I raised earlier was whether it ever makes sense to treat minor gaffes and world-altering errors—the car keys and the WMDs—as comparable phenomena. In their causes and consequences, these errors are so unalike that including them in the same category seems at best unhelpful and at worst unconscionable. But if we're interested in the human experience of error, such comparisons become viable—in fact, invaluable. For example, we are usually much more willing to entertain the possibility that we are wrong about insignificant matters than about weighty ones. This has a certain emotional logic, but it is deeply lacking in garden-variety logic. In high-stakes situations, we should want to do everything possible to ensure that we are right—which, as we will see, we can only do by imagining all the ways we could be wrong. That we are able to do this when it hardly matters, yet unable to do so when the stakes are huge, suggests that we might learn something important by comparing these otherwise very different experiences. The same can be said of comparing our verifiable and unverifiable beliefs—say, the name of that Mets player versus a contested memory. By examining our sense of certainty and our reaction to error in cases where we turn out to be objectively wrong, we can learn to think differently about our convictions in situations where no one will ever have the final say.

This attention to the experience of being wrong resolves some potential objections to my everything-but-the-kitchen-sink approach to error. But two important things remain to be said about the scope and method of this project. And they are two important *big* things: one concerns morality and the other concerns truth. Take morality first. In daily life, we use "wrong" to refer to both error and iniquity: it is wrong to think that the earth is flat, and it is also wrong to push your little brother down the stairs. I'm concerned here only with the former kind of wrongness, but for several reasons, moral issues will be a constant presence in these pages.

One such reason is that moral and intellectual wrongness are connected not by mere linguistic coincidence but by a long history of associating error with evil—and, conversely, rightness with righteousness. (We'll hear more about that history in the next chapter.) Another reason is that some of our most significant experiences of error involve reversing moral course. Sometimes, we conclude that we were wrong about the substance of our ethical convictions: that premarital sex actually isn't morally abhorrent, say, or that vegetarianism isn't morally requisite. At other times, we conclude that we were right about our ethics but wrong about the people or institutions we trusted to uphold them. Thus some Communists abandoned their faith in Stalin (but not in Communism) when he signed his nonaggression pact with Hitler, and some Catholics abandoned their church (but not its teachings) after revelations that it had sought to cover up widespread child abuse by priests. These experiences of being wrong about moral issues are distinct from the other errors in this book in content, but not in form. In every case, we place our faith in an idea (or a policy, or a person) only to realize, either by process or by crisis, that it has failed us.

A third reason morality will crop up in this book is that many moral wrongs are supported and legitimized by factual errors. To take an obvious example, consider phrenology, the now-discredited "science" of determining intelligence and personality through the shape of the skull. Throughout the nineteenth and early twentieth centuries, phrenology was used to defend discrimination against foreigners, Jews, Blacks, and other maligned minorities (to say nothing of women, that maligned majority). Here, as in so many cases, intellectual errors enabled moral wrongs. Of course, the opposite is true, too: preexisting prejudices shaped and sustained phrenology as much as phrenology shaped and sustained those prejudices. But that's the point. Often, our beliefs about what is factually right and our beliefs about what is morally right are entirely inextricable.

There is one final way in which morality is relevant—central, in fact— to this book. This concerns the moral implications of wrongness itself. As I've already noted, the relationship we cultivate with error affects how we think about and treat our fellow human beings—and how we think about and treat our fellow human beings is the alpha and omega of ethics. Do we have an obligation to others to contemplate the possibility that we are wrong? What responsibility do we bear for the consequences of our mistakes? How should we behave toward people when we think that they are wrong? The writer and philosopher Iris Murdoch once observed that no system of ethics can be complete without a mechanism for bringing about moral change. We don't usually think of mistakes as a means to an end, let alone a positive end—and yet, depending on how we answer these questions, error has the potential to be just such a mechanism. In other words, erring is not only (although it is sometimes) a moral problem. It is also a moral *solution*: an opportunity, as I said earlier, to rethink our relationship to ourselves, other people, and the world.

This sketch of the relationship between moral wrongness and error brings us almost to the end of our definitional quagmire. But I confess I have saved the swampiest step for last. This is the truth question: whether "right" and "wrong" reflect the real state of the world or are simply subjective human designations. The conundrum of whether truth exists, how we can arrive at it, and who gets to adjudicate it has preoccupied some of the best thinkers of every culture and era since time immemorial. This obsession has yielded tremendous intellectual and artistic returns, but very little that could truly be called progress, let alone resolution. Safe to say, then, that we aren't going to get to the bottom of these issues here. But we can't just ignore them, either. Socrates was right: no theory of error can exist entirely outside a theory of truth.

It's easy to spot the theory of truth implicit in the traditional philosophical definition of wrongness. If we believe that error involves taking something false to be true, then we are also signing on to a belief in truth. In other words, this definition of wrongness assumes the existence of absolute rightness—a fixed and knowable reality against which our mistakes can be measured. Sometimes, that assumption serves us well. There are, after all, plenty of broadly accepted standards of truth; even a committed relativist will likely concede that we can be just plain wrong about, say, the outcome of an election or the paternity of a child. The trouble with this definition is that the opposite is true, too. Even a committed realist will concede that there are many situations where an absolute standard of truth is unavailable. And yet, confronted with such situations, we often continue to act as if right and wrong are the relevant yardsticks.

Take the issue of aesthetics. We all know that matters of taste are different from matters of fact—that standards of right and wrong apply to facts but not to preferences. Indeed, we are somehow able to sort this out very early in life. Even young children understand that it's not okay if you think the sky is blue and I think the sky is green, but totally okay if your favorite color is blue and my favorite color is green. Yet it is comically easy to find examples of full-grown adults acting like their own taste is the gospel truth. Mac fanatics are famous for treating PC users like the victims of a mass delusion. People who swoon over hardwood floors regard wall-to-wall carpeting in Victorian homes as objectively appalling. Neighbors fulminate—or litigate—over one another's exterior paint colors or inflatable lawn ornaments. It is barely an exaggeration to say that I once almost broke up with someone over the question of whether rhubarb pie qualifies as a great dessert (obviously not) and whether *The Corrections* qualifies as a great novel (obviously so).

Granted, most of us are a bit wry about our tendency to treat our own predilections as the transcendent truth. Still, knowing that this behavior is ridiculous seldom stops us from engaging in it. The late novelist and critic John Updike once noted that the trouble with writing book reviews is that it is "almost impossible to . . . avoid the tone of being wonderfully right." The same goes for our informal reviews of almost everything. It's as if I believe, in some deep-down part of myself, that rhubarb pie radiates a kind of universal ickiness, while *The Corrections*, in some intrinsic way, just *is* brilliant. (And you, my rhubarb pie loving reader, are marveling at how wrong I am.) It follows, then, that anyone sufficiently perceptive and intelligent would respond to these things—to everything—the same way I do.

If this is how we act when we know that right and wrong are irrelevant, you can imagine what happens when there really is a fact of the matter, whether or not we ourselves can ever arrive at it. Forget, for a moment, the obvious but treacherous terrain of religion or politics. You can provoke a deep-seated sense of rightness just as swiftly by, say, asking a bunch of scholars of Elizabethan literature who really wrote *Hamlet*. It's almost impossible to imagine any finding that would settle that question to everyone's satisfaction, just as it is almost impossible to imagine how you would get all parties to agree on the origins of human life, or on the necessity of U.S. intervention in Iraq. Yet it is often precisely these irresolvable issues that arouse our most impassioned certainty that we are right and our adversaries are wrong. To my mind, then, any definition of error we choose must be flexible enough to accommodate the way we talk about wrongness when there is no obvious benchmark for being right.

To find such a definition, we might return to the experience of error. Rather than thinking of being wrong as believing something is true when it is objectively false, we could define it as the experience of rejecting as false a belief *we ourselves* once thought was true—regardless of that belief's actual relationship to reality, or whether such a relationship can ever be determined. This is a tempting fix, for two reasons. First, with a slight tweak to an established definition of error, it puts PAID to any irksome questions about truth. Second, it shines the spotlight on an important and often overlooked corner of human experience, one that is central to this book: the hinge moment when we swing from believing one thing to believing its antithesis. Still, as an overall definition, this one seems unsatisfactory as well, since it fails to capture our everyday notion of error. When we accuse someone of being wrong, we don't mean that she is in the throes of rejecting one of her own beliefs. We mean that her beliefs are at odds with the real state of the world.

In the end, then, neither of these definitions of being wrong—as a deviation from external reality, or an internal upheaval in what we believe—will completely suffice for our purposes. Although I will draw on both ideas, the full human experience of error is too multiform and chameleon to stay put inside either one. In writing about comedy, the French philosopher Henri Bergson argued against "imprisoning the comic spirit within a definition." Instead, he wrote, he hoped to provide his readers with "something more flexible than an abstract definition—a practical, intimate acquaintance, such as springs from a long companionship." This strikes me as an admirable goal, and one that will serve as well for wrongness as for funniness. For better and worse, error is already our lifelong companion. Surely, then, it's time we got to know it.

Most of the rest of this book—into which I promise to release you very soon—is built around stories of people screwing up. These stories involve, among other things, illusions, magicians, comedians, drug trips, love affairs, misadventures on the high seas, bizarre neurological phenomena, medical catastrophes, legal fiascos, some possible consequences of marrying a prostitute, the lamentable failure of the world to end, and Alan Greenspan. But before we can plunge into the experience of being wrong, we must pause to make an important if somewhat perverse point: there *is* no experience of being wrong.

There is an experience of *realizing* that we are wrong, of course. In fact, there is a stunning diversity of such experiences. As we'll see in the pages to come, recognizing our mistakes can be shocking, confusing, funny, embarrassing, traumatic, pleasurable, illuminating, and life-altering, sometimes for ill and sometimes for good. But by definition, there can't be any particular feeling associated with simply *being* wrong. Indeed, the whole reason it's possible to be wrong is that, while it is happening, you are oblivious to it. When you are simply going about your business in a state you will later decide was delusional, you have no idea of it whatsoever. You are like the coyote in the Road Runner cartoons, after he has gone off the cliff but before he has looked down. Literally in his case and figuratively in yours, you are already in trouble when you feel like you're still on solid ground. So I should revise myself: it does feel like something to be wrong. It feels like being right.

This is the problem of error-blindness. Whatever falsehoods each of us currently believes are necessarily invisible to us. Think about the telling fact that error literally doesn't exist in the first person present tense: the sentence "I am wrong" describes a logical impossibility. As soon as we know that we are wrong, we aren't wrong anymore, since to recognize a belief as false is to stop believing it. Thus we can only say "I *was* wrong." Call it the Heisenberg Uncertainty Principle of Error: we can be wrong, or we can know it, but we can't do both at the same time.

Error-blindness goes some way toward explaining our persistent difficulty with imagining that we could be wrong. It's easy to ascribe this difficulty to various psychological factors—arrogance, insecurity, and so forth—and these plainly play a role. But error-blindness suggests that another, more structural issue might be at work as well. If it is literally impossible to feel wrong—if our current mistakes remain imperceptible to us even when we scrutinize our innermost being for signs of them—then it makes sense for us to conclude that we are right. Similarly, error-blindness helps explain why we accept fallibility as a universal phenomenon yet are constantly startled by our own mistakes. The psychologist Marc Green has observed that an error, from the point of view of the person who makes it, is essentially "a Mental Act of God." Although we understand in the abstract that errors happen, our specific mistakes are just as unforeseeable to us as specific tornadoes or specific lightning strikes. (And, as a result, we seldom feel that we should be held accountable for them. By law, after all, no one is answerable for an Act of God.)

If our current mistakes are necessarily invisible to us, our past errors have an oddly slippery status as well. Generally speaking, they are either impossible to remember or impossible to forget. This wouldn't be particularly strange if we consistently forgot our trivial mistakes and consistently remembered the momentous ones, but the situation isn't quite that simple. I can never come across the name of the German writer Goethe without remembering the kindly but amused correction delivered to me by a college professor the first time I said it out loud, as Go-eth. As in pride goeth before a fall. (For readers in my erstwhile boat, it comes closer to rhyming with the name Bertha, minus the H. And the R.) This was a trivial and understandable mistake, yet I seem destined to go to my grave remembering it.

Compare that to an experience recounted by Sigmund Freud in *The Psychopathology of Everyday Life* (itself a book about erring). Once, while settling his monthly accounts, Freud came upon the name of a patient whose case history he couldn't recall, even though he could see that he had visited her every day for many weeks, scarcely six months previously. He tried for a long time to bring the patient to mind, but for the life of him was unable to do so. When the memory finally came back to him, Freud was astonished by his "almost incredible instance of forgetting." The patient in question was a young woman whose parents brought her in because she complained incessantly of stomach pains. Freud diagnosed her with hysteria. A few months later, she died of abdominal cancer.

It's hard to say which is stranger: the complete amnesia for the massive error, or the perfect recall for the trivial one. On the whole, though, our ability to forget our mistakes seems keener than our ability to remember them. Over the course of working on this book, when I had occasion to explain its subject matter to strangers, a certain percentage would inevitably respond by saying, "You should interview me, I'm wrong all the time." I would then ask for an example and, almost as inevitably, their brows would furrow, they would fall silent, and after a while, with some puzzlement, they would admit to drawing a blank. As one such would-be interviewee observed, "It's funny; I can sort of picture many times where I've said, 'oh, no, I'm so wrong, this is so bad or so embarrassing,' and I can even sort of recall losing sleep and missing dinners and being all uptight, but I can't actually remember a single specific instance of being wrong."

Part of what's going on here is, in essence, a database-design flaw. Most of us don't have a mental category called "Mistakes I Have Made." A close friend of mine, one who knew about this book from its earliest stages, wrote to me two years into the process to say that it had suddenly dawned on her that one of the formative events of her childhood was an experience of dramatic wrongness. My friend hadn't forgotten about this event during the previous two years, but it was mentally filed away under other labels (in this case, "times I've been lonely" and "times I've been angry"). As a result—and despite all the vicarious thinking about wrongness she had done on my behalf—the memory hadn't been accessible to her as a story about error.

Like our inability to say "I was wrong," this lack of a category called "error" is a communal as well as an individual problem. As someone who tried to review the literature on wrongness, I can tell you that, first, it is vast; and, second, almost none of it is filed under classifications having anything to do with error. Instead, it is distributed across an extremely diverse set of disciplines: philosophy, psychology, behavioral economics, law, medicine, technology, neuroscience, political science, and the history of science, to name just a few. So too with the errors in our own lives. We file them under a range of headings—"embarrassing moments," "lessons I've learned," "stuff I used to believe"—but very seldom does an event live inside us with the simple designation "wrong."

This category problem is only one reason why our past mistakes can be so elusive. Another is that (as we'll see in more detail later) realizing that we are wrong about a belief almost always involves acquiring a replacement belief at the same time: something else instantly becomes the new right. In light of this new belief, the discarded one can quickly come to seem remote, indistinct, and irrelevant, as if we never took it all that seriously in the first place. This convenient erasure of past errors happens on a societal level as well. Doctors don't teach medical students the theory of bodily humors, and astronomy professors don't teach their students to calculate the velocity of the fifty-five concentric spheres Aristotle thought composed the universe. This is practical and efficient pedagogy, but it shores up our tacit assumption that current belief is identical with true belief, and it reinforces our generalized sense of rightness.

What with error-blindness, our amnesia for our mistakes, the lack of a category called "error," and our tendency to instantly overwrite rejected beliefs, it's no wonder we have so much trouble accepting that wrongness is a part of who we are. Because we don't experience, remember, track, or retain mistakes as a feature of our inner landscape, wrongness always seems to come at us from left field—that is, from outside ourselves. But the reality could hardly be more different. Error is the ultimate inside job. Yes, the world can be profoundly confusing; and yes, other people can mislead or deceive you. In the end, though, nobody but you can choose to believe your own beliefs. That's part of why recognizing our errors is such a strange experience: accustomed to disagreeing with other people, we suddenly find ourselves at odds with *ourselves*. Error, in that moment, is less an intellectual problem than an existential one—a crisis not in what we know, but in who we are. We hear something of that identity crisis in the questions we ask ourselves in the aftermath of error: *What was I thinking? How could I have done that?*

These private questions about the origins of error echo a broader public inquiry that has been under way since time immemorial. If wrongness both haunts and eludes us, we can take comfort from the fact that it has done the same for countless generations of theologians, philosophers, psychologists, sociologists, and scientists. Many of the religious thinkers who tried to understand why we err found their answer at the gates of the Garden of Eden. Thus Thomas Aquinas, the thirteenth-century scholastic, held that we make mistakes because, when we were banished from paradise, we were cut off forever from direct access to divine truth. To Aquinas and many of his fellow theologians, our errors arise from the gap between our own limited and blemished minds and God's unlimited and perfect omniscience.

This same basic idea has received countless secular treatments as well. Plato thought that our primordial soul was at one with the universe, and that we only began to err when we took on our current physical form and forgot those cosmic truths. The Enlightenment philosopher John Locke thought that error seeped into our lives from the gap between the artificiality of words and the reality of the things they name—from the distance between an indescribable essence and the nearest sayable thing. The German philosopher Martin Heidegger thought that error could be explained by the fact that we live in time and space; because we are bound to a particular set of coordinates, we can't rise above them and see reality as a whole, from a bird's-eye (or God's-eye) view. As different as these explanations seem, all these thinkers and many more conceived of error as arising from a gap: sometimes between the particular and the general, sometimes between words and things, sometimes between the present and the primeval, sometimes between the mortal and the divine—but in every case, and fundamentally, between our own mind and the rest of the world.

For the most part, we spend our lives blithely ignoring this gap. And with good reason. Who wants to be reminded of the fall from grace, the separation from truth, the particular and limited nature of our existence? When we get things wrong, however, this rift between internal and external realities suddenly reveals itself. That's one reason why erring can be so disquieting. But another, oddly paradoxical reason is our failure to spot this rift *earlier*. Our mistakes show us that the contents of our minds can be as convincing as reality. That's a dismaying discovery, because it is precisely this quality of convincing-ness, of verisimilitude, that we rely on as our guide to what is right and real.

Yet if we find this mental trickery troubling, we should also find it comforting. The miracle of the human mind, after all, is that it can show us the world not only as it is, but also as it is *not*: as we remember it from the past, as we hope or fear it will be in the future, as we imagine it might be in some other place or for some other person. We already saw that "seeing the world as it is not" is pretty much the definition of erring—but it is also the essence of imagination, invention, and hope. As that suggests, our errors sometimes bear far sweeter fruits than the failure and shame we associate with them. True, they represent a moment of alienation, both from ourselves and from a previously convincing vision of the world. But what's wrong with that? "To alienate" means to make unfamiliar; and to see things—including ourselves—as unfamiliar is an opportunity to see them anew.

For error to help us see things differently, however, we have to see *it* differently first. That is the goal of this book: to foster an intimacy with our own fallibility, to expand our vocabulary for and interest in talking about our mistakes, and to linger for a while inside the normally elusive and ephemeral experience of being wrong. There's an obvious practical reason to do this, which is that our mistakes can be disastrous. They can cost us time and money, sabotage our self-confidence, and erode the trust and esteem extended to us by others. They can land us in the emergency room, or in the dog house, or in a lifetime's worth of therapy. They can hurt and humiliate us; worse, they can hurt and humiliate other people. In short, to the degree that we can prevent them, we probably should. And to do that, we need to understand why we err in the first place.

That said, it should be clear by now that this book isn't intended as a self-help guide for the chronically wrong—*How To Error-Proof Your Life*, say, or *Thirty Days to a Righter You*. On the contrary, it is far more a defense *of* wrongness than a defense against it. This book takes seriously Augustine's suggestion that error is somehow essential to who we are, and sets out to explore just how this is so. In Part One, I trace the history of how we think about wrongness and the emergence of two opposing models of error—models that also reflect our ideas about what kind of creatures we are and what kind of universe we live in. In Part Two, I explore the many factors that can cause us to screw up, from our senses to our higher cognitive processes to our social conventions. In Part Three, I move from why we get things wrong to how we feel when we do so. This part of the book traces the emotional arc of erring, from the experience of realizing we went astray to how that experience can transform our worldviews, our relationships, and—most profoundly—ourselves.

The last part of this book turns from the origins and experience of error to its avoidable hazards and unexpected pleasures. Here, I look at how embracing our fallibility not only lessens our likelihood of erring, but also helps us think more creatively, treat each other more thoughtfully, and construct freer and fairer societies. In the final chapter, I encourage us to see error as a gift in itself—a rich and irreplaceable source of humor, art, illumination, individuality, and change. This book opened with the pleasure of being right, but it will conclude with the more complicated, more interesting, and ultimately more revelatory pleasure of being wrong.

2.

Two Models of Wrongness

Our errors are surely not such awfully solemn things. In a world where we are so certain to incur them in spite of all our caution, a certain lightness of heart seems healthier than this excessive nervousness on their behalf.

—WILLIAM JAMES, "THE WILL TO BELIEVE"

Ross Gelbspan is a colleague of mine, a fellow journalist who has been writing about environmental issues for forty-odd years. Back in 1972, when he was working for the *Village Voice*, he covered a press conference about *The Limits to Growth*, a study of the impact of economic development and population pressures on natural resources. *The Limits to Growth* made headlines all over the world when it was published, and is still the best-selling environmental book of all time.

"It was very interesting, very frightening stuff," Ross recalled. "The press conference was about how all these various factors—increasing population, increasing pollution, diminishing resources—were going to hit a point of exponential takeoff." One of the speakers at the conference was Donella Meadows, a coauthor of the book and a pioneering environmental scientist. Sitting in the audience during her presentation, Ross was struck by the contrast between the grim predictions she was describing and the fact that she was pregnant—that, as he put it, "she had somehow found personal hopefulness in the midst of this really massive gloom and doom." He saw it as a small grace note, a reminder about the possibility of optimism and renewal in even the hardest of times, and he used it as the kicker to his story. The *Voice* printed the article on the front page. That would have been nice for Ross—except that Donella Meadows wasn't pregnant.

Certain mistakes can actually kill us, but many, many more of them just make us want to die. That's why the word "mortify" comes up so often when people talk about their errors. Here is Ross, verbatim: "I was mortified. I mean, *mortified* mortified. I was not a rookie. I'd been a reporter since 1961. I'd worked for the *Philadelphia Bulletin*, I'd worked for the *Washington Post*. But I'd never made an error like that, and I cannot begin to describe the embarrassment. Truth is, I'm still mortified when I talk about it." Nearly forty years have elapsed since Ross's article was published. The world has, in varying degrees, ignored, learned from, and defied the predictions in *The Limits to Growth*. Donella Meadows died in 2001. Even journalism as we know it is on its way out. Ross's embarrassment has outlived it all. When I told him the expected publication date for this book, he said, "Good—with luck I'll be dead by then."

Granted, Ross's mistake was particularly awkward. But it was not particularly consequential—not for Meadows, who was gracious about it; not for Ross; not even for Ross's career. So wasn't wanting to die something of an extreme reaction? Maybe. But if so, it is an extreme reaction to which we all sometimes succumb. Indeed, one of our recurrent responses to error is to wish ourselves out of existence. Describing the moment of realizing certain mistakes, we say that we wanted to crawl into a cave, or fall through a hole in the floor, or simply disappear. And we talk about "losing face," as if our mistakes really *did* cause us to disappear—as if our identity was rubbed out by the experience of being wrong.

In addition to this death-wish response to error, we have another reaction that is less drastic. But more gastric: sometimes, instead of wanting to die, we just want to vomit. Or so one might assume from the strangely culinary vocabulary we use to talk about being wrong. In the aftermath of our mistakes, we eat crow, eat humble pie, eat our hat, or, at the other end of the sartorial menu, eat our shoe. And, of course, we eat our words. These sayings differ in their origins, but the overall implication is clear: error is both extremely unappetizing and very tough to digest. If being right is succulent, being wrong runs a narrow, unhappy gamut from nauseating to worse than death.

This is the received wisdom about error: that it is dangerous, humiliating, distasteful, and, all told, un-fun in the extreme. This view of error— let's call it the pessimistic model—has some merit. As I acknowledged earlier (and as everyone knows), our mistakes really can be irritating or humiliating or harmful, to ourselves as well as to others. To dismiss that fact would be disingenuous, but as an overall outlook on wrongness, the pessimistic one is radically incomplete. To begin with, it obscures the fact that whatever damage can arise from erring pales in comparison to the damage that arises from our fear, dislike, and denial of erring. This fear acts as a kind of omnipurpose coagulant, hardening heart and mind, chilling our relationships with other people, and cooling our curiosity about the world.

Like many fears, the fear of being wrong stems partly from a lack of understanding. The pessimistic model of error tells us *that* wrongness is unpleasant, but it doesn't tell us *why*, and it has nothing at all to say about errors that don't turn out to be disagreeable. To account for the breadth of our real-life experiences with wrongness, we need to pair the pessimistic outlook with another one. In this second, optimistic model of error, the experience of being wrong isn't limited to humiliation and defeat. Actually, in this model, the experience of being wrong is hardly limited at all. Surprise, bafflement, fascination, excitement, hilarity, delight: all these and more are a part of the optimistic understanding of error. This model is harder to recognize around us, since it is forever being crowded out by the noisier notion that error is dangerous, demoralizing, and shameful. But it exists nonetheless, and it exerts a subtle yet important pull both on our ideas about error and on our ideas about ourselves.

These two models of error, optimistic and pessimistic, are in perpetual tension with each other. We could try to study them in isolation—the discomforts and dangers of being wrong over here, its delights and dividends over there—and we could try to adjudicate between them. But it is when we take these two models together, not when we take them apart, that we begin to understand the forces that shape how we think and feel about being wrong.

"Our errors are surely not such awfully solemn things." That cheery quote, which heads this chapter, could be the motto of the optimistic model of wrongness; and its author, the nineteenth-century philosopher and psychologist William James, could serve as its foremost spokesperson. For a representative of the pessimistic model, we might return to Thomas Aquinas, the medieval monk who tipped his hand in the last chapter by associating error with original sin. "The mind being the faculty of truth," wrote the philosopher Leo Keeler, both summarizing and quoting Aquinas, "error cannot be its normal fruit, but will necessarily have the character of a defective byproduct, an accidental disorder, a miscarriage comparable to 'monstrous births' in nature."

Defective, accidental, monstrous, a miscarriage: the message is clear enough. For Aquinas, error was not merely abhorrent but also abnormal, a perversion of the prescribed order of things. William James, had he been around, would have had none of it—none of the revulsion (this was a man whose prescription for error was "a certain lightness of heart"), and none of the business about abnormality, either. Given that all of us get things wrong again and again, how abnormal, he might have asked, can error possibly be?

This debate over whether error is normal or abnormal is central to the history of how we think about wrongness. What's most interesting about the debate isn't what it tells us about wrongness per se, but what it tells us about the kind of creatures we think we are and the kind of world we think we live in. Take Aquinas and James: they fundamentally disagreed, but their disagreement was only secondarily about error. The real issue was Aquinas's claim about "the mind being the faculty of truth." If you believe, as he did, that there is a truth and that (to borrow James's formulation) "our minds and it are made for each other," then error is both deplorable and difficult to explain. On the other hand, if you believe that truth is not necessarily fixed or knowable, and that the human mind, while a dazzling entity in its own right (in fact, *because* it is a dazzling entity in its own right), is not reality's looking glass—if you believe all of that, as James did, then error is both explicable and acceptable.

These competing ideas of error crop up in efforts to define the term, as we saw when we tried to do so ourselves. In the 1600s, France's *Larousse* dictionary defined error, rather beautifully, as "a vagabondage of the imagination, of the mind that is not subject to any rule." Scarcely a hundred years later, in the same country, Denis Diderot's famed *Encyclopédie* defined it, instead, as endemic to *every* human mind, that "magic mirror" in which the real world is distorted into "shadows and monsters." These two definitions suggest two markedly different understandings of human nature. As error goes from being a hallmark of the lawless mind to our native condition, people cease to be fundamentally perfectible and become fundamentally imperfect. Meanwhile, truth goes from being a prize that can be achieved through spiritual or intellectual discipline to a fugitive that forever eludes the human mind.

The history of error is not an account of the shift from one of these frameworks to the other. Instead, it is an ongoing, millennia-long argument between the two. Over that time, this argument has come to be defined by several other questions, in addition and closely related to whether screwing up is basically aberrant or basically normal. One of these questions is whether error is with us to stay or if it can somehow be eradicated. James Sully, a British psychologist whose 1881 *Illusions* constitutes perhaps the most thoroughgoing early investigation of human error, thought that most forms of it would eventually be overcome. Observing that "the power of introspection is a comparatively new acquisition of the human race," Sully concluded that "as it improves, the amount of error connected with its operation may reasonably be expected to become infinitesimal."

A similar sentiment was expressed a half-century later by Joseph Jastrow, an American psychologist who conceived and edited an anthology of folly across the ages that he titled *The Story of Human Error*. A story, it might be observed, traditionally has a beginning, a middle, and an end, and Jastrow clearly thought we were approaching the final chapter in the history of wrongness. Praising "the present peak of scientific achievement," he predicted that "such advances in the uses of mind . . . mark the decisive stages in the elimination of error." Jastrow was inspired to write his book by a visit to the 1933 World's Fair, which was appropriate since such events are themselves often paeans to the perfectibility of the human race. At the 1939 fair in New York, for example, the literature at the "World of Tomorrow" exhibit reproved its visitors for "still grant[ing] to belief or opinion the loyalty which should go only to fact," while prophesying that in the future, "we will behave as the trained scientist behaves today. We will welcome the new, test it thoroughly, and accept it joyously, in truly scientific fashion."

Inevitably, from the present vantage point, these rosy predictions sound hopelessly dated and naïve. But the idea that we can eradicate error—through evolutionary advancement, technological innovation, establishing an ideal society, or spreading the word of God—has a timeless hold on the human imagination. Implicit in this idea is the belief that we should *want* to eradicate error. And, sometimes, we should: we'd all be happy to see mistakes permanently disappear from, say, the nuclear power industry. But eradicating the entirety of error is another matter. Practicality aside, such an objective presents three problems. The first is that, to believe we can eradicate error, we must also believe that we can consistently distinguish between it and the truth—a faith squarely at odds with remembering that we ourselves could be wrong. Thus the catch-22 of wrongology: in order to get rid of error, we would already need to be infallible.

The second problem with this goal is that virtually all efforts at eradication—even genuinely well-intentioned ones—succumb to the law of unintended consequences. Take the pests out of their ecological niche, and pretty soon you won't have any hummingbirds or marmots or mountain lions, either. Even if you can't be brought to believe that error itself is a good thing, I hope to convince you by the end of this book that it is inseparably linked to other good things, things we definitely do not want to eliminate—like, say, our intelligence.

The final problem with seeking to eradicate error is that many such efforts are *not* well intentioned—or if they are, they tend in the direction for which good intentions are infamous. Here, for instance, is Sully, averring that error's "grosser forms manifest themselves most conspicuously in the undisciplined mind of the savage and the rustic." And here is the anthropologist Ralph Linton, a contributor to Jastrow's anthology, observing (critically) that at one time, "all heathen cultures were [regarded as] at best examples of human error, while at worst they were devices of Satan, devised to keep damned souls securely in his net. In either case it was the duty of Christians to destroy them." As these quotations make clear, it is alarmingly easy to impute error to those whose beliefs and backgrounds differ from our own. And, as they also show, there is a slippery slope between advocating the elimination of putatively erroneous beliefs, and advocating the elimination of the institutions, cultures, and—most alarmingly—people who hold them.

The idea that error can be eradicated, then, contains within it a frighteningly reactionary impulse. And yet, at heart, it is an idea about progress: a belief that there is an apex of human achievement, and that the way to reach it is through the steady reduction and eventual elimination of mistakes. But we have another, competing idea of progress as well—one that rests not on the elimination of error but, surprisingly, on its perpetuation. This idea began to emerge during the Scientific Revolution, through that era's hallmark development, the scientific method. It is a measure of the method's success (and its simplicity, in theory if not in practice) that, some 400 years later, virtually every reader of this book will have learned it in junior high school. The gist of the scientific method is that observations lead to hypotheses (which must be testable), which are then subjected to experiments (whose results must be reproducible). If all goes well, the outcome is a theory, a logically consistent, empirically tested explanation for a natural phenomenon.

As an ideal of intellectual inquiry and a strategy for the advancement of knowledge, the scientific method is essentially a monument to the utility of error. Most of us gravitate toward trying to verify our beliefs, to the extent that we bother investigating their validity at all. But scientists gravitate toward falsification; as a community if not as individuals, they seek to disprove their beliefs. Thus, the defining feature of a hypothesis is that it has the potential to be proven wrong (which is why it must be both testable and tested), and the defining feature of a theory is that it hasn't been proven wrong yet. But the important part is that it can be—no matter how much evidence appears to confirm it, no matter how many experts endorse it, no matter how much popular support it enjoys. In fact, not only *can* any given theory be proven wrong; as we saw in the last chapter, sooner or later, it probably will be. And when it is, the occasion will mark the success of science, not its failure. This was the pivotal insight of the Scientific Revolution: that the advancement of knowledge depends on current theories collapsing in the face of new insights and discoveries. In this model of progress, errors do not lead us away from the truth. Instead, they edge us incrementally toward it.

During and after the Scientific Revolution, the leading minds of Western Europe took this principle and generalized it. As they saw it, not only scientific theories but also political, social, and even aesthetic ideas were subject to this same pattern of collapse, replacement, and advancement. In essence, these thinkers identified the problem of error-blindness on a generational and communal scale. We can no more spot the collective errors of our culture than we can spot our own private ones, but we can be sure that they are lurking somewhere.

The thinkers responsible for this insight came by it honestly. They lived at a time when fifteen centuries of foundational truths had lately been disproved or displaced by a staggering influx of new information: about previously unknown plants and animals, about geology and geography, about the structure of the universe, about the breadth and diversity of human culture. In our own globally intimate, Google-mapped era, it is almost impossible to fathom the degree of intellectual and emotional disruption all that new information must have occasioned. I suppose that if tomorrow a UFO landed in Pittsburgh, I might experience a comparable combination of stunning error and thrilling possibility. Certainly I would have to rebuild my understanding of the cosmos from the ground up.

Faced with that task, many of these thinkers concluded that the best and safest tool for this sweeping intellectual reconstruction was doubt: deep, systematic, abiding, all-encompassing doubt. Thus Michel de Montaigne, the great Renaissance philosopher and essayist, inscribed above the door of his study *que sais-je?*—what do I know? And thus Descartes set himself the task of doubting *everything*, up to and including his own existence (a project we'll hear more about later). These thinkers weren't nihilists, nor even skeptics. They believed in truth, and they wanted to discover it. But they were chastened by the still-palpable possibility of drastic error, and they understood that, from a sufficiently distant vantage point, even their most cherished convictions might come to look like mistakes.

What was new and radical about this perspective wasn't the recognition of how difficult it is to distinguish error from truth. That idea is at least as old as Plato. It appears in the Bible as well—for instance, as the question of how to tell false prophets from true. ("For Satan himself masquerades as an angel of light," we read in 2 Corinthians.) Renaissance and Enlightenment thinkers would also have been familiar with this idea from the work of their medieval counterparts, who often characterized errors as *ignes fatui*—literally fool's fires, although often translated as false or phantom fires. Today we know these false fires as will o' the wisps: mysterious wandering lights that, in folklore, lead unwary travelers astray, typically into the depths of a swamp or over the edge of a cliff. Less romantically, false fires also referred to the ones lit by bandits to fool travelers into thinking they were approaching an inn or town. In either case, the metaphor says it all: error, disguised as the light of truth, leads directly into trouble. But Enlightenment thinkers mined a previously unnoticed aspect of this image. Error, they observed, wasn't simply darkness, the absolute absence of the light of truth. Instead, it shed a light of its own. True, that light might be flickering or phantasmagoric, but it was still a source of illumination. In this model, error is not the opposite of truth so much as asymptotic to it—a kind of human approximation of truth, a truth-for-now.

This is another important dispute in the history of how we think about being wrong: whether error represents an obstacle in the path toward truth, or the path itself. The former idea is the conventional one. The latter, as we have seen, emerged during the Scientific Revolution and continued to evolve throughout the Enlightenment. But it didn't really reach its zenith until the early nineteenth century, when the French mathematician and astronomer Pierre-Simon Laplace refined the theory of the distribution of errors, illustrated by the now-familiar bell curve. Also known as the error curve or the normal distribution, the bell curve is a way of aggregating individually meaningless, idiosyncratic, or inaccurate data points in order to generate a meaningful and accurate big picture.

Laplace, for instance, used the bell curve to determine the precise orbit of the planets. Such movements had been recorded since virtually the beginning of history, but those records were unreliable, afflicted by the distortion intrinsic to all human observation. By using the normal distribution to graph these individually imperfect data points, Laplace was able to generate a far more precise picture of the galaxy. Unlike earlier thinkers, who had sought to improve their accuracy by getting rid of error, Laplace realized that you should try to get *more* error: aggregate enough flawed data, and you get a glimpse of the truth. "The genius of statistics, as Laplace defined it, was that it did not ignore errors; it quantified them," the writer Louis Menand observed. ". . . The right answer is, in a sense, a function of the mistakes." For thinkers of that particular historical moment, who believed in the existence of an ordained truth while simultaneously recognizing the omnipresence of error, the bell curve represented a kind of holy grail: wrongness contained, curtailed, and coaxed into revealing its opposite.*

---

* If Laplace helped catapult the bell curve into fame, another astronomer, the Belgian Adolphe Quetelet, helped it achieve something closer to infamy. Quetelet gathered data about people—about our heights and criminal records and number of children and age at death—and graphed them the way Laplace had graphed the stars. In the theory of the distribution of errors, he realized, the particular quirks and characteristics of any given human represented the errors: deviations from a norm that only became visible when all those quirks were aggregated. This innovation solidified an association, implicit since antiquity, between being deviant and being wrong—and, conversely, between being

A century later, the idea that errors reveal rather than obscure the truth gained a powerful new proponent in Freud. But while earlier thinkers had been interested primarily in external truths—in the facts of the world as ordained by nature or God—Freud's domain was the internal. The truths he cared about are the ones we stash away in our unconscious. By definition, those truths are inaccessible to the reasoning mind—but, Freud argued in *The Psychopathology of Everyday Life*, we can catch occasional glimpses of them, and one way we do so is through error. Today, we know these truth-revealing errors as Freudian slips—as the old saw goes, saying one thing and meaning your mother. According to Freud, these seemingly trivial mistakes are neither trivial nor even, in any standard sense, mistakes. That is, they aren't the result of accident or absentmindedness or the misfiring of a stray neuron or any such mundane cause. Instead, they arise from—and therefore illuminate—a submerged but significant psychic truth. In this view, such errors are envoys from our own innermost universe; and, however garbled their messages may be, they contain valuable information about what's really going on in there.

In addition to these slips, Freud also thought there were a few other avenues by which the secret truths of the unconscious could seep out. One of these, dreams, is relevant to us all. Another, relevant only to the unfortunate few, is insanity. At first, dreams and madness might not seem terribly germane to this book. But what these two conditions have in common with each other is the misperception of reality—which, you'll recall, is also one definition (indeed, the earliest and most pervasive one) of being wrong. To better understand our mundane misperceptions, it pays to look closely at our extreme ones. So that is where I want to turn now—to dreams, drug trips, hallucinations, and madness; and, by way of those examples, to a closer look at the notion that, through error, we perceive the truth.

. . .

normal and being right. (It was Quetelet who came up with that stock character of statistics, the "average man.") For more on the potential insidiousness of this innovation, I refer the reader to the notes.

However far-fetched this connection between wrongness and whacked-outness might seem, you yourself invoke it routinely. I say this with some confidence, because our everyday ways of thinking and talking about error borrow heavily from the argot of altered states. For starters, we commonly (if crudely) compare being wrong to being high. Try saying something patently erroneous to a member of my generation, and you'd better be prepared to hear "what are you smoking?" or "are you on crack?" Likewise, we seldom hesitate to impute insanity to people who strongly hold beliefs that we strongly reject. (Witness all the mudslinging about "liberal lunatics" and "right-wing wingnuts.") Finally, we talk about snapping out of our false beliefs as if they were trances and waking up from them as if they were dreams.

Of all these analogies, the association between erring and dreaming is the most persistent and explicit. "Do you not see," asked the eleventh-century Islamic philosopher and theologian Abu Hamid Muhammad al-Ghazali, "that while asleep you assume your dreams to be indisputably real? Once awake, you recognize them for what they are—baseless chimeras." The same could be said, he observed, of our waking beliefs. "In relation to your present state they may be real; but it is possible also that you may enter upon another state of being"—and from the vantage point of that future state, he continued, your present one will seem as self-evidently false as your dreams do when you awake.

Although we treat errors and altered states as analogous in certain ways, there is one important respect in which we treat them very differently. As I began this chapter by noting, mistakes, even minor ones, often make us feel like we're going to be sick, or like we want to die. But altered states—some of which really *can* sicken or kill us—frequently enthrall us. We keep journals of our dreams and recount them to our friends and family (to say nothing of our therapists). We feel that our lives are illuminated and enriched by them, and we regard those who seldom remember theirs as, in some small but important way, impoverished. We are highly motivated to seek out the reality-altering power of drugs, despite the danger of overdose, addiction, or arrest. The delirium of extreme illness is arguably even riskier, not to mention harder to come by and all-around less desirable. Yet I will say this:

once, while running a very high fever in a tropical rainforest, I carried on a long conversation with the poet Samuel Taylor Coleridge, who was sitting on the end of my bed, knitting. Coleridge, of course, was long dead, and as for me, I've never been sicker. But I've almost never been so mesmerized or elated, either—and, since then, I haven't once taken medicine to reduce a fever. If, on those occasions when I'm already sick anyway, I could take a pill to *increase* my temperature instead, to nudge it up just into the zone of hallucination, I would seriously consider doing so. Granted, it's not what the doctor ordered—in fact, it's plainly idiotic—but that's the point. Altered states are so compelling that we often do what we can, wisely or otherwise, to produce, reproduce, and prolong them.

The attraction of an altered state is not, as one might initially imagine, just its pure weirdness—how far it diverges from everyday life. Instead, it is the combination of this weirdness and its *proximity* to everyday life. What is altered, in an altered state, are the elements of the world, the relations among them, and the rules that govern them. But the way we experience these states remains essentially unchanged. The tools we use to gauge and understand the sober world—our reason, our emotions, and above all our senses—are largely unimpaired and sometimes even enhanced in the trippy one. As a result, these false worlds have all the intimacy, intensity, and physicality—in short, all the indicators of reality—of the true one.

What does it mean about the realness of reality if it is so susceptible to alteration—by a dream, a drug, a difference of just a few degrees in body temperature? And, conversely, what does it mean about the supposedly unreal if it is so easy to conjure and so intensely convincing? These questions have haunted our collective imagination from *A Midsummer Night's Dream* to *The Matrix* (both of which, incidentally, hinge on drug trips). One of the most consistent answers—and the crucial one, for my purposes—is that the false and the true are reversed: that the unreal is, so to speak, the real real. Freud, as I've already noted, believed that the false worlds of our dreams reveal deep and hidden truths about ourselves. So did the writer Artemidorus Daldianus, who, almost two thousand years earlier, penned the *Oneirocritica*—a Greek *Interpretation of Dreams*. And they weren't alone. Virtually every culture in every era has believed that dreams express otherwise inaccessible truths about the dreamer: about her forgotten or unknown past, her secret beliefs and desires, her destiny. In the same vein, virtually every culture in every era (with the halfway exception of the industrialized West) has regarded visions and hallucinations as revealing the otherwise inaccessible truths of the universe. From Siberian shamans to Aztec priests to the Merry Pranksters to spiritually inclined potheads the world over (ancient Christians, early Jews, Scythians, Sikhs, Sufis, and Rastafarians, to name just a few), we have regarded our drugs as entheogens—substances that can lay bare the truth of the cosmos and show us the face of God.

If dreams and drug states create acute but temporary alterations in our understanding of reality, the acute and ongoing version is insanity. You might think (and hope) that insanity would take us even further away from everyday error, but instead it brings us full circle. Diderot's *Encyclopédie* defined madness as the act of departing from reason "with confidence and in the firm conviction that one is following it." Maybe so, but if that's how we go crazy, it is also how we go wrong. The more recent French philosopher and historian Michel Foucault called insanity "the purest and most complete form of *quid pro quo*"—of taking one thing for another. To take something for something it is not: If that's not error, what is?

Ultimately, only three factors seem to distinguish the false reality of madness from the false reality of wrongness. The first is purity, as in Foucault's "purest form": insanity is error undiluted. The second is consistency: one noted early classifier of disease, the eighteenth-century physician François Boissier de Sauvages, described the insane as those "who persist in some notable error." The third factor concerns substance: which *quid* you take for which *quo*. We can be wrong about all manner of things, even persistently and purely wrong about them, while still retaining our claim to sanity—just so long as enough other people are wrong about them, too. This point is made by the medical definition of delusion ("a false belief *not shared by others*"), but not nearly as well as it was made by the Renaissance scholar Desiderius Erasmus in *The Praise of Folly*. "The reason a person who believes he sees a woman when in reality he is looking at a gourd is called crazy is because this is something beyond usual experience," he wrote.

"However, when a person thinks his wife, who is enjoyed by many, to be an ever-faithful Penelope, he is not called insane at all"—although he *is* called wrong—"because people know that this is a common thing in marriage." In other words, error in extremis—extremely pure, extremely persistent, or extremely peculiar—becomes insanity. Madness is radical wrongness.

Like all equations, this one is reversible. If madness is radical wrongness, being wrong is minor madness. Thus Sully, the author of *Illusions*, conceived of error as a "border-land between perfectly sane and vigorous mental life and dementia." Something of the same attitude is reflected in the Romance languages, in which being right is rendered as being sane: in French, *j'ai raison*; in Spanish, *tengo razon*. Translation: I have reason on my side, I'm in possession of my senses—whereas you, my errant friend, are straying near the borders of crazy. Minor madness can also be an apt description of how being wrong actually *feels*. We will meet more than one person in this book who characterizes his or her experience of error as scarily similar to insanity.

We already saw that hallucinations and dreams are widely regarded as revealing greater truths. So too with madness. Societies throughout the ages have nurtured the belief that the insane among us illuminate things as they truly are, despite their own ostensibly deranged relationship to reality. That's why, in literature, it is always the fools (those who never had any sense in the first place) and the madmen (those who lost it) who speak truth to power. (Children—i.e., those who have not yet reached the age of reason—sometimes play this role as well.) This narrative of wrongness as rightness might have achieved its apotheosis in *King Lear*, a play that features a real madman (Lear, after he loses it), a sane man disguised as a madman (Edgar), a blind man (Gloucester), and a fool (the Fool). I don't know where else so many characters have been set in orbit around the idea of truth, or where else truth itself has been so set on its head. Here, wisdom is folly ("for wise men are grown foppish," observes the Fool), and folly is wisdom ("This [Fool] is not altogether fool, my lord," the king's courtier dryly notes). Blindness is insight: "I stumbled when I saw," says Gloucester, who perceives the truth only after he has lost his eyes. And insanity is intellectual and moral clarity: it is only after Lear loses his daughters and his senses that he understands what he has done and can feel both loss and love.

This idea—that from error springs insight—is a hallmark of the optimistic model of wrongness. It holds even for mundane mistakes, which is why proponents of this model (myself included) see erring as vital to any process of invention and creation. The example of altered states simply throws this faith into relief: make the error extreme enough, depart not a little way but all the way from agreed-upon reality, and suddenly the humdrum of human fallibility gives way to an ecstasy of understanding. In place of humiliation and falsehood, we find fulfillment and illumination. We hear this strangely intimate relationship between error and truth in the double meaning of the word "vision," which conveys both delusion and revelation.

Unfortunately, as proponents of the pessimistic model of wrongness will be quick to point out, the reassuring notion that error yields insight does not always comport with experience. Sometimes, being wrong feels like the *death* of insight—the moment when a great idea or a grounding belief collapses out from under us. And sometimes, too, our mistakes take too great a toll to be redeemed by easy assurances of lessons learned. Here, as everywhere, the pessimistic and optimistic models part ways on the fundamental meaning of wrongness. Our errors expose the real nature of the universe—or they obscure it. They lead us toward the truth, or they lead us astray. They are the opposite of reality, or its almost indistinguishable approximation—certainly as close as we mere mortals can ever hope to get. They are abnormalities we should work to eliminate, or inevitabilities we should strive to accept. They are essentially "monstrous." They are quintessentially human.

Together, these two conflicting models form the backbone of our understanding of error. Even if we've never contemplated them before, they account for the contradictions in how we think about being wrong, and for the varying ways we experience it. Before we turn to those experiences, I want to introduce two figures who vividly embody these different models of wrongness. Unlike the various error-stricken individuals we'll meet in the rest of this book, these figures do not actually exist. They are creatures of mythology, and they do not so much err as animate—and illuminate—the ways we think about error.

In ancient Indo-European, the ancestral language of nearly half of today's global population, the word *er* meant "to move," "to set in motion," or simply "to go." (Spanish speakers will recognize it as *ir*.) That root gave rise to the Latin verb *errare*, meaning to wander or, more rakishly, to roam. The Latin, in turn, gave us the English word "erratic," used to describe movement that is unpredictable or aimless. And, of course, it gave us "error." From the beginning, then, the idea of error has contained a sense of motion: of wandering, seeking, going astray. Implicitly, what we are seeking—and what we have strayed from—is the truth.*

In the two archetypal wanderers of Western culture, we see clearly the contrasting ideas that shape our understanding of error. One of these is the knight errant and the other is the *juif errant*—the wandering Jew. The latter figure, a staple of anti-Semitic propaganda, derives from a medieval Christian legend in which a Jew, encountering Jesus on the road to the crucifixion, taunts him for moving so slowly under the weight of the cross. In response, Jesus condemns the man to roam the earth until the end of time. As the historian David Bates has observed, the wandering Jew "literally embodied, for Christian Europeans, the individual separated from the truth." In this model, erring is inextricably linked to both sin and exile. To err is to experience estrangement from God and alienation among men.

The knight errant is also a staple of medieval legend, but otherwise he could scarcely be more different. Where the wandering Jew is defined by his sin, the knight errant is distinguished by his virtue; he is explicitly and unfailingly on the side of good. His most famous representatives include Galahad, Gawain, and Lancelot, those most burnished of knights in shining armor. (A bit further afield, they also include Don Quixote, who, as

---

* Here, too, we can detect the intertwined histories of wrongness and madness. The word "hallucinate" comes from the Latin meaning to wander mentally, while "raving" comes from "roving."

both knight errant and utter lunatic, deserves his own special place in the pantheon of wrongology.) Although far from home, the knight is hardly in exile, and still less in disgrace. Unlike the *juif errant*, who is commanded to wander and does so aimlessly and in misery, the knight errant is on a quest: he wanders on purpose and with purpose, as well as with pleasure. He is driven, like all travelers, by curiosity, by the desire to experience something more of the world.

It will be clear, I hope, that I am not invoking these archetypes to endorse their obvious prejudices. Instead, I'm interested in the way those prejudices lend meaning to our two main models of wrongness. As embodied by the wandering Jew, erring is both loathsome and agonizing—a deviation from the true and the good, a public spectacle, and a private misery. This image of wrongness is disturbing, especially given the all-too-frequent fate of the non-mythological Jews: abhorred, exiled, very nearly eradicated. Yet it far more closely resembles our everyday understanding of wrongness than do the virtue and heroism of the knight errant. If this bleak idea of error speaks to us, it is because we recognize in the wandering Jew something of our own soul when we have erred. Sometimes, being wrong really does feel like being exiled: from our community, from our God, even—and perhaps most painfully—from our own best-known self.

So we should acknowledge the figure of the wandering Jew as a good description of how it can feel to be wrong. But that doesn't mean we need to accept it as the final word on error's essential meaning and moral status. For one thing, it's hard to claim *any* fixed meaning or moral status for error when we have such radically competing ideas about it. In light of that, why cleave any more closely than necessary to the most disagreeable vision of wrongness around? We have, after all, a better alternative. In fact, the idea of erring embodied by the wandering knight is not just preferable to the one embodied by the wandering Jew. It is also, and somewhat remarkably, preferable to not erring at all. To err is to wander, and wandering is the way we discover the world; and, lost in thought, it is also the way we discover ourselves. Being right might be gratifying, but in the end it is static, a mere statement. Being wrong is hard and humbling, and sometimes even dangerous, but in the end it is a journey, and a story. Who really wants to stay home and be right when you can don your armor, spring up on your steed and go forth to explore the world? True, you might get lost along the way, get stranded in a swamp, have a scare at the edge of a cliff; thieves might steal your gold, brigands might imprison you in a cave, sorcerers might turn you into a toad—but what of that? To fuck up is to find adventure: it is in that spirit that this book is written.

PART II

THE ORIGINS OF ERROR

3.

Our Senses

A lady once asked me if I believed in ghosts and apparitions. I answered
with truth and simplicity, No, madam, I have seen far too many myself.
—Samuel Taylor Coleridge

In April of 1818, the Scottish explorer John Ross sailed west from London
with two ships, thirty years of naval experience, and a mandate from the
British Admiralty to find the Northwest Passage—the much sought-after
water route across or around North America. The existence of such a route
was an open question, but its potential economic significance was beyond
dispute. Because virtually all commercial goods were transported by water
at the time, faster transit between Europe and Asia would fuel a surge in
global trade. Small wonder, then, that the quest for the Northwest Passage
had become an international obsession—a spur to exploration, a screen for
the projection of wild fantasies about the New World, and the crucible in

which men's fortunes and reputations were made or broken. By the time the 1818 expedition set sail, explorers and fortune seekers had been looking for the route for more than 300 years. For the last seventy-five of those, the British government had offered a standing prize of £20,000—about $2 million in today's money—to anyone who could find it.

A decade or so before Ross left port, Meriwether Lewis and William Clark's celebrated trek across the United States had shown that there were no navigable rivers connecting the two coasts, so subsequent explorers looked north, to the waters of the Canadian Arctic. This was a place Ross had never been. Although he had joined the navy at the age of nine, his northernmost service prior to 1818 had been in Sweden; the rest had been in the English Channel, the West Indies, and the Mediterranean. It might seem odd to select a man with no regional experience to captain such a pivotal expedition, but as it happened, John Barrow, the subsecretary of the British Admiralty who sponsored the voyage, had little choice. Virtually no explorers had sailed to the Arctic from England since William Baffin, fully 200 years earlier, making Ross's journey the inaugural Arctic expedition of the modern Royal Navy.

From Baffin's maps and reports, Ross knew of the eponymous Baffin Bay and of three large sounds—Smith, Jones, and Lancaster—in its northwestern reaches. Given wide latitude by Barrow to conduct the expedition as he saw fit, Ross determined to explore those sounds to see if any of them gave out onto the hoped for Northwest Passage. In July, after three months at sea, he and his crew reached Baffin Bay—something of a triumph itself, since Barrow, for one, had openly doubted its existence. After concluding that Smith Sound and Jones Sound were impassable, they turned their attention to Lancaster, which Ross had considered the most promising of the three. When they arrived there at the end of August, however, the sound was socked in by thick fog, and there was nothing to do but wait. Finally, at three o'clock on the afternoon of August 31, an officer knocked on Ross's cabin door to report that the skies were clearing, and the captain immediately headed for the deck. Shortly thereafter, the fog lifted completely and, Ross wrote in his account of the voyage:

I distinctly saw the land, round the bottom of the bay, forming a chain of mountains connected with those which extended along the north and south sides. This land appeared to be at the distance of eight leagues [about 27 miles]; and Mr. Lewis, the master, and James Haig, leading man, being sent for, they took its bearings, which were inserted in the log. . . . The mountains, which occupied the centre, in a north and south direction, were named Croker's Mountains, after the Secretary to the Admiralty.

So Lancaster "sound" was only an inlet. Instead of opening westward onto a waterway out of Baffin Bay and onward to the Pacific, it ended in land—a vast expanse of ice and high peaks. It also ended Ross's voyage to the Arctic. Disappointed, but having fulfilled the terms of his naval mandate, the commander returned to England.

But something odd had happened. Ross's second-in-command, one William Parry, had been following at a distance in the other ship, and he hadn't seen the mountains that Ross claimed blocked the way out of Lancaster Sound. When he got home, he made this fact known to John Barrow. As the backer of the trip and England's leading champion of the quest for the Northwest Passage, Barrow naturally preferred the idea of the mountains not existing to the idea of their existing. Trusting Parry's word, he concluded that the commander had been wrong. A cloud of mistrust and derision began to gather around Ross, even though, by most measures, he had achieved the extraordinary. Chief among his accomplishments was navigating a British ship through the treacherous waters of the eastern Arctic and returning it safely home. At the same time, he had verified William Baffin's previously disputed travel report, opened up Baffin Bay for the British whaling industry, documented the first known encounter between Westerners and the regional Inuit population, gathered important information about tides, ice, and magnetism, and brought back any number of biological and geological specimens. But in the face of the fervor over the Northwest Passage, none of that carried much weight. Ross's reputation was tarnished, and it was soon to tank. Less than a year after the 1818 expedition returned,

Barrow sent Parry back to Lancaster Sound for a second look. This time, Parry *did* see the Croker range—and then he sailed right through it. The mountains were a mirage.

John Ross had fallen victim to one of the stranger and more fascinating optical phenomena on earth. Anyone who has been in a car on a hot day is familiar with the mirage in which a pool of water seems to cover the highway in the distance but disappears as you approach. This is called an inferior mirage, or sometimes a desert mirage, since the same phenomenon causes nonexistent oases to appear to travelers in hot, sandy lands. But very few of us are familiar with mirages of the kind Ross saw, because the conditions necessary to produce them are usually found only near the earth's poles. This type of mirage is known as a superior (or arctic) mirage. Inferior mirages show us things that don't exist—puddles on the road or pools in the desert. But superior mirages show us things that do exist. The mountains that Ross saw were real. The trouble is, they weren't twenty-five miles west of him in Lancaster Sound. They were *two hundred* miles west of him, on a distant island in the Canadian Arctic.

Needless to say, under normal circumstances, we don't see mountains from 200 miles away and conclude that they are nearby. In fact, barring optimal conditions, we don't see mountains from 200 miles away, period. But by bending light rays from beyond the horizon up toward us, superior mirages lift objects into our field of vision that are usually obscured by the curvature of the earth. Such mirages begin with a temperature inversion. Normally, air temperatures are warmest near the surface of the earth and start dropping as you go up. (Think about how much colder it is on top of a mountain than in the valley below.) But in a temperature inversion, this arrangement reverses. A cold layer of air close to the earth—say, directly above the polar land or sea—meets a higher, warmer layer of air created by atypical atmospheric conditions. This inverted situation dramatically increases the degree to which light can bend. In the Arctic or Antarctic, where surface air temperatures are extremely cold, light sometimes bends so much that the photons that eventually strike any available human retinas can be reflected from objects up to several hundred miles away. The result

The illusory Croker Mountains, as drawn by John Ross in his travel journal.

is, in essence, another kind of false fire—a trick of the light that leads unwary travelers astray.

Ross was by no means the first or last seafarer to be fooled by an Arctic mirage. The Celts, who sailed from the Norwegian Sea's Faroe Islands in the eighth century and made landfall on what is now Iceland, were probably tempted into their boats by mirages that made the distant land appear far closer than it was. Likewise, historians speculate that the Vikings ventured to North America (where they landed sometime around AD 1000) after spotting a superior mirage of the mountains of Baffin Island from the coast of Greenland. As these examples suggest, superior mirages are particularly likely to consist of mountains and other large land masses. But because such mirages can show us anything that actually exists, rather than the shimmering illusion of water that is the inferior mirage's only trick, their subject matter is, in theory, almost unlimited. Accordingly, sailors have also reported seeing arctic mirages of relatively small objects, including icebergs, pack ice, and—most hauntingly—other ships.*

---

* History's largest recorded mirage is of an entire continent. In 1906, the American explorer Robert Peary was exploring far northern Canada on foot when he looked out to sea and saw, at a distance he estimated to be 120 miles, a land mass that spanned so much of the horizon that he concluded that it must be a continent. The nomenclature of

To get a sense of just how compelling such mirages can be, consider the comparatively recent experience of the Canadian captain Robert Bartlett. On July 17, 1939, while sailing between Greenland and Iceland, Bartlett suddenly spotted the coast of the latter country, looming so large that he could easily make out many familiar landmarks. Like John Ross, Bartlett estimated the apparent distance of the coast at twenty-five or thirty miles away. But he knew its actual distance was more than ten times that, since his ship was positioned roughly 350 miles from the Icelandic coast. That he could see land at all is astonishing—akin to seeing the Washington Monument from Ohio. And yet, Bartlett wrote, "If I hadn't been sure of my position and had been bound for Reykjavik, I would have expected to arrive within a few hours. The contours of the land and the snow-covered summit of the Snaefells Jökull [glacier] showed up unbelievably near."

Only 125 years' worth of improvements in navigational tools and geographic knowledge prevented Bartlett from making virtually the same mistake as Ross. Thanks to those advances in technology, including information technology, Bartlett was able to override his own judgment. His resources may have been better, but his senses were equally, spectacularly deceived.

---

polar exploration gets rather confusing at this point, because Peary (not to be confused with Parry, John Ross's second-in-command) named the place he saw Crocker Land (not to be confused with Ross's Croker Mountains). Peary reported the discovery upon his return to the United States, and, seven years later, one of his former lieutenants, Donald MacMillan, set forth to explore the new continent. MacMillan made camp in the Canadian Arctic, and, once the Polar Sea had frozen, set across it. After slogging almost 600 miles by foot and dogsled, he and his men spotted a vast terrain that perfectly matched Peary's description. But as they continued toward it, the land seemed to change, and when the sun dropped down in the night sky, it disappeared entirely. The men pressed on anyway, past the point where they should have reached the mysterious continent, but they never encountered land. Since, as we now know, no vast continent lurked a few hundred miles further on, this was not precisely an arctic mirage, but rather a fata morgana—an illusion of magnification and distortion. The explorers were actually seeing only the corrugated surface of the frozen sea itself, thrown radically out of proportion by the capricious polar light.

. . .

Of the very long list of reasons we can get things wrong, the most elementary of them all is that our senses fail us. Although these failures sometimes have grave consequences (just ask Captain Ross), we usually think of sensory mistakes as relatively trivial. In fact, we often don't think of them as mistakes at all. And yet, in many respects, failures of perception capture the essential nature of error. There's a reason that James Sully, that early chronicler of wrongness, took *Illusions* as both the title of his book and the template for all other forms of error.

The rest of us do this, too, albeit mostly without realizing it. When we discover that we have been wrong, we say that we were *under an illusion*, and when we no longer believe in something, we say that we are *disillusioned*. More generally, analogies to vision are ubiquitous in the way we think about knowledge and error. People who possess the truth are *perceptive, insightful, observant, illuminated, enlightened,* and *visionary*; by contrast, the ignorant are *in the dark*. When we comprehend something, we say *I see*. And we say, too, that the scales have fallen from our eyes; that once we were blind, but now we see.

This link between seeing and knowing is not just metaphorical. For the most part, we accept as true anything that we see with our own eyes, or register with any of our other senses. We take it on faith that blue is blue, that hot is hot, that we are seeing a palm tree sway in the breeze because there is a breeze blowing and a palm tree growing. As I've already suggested, and as we'll see in more detail in the upcoming chapters, we are all prone to regarding the ideas in our own heads as direct reflections of reality, and this is particularly true in the domain of perception. Heat, palm trees, blueness, breeziness: we take these to be attributes of the world that our senses simply and passively absorb.

If that were the case, however, it is unclear how our senses could ever deceive us—which, as we've just seen, they are eminently capable of doing. Moreover, they are capable of doing so under entirely normal circumstances, not just under exceptional ones like those John Ross experienced. Consider what happens when you step outside on a cloudless night. For the purpose

"Landing the Treasures, or Results of the Polar Expedition!!!," a 1819 cartoon by George Cruikshank ridiculing the Ross voyage. The man on the far left is saying, "I think as how we have bears, gulls, savages, chump wood, stones, and puppies enough without going to the North Pole for them." Ross and his crew are depicted without noses, a reference to an Inuit practice of pulling noses in place of shaking hands. (The man carrying the rear end of the polar bear is saying, "It's a good thing I've lost my nose.")

of this thought experiment, imagine that you step outside not in Chicago or Houston, but in someplace truly dark: the Himalayas, say, or Patagonia, or the north rim of the Grand Canyon. If you look up in such a place, you will observe that the sky above you is vast and vaulted, its darkness pulled taut from horizon to horizon and perforated by innumerable stars. Stand there long enough and you'll see this whole vault turning overhead, like the slowest of tumblers in the most mysterious of locks. Stand there even longer and it will dawn on you that your own position in this spectacle is curiously central. The apex of the heavens is directly above you. And the land you are standing on—land that unlike the firmament is quite flat, and unlike the stars is quite stationary—stretches out in all directions from a midpoint that is you.

Occasional bad weather and a hundred-odd years of artificial illumination aside, this is the view that we as a species have been looking at for 73 million nighttimes. It is also, of course, an illusion: almost everything we see and feel out there on our imaginary Patagonian porch is misleading. The sky is neither vaulted nor revolving around us, the land is neither flat nor stationary, and, sad to say, we ourselves are not the center of the cosmos.

Not only are these things wrong, they are *canonically* wrong. They are to the intellect what the *Titanic* is to the ego: a permanent puncture wound, a reminder of the sheer scope at which we can err. What is strange, and not a little disconcerting, is that we can commit such fundamental mistakes by doing nothing more than stepping outside and looking up. No byzantine theorizing was necessary to arrive at the notion that the stars move and we do not. (In fact, it's the byzantine theorizing that is gradually nudging us toward a more accurate understanding of the universe.) We simply saw the former, and felt the latter.

The fallibility of perception was a thorn in the side of early philosophers, because most of them took the senses to be the main source of our knowledge about the world. This raised an obvious question: if we can't trust our senses, how can we trust our knowledge? One early and clever solution to this problem was to deny that there *was* a problem. That was the fix favored by Protagoras, the leader of a group of philosophers known as the Sophists, who held forth in ancient Greece around the fifth century BC. Protagoras agreed that the senses were the source of all knowledge, but he categorically denied that they could be wrong. You might imagine that this conviction would lead to a kind of absolute realism: the world is precisely as we perceive it. But that only works if we all perceive the world exactly the same way. Since we don't, Protagoras wound up espousing radical relativism instead. To borrow an example from Plato (whose extensive rebuttal of the Sophists is the chief reason we know what they believed): if a breeze is blowing and I think it is balmy and you think it is chilly, then what temperature is it really? Protagoras would say it is warm to me and cold to you, and that's that. There is no reality "out there" for the senses to perceive or misperceive; the information provided by our senses *is* reality. And if my senses happen to contradict yours—well, then our realities must differ. In matters of perception, Protagoras argued, everyone was always right.

Protagoras deserves recognition for being the first philosopher in Western history to explicitly address the problem of error, if only by denying its existence. For most of us, though, his position on perception is intrinsically unsatisfying (much as relativism more generally can seem frustrat-

ingly flaccid in the face of certain hard truths about the world). Plato, for
one, thought it was nonsense. He noted that even a breeze must have its
own internal essence, quite apart from whoever it blows on, and essentially
advised Protagoras to get a thermometer. But Plato also rejected the whole
notion that our senses are the original source of knowledge. Since, as I
mentioned earlier, he thought our primordial souls were at one with the
universe, he believed that we come to know the basic truths about the world
through a form of memory. Other philosophers agreed with Protagoras
that the senses are a crucial conduit of information, but, unlike him, they
acknowledged that perception can fail. This seems like a reasonable position, and one we are likely to share, but it raises two related and thorny
questions. First, how exactly do our senses go about acquiring information
about the world? And second, how can we determine when that information is accurate and when it is not?

Early philosophers regarded the first question as, essentially, a spatial-
relations problem. The world is outside us; our senses are within us. How,
then, do the two come together so that we can know something? Obviously
our senses can't go forth and drag an actual chunk of the world back to their
internal lair, intact and as is, for the benefit of the rest of the brain. But—
outside of dreams, hallucinations, and madness—most perceptions aren't
produced solely by our minds either. Instead, our senses must somehow
bridge the gap I described in Chapter One: the rift between our own minds
and everything else. One way to understand how they do this is to think
of sensing as two different (although not normally separable) operations.
The first is sensation, in which our nervous system responds to a piece of
information from our environment. The second is perception, in which
we process that information and make it meaningful. Perception, in other
words, is the interpretation of sensation.

Interpretation implies wiggle room—space to deviate from a literal
reading, whether of a book or of the world. As that suggests, this model
of perception (unlike the one in which our senses just passively reflect our
surroundings) has no trouble accommodating the problem of error. Every
step in the interpretative process represents a point of potential divergence

between our minds and the world—a breach where mistakes can sneak in. This model also answers the second question I asked about perception: How can we determine when it is accurate and when it is not? Unfortunately, the answer is that we cannot. Since we generally have no access to the objects of our sensory impressions other than through our senses, we have no independent means of verifying their accuracy. True, we can seek confirmation from other people's senses, but there's no way to be sure that theirs aren't failing them in the same way. As a result, there is no guarantee that we aren't as wrong about a basic perception right now as most people were for most of history about the nature of the night sky.

This isn't to say that every act of interpretation is an act of misinterpretation. In perception, as in so many things in life, departing from literalism often serves us uncommonly well—serves, even, a deeper truth. Consider a mundane visual phenomenon: when objects recede into the distance, they appear to get smaller. If we had sensation without interpretation, we would assume that those objects were actually shrinking, or perhaps that we were growing—either way, a bewildering, Alice-in-Wonderland-esque conclusion. Instead, we are able to preserve what is known as size constancy by automatically recalibrating scale in accordance with distance. We know that planes don't get smaller after they take off, and that the buildings in our rearview mirror don't sink into the earth as we drive away.

For a different example of the utility of interpretation, consider your blind spot—the literal one, I mean. The blind spot is that part of the eye where the optic nerve passes through the retina, preventing any visual processing from taking place. If perception were just unembellished sensation, we would experience a chronic lacuna where this nerve interrupts our visual field. But we do not, because our brain automatically corrects the problem through a process known as coherencing. If the blind spot is surrounded by blue sky, we will "see" blue sky there as well; if it is surrounded by Times Square, we will "see" tourists and taxis. These, then, are instances—just two of many—in which the interpretative processes of perception sharpen rather than distort our picture of the world.

No matter what these processes do, though, one thing remains the same: we have no idea that they are doing it. The mechanisms that form our perceptions operate almost entirely below the level of conscious awareness; ironically, we cannot sense how we sense. And here another bit of meta-wrongness arises. Because we can't perceive these processes in action, and thereby take note of the places where error could enter the picture, we feel that we cannot be wrong. Or, more precisely, we cannot feel that we could be wrong. Our obliviousness to the act of interpretation leaves us insensitive—literally—to the possibility of error. And that is how you and I and everybody else in the world occasionally winds up in (you will pardon the expression) Captain John Ross's boat.

I can't whisk you off to the Arctic to see a superior mirage, but I can easily get you to think you see something you don't. Look:

This is one of my favorite optical illusions, not because it is particularly dazzling but because it is particularly maddening. The trick is that the square labeled A and the square labeled B are identical shades of gray. No, really. In fact, if you think of this image as a checkerboard, then all the "white" squares that fall within the shadow of the cylinder (like B) are the same color as all the "black" squares that fall outside the shadow (like A).

You don't believe me, for the very good reason that you *do* believe your eyes, and your eyes are telling you that these squares look completely different. Actually, it's not your eyes that are telling you this; it's a handful of interpretative processes of the kind I just described. These processes are in play because, when it comes to determining the color of objects around us, our visual system can't afford to be too literal. If it were, it would do nothing but measure the wavelength of light reflecting off a given object. In that case, as the psychologist Steven Pinker has pointed out, we would think that a lump of coal sitting in bright sunlight was white, and that a lump of snow inside a dark house was black. Instead, we're able to correct for the presence of light and shadow so that the coal still appears fundamentally black and the snow still appears fundamentally white.

One way we do this is through local contrast. In nature, if something is lighter than its immediate surroundings, it's probably light in an absolute sense, rather than just because of the way the sun is or isn't striking it. That's one reason why, in this illusion, we read Square B (which is lighter than the dark checks around it) as light, period. The same phenomenon applies in reverse, so that we read Square A (which is darker than the squares around it) as dark, period. This interpretation is reinforced by several other interpretative processes, including the fact that we automatically adjust for cast shadows, mentally lightening whatever objects they fall on—in this case, Square B.

The net effect of these visual "corrections" is an illusion that is absolutely unshakeable. When I first saw it, I was so incredulous that I finally took a pair of scissors and cut the picture apart—whereupon, lo and behold, the A and B squares became indistinguishable from each other. In an effort to discourage you from mutilating this book, I offer a second image:

Not quite as convincing as slicing and dicing, perhaps, but a good start. (If you must cut it apart yourself to be persuaded, the original image—and a lot of other fun stuff—is available on the website of its creator, Edward Adelson, a professor of vision science at MIT.)

What makes this illusion both irksome and fascinating is that knowing how it works does not prevent it from working. No matter how many times you read the above explanation (or how many copies of the image you cut to pieces), the two shades of gray will still look strikingly different to you. Likewise, Robert Bartlett's knowledge that he was 350 miles from Iceland could keep him from getting lost, but it was powerless to prevent him from seeing the Icelandic coast looming up before him. This is one of the defining features of illusions: they are robust, meaning that our eyes fall for them even when our higher cognitive functions are aware that we are being deceived. A second defining feature is that they are consistent: we misperceive them every time we come across them. Finally, they are universal: all of us misperceive them in precisely the same way.*

These characteristics make sense when you recall that illusions are the product of unconscious and universal perceptual processes. But here's the important part: those same processes—the ones that cause us to screw up when we encounter illusions—serve us extremely well in everyday life. This helps explain why a scientist at one of the most respected academic institutions in the world is paid to sit around developing optical illusions.

---

* I'm focusing here on universal perceptual mistakes, but our senses can also err in individual, idiosyncratic ways. One person who thought seriously about this was the eighteenth-century German philosopher Immanuel Kant. Most of the ancient philosophers who studied perception (Plato and Protagoras, et al.) were concerned primarily with physical operations: with how the mechanisms of touch, taste, vision, olfaction, and audition interact with the properties of the world. But Kant was interested primarily in psychological processes, and he argued that our beliefs, desires, thoughts, and feelings also influence the way we perceive our environment. This contribution to the philosophy of perception was crucial, because it explained how we could get not just universal errors like mirages, but also individual sensory mistakes—how two people who see or hear the same thing can walk away with two entirely different impressions of it. Protagoras explained this by saying that reality varied. Kant said no, it is people who vary, right down to our ways of perceiving the world.

The real object of study is not the illusions themselves but the processes that give rise to them—processes that would be far harder to study (or even know about) if they didn't occasionally produce surprising and erroneous results. Moreover, because illusions trick all of us (rather than, say, only stroke victims or only children), they help us understand how visual perception operates in a healthy, mature brain. In studying illusions, scientists aren't learning how our visual system fails. They are learning how it works.

This point merits some emphasis: being wrong is often a side effect of a system that is functioning exactly right. Remember size constancy, our automatic ability to recalibrate scale according to distance? This is a handy trick 99.99 percent of the time. The other 0.01 percent occurs when, say, you find yourself on a ship in the Arctic looking at very large mountains, which you therefore conclude are very nearby. In this case (and in many others, as we'll see), mistakes arise when a basically reliable system leads us astray. That's part of what makes optical illusions, and errors more generally, so unforeseeable and surprising: not only do they arise from processes we can't feel, they arise from processes that, under normal circumstances, work to our advantage.

Illusions, then, are the misleading outcomes of normal (and normally beneficial) perceptual processes. This isn't just true of the visual kind. If you've ever seen a ventriloquist, you've been duped by another of these processes—in this case, one that automatically integrates information from your visual and auditory systems. (Thus if you hear speech and see a moving mouth, you'll register the speech as coming from that mouth—even if it belongs to a three-foot tall wooden puppet.) Other auditory illusions are even more common. If you have either a cell phone or a baby, you are familiar with the experience of hearing your particular phone ringing, or your particular baby crying, when in fact it is (for once) quiet. Then there are tactile illusions, of which by far the most famous is that of the phantom limb: the amputee's persistent, unshakable sense of experiencing sensation in his or her missing body part. Those of us fortunate enough to have all our limbs sometimes experience a similar if sillier feeling known as—no joke—the phantom hat. In this illusion, we continue to feel the presence of a tightly worn accessory, bandage, or article of clothing for some time after it has been removed.*

As this brief catalogue makes clear, and as I suggested earlier, most sensory illusions are not terribly important. Unless you are a vision scientist or an amputee or Captain John Ross, they have pretty much the status of parlor tricks. Occasionally, though, the quirks of our perceptual system leave us vulnerable to more serious errors. Take, for instance, a phenomenon known as inattentional blindness. There is a rather amazing experiment—which I'm about to ruin for you—in which subjects are shown a video of a group of people playing a fast-paced ball game and are asked to count how many times the ball is passed back and forth. At some point during the video, a gorilla (more precisely, a person in a gorilla costume) wanders into the middle of the group of players, stands around for a bit, beats its chest a few times, and then wanders off again. Here's the amazing part: between 33 and 50 percent of subjects don't see this happen. Perhaps this bears repeating: one-third to one-half of people instructed to pay close attention to a video fail to see a gorilla beating its chest in the middle of it.

This is inattentional blindness in action. It turns out that when we ask people to look for something specific, they develop a startling inability to see things in general. This cognitive peculiarity has been recorded since at least the 1970s, but you have to hand it to the designers of this study—the psychologists Daniel Simons and Christopher Chabris—for going well beyond what less inspired thinkers might have imagined was the logical extreme in order to demonstrate its potency. (The video is available on the website of the Visual Cognition Lab of the University of Illinois. But be warned: having read this paragraph, you will not fail to see the gorilla. It's as if, rather than asking you to count the number of basketball passes, I've asked you to count the number of great apes. However, close to half your friends can still be duped.)

---

* The phantom limb and the phantom hat illustrate an important point, which is that we react to and interpret not just information from the outside world, but from our interior world as well. And sometimes—as in these phantom sensations—we misinterpret it. We will see another, even more dramatic example of this in the next chapter.

Like other automatic perceptual processes, inattentional blindness is generally quite useful. Without it, we wouldn't be able to tune out the noise in our environment and focus on the task at hand. But when this process works against us, the consequences can be grave. In 1972, Eastern Airlines Flight 401 was preparing to land in Miami when a light on the control panel failed to illuminate. The three crewmembers in the cockpit became so focused on the problem that they didn't notice that the plane was continuing its descent on autopilot. The flight crashed in the Everglades, killing a hundred people. Analysis of the cockpit voice recorder showed that none of the crew noticed the impending crisis until just seconds before the crash. Similarly, inattentional blindness is thought to be a culprit in many car accidents, especially those involving pedestrians and cyclists—who, no matter how visible they make themselves, are less likely to be anticipated by drivers, and thus less likely to be seen. On a less frightening but still frustrating note, inattentional blindness is commonly exploited by thieves who work in pairs or groups to create a distraction, thereby drawing their target's attention away from what would otherwise be the obvious pilfering of his or her possessions.

This deliberate exploitation of systemic perceptual glitches has a long and occasionally disreputable history, especially within religion and politics. One early account of the use of illusions for such purposes comes from David Brewster, a Scottish polymath and the author of the 1833 *Letters on Natural Magic*. Brewster was interested in "the means by which [ancient governments] maintained their influence over the human mind—of the assistance which they derived from the arts and the sciences, and from a knowledge of the powers and phenomena of nature." If you've ever wondered about the origins of the phrase "smoke and mirrors," Brewster provides a detailed description of how to use pieces of concave silver to throw human images against a background of smoke, thereby making gods (or rulers, or enemies) seem to dance and writhe in the center of a fire. His catalog of auditory illusions includes, among others, explanations of the mechanisms behind "the golden virgins whose ravishing voices resounded through the temple of Delphos; the stone from the river Pactolus, whose trumpet notes scared the robber from the treasure which it guarded; the speaking head which uttered its oracular responses at Lesbos; and the vocal statue of Memnon, which began at the break of day to accost the rising sun."

As these examples suggest, dominion over perception is power. This is not a truth limited to ancient times. In fact, the most crystalline example of it might come from Brewster's own era, in the form of a footnote to the history of colonial Africa. In the mid-nineteenth century, France was experiencing difficulty in Algeria. The region's Islamic holy men were using their status—and supposedly their supernatural powers—to encourage resistance to colonial rule, and the resulting rebellion was proving difficult to quell. Deciding to fight fire with fire, Napoleon III turned to one Jean Eugène Robert-Houdin, an erstwhile watchmaker who had become an extraordinarily inventive and convincing illusionist. (Today Robert-Houdin is recognized as the father of modern magic, an honor that comes complete with a kind of figurative primogeniture. In 1890, an aspiring young magician named Ehrich Weiss, seeking to pay homage to his hero, changed his name to Houdini.) Napoleon sent Robert-Houdin to Algeria with instructions to out-holy the holy men, and so he did. Wielding the full panoply of contemporary illusions—plucking cannon balls from hats, catching bullets between his teeth, causing perfectly incarnate chieftains to vanish without a trace—the magician convinced his audience that the more powerful gods were on the side of the empire, and that the French, accordingly, were not to be trifled with.*

Our perceptual glitches, then, can leave us vulnerable to exploitation, whether by politicians or pickpockets. They can make us dangerous unto ourselves and others, as in the crash of Eastern Airlines Flight 401. They can be disruptive, whether slightly (as when we realize that our eyes are misprocessing an image of a checkerboard) or massively (as when we discover that the sun does not revolve around the earth). They can be con-

---

* Robert-Houdin's work in Algeria is essentially an antecedent to modern military psychological operations, or psy-ops. Not all psy-ops involve the manipulation of perception, but many do. The Iraq War provides (at least) two memorable examples: the highly choreographed toppling of the statue of Saddam Hussein in Baghdad, and the much-publicized distortion and dramatization of the "saving" of Private Jessica Lynch.

sequential (as when an imaginary mountain chain scuttles your career) or trivial (as when a puddle on the road evanesces as you approach). And they can be pleasurable, as when we gape at optical illusions or flock to magic shows.

Dangerous, disruptive, consequential, trivial, pleasurable: as tangential to error as they initially seem, perceptual failures turn out to showcase virtually the entire practical and emotional range of our mistakes. That's one reason why I claimed earlier that they are the paradigmatic form of wrongness. But another and more important reason is this: illusions teach us how to think about error. Intellectually, they show us how even the most convincing vision of reality can diverge from reality itself, and how cognitive processes that we can't detect—and that typically serve us quite well—leave us vulnerable to mistakes. Emotionally, illusions are a gateway drug to humility. If we have trouble acknowledging our own errors and forgiving those of others, at least we can begin by contemplating the kind of mistakes to which we all succumb.

Illusions make this possible, but they also make it palatable. In defiance of the pessimistic model of error—which can't account for illusions, and therefore claims that they don't count—we experience these sensory errors as fun, and pleasurable, and just about endlessly fascinating. This fascination begins very young (optical illusions, like knock-knock jokes, are a particular passion of elementary school kids) and doesn't appear to diminish with age. In other words, illusions are not just universally experienced. They are universally *loved*.

This attraction to illusions upends our conventional relationship to wrongness. We are usually happiest when we think that we understand and have mastery over our environment. Yet with illusions such as mirages, we take pleasure in the ability of the world to outfox us, to remind us that its bag of tricks is not yet empty. We usually like to be right. Yet in illusions such as Edward Adelson's checkerboard (where we can neither see the image correctly nor fathom how we could be seeing it wrong), we experience an agreeable astonishment that there was room for error after all. We usually dislike the experience of being stuck between two conflicting theories. Yet in another class of illusions—including the famous vases/faces and old woman/young woman images*—our pleasure lies precisely in being able to toggle back and forth between two different and equally convincing visions of reality. Finally, we usually do not care to dwell on our mistakes after they happen, even if it would behoove us to do so. Yet illusions command our attention and inspire us to try to understand them—and to understand, too, the workings and failings of our own minds.

Granted, it is easy, at least comparatively, to find pleasure in error when there's nothing at stake. But that can't be the whole story, since all of us have been known to throw tantrums over totally trivial mistakes. What makes illusions different is that, for the most part, we enter into them by consent. We might not know exactly how we are going to err, but we know that the error is coming, and we say yes to the experience anyway.

In a sense, much the same thing could be said of life in general. We can't know where our next error lurks or what form it will take, but we can be very sure that it is waiting for us. With illusions, we look forward to this encounter, since whatever minor price we pay in pride is handily outweighed by curiosity at first and by pleasure afterward. The same will not always be true as we venture past these simple perceptual failures to more complex and consequential mistakes. But nor is the willing embrace of error always beyond us. In fact, this might be the most important thing illusions can teach us: that it is possible, at least some of the time, to find in being wrong a deeper satisfaction than we would have found in being right.

---

* Both of these illusions feature a single image that can be interpreted in two different ways. In the first, focusing on the (white) foreground reveals a vase, while focusing on the (black) background reveals two faces; in the second, focusing on certain details reveals the profile of a beautiful young woman, while focusing on others reveals a distinctly less attractive older woman. I've reproduced both illusions in the endnotes.

4.

Our Minds, Part One: Knowing, Not Knowing, and Making It Up

> "I know" seems to describe a state of affairs which
> guarantees what is known, guarantees it as a fact. One
> always forgets the expression, "I thought I knew."
> —LUDWIG WITTGENSTEIN, *ON CERTAINTY*

In 1992, a forty-six-year-old woman whom I'll call Hannah underwent a neurological examination at a hospital in Vienna, Austria. The neurologist, Georg Goldenberg, began by asking Hannah to describe his own face. It was an odd question, but Hannah complied. The doctor had short hair and was clean shaven, she said; he wasn't wearing glasses, and he looked like he had a bit of a tan. Goldenberg next asked Hannah about an object in front of her. It was a notebook, she answered, like the kind schoolchildren use, with a brown cover and some writing in Latin script that she couldn't quite make out. And where exactly was the book located, the doctor asked her. He was holding it up in his left hand, Hannah replied, at just about eye level.

The trouble was this: Goldenberg's face was concealed behind a screen, the object in front of his patient was a comb, and before asking about its location, he'd hidden it beneath the table in front of him. Hannah was blind. One month earlier, she had suffered a stroke that destroyed virtually her entire visual cortex and left her all but unable to move, owing to loss of muscle coordination and chronic, epilepsy-like contractions, especially on the left side of her body. All that was bad enough. But Hannah was also left with a rarer and stranger problem: she didn't know that she was blind.

To be blind without realizing our blindness is, figuratively, the situation of all of us when we are in error. As a literal predicament, however, it is all but impossible to fathom. It is weird enough to see a mountain when there is no mountain, as Captain John Ross did. But it is *really* weird to see a mountain when you cannot see. And yet, this blind-to-our-own-blindness condition exists. It is called Anton's Syndrome, and it belongs to a group of similar neurological problems collectively known as anosognosia, or the denial of disease. The most common form of anosognosia—far more common than Anton's Syndrome, although equally hard to imagine—is the denial of paralysis. Like denial of blindness, denial of paralysis typically (although not exclusively) occurs in stroke victims. Just as Hannah unhesitatingly described people and objects she couldn't see, these patients will confidently tell their doctors or family members that of course they are able to move—or that they just did move, or even that they are currently doing so. One illustrious (and illustrative) victim of this strange syndrome, the late Supreme Court Justice William Douglas, claimed that he had no physical problems and cheerfully invited a reporter covering his stroke to join him for a hike.

Anton's Syndrome and denial of paralysis are, to put it mildly, bizarre. There are plenty of physical conditions that can afflict us without our knowledge: heart disease, cancer, autoimmune disorders—all the terrible sleeper cells of the body. But blindness and paralysis are not normally among them. Whether or not we can see, whether or not we can move: this kind of intimate knowledge of our own body isn't usually subject to uncertainty, let alone error. In fact, it doesn't even sound quite right to describe these things as knowledge of our body. Noticing that we have a sore throat or recognizing that our knees aren't quite as reliable as they used to be are clearly instances of bodily knowledge. But sore throats and bum knees are pretty much *only* about our bodies. They don't bear very deeply on our sense of who we are, whereas the abilities to see and to move definitely do. Moreover, these abilities bear on the most basic kind of selfhood there is—not the complex, striated, narrative identity we build up over time, but the one we have from birth: the unspoken but profoundly central sense that we are *this* kind of being, with *this* kind of relationship to the world.

In a sense, then, people with anosognosia are as wrong as it is possible to be. Other errors might be more sweeping in their consequences or more emotionally devastating: being wrong about your family history, say, or committing wholeheartedly to a theology, ideology, or person you later wholeheartedly reject. But no other error requires us to concede quite so much ground to the sheer possibility of being wrong. If mistakes arise from the gap between our inner picture of the world and the world as it really is, anosognosia shows us that this gap never fully closes, even when we can least fathom its existence. It is all but impossible to imagine that, for instance, my belief that I'm moving my arm could be at odds with what my arm is actually doing. There seems to be no room for doubt, no plausible way I could be wrong. Indeed, we use our certainty about our own bodies to emphasize the depths of our other convictions: we say that we know something like the back of our hands, or that it's as plain as the nose on our face. Yet neurologists suspect that precisely what goes awry in denial of paralysis and Anton's syndrome is that the brain mistakes an idea in the mind (in the former case, thinking about moving a limb; in the latter, remembering or imagining a visual landscape) for a feature of the real world. What anosognosia shows us, then, is that wrongness knows no limits—that there is no form of knowledge, however central or unassailable it may seem, that cannot, under certain circumstances, fail us.

This fallibility of knowledge is gravely disappointing, because we really, really love to know things. One of my nieces, who is not yet eighteen months old, recently uttered her first sentence. It was "I know." To have such scanty experience of the world and so much implacable assurance is pretty impressive—but my niece, as much as I adore her, is not exceptional in this regard. From the time we learn to talk until death finally silences us, we all toss around claims to knowledge with profligate enthusiasm. We know, or think we know, innumerable things, and we enjoy the feeling of mastery and confidence our knowledge gives us.

Unfortunately, as we just saw, this knowledge is always at risk of failing. Moreover (as we'll see next) the barometer we use to determine whether we do or don't know something is deeply, unfixably flawed. By contrast—although not reassuringly—our capacity to ignore the fact that we don't know things works wonderfully. In sum: we love to know things, but ultimately we can't know for sure that we know them; we are bad at recognizing when we *don't* know something; and we are very, very good at making stuff up. All this serves to render the category of "knowledge" unreliable—so much so that this chapter exists largely to convince you to abandon it (if only temporarily, for the purpose of understanding wrongness) in favor of the category of belief.

We'll look at that category more closely in the next chapter, but for now, suffice it to say that it includes just about every idea you have about the world—whether or not you know you have it, and whether or not it is true. For several millennia, philosophers have tried to identify criteria by which some of those beliefs could be elevated into the loftier category of knowledge: things we can reasonably claim to know beyond a shadow of a doubt. The most enduring suggestion was offered by Plato, who defined knowledge as "justified true belief." To his mind, you could only claim to know something if A) it was true; and B) you could come up with a good explanation for why it was true. That ruled out false beliefs with strong explanations (such as the claim that the sun revolved around the earth), as well as true beliefs with weak explanation (such as my claim that I'm holding the winning raffle ticket—which it turns out that I am—because "I can feel it in my bones").

Plato's definition kicked off 2,500 years of debates about the nature of knowledge. The earliest objection to it came from the Skeptics, who argued that *no* beliefs are verifiably true, and that therefore (my niece notwithstanding) we can't rightly claim to know anything. Other philosophers, by contrast, feel that we can claim to know some things, but argue that Plato didn't go far enough in specifying which ones. For these thinkers, knowledge is belief with a bunch of backup: belief that is not only justified and true, but also *necessarily* true, impossible to disprove, arrived at in a certain fashion, and so forth.

For my purposes, there are two important things to be learned from these debates. The first is that knowledge is conventionally viewed as belief plus a bunch of credentials, an idea we'll return to at the end of this chapter. The second is that even if you happen to be a professional philosopher, it is very difficult to figure out what, if anything, you can rightly claim to know. This isn't an issue that particularly troubles the rest of us, not because we are such brilliant natural philosophers but because the experience of knowing something seems relatively straightforward. For most of us, whether or not we know a particular fact isn't something we think about; it is something we feel. As William James wrote, "Of some things we feel that we are certain: we know, and we know that we do know. There is something that gives a click inside of us, a bell that strikes twelve, when the hands of our mental clock have swept the dial and meet over the meridian hour."

James did not mean this as a compliment. The feeling of knowing something is incredibly convincing and inordinately satisfying, but it is not a very good way to gauge the accuracy of our knowledge. Blind Hannah presumably "knew" that she could see, but *we* know that she was wrong. That's the problem with the feeling of knowing: it fills us with the conviction of rightness whether we're right or not. Perhaps the most vivid way to see this problem in action is within the domain of memory, where all of us have experienced the sensation of a powerful inner certainty, and where the feeling of knowing has received some of the most extensive attention. In this domain, the "knowledge" in question is knowledge of what happened in the past—except when it turns out not to be knowledge at all.

On December 7, 1941, a thirteen-year-old boy named Ulric Neisser was listening to the radio when he learned that the Japanese had just attacked Pearl Harbor. The experience made a huge impression on the child. For decades to come, he would carry around the memory of a radio announcer interrupting the baseball game he'd been listening to with a bulletin about the bombing.

In its vividness, intensity, and longevity, Neisser's recollection was typical of how our minds react to unusually shocking events. Think about your own memories of a different national tragedy—the terrorist attacks of September 11, 2001. If you are American, I will bet my bank account that you know what you were doing that day: how you learned the news, where you were at the time, how you felt, who you talked to, what you thought about what had happened. I will further bet that those memories are unusually vivid and detailed (certainly far more so than your memories of, say, September 5, 2001, which probably don't even exist), and that you have a high degree of confidence in their accuracy. But—one last wager—I will also bet that, to one degree or another, you're wrong. Neisser certainly was. Forty years after the fact, something suddenly dawned on him: professional baseball isn't played in December.

By then, as fate would have it, the thirteen-year-old baseball fan had become a psychology professor at Emory University, and, in 1989, he published a groundbreaking study on memory failures like the one he had experienced. Before Neisser's work, the going theory was that we are able to remember surprising and traumatic events far more accurately than we can recall their more mundane counterparts—a theory that accords with how it feels to remember them. Such recollections are called "flashbulb memories," since they seem to have the perfect fidelity of photography. Psychologists speculated that these memories stemmed from unique evolutionary imperatives and were formed through different neurological processes than we use to recall everyday life. But while the unusual vividness and specificity of such memories were well established (thanks largely to a 1977 study of people's recollections of the assassination of John F. Kennedy), no one had ever put their accuracy to the test.

National tragedy is good to memory researchers. In 1986, when the space shuttle *Challenger* exploded, Neisser saw an opportunity to remedy this gap in the memory literature, and to find out whether his own mistaken Pearl Harbor recollection was an anomaly. He surveyed his students about their memories of the disaster the day after it happened, and then again three years later. The results spelled the end of conventional flash-bulb memory theory. Less than 7 percent of the second reports matched the initial ones, 50 percent were wrong in two-thirds of their assertions, and 25 percent were wrong in every major detail. Subsequent work by other researchers only confirmed the conclusion. Our flashbulb memories might remain stunningly vivid, but research suggests that their accuracy erodes over time at the same rate as our everyday recollections—a decline so pre-cise and predictable that it can be plotted on a graph in what is known, evocatively, as the Ebbinghaus curve of forgetting. (For the record, a group of cognitive scientists and psychologists working together as the 9/11 Mem-ory Consortium repeated and expanded on Neisser's study after September 11, with roughly the same results.)

There is a vast body of literature, most of it in neuroscience and psy-chology, about how our memories come to be riddled with errors. But what interests me is why these wrong memories continue to feel so right—or, put differently, why they produce such a strong feeling of knowing. The subjects in the 1977 study of the Kennedy assassination described their recollections of that event as "burned on their brain," and as vivid "as if it happened yesterday." More strikingly, when Neisser showed one of his sub-jects her initial report of the *Challenger* disaster—a report that didn't match her memory of it—she responded by saying, "I know that's my handwriting, but I couldn't possibly have written that." Likewise, despite everything you just read, you probably remain powerfully confident in your memories of September 11.

You might be wrong, but you are not alone. None of us capture our memories in perfect, strobe-like detail, but almost all of us believe in them with blinding conviction. This conviction is most pronounced with respect to flashbulb memories, but it isn't limited to them.* Even with compara-

---

* As that suggests, memories don't need to be traumatic to induce the feeling of know-ing. In fact, they don't even need to be real. That's the startling and provocative conclu-sion of false memory studies. In these studies, subjects are convinced, over a series of meetings with a psychologist, and with the consent and participation of their families, that they experienced something as a child which they did not: getting lost in a store,

tively trivial matters, we believe in our recollections with touching sincerity and defend them with astounding tenacity. We squabble with our sister over who shrank the sweater back in 1984, we disagree with our lover of fifteen years about the location of our third date, and we simply can't let it go. We might drop the subject, but—barring clear-cut evidence against us—we retain the deep inner certainty that we are right.

How can we square this feeling of rightness with the very real possibility that we are wrong? This is a question that haunts all of wrongology, not just errors of memory. The problem is suggested by the very phrase "the feeling of knowing." In life, as in language, we begin with a psychological state (the "feeling" part) and end up with a claim about the truth (the "knowing" part). In other words, we feel that we are right because we *feel* that we are right: we take our own certainty as an indicator of accuracy. This isn't completely foolish of us, since studies show that there is some correlation between confidence and correctness. But it isn't completely foolproof, either. As the case of flashbulb memories makes clear, our certainty reflects the existence of a particularly vivid inner picture. But nothing in life guarantees that this picture reflects the real state of affairs.

This reliance on a vivid inner picture helps explain why memories are particularly apt to trigger the feeling of knowing. Two thousand years ago,

---

say, or taking a hot-air balloon ride. Overall, about one in four subjects will accept a false memory. (Among young children, the figure is significantly higher, ranging from 30 to 60 percent.) For these participants, the implanted "memories" become largely indistinguishable from reality—so much so that it can be difficult to convince them later that the event never happened. One fourteen-year-old subject named Chris, who was led to believe that he had gotten lost in a shopping mall as a child, responded to the debriefing of the experiment with incredulity. "I thought I remembered being lost . . . and looking around for you guys. I do remember that," he insisted. "And then crying, and Mom coming up and saying 'Where were you? Don't you—don't you ever do that again.'" Although the event was fabricated, when Chris searched his mind, he somehow encountered the affirmative feeling that he had been lost. In a sense, these false memories are no different from errors in flashbulb memories; Ulric Neisser "remembered" something that hadn't happened to him, too. But most of us find them more disturbing, since they suggest just how baseless the feeling of knowing can be—and, accordingly, how radically our memories can be manipulated, deliberately or otherwise.

Plato proposed a model of how memory works that is both radically out-dated and remarkably timeless. Imagine, he suggested, that you have in your mind a wax tablet—"a gift of Memory, the mother of the Muses." Everything you experience, from your own thoughts and sensory impressions to interactions with others, creates an imprint in that wax, like an insignia pressed into the seal on a letter. In this model, our memories are the marks in the wax: an unchanging mental replica of the events of the past, captured at the moment they occurred.

If Plato's medium has fallen into obsolescence, his metaphor has endured. Every generation's cutting-edge recording technology has been pressed into service to symbolize the workings of memory. Flashbulb memories are part of this tradition, as are books, gramophones, movies, and, most recently, computers. (This last analogy is in many ways the most explicit, not least because it is bidirectional: we speak of our memories as being like computers, but also of our computers as having memory—a locution that's become so natural that we forget it is a metaphor.) Within this recording-technology model of memory, the vividness of an inner picture really *does* vouchsafe its accuracy. We don't question the integrity of stored data if the photos aren't faded or missing and the book hasn't fallen apart at the seams.

The trouble is, this model of memory is simply wrong. Plato knew it was philosophically unsound, and, in his inimitable fashion, he proposed it only in order to genially eviscerate it. Later thinkers saw that it was scientifically flawed as well, and suggested successively more sophisticated (if still tentative) descriptions of how the brain remembers and forgets. Most contemporary neuroscientists agree that memory is not a single function but multiple distinct processes: remembering people, facts, particular times and places, how to perform physical actions, and so on. Similarly, they agree that these tasks are not accomplished by a single structure—the wax tablet or Polaroid or PC in the brain—but rather by many different ones, whose responsibilities range from face recognition to emotional processing. Perhaps most tellingly, they also agree that a memory is not so much stored intact in one part of the brain as reassembled by all these different structures each time we call it to mind.

So much for the recording-device model of memory. But once we dispense with the model, we also have to dispense with the idea that vividness is a good indicator of accuracy. If, instead of pulling our memories out of storage when we need them, we rebuild them afresh every time, then vividness could just be a feature that we build into some but not others. Alternatively, it could be a side effect of the building process itself. The neuroscientist William Hirst (one of the co-chairs of the 9/11 Memory Consortium) explained that some memories might strike us as convincing not because they are necessarily accurate but because of how often we call them to mind (i.e., reassemble them) and how easy it is do so. Hirst also suggests that some memories might feel particularly persuasive because of what he calls our "meta-theories about the kind of things we will or will not remember." That is, some memories might feel "burned on our brain" because it is psychologically or culturally unacceptable to forget them. Think about all those "Never Forget" bumper stickers that appeared after 9/11. As Hirst points out, "sometimes, remembering becomes a moral imperative."

This newer model of memory is imperfect. There are still many things we don't understand about how our minds store, retrieve, and reconstruct information from the past. But the real question about this model might simply be whether the nonscientists among us can be brought to believe in it. There's a reason that Plato's wax tablet remains our most pervasive and intuitive model of memory: although it is a bad description of how remembering works, it is an excellent description of how remembering *feels*. Since we can't sense our minds reconstructing memories from across multiple regions of our brain, we run into the same problem with memory that we had with perception. We can't feel the process, so we can't feel the places in that process where distortions and errors can creep in.

This tendency to conflate feeling we know with actually knowing is not limited to the domain of memory. It can be evoked by any sufficiently powerful belief—and, as we'll see in the next chapter, we have powerful beliefs about many, many things. We'll also see in subsequent chapters how the feeling of knowing is reinforced by other factors, ranging from who we hang out with to how our brains work. For now, though, I want to look at what happens when this feeling of knowing collides with the reality of not knowing. And for that, we need to go back to where we started—to blind Hannah, who "knows" that she can see.

No doubt about it: it's weird for a blind person to think that she can see. As it turns out, though, this particular problem—Anton's Syndrome—is just the beginning of the weird things going on for Hannah. What's even stranger is that she goes on to confidently describe her doctor's clean shave and fetching tan, not to mention the location and characteristics of a non-existent notebook. Likewise, as Justice Douglas demonstrated, many people who deny their paralysis do not stop there. If they have somehow accomplished a tricky task with one hand—say, buttoning their shirt—they will report that they did it with both. If you invite them to get up and stroll around the room with you, they'll decline, but not by saying they can't move. Instead, they'll say that they would love to but their arthritis is acting up, or they slept poorly the night before, or they are a bit tired because they just returned from a round of golf. These responses are patently untrue, not to mention crazy-sounding, and yet the patients themselves are neither dishonest nor insane. They don't set out to deceive anyone, and they don't have any awareness that what they are saying is false. Furthermore, many of them are lucid, intelligent, articulate, and, right up until the subject of their disability arises, entirely in touch with reality. So what is going on with these people?

The answer is that they are confabulating. To confabulate means, basically, to make stuff up; the most relevant etymological ghost is the word "fable." The confabulations that arise from brain damage are spontaneous fables. They explain things, as many fables do, but they are manifestly works of fiction. Like many works of fiction—the magical realism of Gabriel García Márquez, say, or the novels of Haruki Murakami—confabulations seamlessly blend the mundane with the incredible. And confabulation has another thing in common with literature as well: both are manifestations of our unstoppable drive to tell stories that make sense of our world.

We'll hear a lot more about that drive in the next chapter. For the moment, though, the important point is that, under normal circumstances, the stories we generate are subject to a fairly extensive process of verification. But not so with confabulators. "The creative ability to construct plausible-sounding responses and some ability to verify those responses seem to be separate in the human brain," wrote the philosopher William Hirstein (not to be confused with the memory scientist William Hirst) in his 2005 book on confabulation, *Brain Fiction*. "Confabulatory patients retain the first ability, but brain damage has compromised the second."

Imagine, by way of analogy, that each of us possesses an inner writer and an inner fact-checker. As soon as the writer begins devising a story, the fact-checker gets busy comparing it with the input from our senses, checking it against our memory, examining it for internal inconsistencies, thinking through its logical consequences, determining if it contradicts anything in our database of facts about the world, and, once we utter it, gauging other people's reactions to assess its credibility. True, our stories can still wind up being inaccurate—sometimes even outlandish—but they are nonetheless constrained in certain crucial ways.

When the fact-checker falls asleep on the job, however, our theories about the world can become wholly unmoored from reality. All of us have experienced this, because the one time our fact-checkers reliably fall asleep is when we do, too. Think about dreams again for a moment, and about how weird even just the averagely weird ones can be: you are in the house you grew up in, say, only it's in Copenhagen instead of Cleveland, and for some reason there's an Olympic-sized pool in the backyard, where your current boss (who is also sort of your second-grade teacher) is teaching you to swim. Now, two bizarre things are going on here. The first is that your brain is generating representations of the world that are only lightly tethered to the real, or even to the possible. The second is that you are completely untroubled by this fact. This inexplicable nonchalance is nicely captured in Gilbert and Sullivan's comic opera *Iolanthe*, which features a character recounting a convoluted dream about crossing the English Channel. "Bound on that journey," he sings, "you find your attorney, who started that morning from Devon. / He's a bit undersized and you don't feel surprised when he tells you he's only eleven."

You don't feel surprised: this is the defining emotional absence in dreams.

Surprise is a response to the violation of our expectations, an emotional indicator that our theories were in error. But we have no intimation of error in dreams, because we are cut off from all the usual ways to assess the plausibility of our beliefs. Asleep, we have minimal input from our senses, minimal logical processing, no reality-monitoring functions, and no one else around to look at us like we're crazy. Thus no matter how askew or improbable things get (swimming lessons from our boss, prepubescent attorneys), we remain unfazed; the erroneous and the impossible simply have no meaning in the dreamscape. (In our dreams, too, we are paralyzed but think we can move, and blind but think we can see.) It's only when we wake up—when our inner fact-checker jolts back into consciousness, and asks our inner writer what on earth she has been up to—that we are able to recognize the implausibility of what we've just experienced.

The fact that we abandon reality when we sleep is not a problem. On the contrary: as I pointed out in Chapter Two, it is an anti-problem, one of our species' consistent sources of fascination, inspiration, and pleasure. The difficulty commences when our inner writer operates in a similarly unconstrained fashion when we are awake. This is what happens to confabulators. As Hirstein put it in *Brain Fiction*, "One of the characters involved in an inner dialogue has fallen silent, and the other rambles on unchecked."

One of the clearest examples of the confabulation that occurs when this inner dialogue is disrupted comes not from anosognosics but from people with a different neurological problem: epilepsy. In the 1960s, the neuroscientist Michael Gazzaniga and his colleagues conducted a series of experiments on split-brain patients—people whose epilepsy is so severe that the two hemispheres of their brain have been surgically separated to control life-threatening seizures. Using a special process to display images to one side of the brain but not the other, the scientists flashed commands to the right hemisphere of these patients. When the patients obeyed the commands, they were asked to explain their behavior. The resulting answers were bizarre. When a subject who had been commanded to laugh was asked why he was doing so, he told the experimenters, "Oh, you guys are too much." When another subject who had been told to walk was asked why she had stood up, she replied that she was thirsty and was going to get a drink.

These confabulatory answers were the left brain's solution to a strange problem. That side of the brain is heavily linguistic, and as such it is responsible for crafting our narratives about the world. The right brain, by contrast, is only minimally linguistic; it can understand commands and initiate actions, but it can't generate explanations. In healthy human beings, this division of labor isn't a problem, because information is constantly shuttled back and forth between the two hemispheres. In split-brain patients, however, the two sides have no way to communicate with each other. As a result, when Gazzaniga's subjects were asked to account for their behavior, the right side of the brain (which had seen and responded to the commands) lacked the ability to explain what was going on, while the left side of the brain (which was able to generate explanations) lacked the requisite information. In other words, the left hemisphere literally had no idea why its own self was acting as it was. All it could do was theorize backwards from the subject's behavior, and it proved extremely adept at doing so. With no apparent befuddlement, no noticeable time lag, and no appearance of doubt or intent to deceive, the left side of the brain consistently generated completely plausible—although, of course, completely wrong—explanations.

If confabulation occurred only as the result of brain damage or drastic surgical intervention, it would just be a freakish footnote to neuroscience.* In fact, though, it's strikingly easy to get healthy people to confabulate. In 1977, the psychologists Richard Nisbett and Timothy Wilson set up shop in a department store in Michigan, where they asked people to compare

---

* Two far more common neurological problems, Alzheimer's disease and dementia in general, are also associated with confabulation. Older adults who suffer from these conditions often seem to confabulate in response to memory loss, as when your ninety-two-year-old mother fabricates her medical history for her doctor, or claims that someone has stolen the purse whose location she has forgotten. In fact, memory deficits are neither necessary nor sufficient to produce confabulation, but the two conditions are correlated. We know, for instance, that amnesiacs (people with severe, short-term memory loss) often generate fictitious narratives to fill in the gaping holes in their past. Hirstein tells the story of one such patient who replied to a doctor's inquiry about his weekend by recounting the details of a professional conference he had attended in New York. In reality, the patient had been in the hospital not merely throughout the weekend but for the previous three months.

what they claimed were four different varieties of pantyhose. In reality, all the hose were the same, but that didn't prevent shoppers from showing a preference for one of them. Moreover, it didn't stop them from *explaining* their preference, by claiming that (for instance) this color was just a little more appealing or that fabric was a little less scratchy.

In a sense, this is blind Hannah all over again. It's weird enough that these shoppers chose between identical pantyhose in the first place, but it is even weirder that they generated explanations for those choices. After all, they could have just shrugged and declined to explain their decisions. We are expected to be able to justify our beliefs, but not so our taste. "I just like that one; I couldn't tell you why" is a perfectly acceptable explanation for why we're attracted to a particular pair of pantyhose (or a particular shade of blue, or a particular flavor of ice cream). In fact, it might be the *only* acceptable explanation: as we say, there's no accounting for taste. Yet these shoppers insisted on providing accounts anyway. Since there were no differences among the pantyhose, these accounts couldn't have been the real reasons behind the shoppers' choices; they could only be post-hoc justifications. Their real motivations remain mysterious. The one factor the researchers could identify was the influence of position, since almost four out of five shoppers preferred the hose on the far right-hand side of the display over those on the far left-hand side. But of course, none of the shoppers explained their choice by reference to location. Instead, like split-brain patients, they confabulated explanations for a decision whose actual origins was buried in an unreachable part of the brain.

At first, this experiment seems to demonstrate a strange but basically benign quirk of human cognition: we like to explain things, even when the real explanation eludes us. But it has a sobering epilogue. When Nisbett and Wilson revealed the nature of the experiment to its unwitting subjects, many of them refused to believe that the pantyhose were identical. They argued that they could detect differences, and they stuck by their original preferences. Likewise, people who work with clinical confabulators report that the most striking thing about them isn't the strangeness of their erroneous beliefs, nor even the weirdness of the confabulations they generate to cover them, but rather the fact that these confabulations are uttered as if they were God's word. A hundred years ago, the German psychiatrist Emil Kraepelin marveled at the "rocklike certitude" with which confabulators delivered their untruths. Hirstein, the author of *Brain Fiction*, echoed that sentiment. "Perhaps what is most troubling about witnessing such confabulations," he wrote, "is the rock-jawed certainty with which they are offered up."

Hirstein noted something else peculiar about confabulators as well. Whenever any of us is asked a question, we can respond in one of three ways (assuming that we are not out to deceive anyone). If we know the answer, we will respond correctly. If we don't know the answer, and we realize that we don't know it, we will admit to being stumped. Finally, if we think we know the answer when we do not, we will respond confidently but incorrectly.

For anosognosic confabulators, the first possibility is ruled out: they are neurologically unable to provide the right answers to questions about their impairment. But, Hirstein observed, they are also unable to recognize that they don't know the right answers. "Apparently," he wrote, "admitting ignorance in response to a question, rather than being an indication of glibness and a low level of function, is a high-level cognitive ability, one that confabulators have lost. 'I don't know,' can be an intelligent answer to a question, or at least an answer indicative of good cognitive health." Maybe so, but this same inability to say "I don't know" also afflicted the majority of participants in Nisbett and Wilson's study—confabulators who, to all appearances, enjoyed perfectly fine cognitive health.

It's not exactly news that most people are reluctant to admit their ignorance. But the point here is not that we are bad at saying "I don't know." The point is that we are bad at *knowing* we don't know. The feeling of not knowing is, to invert James's formulation, the bell that fails to chime—or, at any rate, the one whose chime we fail to hear. The problem, I suspect, is that we are confused about what ignorance actually feels like. At first blush, it seems that the feeling should be one of blankness, of nothing coming to mind when an answer is required. And sometimes, as when the question we face is a simple matter of fact, this *is* how ignorance feels: if you ask me who the prime minster of Kyrgyzstan is, I will have no trouble recognizing that I haven't the foggiest idea. For the most part, though, the feeling of blankness is a lousy guide to ignorance—because, thanks to our aptitude for generating stories, stuff is almost always coming to mind. As a result, to know that we don't know, we can't just passively wait around to see if our mind comes up empty. Instead, we need to actively identify and reject all the incorrect or ill-grounded hypotheses our inner writer is madly generating.

How good we are at doing this varies significantly from person to person. Some of us have voluble and inventive inner writers, some of us have meticulous inner fact-checkers, and a lucky few have both. Most of us, however, are noticeably better at generating theories than at registering our own ignorance. Hirstein says that once he began studying confabulation, he started seeing sub-clinical versions of it everywhere he looked, in the form of neurologically normal people "who seem unable to say the words, 'I don't know,' and will quickly produce some sort of plausible-sounding response to whatever they are asked." Such people, he says, "have a sort of mildly confabulatory personality."*

Actually, *all* of us have mildly confabulatory personalities. Take (just for example) me. Not long ago, I found myself participating in a lively discussion about the likely accuracy of string theory. The contributors to this conversation included a lawyer, a labor organizer, an environmental consultant, a graduate student in philosophy, and a journalist (me). One of us (me again) had a friend who was a real-live string theorist. All of us had read a recent *New York Times* piece describing some recent disputes among theoretical physicists about the future of the field. All of us had also read or heard something else on the subject, at some point, by someone or other— or at least so we claimed in the course of the conversation. None of us had taken a physics course since high school. I sincerely doubt that any of us were capable of solving so much as a quadratic equation.

---

* There's some evidence that mildly confabulatory people are at risk of becoming majorly confabulatory people. In a 1996 study, the psychologist E. A. Weinstein asked the family members of anosognosics—some of them also confabulators, some of them not—to describe their afflicted relative's personality before the onset of disease. He found that the confabulators in the group were consistently characterized as having previously been "stubborn, with an emphasis on being right."

This was a conversation to give the phrase "theoretical physics" a whole new meaning. My friends and I were the most outrageously unqualified group of string theorists ever assembled. In fact, we could far more aptly have been called shoestring theorists: virtuosos of developing elaborate hypotheses based on vanishingly small amounts of information. The Chicago Public Radio show *This American Life* once dedicated an entire episode to this kind of mild confabulation, in the course of which they did us all a favor by coining a vastly better term for it. Actually, it's more accurate to say that they launched an imaginary magazine devoted to covering it—a magazine they called *Modern Jackass*.

Modern Jackass: once you learn the phrase, it's easy to find yourself using it all the time, which says everything you need to know about the pervasiveness of mild confabulation. One of the producers of the show, Nancy Updike, joked that she herself is a frequent contributor to *Modern Jackass: Medical Edition*—you know, the one where you bullshit your way through an explanation of the merits of antioxidants or the evils of partially hydrogenated vegetable oil. I introduced the Modern Jackass concept to my family and within a matter of hours they were turning around and congratulating me on my cover story for the magazine. (It was about the origins of ethnic tension in the former Yugoslavia, about which I know only slightly more than I do about string theory.) And I recently offered a friend a position as a staff writer, after he tried to explain the difference between alternating and direct current, and, immediately thereafter, why the Americans and the British drive on different sides of the road.

As ill-informed as these ad hoc, out-loud musings can be, such Modern Jackass moments can play a useful role in our lives. Assuming we have the internal flexibility (and the communal permission) to backtrack and revise, they can help us solve problems, arrive at answers, and figure out what we *really* believe. But, much like the pantyhose experiment, these intellectual improvisations can have a troublesome outcome. For us, as for those shoppers, something in the alchemy of the interaction often causes our half-baked hypotheses to congeal on the spot. Thus one extremely good way to become wedded to a theory you've just idly expressed is to have it contradicted by, say, your mother. I myself have gone from noncommittal to evangelical in a matter of milliseconds using this technique. Likewise, an acquaintance once confessed to me that when his spouse contradicts a theory he's just hatched, he begins spontaneously generating "facts" to support it—even when he realizes that she is right and he is wrong. In cases like these, we actually *do* know the limits of our knowledge; we just can't stop ourselves from barreling right past them. As with our individual and collective difficulty with saying "I was wrong," we aren't very good at saying, "I don't know."

This ineptitude creates all kinds of friction that should, in theory, be avoidable. Imagine how many unnecessary conflicts we'd all have to endure if we didn't have the ability to say "excuse me" when we needed to get past someone in a crowded space, and "I'm sorry" when we accidentally bumped into them instead. These are simple tools, but it is precisely their simplicity that makes them so valuable, since it makes them easy to remember and deploy when we need them.

An equally convenient way to acknowledge our ignorance would improve our lives on three fronts. First, it would give us a relatively humiliation-free means to rescue ourselves from our own ridiculousness. Second, it would help us de-escalate all those unwinnable battles over crumb cake. Finally, and perhaps most important, it would give us a new category for a common experience. In providing a way to notice and classify all those moments when we wander out onto shaky limbs, a handy rhetorical device—calling ourselves a Modern Jackass, slapping ourselves on the head, anything— would give us a sense of just how common this behavior is, in ourselves as well as in others. As such, it could help us get better at exactly the thing we're so bad at: recognizing the limits of our own knowledge.

This is an admirable goal. After all, knowing what we don't know is the beginning (and, in some religious and intellectual traditions, the entirety and end) of wisdom. Unfortunately, as we have seen, recognizing the limits of our knowledge is extremely difficult. The philosophical options— vetting our beliefs to figure out if they are justified, true, necessary, and so forth—are controversial even among philosophers, and impractical as a way to get through life. And the lay option—relying on the feeling of knowing, and trusting the theories that so constantly come to mind—leads us too easily into error. In other words, we have no sound method for knowing what we know—which means that, strictly speaking, we don't *know* much of anything.

This doesn't mean that we are dumb, or that all our ideas about the world are useless, or that the only honorable course of action is to throw up our hands and throw in our lots with the Skeptics. "When one admits that nothing is certain," proposed the philosopher Bertrand Russell, "one must, I think, also add that some things are much more nearly certain than others." Those are sound words to live by. And yet, as the example of blind Hannah reminds us, we must also accept that we can't ascertain in advance which of the things we think we know will turn out not to be knowledge after all—will turn out, instead, to be wrong.

As that suggests, the idea of knowledge and the idea of error are fundamentally incompatible. When we claim to know something, we are essentially saying that we can't be wrong. If we want to contend with the possibility that we *could* be wrong, then the idea of knowledge won't serve us; we need to embrace the idea of belief instead. This might feel like an unwelcome move, since all of us prefer to think that we know things rather than "merely" believing them. That preference accords with the conventional view of knowledge and belief, in which the former is the loftier of the two concepts. In that view, knowledge is, you will recall, belief *plus:* plus all the conditions the philosophers put on it, and all the faith that we ourselves put in it.

In the end, though, it is belief that is by far the broader, more complex, and more interesting category. It is, I will argue, the atomic unit of our intelligence—the thing that differentiates us from machines, and that lets us navigate the world as deftly as we do. But it is true (and not coincidental) that belief is also the atomic unit of error. Whether we wrongly think we can see or wrongly remember what we did on September 11, whether we are mistaken about pantyhose or mistaken about string theory, what we are ultimately wrong about is always a belief. If we want to understand how we err, we need to look to how we believe.

5.

Our Minds, Part Two: Belief

'Tis with our judgments as our watches, none
Go just alike, yet each believes his own.
—ALEXANDER POPE, "AN ESSAY ON CRITICISM"

On October 23, 2008, Alan Greenspan, the former chair of the Federal Reserve, appeared before a committee of the U.S. House of Representatives to testify about the financial crisis that had lately engulfed more or less the entire planet. Not surprisingly, the atmosphere was somber, and Henry Waxman, the California Democrat who chaired the committee, was not in the mood to pull his punches. "The Federal Reserve had the authority to stop the irresponsible lending practices" that had fueled the crisis, Waxman reminded those in attendance. But, he continued, "its long-time chairman, Alan Greenspan, rejected pleas that he intervene." Then he addressed Greenspan directly, and reproachfully: "those who trusted the market to regulate itself, yourself included, made a serious mistake."

This was hardly the kind of congressional welcome to which Greenspan was accustomed. Throughout his five terms as Fed chief, Greenspan had regularly been referred to as "the greatest central banker in history," "the most powerful man in the world," and, simply, "the maestro." His fame extended beyond the United States (France awarded him the Legion of Honor; Great Britain made him an honorary knight), as well as beyond financial and political circles. In the words of the *Economist* magazine, Greenspan enjoyed "almost rock-star status" among ordinary Americans—a remarkable and somewhat baffling achievement for a famously tight-lipped financier in charge of a blindingly complex aspect of government. His autobiography, presciently titled *The Age of Turbulence*, reportedly sold for $8.5 million dollars, second only to Bill Clinton's memoir and tied with Pope John Paul II's. When the book came out, in the summer of 2007—right around the time when the financial fault lines began to tremble—it topped both the *New York Times* and the Amazon.com bestseller lists.

By October 23, though, all that was in the past. The economy had been in bad shape for over a year, and in the spring of 2008, with the collapse of the global investment giant Bear Stearns, it had entered a virtual freefall. What began as a subprime mortgage crisis (triggered by the now-infamous practice of offering mortgages to people with limited or troubled credit histories) had broadened into a liquidity crisis, a credit crisis, a banking crisis, a currency crisis, a trade crisis—just about every kind of economic crisis you could name. In the United States, the stock market had fallen 37 percent since the start of the year. The American economy had lost 1.5 million jobs (a figure that would rise to over 5 million by early 2009), and the unemployment rate was marching toward double digits in the worst-hit states and sectors. Globally, the situation was even grimmer. The International Labor Organization predicted that, worldwide, between 18 and 50 million jobs would vanish into the maw of the crisis. Six months after Greenspan spoke, the Blackstone Group, a financial services company, reported that between 40 and 45 percent of global wealth had evaporated in under a year and a half.

For anyone with so much as a toe in the global economy, the crisis came as a massive financial and emotional shock—disturbing if you were lucky, devastating if you weren't. But for those who were charged with actually understanding and directing that economy, the collapse occasioned a massive ideological crisis as well. One of the primary jobs of economists is to create models of how financial systems work, and while those models are, by definition, simplifications and estimations as compared to the real thing, they are nonetheless supposed to be useful for making predictions, not to mention policy. (That's why economists create them, after all.) As Waxman pointed out, Greenspan's economic model was based on the premise that markets could be trusted to regulate themselves—and, as a corollary, that governments should not do so instead. Since Greenspan's model had essentially been the global model for close to twenty years, the doctrine of market self-regulation had become all but holy writ. As Waxman put it, "trust in the wisdom of the markets was infinite."

Then the markets imploded—and, with them, the model. As Greenspan told the committee, "the whole intellectual edifice collapsed." He had, he continued, "found a flaw in the model that I perceived is the critical functioning structure that defines how the world works." If that wasn't clear enough, Waxman offered a blunt translation: "you found that your view of the world, your ideology, was not right." It is a measure of how completely and publically Greenspan's model had failed that he was forced to concur. "Precisely," he replied. "That's precisely the reason I was shocked, because I had been going for forty years or more with very considerable evidence that it was working exceptionally well." The demise of his doctrine that the market would always protect investors had left him, he said, "in a state of shocked disbelief."

In that, Greenspan was hardly alone. One of the most striking features of the economic catastrophe was the sheer number of financiers wandering around in a state of stunned bewilderment, trying to grasp how their understanding of the world had served them so poorly. As the hedge fund manager Steve Eisman told the financial writer Michael Lewis (he of *Moneyball* and *Liar's Poker* fame), being an investment banker in the early twenty-first century was "like being a Scholastic, prior to Newton. Newton comes along, and one morning you wake up: 'Holy shit, I'm wrong!'"

Still, one could argue—and many did—that Greenspan, at least, had no business being quite so shocked. Over the years, countless people had challenged his deregulatory dogma, including (to name just a few) Joseph Stiglitz and Paul Krugman, both Nobel Prize–winning economists, and Brooksley Born, who was head of the Commodity Futures Trading Commission from 1996 to 1999. Born eventually became something of a Cassandra figure for the crisis, since she repeatedly called for regulating the market for derivatives, those ultracomplex financial products that eventually helped bring down the economy. Those calls were silenced when Greenspan, along with then-Treasury Secretary Robert Rubin and then-Securities and Exchange Commission Chair Arthur Levitt, took the extraordinary step of convincing Congress to pass legislation forbidding Born's agency from taking any action for the duration of her term. In a joint statement issued at the time, Greenspan defended the move on the grounds of "grave concern about this [proposed regulatory] action and its possible consequences." Merely discussing the option of government regulation, he asserted, could destabilize the markets and send capital surging out of the United States.

If Greenspan was reduced to "shocked disbelief" when the markets failed to regulate themselves and slid into chaos, it was not because he'd never been warned of the possibility. Nor was it because his own model had never been criticized (it had), or because alternative models had never been floated (they had). The problem, instead, was that his faith in the ability of markets to regulate themselves was, in Born's word, "absolutist." Greenspan was as figuratively invested in unregulated markets as the rest of us were literally invested in them. He had a model of how the world worked, and his confidence in it was all but immoveable.

Actually, Greenspan had many thousands of models of how the world worked. He must have, because we all do. These models are our beliefs, and they cover everything from how we should invest our money to where we left our wallet. We believe in some of these models only tentatively—personally, I'm only about 50 percent sure of the whereabouts of my wallet right now—and some of them absolutely. But no matter how unshakably we believe in them, the models themselves can be shaken; that is what differentiates belief from the imaginary ideal of knowledge. Knowledge, as we have seen, cannot make room for error, and therefore could not have failed Greenspan. But beliefs can, and his did. In fact, it failed us all.

This book is about our Greenspan moments: about what happens when our beliefs, including our most fundamental, convincing, and important ones, fail us. To understand how beliefs fail, though, we first need to understand how they work. And to understand that, we need to start with the most basic question of all: just what *is* a belief, anyway?

When we talk about beliefs in casual conversation, we usually mean our overt convictions about important matters: about religion or morality or propriety, politics or economics, ourselves or other people. These beliefs are explicit, in the sense that we are aware of having them, and can articulate and defend them if called upon to do so. Put differently, there is an experience associated with holding them. It felt like something for Alan Greenspan to believe in market self-regulation, just as it feels like something for you to believe in God, or in universal healthcare, or that your father-in-law dislikes you.

By contrast, when philosophers talk about belief (which they do often; it is an occupational hazard), they mean something markedly different. Or rather, they mean something *more:* they agree that our overt convictions about financial markets and so forth deserve to be called beliefs, but they think a lot of other things merit the term as well. Suppose you are reading this book in bed at midnight with the blinds drawn. Philosophers would say that your set of beliefs right now includes the following: that it is dark outside; that the sun will not rise for many more hours; that when it does, it will do so in the east; that the mattress underneath you is a solid object; that a flying saucer is not about to crash through your bedroom window; that you will wake up tomorrow as the same person you are today, and so on.*

---

* And on and on: one implication of the philosophical definition of belief is that, technically, the set of beliefs each of us holds is infinite. (If you believe there isn't a monster under your toddler's bed, you also believe there aren't two monsters under her bed, or three monsters, or . . . et cetera.) Needless to say, no one actually holds an infinite number of beliefs in the conscious mind. But the point of this definition of belief is that consciousness doesn't matter. What matters is that our everyday actions are grounded

What makes these additional beliefs seem so strange—what makes them seem, in fact, so unbelief-like—is that there is no experience associated with holding them. Believing that my mattress is solid doesn't feel like believing in God, largely because believing that my mattress is solid doesn't feel like *anything*. I am completely unaware of believing it. Left to my own devices, I'm extremely unlikely to characterize it as a belief, and, if I'm called upon to defend it, I will be both baffled as to why I should do so and at a loss as to how to go about it. In other words, almost everything we normally associate with the experience of believing—consciousness, conviction, emotion, explanation—is absent from these other, implicit beliefs.

Psychologically, then, the everyday concept of belief and the philosophical one differ from each other in the most salient way imaginable: in how we experience them. Functionally, however, they are virtually indistinguishable. Whether we are aware of our beliefs or not, they are all, like Greenspan's free-market philosophy, models of the world. In the literal sense, a model of the world is a map, and that's basically what beliefs are, too: mental representations of our physical, social, emotional, spiritual, and political landscapes. My explicit belief that my father-in-law dislikes me is crucial to my mental representation of my family, just as my implicit belief that my mattress is solid is crucial to my mental representation of my bedroom. Both serve the same maplike function of helping me figure out where I might or might not want to sit when I enter a certain room. Both, in other words, are necessary pixels in my picture of the world. Whether or not I can feel that pixel light up in my head is irrelevant. Think about what happens when I walk into an unfamiliar hotel room at night: in order to decide where to lie down, I need a mental image of the kind of things on which I can sleep, but I don't need to know that I have that image. The model of the world—the belief—is vital, but awareness of the belief is dispensable. In fact, lack of awareness is the norm. From the anticipated behavior of inanimate objects to the presumed identity of our parents to whether we can see a mountain chain or see at all, the vast

in an essentially limitless number of implicit convictions.

majority of our mental models are implicit: entirely unfelt, yet essential to how we make sense of ourselves and the world.

Just as implicit and explicit beliefs function in the same way, they also fail in the same way. However different they might seem to us under normal circumstances, in the moment of error, they are identical. Or rather, they *become* identical: the instant an implicit assumption is violated, it turns into an explicit one. Imagine for a moment a scene worthy of a Marx Brothers movie. It's nighttime, I emerge from the bathroom in my pajamas, pick up my book, lie down on my bed—and, wham, fall straight through the mattress onto the floor. Should this exceedingly unlikely scenario somehow transpire, three things will have collapsed. The first is my mattress. The second is my belief in the solidity of that mattress. The third—and here is the point I am trying to make—is the implicitness of that belief. If I find myself sprawled on the floor, all of my previously unconscious convictions about mattresses will suddenly surge into consciousness. In the moment of error, our implicit beliefs are simultaneously contravened and revealed.

Once we acknowledge that implicit assumptions and explicit convictions are just subsets of the single category of belief, we can go further and acknowledge that even the distinction between them is suspect. All of us have plenty of beliefs that we are somewhat aware of holding, or that we can become aware of holding when necessary. (I don't believe anything about the location of my sunglasses in December, but come June, when I can't find them, I believe that my sister borrowed them.) Still, however tenuous this distinction might be, it is relevant to this book in at least one respect. While many of our beliefs fall somewhere in the middle of the implicit-explicit spectrum, it is those that lie at the extreme ends that collapse most spectacularly in the event of error. If anything can rival for sheer drama the demise of a belief that we have adamantly espoused, it is the demise of a belief so fundamental to our lives that we never even registered its existence.

Our beliefs, then, are models of the world—but they aren't just models for models' sake. Like economic models, our mental ones exist to help us make predictions and policies. In the words of William James, beliefs "are really rules for action." One obvious corollary to this is that our beliefs have consequences. I don't mean that being *wrong* about them has consequences, although that's also true: as we just saw, a flawed belief helped eradicate nearly half the world's wealth. I mean that simply *holding* a belief can have consequences.

Consider another financial example. Since 1992, CalTech and MIT have been collaborating on a project known as the Laser Interferometer Gravitational-Wave Observatory. The observatory is the single most expensive project ever funded by the National Science Foundation. It took ten years and $300 million to build, and costs $30 million per year to operate. Its mission is to find gravitational waves ("ripples in the fabric of space-time [that] are produced by violent events throughout the universe," says the NSF, if that helps), and it had better succeed, because the existence of those waves is posited by nothing less than the general theory of relativity. As the science writer Margaret Wertheim has noted, this is an instance where "belief has brought into being a half-billion-dollar machine."

A half-billion dollars is a bundle of money, but pricey machines are just the tip of the iceberg. Housing bubbles, holy wars, the 1964 Civil Rights Act, the lunar landing: all of these came about as the result of belief. Plainly, then, our beliefs don't just have financial and material consequences. They also have political, legal, intellectual, cultural, and even corporeal ones. And, crucially, they have emotional and psychological consequences as well. Again, I'm not talking about the emotional consequences of being wrong about a belief, a topic we'll get into later. I'm talking about the emotional consequences of merely believing it—the way that building a gravitational-wave observatory is a consequence of believing in general relativity (whether or not it is correct), and investing in the stock market is a consequence of believing that it is sound (whether or not it is).

Some of the emotional consequences of our beliefs are pretty straightforward. If you believe that your true love is nervous during dinner because he plans to propose to you over dessert, you will be excited and happy; if you believe that he is nervous because he plans to break up with you, you will be anxious and upset. But examples like that don't get at either the scope or the significance of the psychological repercussions of our beliefs. To grasp that scope, you have to grasp the scope of belief itself. Our models of the world extend beyond markets and mattresses and the general theory of relativity, into a kind of General Theory of Us: whether we think we are attractive and intelligent, competent or inept, better or worse off than other people; whether we think our parents loved us; whether we think a God is watching over us; whether we think we are basically safe and cared for in the world.

Convictions like these organize our idea of who we are, as well as how we relate to our environment. As that suggests, and as we'll see throughout this book, our beliefs are inextricable from our identities. That's one reason why being wrong can so easily wound our sense of self. And it's also why psychotherapy often focuses on helping people to examine—and, when necessary, change—their beliefs about themselves and others. Regardless of whether those beliefs are conscious or unconscious, regardless of whether they are right or wrong, they determine how we feel and how we behave every day of our lives.

Here is what we have learned so far in our quest to understand beliefs: they are models of the world; they help us take action; and accordingly, they incur consequences. Good enough—except why, then, do we have so many beliefs that we will never be able to act on? This is sometimes known as the problem of distal beliefs. "Distal," in this case, means far from the self; a distal belief is one that pertains to things remote from us in time or space or relevance. If we believe in the soundness of markets, the solidity of mattresses, or the existence of God, those beliefs will guide our actions in the world. But what about the belief that string theory is right, that South Africa's AIDS policy is wrong, and that Alpha Centauri C is the closest star to the earth? As we'll see in Chapter Seven, merely espousing such beliefs might be socially prudent or advantageous, regardless of whether they are relevant, or even right. But unless you are a physicist or a public health expert or an interstellar traveler, they will not enable you to take any action in the world.

Why, then, do we bother having distal beliefs? One way to answer this question—certainly the most fun way—is to think about sex. The reason we have a sex drive is to ensure that we reproduce, but the vast majority of our sexual activity does not result in offspring. We simply have an instinct to copulate, with the consequence that we have enough babies and (evolutionarily speaking) way more than enough sex. For at least a century, psychologists and philosophers have suggested that our urge to explain the world is analogous to our urge to populate it. Like making babies, they argue, making theories is so crucial to our survival that we have a natural drive to do so—what William James called a "theoretic instinct."* This is the impulse I gestured toward in the last chapter: the one that compels us to generate stories and explanations all the time, even at the risk of being featured in a magazine called *Modern Jackass*.

It's easy to see why a theory drive would be evolutionarily advantageous. Imagine that you are your own earliest ancestor, trying to make your way in the world some 200,000 years ago. Somehow, you have to figure out that shaking a certain kind of tree will make edible fruit fall to the ground. You have to learn that berries of specific shapes and colors are nourishing, while other very similar berries can kill you. Upon hearing a rustling in the bushes, you have to be able to infer—pretty damn quickly—the presence of a predator, or of dinner. In other words, you must be extraordinarily adept at guessing what's going on in your environment and why. This is precisely the skill set covered by theorizing, and its utility has not diminished over time. While my concerns about predators might be greatly diminished these days, I now need to be able to determine whether the stranger striding toward me wants to ask me for a light or relieve me of my wallet, whether the explosions

---

* At the risk of further muddying some already murky lexical waters, I use the words "belief" and "theory" almost interchangeably in this book. Some thinkers have called for a distinction between the two terms, arguing that theories are more explicit, more developed, or more explanatory than beliefs. But such distinctions are largely untenable, or at any rate extremely slippery. For instance, try applying them to the statement "I believe in God." If you are a five-year-old, that statement almost certainly represents a belief: a not very developed, probably not very explanatory, and possibly not even very explicit conviction. On the other hand, if you are the pope, it is clearly a theory. Moreover—and more important for my purposes—none of the differences we can posit between beliefs and theories have any bearing on their function. Theories, like beliefs, exist to represent the world around us.

outside are a threat to my life or merely a fireworks display, and whether or not my two-year-old just ate the Lego that is suddenly nowhere to be seen. Theorizing, like fornicating, is of timeless use to our species.

The evolutionary utility of theorizing helps explain why we have such a hyper-abundance of beliefs—including those, like distal beliefs, that serve no obvious purpose. Just as our reproductive instinct somehow produced Paris Hilton videos and our language instinct somehow produced Proust, our theorizing instinct has long since exceeded the barebones requirements of survival. Because we needed to be able to theorize about some things (unfamiliar berries, rustling bushes), we wound up able to theorize about everything. And we do. How supernovas are formed, why autism is on the rise, what was going on with that married couple at the cocktail party, why we like one pair of pantyhose more than another: there is virtually no subject—no matter what domain of life it concerns, how pressing or trivial it may be, and how much or little we know about it—that is not suitable fodder for our theory-happy minds.

The evolutionary urgency of theorizing also helps explain why we form beliefs both constantly and unconsciously. Of course, we are capable of theorizing intentionally, too, and we do so all the time—both informally (as when we spend happy hour trying to figure out why our boss was in such a foul temper that afternoon) and formally (as when we spend our career trying to figure out what causes cancer). What we aren't capable of doing is *not* theorizing. Like breathing, we can ignore the belief-formation process or control it—or even refine it—but whatever we do, it will keep on going for as long as we keep on living. And with good reason: if we want to eat dinner rather than be dinner, we are well served by a process so rapid and automatic that we don't need to waste time deliberately engaging it.

As with our perceptual processes, this automatic theorizing generally careens into consciousness only when something goes wrong. For instance: not long ago, I arranged to meet an interview subject for coffee in Manhattan. When I walked into the café and she stood up to introduce herself, I had the common yet always somewhat startling experience of realizing that she looked nothing like what I had expected. What was strange about this experience—what is always strange about such experiences—is that, prior to meeting this woman, I had no idea that I had any mental image of her at all. And yet, somewhere in the back of my mind, I had generated a picture of her, without any conscious awareness of doing so. Moreover, this process must have been quite sophisticated, since when I went back and thought about it, I realized that not only could I describe the person I had expected to see, I could pinpoint some of the factors that led me to draw my mistaken portrait: a name I associated with a certain era and ethnicity, a scrap of information that suggested a certain aesthetic, and so forth. In short, some very sophisticated theory making was going on in my mind, entirely without my awareness. This is true for all of us, all the time. Below the level of conscious thought, we are always amassing information from our environment and using it to add to or rearrange our model of the world.

As with the much-debated language instinct, the theorizing instinct is, itself, just a theory. No one knows if our capacity to generate hypotheses about the world is truly hard-wired. We do know, though, that it kicks in very early. For instance, there is suggestive evidence that babies as young as seven months are already theorizing about basic physical properties such as gravity. That might seem hard to believe, but tack on a few more months and you've got a toddler—and toddlers are infamous theorizers. Armed with not much more than an insatiable drive for physical exploration and an enthusiasm for the word "why," the average two-year-old seems determined to take on the whole world. And that's exactly what he or she is doing. It is in childhood, after all, that our environment is most mysterious to us, and most urgently in need of mapping. The Berkeley psychologist Alison Gopnik has even posited that the theory drive exists specifically for early childhood, although it operates throughout our lives—just as the sex drive exists specifically for our fertile years, even though we are sexual long before and long after.

Whether the idea of a theory instinct turns out to be sound biology or just apt analogy, belief formation is clearly central to our species. Its survival value aside (as if survival were the kind of thing we could set aside), it defines the way we inhabit our environment, inarguably for the better. I invoke again the analogy to sex and language: it is good to make babies and shout warnings, but it is *really* good to make love and read Shakespeare.

So too with theorizing: the instinct is about staying alive, but the excess is about living. It enriches our everyday life (those happy-hour debriefs about the boss) and enables our most extraordinary achievements (that hoped-for cure for cancer). Without it, we would be bereft of virtually all our hallmark human endeavors: religion, science, and storytelling; curiosity, exploration, and discovery. With it, we are able to venture beyond the known world and toward the terrain of all that is hidden from us—the past and the future and the far-flung, the cloaked machinery of nature, other people's inner lives. It is the gift that beckons us beyond the eked-out existence of mere survival.

There is, predictably, a problem. Although we are highly adept at making models of the world, we are distinctly less adept at realizing that we have made them. As I suggested in my discussion of perception, our beliefs often seem to us not so much constructed as reflected, as if our minds were simply mirrors in which the truth of the world passively appeared.

Psychologists refer to this conviction as naïve realism. Naïve realism is an automatic tendency, not an intentional philosophical position. If you actually believed that the world was precisely as you experienced it, you would be an intentional naïve realist, but as far as I know, no one has seriously subscribed to this position in the entire history of humanity. Even the most impassioned realist, the kind that regards relativists as dangerous loons from Planet France, recognizes that our experience of the world is not identical with the world itself. To take only the simplest examples: there is no such thing as red if you are a bat, and no such thing as loud if you are a rock, and (so far as we currently know) no such thing as triumph or regret if you are a Shetland pony. Color and sound and emotion are all central to how we experience and make sense of the world, but they can't inhere in the world itself, because they cease to exist the moment you take minds out of the picture. Conversely, plenty of things exist in the world that the human mind cannot experience directly: the infrared spectrum, the structure of molecules, and very possibly a dozen or so extra dimensions.

With good reason, then, there are no proponents of naïve realism. But that doesn't mean there are no naïve realists. On the contrary, there are tons of them—starting, research suggests, with everyone under the age of four. Very young children seem to believe, truly and ardently, that our minds and the world never diverge from each other. As a result—and this is why naïve realism matters so much to this book—they think we can't believe things that are wrong.

We know this about little kids courtesy of one of the classic experiments of developmental psychology. The experiment is known as the false belief test, or, informally, as the Sally-Ann task, after the most famous of its many variations. If you count among your acquaintances a child under the age of four, you can replicate it yourself—and you should, because until you've seen the results firsthand, it's hard to grasp their weirdness, and harder still to believe them. All you need to do is stage a simple puppet show. One character (Sally, in the classic version) takes a candy bar, puts it in a basket, closes the lid, and leaves the room. As soon as she disappears, another character (Ann) takes the candy bar out of the basket and hides it in a cupboard. Now ask the child this: when Sally returns, where will she look for her candy bar?

If the child you've enlisted for this experiment is your own, you already know that kids of this age are stupendous thinkers. They speak and understand their native language (or languages) with ease, and add words and concepts with a rapidity that is the envy of every adult. They are insatiably curious, highly attentive to the world around them, and capable of impressive feats of memory and concentration. They understand cause and effect and can reason about when, why, and how things happen. They make inferences about the world around them that, even when wrong, display a remarkable attentiveness to their environment. They play games, not to mention invent them. They negotiate complex social interactions, and they understand that different people can have different needs, desires, and emotions. Depending on the family they were born into, they may already be reading about star-bellied sneetches or learning to play hockey or studying the violin. And yet, without fail, these same brilliant children will confidently report that Sally will look for her candy bar not in the basket where she put it, but where it actually is: in the cupboard where it was hidden while she was out of the room.

To adults (or, for that matter, six-year-olds), this answer is baffling. We understand that there is no way Sally could know the real whereabouts of her candy bar—literally no mechanism by which she could acquire that knowledge—because she wasn't around to witness Ann relocating it. But this experiment suggests that young children don't care about such mechanisms. For them, it seems, the world and the mind enjoy an automatic correspondence: Sally thinks the candy bar is in the cupboard because the candy bar *is* in the cupboard. Adults, whether they are realists or relativists, recognize that the mind contains a kind of personalized representation of reality—the world as rendered by you or me or Sally. Kids, by contrast, seem to think the mind contains a *replica* of reality: the world as rendered by Xerox. Apparently, they don't yet understand that beliefs about the world can be at variance with the world itself.*

If the Sally-Ann test doesn't seem like conclusive proof of this claim, consider the following, even more astonishing variant of it. In this version, children are shown a box with a picture of candy on the front and asked what they think is inside. Reasonably enough, they say "candy." When they open it, however, they find (presumably to their disappointment) that it is full of pencils. Here's the astonishing part: if you then ask the children what they thought was in the box before they opened it—that is, about twenty seconds earlier—they will insist that they thought it contained pencils. What children maintain about the imaginary Sally they also maintain about themselves: that their beliefs about the world cannot deviate from the world as it really is.

This faith in the perfect accuracy of our beliefs is fleeting. By the age of five, virtually all children can pass the Sally-Ann test with ease. In coming

---

* Remember the Pessimistic Meta-Induction from the History of Science? Here it is in action. While I was writing this book, the once uncontroversial claim that young children can't grasp the existence of a gap between the mind and the world suddenly came up for debate. Recent evidence from infancy experiments (where eye gaze is used as a measure of babies' beliefs) suggests that children might understand more about false beliefs than psychologists previously thought. Although three- and four-year-olds still reliably fail the Sally-Ann task, it now appears that fourteen-month-olds can pass it. It remains to be seen how these findings will be reconciled.

to do so, these children have acquired what developmental psychologists call "representational theory of mind." That is, they've figured out what a mind is, at least in general terms—not a photocopy of reality but a private and somewhat idiosyncratic means for making sense of the world—and they've figured out that everybody has one. This changed understanding leads to striking new insights: that beliefs about the world can be at odds with the world itself; that my beliefs can be at odds with yours; that other people don't necessarily know everything I know; and, conversely, that I don't necessarily know everything other people know.

These insights seem so obvious to adults that it is easy to overlook their importance. The ability to grasp what minds do, to understand that people can hold beliefs that are mistaken or different from our own, subtends a vast swath of mature thinking. It allows us to "read minds," not as psychics use the term but as psychologists do—to infer people's thoughts and feelings based on their words, actions, or circumstances. Rebecca Saxe, a neuroscientist at MIT and one of the leading contributors to our understanding of the brain structures underlying theory of mind, offers the example of *Romeo and Juliet*. As audience members, we know that the seemingly lifeless Juliet is not actually dead, as Romeo believes, but has merely taken a sleeping potion. But if we didn't have theory of mind, we wouldn't be able to set aside our own knowledge and see the scene as Romeo does—and so we wouldn't understand why he kills himself. The false belief on which the whole tragedy turns would be completely lost on us.

So, too, would entire expanses of the social landscape. Without theory of mind, we wouldn't be able to register the subtleties of a flirtation, recognize our accidental offenses against a friend, or foresee that coming home two hours late might alarm and anger our family. As these examples suggest, theory of mind is vital to our emotional, intellectual, and moral development. (Tragically, we have some idea of how compromised we would be without it, because its absence or diminution is characteristic of people with autism and Asperger's syndrome.*)

---

* Another variant of the Sally-Ann task provides a particularly poignant illustration of the difference between healthy and autistic children's ability to understand other

Once you acquire theory of mind, there is no going back; barring serious brain injury, you will never fail the Sally-Ann test again. But the attraction of naïve realism never wholly fades. Granted, we come to understand, in the abstract, that our beliefs can be skewed by any number of factors, ranging from the silent nudgings of self-interest to the limits of omniscience—the fact that, like Sally, sometimes we just aren't in the right room at the right time. When it comes to our specific convictions about the world, however, we all too easily lapse back into the condition of toddlers, serenely convinced that our own beliefs are simply, necessarily true.[†]

Why do we do this? The most obvious answer is that we're so emotionally invested in our beliefs that we are unable or unwilling to recognize

---

people's minds. In this version, the experimenter shows the child a Polaroid camera, explains what it does, takes some sample pictures, and allows the child to play with it until he or she is familiar with how it works. Then the puppet show proceeds as in the original experiment—except that, when Sally puts the candy bar in the basket, the experimenter takes a picture of it there. At the end of the show, after Sally has left the room and Ann has moved the candy bar to the cupboard, the child is asked not where Sally thinks the candy bar is, but where it will appear in the photograph. Although this test and the original Sally-Ann experiment seem identical in the determination that children are asked to make, neuroscientists have shown that we use different parts of the brain to reason about minds than about objects. Healthy children find the Polaroid version of the false-belief task *harder* than the original one: they continue to fail it for some months after they've begun to reason correctly about other people's beliefs. Autistic children, by contrast, can pass the false-belief test when it involves Polaroid pictures, but not when it involves other people's minds. The workings of the former, a mechanical object, are transparent to them. It is the latter that is the black box.

† Our habit of treating many of our beliefs like facts can be seen, in somewhat sidelong fashion, in the specialized way we use the expression "I believe." When I flag a statement as a belief, I'm not emphasizing the depths of my conviction; I'm taking pains to convey my doubt. Imagine that you and I are at a party when a distant acquaintance walks through the door. You nudge me and ask me to remind you of his name. If I say, "His name is Victor," there's a good chance that you'll exclaim, "Victor! Good to see you again." But if I say, "I believe his name is Victor," you will probably have the sense to hold back. You will rightly hear, in that "I believe," an implicit caveat: "this is *just* a belief; I could be wrong." We attach no such caveats when we feel no uncertainty, which is why we say "Rudy Giuliani is a reactionary control freak," not "I believe that Rudy Giuliani is a reactionary control freak."

them as anything but the inviolable truth. (The very word "believe" comes from an Old English verb meaning "to hold dear," which suggests, correctly, that we have a habit of falling in love with our beliefs once we've formed them.) There's a lot to be said for that answer, and much of it *will* get said in the coming pages. For now, though, I want to propose another, less obvious theory about why we act like our beliefs are necessarily true—which is that we are logically obliged to do so. Philosophers have a name for this theory, but, unfortunately, it's a name that only a philosopher could love: the First Person Constraint on Doxastic Explanation. "Doxastic" means "pertaining to beliefs"; that strange syllable, *dox*, is the same one that shows up in words like "orthodox" ("believing correctly") and "paradox" ("contrary beliefs"). In lay terminology, the phrase means that each of us has limited options for how to explain why we believe the things we do.

I'm going to jettison this cumbersome name and (for reasons that will become obvious in a moment) call this idea the 'Cuz It's True Constraint. Here's how it works. Let's say I believe that drinking green tea is good for my health. Let's also say that I've been drinking three cups of green tea a day for twenty years, that I come from a long line of green tea drinkers, and that I'm the CEO of a family-owned corporation, Green Tea International. An impartial observer would instantly recognize that I have three very compelling reasons to believe in the salubrious effects of green tea, none of which have anything to do with whether those effects are real. First, having ingested vast quantities of it, at least partially in the conviction that I was boosting my chances at a long and healthy life, I'm going to be resistant to any suggestion that all that tea had zero effect on me (or, worse, a deleterious one). Second, because my allegiance to green tea is part of an entrenched and presumably sacrosanct family tradition, questioning it could seriously damage my most intimate relationships, not to mention my share of the family fortune. Finally, I have staked my financial and professional status on the belief that green tea is good for one's health.

In short, I have powerful social, psychological, and practical reasons to believe in the merits of green tea. The gist of the 'Cuz It's True Constraint is that I myself can't believe that these reasons contribute in any significant way to my conviction that green tea is good for me. Instead, I must believe that this conviction is based on the facts: in this case, on the physical (rather than emotional, financial, or familial) benefits of green tea. In other words, I must believe that I believe it *'cuz it's true.* As the philosopher Ward Jones said, "It simply does not make sense to see myself as both believing that P is true"—where "P" stands for any proposition—"and being convinced that I do so for reasons having nothing to do with P's being true."

Viewed in a certain light, the 'Cuz It's True Constraint can appear self-evident, or even circular. *Of course* we have to think our beliefs are true: that's what it means to believe them. Fair enough. But one of the strengths of philosophy lies in looking closely at the self-evident—and when you look closely at the 'Cuz It's True Constraint, you see the origins of some of the most important aspects of our relationship to wrongness. Specifically, you begin to see why we are so convinced that our own beliefs must be right, and why we feel no need to extend that assumption to other people.

So let's look closely. The 'Cuz It's True Constraint has several stipulations, the first of which is that it applies only to beliefs I currently hold. I can readily concede that beliefs I *used* to hold weren't based on the facts—that, say, my conviction about adulterers burning in eternal hellfire was just a product of my evangelical upbringing, or that my stint with the International Socialist Organization was just a way to rebel against my conservative parents. What's more, once I've rejected a belief, I can often *only* perceive the self-serving reasons I believed it, and can no longer recognize any evidence for it as rationally compelling.

The second stipulation of the 'Cuz It's True Constraint is that it applies only to specific beliefs—not to my entire set of beliefs, nor to how I feel about the nature of believing in general. As I already mentioned, most of us can acknowledge, in the abstract, that beliefs are influenced by all kinds of non-objective factors. We can even go further and admit that, at this very moment, some of our own beliefs are doubtless swayed by such factors as well. It is only when we are confronted about a specific and active belief that the constraint kicks in. Ask me whether I think my beliefs in general are affected by personal biases and I'll say sure. Ask me about the fidelity of my girlfriend or the safety of my health regimen or the accuracy of the data I just published in that prominent journal, and—ah, well, I assure you that I believe in *those* things not because they are comforting or convenient, but because, by God, they are true.

Finally, consider the most important stipulation of the 'Cuz It's True Constraint. This is the one suggested by the "first person" part of its proper name: it applies only to our own beliefs, not to those of other people. Nothing about the constraint prevents me from thinking that Ellen believes in God to ameliorate her fear of death, or that Rudolf opposes gun control because his father sits on the board of the NRA, or that you believe behaviorism is baloney because your entire tenure committee does, too. On the contrary, we impute biased and self-serving motives to other people's beliefs all the time. And, significantly, we almost always do so pejoratively. If I suggest that the CEO of Green Tea Incorporated stands to gain financially by believing in the benefits of green tea, I'm at the very least implying that she isn't qualified to judge the truth of her belief—and, more likely, I am implying that there *is* no truth to her belief.* In other words, if we want to discredit a belief, we will argue that it is advantageous, whereas if we want to champion it, we will argue that it is true. That's why we downplay or dismiss the self-serving aspects of our own convictions, even as we are quick to detect them in other people's beliefs.

Psychologists refer to this asymmetry as "the bias blind spot." The bias blind spot can be partly explained by the Lake Wobegon Effect, that endlessly entertaining statistical debacle whereby we all think that we are above average in every respect—including, amusingly, impartiality. But a second factor is that we can look into our own minds, yet not into anyone else's. This produces a methodological asymmetry: we draw conclusions about other people's biases based on external appearances—on whether their beliefs *seem* to serve their interests—whereas we draw conclusions about our own biases based on introspection. Since, as we've seen, much of belief-formation neither takes place in nor leaves traces in conscious thought, our conclusions about our own biases are almost always exculpatory. At most,

---

* This is a logical fallacy. The fact that I benefit from a given belief might raise questions about my capacity to assess it objectively, but it doesn't bear on the truth of the belief itself. After all, people benefit from true beliefs as well as false ones.

we might acknowledge the existence of factors that could have prejudiced us, while determining that, in the end, they did not. Unsurprisingly, this method of assessing bias is singularly unconvincing to anyone but ourselves. As the Princeton psychologist Emily Pronin and her colleagues observed in a study of the bias blind spot, "we are not particularly comforted when others assure us that they have looked into their own hearts and minds and concluded that they have been fair and objective."

So we look into our hearts and see objectivity; we look into our minds and see rationality; we look at our beliefs and see reality. This is the essence of the 'Cuz It's True Constraint: every one of us confuses our models of the world with the world itself—not occasionally or accidentally but *necessarily*. This is a powerful phenomenon, and it sets in motion a cascade of corollaries that determines how we deal with challenges to our belief systems—not, alas, for the better.

The first such corollary is the Ignorance Assumption. Since we think our own beliefs are based on the facts, we conclude that people who disagree with us just haven't been exposed to the right information, and that such exposure would inevitably bring them over to our team. This assumption is extraordinarily widespread. To cite only the most obvious examples, all religious evangelism and a good deal of political activism (especially grassroots activism) is premised on the conviction that you can change people's beliefs by educating them on the issues.

The Ignorance Assumption isn't always wrong; sometimes our ideological adversaries *don't* know the facts. But it isn't always right, either. For starters, ignorance isn't necessarily a vacuum waiting to be filled; just as often, it is a wall, actively maintained. More to the point, though, the Ignorance Assumption can be wrong because *we* can be wrong: the facts might contradict our own beliefs, not those of our adversaries. Alternatively, the facts might be sufficiently ambiguous to support multiple interpretations. That we generally ignore this possibility speaks to the powerful asymmetry of the Ignorance Assumption. When other people reject our beliefs, we think they lack good information. When we reject their beliefs, we think we possess good judgment.

When the Ignorance Assumption fails us—when people stubbornly

persist in disagreeing with us even after we've tried to enlighten them—
we move on to the Idiocy Assumption. Here, we concede that our opponents know the facts, but deny that they have the brains to comprehend
them. This assumption can be a narrow judgment, applied to a specific
person on a specific issue, or it can be a sweeping assessment of any individual or group we regard as the opposition. In the course of working on
this book, I spoke with a left-wing lawyer who described growing up in a
politically progressive environment and then attending a liberal (in every
sense) arts college. As a consequence, she told me, "it wasn't until I went
to Yale Law School that I met people I disagreed with, ideologically, who
were incredibly smart. This is going to sound ridiculous, but it wasn't until
then that I realized that conservatives could be intelligent." It would be
nice if that statement *did* sound ridiculous, but we hear variations on it so
often that this one scarcely registers as surprising (except, perhaps, in its
forthrightness). Think, for instance, of the countless times we say things
like "what kind of idiot could actually believe . . ."

One of the most common answers to that question is: the wicked kind.
This is the Evil Assumption—the idea that people who disagree with us
are not ignorant of the truth, and not unable to comprehend it, but have
willfully turned their backs on it. The Evil Assumption has a longstanding relationship with religion, where "unbeliever" is all but synonymous
with "evildoer." But it is almost equally common in politics. In *The Prelude*,
the poet William Wordsworth acidly described the French Revolution as
a cause that, ostensibly, "no one could stand up against, / who was not lost,
abandoned, selfish, proud, / mean, miserable, willfully depraved, / hater perverse of equity and truth." (Wordsworth was largely condemning his own
doctrinaire past; the poem is subtitled *Growth of a Poet's Mind*.) As those lines
suggest, clashes of belief that engender violent conflict are especially good
at provoking the Evil Assumption. And, conversely, the Evil Assumption is
especially good at provoking violent conflict. (If beliefs have consequences,
consider the likely consequences of believing that those who disagree with
you are wicked.) But those who disagree with you don't have to reject your
God or threaten your life for you to conclude that they are depraved. These

days, you can't punch the scan button on your radio without coming across an invocation of the Evil Assumption: hosts or guests or callers describing their ideological opponents as morally depraved reprobates bent on the destruction of civilization as we know it.

That's quite a charge to lay at the feet of people who don't agree with us. And yet it has a certain dark logic, given our tendency to confuse our models of reality with reality itself. Think about the accusation that people who disagree with us "don't live in the real world." What we really mean is that they don't live in our model of the world; they don't share our vision of how things are. By failing to see the world as we do, they actually *are* undermining its reality and threatening its destruction—at least, unto us. But, of course, we are doing the same to them. Implicitly or explicitly, we are denying that they possess the same intellectual and moral faculties that we do—and denying, too, the significance and value of their life experiences, from which, inevitably, many of their beliefs arise.

Of these three assumptions—the Ignorance Assumption, the Idiocy Assumption, and the Evil Assumption—the last is the most disturbing. But the first is the most decisive. We assume that other people are ignorant because we assume that we are not; we think we know the facts, and (as the 'Cuz It's True Constraint mandates) we think those facts determine our beliefs. Put differently, we think the evidence is on our side. It is almost impossible to overstate the centrality of that conviction to everything this book is about, which is why we are going to turn next to the topic of evidence. Our faith in our own reading of the facts undergirds our certainty that we are right, our shock when we turn out to be wrong, and our willingness to deny the perspicacity, intelligence, and moral worth of everyone who disagrees with us.

What is alarming is how naturally this cascade of assumptions comes to us—and not just to the extremists in our midst. I wouldn't characterize Alan Greenspan as a rabid ideologue, and I'd venture to guess that he doesn't routinely use the word "evil" to describe people who disagree with him about economic policy. But he *did* regard such people as dangerous, and (as countless real extremists have likewise done) he did seek to silence them.

Those are not the actions of a man who has contemplated the possibility that his own model could be in error—or that, this time, his beliefs could be the dangerous ones.

This is the grim flip side of our passion for inventing theories. Like toddlers and tyrants, we are quick to take our own stories for the infallible truth, and to dismiss as wrongheaded or wicked anyone who disagrees. These tendencies are most troubling for the way they fuel animosity and conflict. But they are also troubling because they make it extremely difficult to accept our own fallibility. If we assume that people who are wrong are ignorant, or idiotic, or evil—well, small wonder that we prefer not to confront the possibility of error in ourselves.

6.

Our Minds, Part Three: Evidence

ROSENCRANTZ: That must be east, then. I think we can assume that.

GUILDENSTERN: I'm assuming nothing.

ROSENCRANTZ: No, it's all right. That's the sun. East.

GUILDENSTERN (*looks up*): Where?

ROSENCRANTZ: I watched it come up.

GUILDENSTERN: No . . . it was light all the time, you see, and you
opened your eyes very, very slowly. If you'd been facing
back there, you'd be swearing *that* was east.

—TOM STOPPARD, *ROSENCRANTZ AND GUILDENSTERN ARE DEAD*

In 1692, Judge William Stoughton, one of the most venerable lawmakers
in Colonial America, found himself facing an unusual procedural question:
Should visitations by evil spirits be admitted as evidence in a court of law?
Stoughton was presiding over the Salem witch trials and—unfortunately for
the 150 people who were imprisoned and the nineteen who were hanged by

the end of the ordeal—he determined that such evidence was permissible. If you had been alive at the time, and dreamed one night that the ill-fated Goody Proctor was in your bedroom attempting to throttle you, you could have presented your dream as evidence before the court—"as though there was no real difference between G. Proctor and the shape of G. Proctor," in the disapproving words of a contemporary observer.

It is a testament to how far the legal profession has come that few things seem more antithetical to the spirit of justice today than the admission of so-called spectral evidence. Yet the questions Stoughton faced remain central to the practice of law. What counts as evidence? How must it be gathered? Under what circumstances is it admissible? How do certain kinds of evidence compare to other kinds? How much weight should be given to each? How we answer these questions goes a long way toward determining whether justice will be served. Indeed, the fair and consistent practice of law hinges, to a huge degree, on developing a fair and consistent relationship to evidence. (We have names for situations where that relationship doesn't exist or is disregarded, and one of them is "witch trial.")

What is true within the law is also true far beyond it. Although we seldom think of it this way, evidence is immensely central to our lives. We rely on it in science to expand our technological capacity and advance our understanding of the world. We rely on it in journalism to keep us accurately informed and to hold individuals and institutions accountable for their actions. We rely on it in politics to determine which laws to pass, which policies to implement, and which wars to fight. And we rely on it in medicine to sustain our health and save our lives.

These are all public institutions, and, like the law, they have all developed specific and formal ideas about evidence—what kind of information qualifies, how to gather it, how to evaluate it. But evidence is also central to the private, non-institutional entity that is each of us. We know from the last chapter that we can't function without our beliefs, that they tell us where we are, who we are, and what to do next. But these beliefs don't come to us willy-nilly. We form them, as judges form their opinions and juries reach their decisions, based on the evidence. Of course, we don't necessarily form *accurate* beliefs based on *good* evidence. As we've already seen, I'm perfectly capable of forming very iffy notions about string theory based on very scanty secondhand information, and Hannah was perfectly capable of concluding that she could see based on faulty signals from her own brain. In other words, the same goes for us as for the law: how well we gather and evaluate evidence determines how fair or unfair, right or wrong our theories will be. An article in the paper, a weird smell in the basement, the look on your mother's face, your own gut intuition—everything that registers on the sensitive machinery of your brain must be counted in favor of or against your beliefs.

In a perfect world, how would we go about evaluating all this evidence? As it turns out, we have fairly strong and uniform opinions about this. By rough consensus, the ideal thinker approaches a subject with a neutral mind, gathers as much evidence as possible, assesses it coolly, and draws conclusions accordingly. By a further rough consensus, this is not only how we *should* form our beliefs, but how we actually do so. To quote Rebecca Saxe, the neuroscientist from the previous chapter, "we share the conviction that, in general, beliefs follow from relatively dispassionate assessment of facts-of-the-matter and logical reasoning."

This model of how our minds work is a significant step up from naïve realism. Instead of thinking, as toddlers do, that the world is exactly as we perceive it, we recognize that we only perceive certain bits of it—pieces of evidence—and that therefore our understanding might be incomplete or misleading. Unlike naïve realism, then, this model of cognition makes room for error. At the same time, it contains an implicit corrective: the more evidence we compile, and the more thoroughly and objectively we evaluate it, the more accurate our beliefs will be. In this vein, Descartes defined error not as believing something that isn't true, but as believing something based on insufficient evidence.

That definition of error has, at first glance, the virtue of being practical. You can't very well caution people against believing things that aren't true, since, as we've seen, all of us necessarily think our beliefs are true. By comparison, it seems both easy and advisable to caution people against believing things without sufficient evidence. But this idea quickly runs into trouble. First, how are we supposed to know when a body of evidence crosses the threshold from "insufficient" to "sufficient"? Second, what are we supposed to do in situations where additional evidence is not necessarily forthcoming? Augustine, who arrived at Descartes' idea of error some 1,200 years earlier, rejected it when he perceived these problems, and in particular their theological implications. If you encourage people to withhold assent from any proposition that lacks sufficient evidence, he realized, you are inevitably encouraging them to withhold assent from God.*

Augustine needn't have worried. You can urge people not to believe anything based on meager evidence until you are blue in the face, but you will never succeed—because, as it turns out, believing things based on meager evidence is what people *do*. I don't mean that we do this occasionally: only when we are thinking sloppily, say, or only if we don't know any better, or only en route to screwing up. I mean that believing things based on paltry evidence is the engine that drives the entire miraculous machinery of human cognition.

Descartes was right to fear that this way of thinking would cause us to make mistakes; it does. Since he was interested in knowing the truth, and knowing that he knew it, he tried to develop a model of thinking that could curtail the possibility of error. (We'll hear more about his model later.) In fact, curtailing error was the goal of most models of optimal human cognition proposed by most thinkers throughout most of history, and it is the goal behind our own broadly shared image of the ideal thinker. Some of

---

* Monotheistic religions have a particularly interesting and troubled relationship to the idea of evidence. Belief in God is explicitly supposed to be based on faith, not proof: "Blessed are they who have not seen and yet have believed," Jesus says to doubting Thomas in John 20:29. Yet the devout have tried to muster evidence for their beliefs since time immemorial. The shroud of Turin is cited as proof of Jesus' crucifixion, weeping statues of the Virgin Mary serve to substantiate her holiness, the Catholic Church has a formal process for verifying miracles as evidence of God's work, and—before modern science made the claim untenable—volcanoes, hot springs, and geothermal vents were cited as evidence of the existence of hell. More generally, the whole remarkable sweep of creation, from the human eye to the shells on a beach, is often cited as evidence of God the creator. This religious relationship to evidence might be inconsistent, but it isn't surprising. As I suggest at the end of this chapter, we all recognize the value of evidence in grounding our beliefs, and we'd all just as soon have it on our side.

these models, like Descartes', sought to curtail error through radical doubt. Others sought to curtail it through formal logic—using valid premises to derive necessarily valid conclusions. Others, including our shared one of the ideal thinker, seek to curtail it through a kind of general due diligence: careful attention to evidence and counterevidence, coupled with a prudent avoidance of preconceived notions.

By these standards, the cognitive operating system we actually come with is suboptimal. It has no use for radical doubt. It does not rely on formal logic. It isn't diligent about amassing evidence, still less so about counterevidence, and it couldn't function without preconceived notions. It is eminently capable of getting things wrong. In short, our mind, in its default mode, doesn't work anything like any of these models. And yet—not despite but *because* of its aptitude for error—it works better than them all.

Here, I'm going to prove it to you. Actually, I'm going to get *you* to prove it to *me*. Below you will find a very brief multiple-choice test. Please take it. If you still have that four-year-old handy from the last chapter, have her take it, too. You can reassure her that these aren't meant to be trick questions, so neither of you should overthink anything. Here goes:

1. What is behind the shaded rectangle?

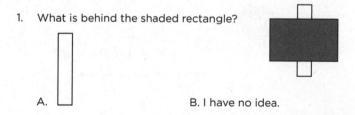

    A. ☐   B. I have no idea.

2. You are traveling in the country of Quine. A speaker of Quinean shows you this picture and says, "This is a Gavagai." What is a Gavagai?

    A. A rabbit.   B. How should I know?

3. Complete the following sentence: "The giraffe had a very long _____."

   A. Neck   B. I'm stumped.

Congratulations; you got all three answers right. You also found this quiz so easy that you don't think congratulations are called for. But here's the thing: this quiz is not easy. At least, it is not *intrinsically* easy. True, you could do it, and so can I, and so can any reasonably attentive four-year-old. Yet computers—which can calculate pi out to a thousand digits while you sneeze—are completely stymied by problems like these. So here is a non-easy question for you: Why is something that is so effortless for a person all but impossible for a machine?

To get a sense of the answer, consider just a tiny fraction of the possibilities a computer has to contemplate when taking this quiz[*]:

1. What is behind the shaded rectangle?

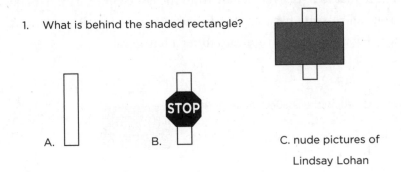

   A.   B.   C. nude pictures of
                                                  Lindsay Lohan

[*] The overall concept of this quiz and its second question come from the philosopher Willard Van Orman Quine, who worked on, among other things, language and episte-mology. Imagine that a field linguist who is trying to translate an unknown language watches as a native speaker points to a rabbit and says "gavagai." The natural conclusion would be that "gavagai" means "rabbit"—but, Quine pointed out, it could also mean, "let's go hunting" or "there's a storm coming" or any number of other things. Quine called this problem "the indeterminacy of translation."

2. You are traveling in the country of Quine. A speaker of Quinean shows you this picture and says, "This is a Gavagai." What is a Gavagai?

   A. grass   B. rabbit plus grass   C. dinner

3. Complete the following sentence: "The giraffe had a very long _____."

   A. tongue   B. flight from Kenya   C. history of drug abuse

These answers strike us as patently absurd. But computers don't have a patent-absurdity monitoring function; they can't rule out these answers (or millions of others like them) because nothing in logic prevents such answers from being right. For that matter, nothing in *life* prevents such answers from being right, either. It is perfectly possible that someone, somewhere—a zookeeper, a veterinarian, a children's book author, someone enjoying a long history of drug abuse—has uttered a sentence about a giraffe's long flight from Kenya. Likewise, it is perfectly possible (although perhaps less probable than some readers would like) that there are naked pictures of Lindsay Lohan behind that shaded rectangle. For that matter, it's perfectly possible that there is a naked picture of *you* behind that rectangle—or of one of the other 7 billion people on the planet, or two pictures of three people, or ten pictures of seven people, or . . . you get the point: there are an infinite number of logically valid, theoretically possible answers to all these questions. Computers recognize this, and therefore can't answer the questions at all.

Human beings, on the other hand, have no trouble answering these questions, because we don't care about what is logically valid and theoretically possible. We care about what is *probable*. We determine what is probable based on our prior experience of the world, which is where evidence comes in: we choose the most likely answer to any given question based on the kinds of things we have (and haven't) experienced in comparable situations before. Over the course of our lifetimes, we've observed some things about giraffes, sentences, and sentences about giraffes, and based on those observations, we make an educated guess about this particular sentence concerning this particular giraffe. Significantly, it doesn't matter how *much* we've observed about sentences and giraffes. Unlike Descartes, we aren't interested in whether we have ample evidence to support a given conclusion—which is just as well, since, as the computer's conundrum shows, we almost certainly do not. All we're interested in is whether whatever evidence we *do* have supports one conclusion better than another. That's why four-year-olds can answer this question, despite their comparatively limited experience with sentences and (one assumes) even more limited experience with giraffes.

This strategy of guessing based on past experience is known as inductive reasoning. As we've seen, inductive reasoning makes us vastly better than computers at solving problems like the ones in this quiz. But it also makes people like Descartes nervous, because it means that our beliefs are not necessarily true. Instead, they are *probabilistically* true. This point was made (and made famous) by the philosopher David Hume, who was arguably the first thinker to fully grasp both the import and the limitation of inductive reasoning. To borrow his much-cited example: How can I be sure that all swans are white if I myself have seen only a tiny fraction of all the swans that have ever existed? If the world were always uniform, consistent, and predictable, I could trust that I am right about this induction (and about all inductions). Unfortunately, as Hume noted, nothing in logic requires the world to be that way, and we know from experience that it isn't always so. I can keep my eyes open for more white swans, but no matter how many I spot, I'll only be adding to my body of evidence, rather than actually proving something about the necessary color scheme of swans. In other words, inductions are necessarily impossible to substantiate. We can know that they are wrong—as Hume's example turned out to be, when a species of black swan was discovered in Australia after his death—but we can't know that they are right. All we know is that they are at least somewhat more likely to be right than the next best guess we could make.

When it comes to multiple-choice quizzes, we are all comfortable with the idea that we make the best guess we can based on whatever evidence we already have. We ought to be, since we've been doing so since grade school. But our use of inductive reasoning isn't limited to that kind of low-stakes situation. On the contrary: psychologists and neuroscientists increasingly think that inductive reasoning undergirds virtually all of human cognition. You make best guesses based on your cumulative exposure to the evidence every day, both unconsciously (as when the motor fibers in your arm estimate where to swing for a baseball) and consciously (as when you bet against the Red Sox, and on the best time to tell your partner how much you lost on that bet).

This kind of guesswork is also how you learned almost everything you know about the world. Take language. Your parents didn't teach you to talk by sitting you down and explaining that English is a subject-verb-object language, that most verbs are converted to the past tense by adding the suffix "-ed," that adjectives generally go before the nouns they modify, and so forth. Mercifully for everyone involved, they didn't have to. All they had to do was keep on chatting about how Mommy poured the milk and Laura painted a pretty picture, and you figured it out by yourself—where "it" is, amazingly, the entire complex grammatical infrastructure of the English language. Not only that, but you did the bulk of this work between birth and four years of age, and you did it despite having heard only the tiniest fraction of all the possible words and combinations of words our language permits.* If there is a better rebuttal to Descartes' claim that we should

---

* One reason the great linguist Noam Chomsky thought language learning must be innate is that the entire corpus of spoken language (never mind the subset spoken to children under four) doesn't seem to contain enough evidence to learn all of grammar. He called this problem "the poverty of the stimulus." In particular, he pointed out, children never hear examples of grammatical structures that aren't permissible in their language, such as "Mommy milk poured" or "picture pretty painted Laura." This raises the question of how kids *know* such structures aren't permissible, since, in formal logic, never hearing such sentences wouldn't mean that they don't exist. (As logicians say, lack of evidence is not evidence of a lack.) But if we learn language inductively, the poverty of the stimulus might not be a problem after all. It's a good bet that if you've been paying attention to language for four years and you've never heard a certain

avoid drawing sweeping conclusions from scanty evidence, I'm not sure what it is.

There are certainly other rebuttals, though, because language isn't the only crucial skill you learned this way. You also used inductive reasoning to learn how to divide the world into categories and kinds—which is why you were somehow able to grasp the concept of "dog" based on a sample population consisting solely of, say, a golden retriever, a shih tzu, and Scooby Doo. Likewise, you used inductive reasoning to learn about the relationships between causes and effects. Just as no one had to teach you the general principles of grammar or the general principles of dogginess, no one had to teach you that, say, lights are usually turned on by flipping switches. You just saw it happen a few times, and in very short order, the relationship between switches and lights was cemented in your mind. (As an adult, if you're standing around indoors and a light suddenly goes on, you'll immediately look around to see who flipped the switch.)

What is true of physical causes and effects is also true of biological and emotional causation. Thanks to inductive reasoning, we are able to determine very quickly that experiencing a strange itchy sensation in our nose means that we are about to sneeze, and that using the F word makes Mom angry. As the latter example suggests, induction is central to how we learn about people, including ourselves. Indeed, much of psychoanalytic theory is based on the belief that our earliest interactions with a tiny number of people permanently shape our theories about who we are, what other people are like, and what kind of treatment we can expect to receive throughout our lives.

Language, categorization, causality, psychology: without expertise in these domains, we would be sunk. And without inductive reasoning—the capacity to reach very big conclusions based on very little data—we would never gain that expertise. However slapdash it might initially seem, this best-guess style of reasoning is critical to human intelligence. In fact, these

---

grammatical form before, you are never going to hear it. Inductively, lack of evidence actually *is* evidence of a lack.

days, inductive reasoning is the leading candidate for actually *being* human intelligence.

But score a point for Descartes: inductive reasoning also makes us fundamentally, unavoidably fallible. As I said, the distinctive thing about the conclusions we draw through induction is that they are probabilistically true—which means that they are possibly false. The theory that you should add the suffix "-ed" in order to form a past-tense verb is a brilliant inductive inference. It is largely correct, it teaches you a huge number of words in one fell swoop, and it's a lot less painful (not to mention a lot more possible) than separately memorizing the past tense of every single verb in the English language. But it also means that sooner or later you are going to say things like drinked and thinked and bringed and runned. Those are trivial errors, and eventually overcome. As we are about to see, however, inductive reasoning is also responsible for some very non-trivial, deeply entrenched mistakes.

Before we look at those specific errors, I want to return briefly to error in general. If the goal of this book is to urge us to rethink our relationship to wrongness, inductive reasoning makes it plain why we should do so. We tend to think of mistakes as the consequence of cognitive sloppiness—of taking shortcuts, cutting corners, jumping to conclusions. And, in fact, we *do* take shortcuts, cut corners, and jump to conclusions. But thinking of these tendencies as problems suggests that there are solutions: a better way to evaluate the evidence, some viable method for reaching airtight verdicts about the world. Yet we've already seen what it takes to thoroughly evaluate evidence and reach airtight verdicts. It takes memorizing tens of thousands of separate past-tense verbs. It takes sitting around wondering about the giraffe's long something-or-other until you've run out of time on the test—and on all of life's other, figurative tests, too. So, yes, there are other ways to reason about the world, but those other ways aren't better. The system we have *is* better. The system we have is astonishing.

This is the lesson we learned with optical illusions, and it is the fundamental lesson of inductive reasoning as well: our mistakes are part and parcel of our brilliance, not the regrettable consequences of a separate and deplorable process. Our options in life are not careful logical reasoning, through which we get things right, versus shoddy inductive reasoning, through which we get things wrong. Our options are inductive reasoning, which probably gets things right, and inductive reasoning, which—*because* it probably gets things right—sometimes gets things wrong. In other words, and appropriately enough, Descartes was half right. Believing something on the basis of messy, sparse, limited information really is how we err. But it is also how we think. What makes us right is what makes us wrong.

That's the good news. The bad news is that inductive reasoning doesn't just sometimes make us wrong. It makes us wrong in ways that are a complete embarrassment to our self-image as clear-eyed, fair-minded, conscientious, reasonable thinkers.

Take a story that was told to me by a man named Donald Leka. Back in 1978, when his two children were in elementary school, Don volunteered to help out at a PTA fundraiser. In the interest of earning a laugh as well as some money, he set up a booth advertising legal advice for 25 cents—a sort of lawyerly version of Lucy's advice booth in *Peanuts*. The booth was obviously something of a jest, but as a responsible lawyer, Don was careful to staff it with practicing members of the bar. So he was alarmed to learn that a guest had gotten legal advice about a healthcare issue not from a colleague who was among those appointed to give such advice, a man named Jim, but from Jim's wife. "I grew quite concerned," Don recollected, "because even though this was lighthearted, I didn't want people's wives just going around giving advice. As soon as I could, I located Jim and told him what his wife was doing"—at which point, Jim informed Don that his wife was general counsel of the largest HMO in the city.

Needless to say, this story is cringe inducing. Also needless to say, the person who has cringed the most is Don, who chalked up his mistake to "ignorant sexism" and still winces about it today. But the reason we make mistakes like this isn't *just* ignorant sexism. It is also because of the pitfalls of inductive reasoning. Even in 2007, when Don told me this story, only a quarter of the lawyers in the United States were women. In the 1970s, the figure was in the low single digits, and Don's experiences bore that out. When he graduated from Harvard Law in 1967, twenty-six of his 525 classmates were women—just over 5 percent. When he took his first job, he had one female colleague out of twenty-three lawyers—just under 5 percent. In Don's experience, 95 percent of lawyers were male. Most of us would be willing to put some money on 95 percent odds, and in essence that's what happened at the PTA event. Unbeknownst to Don, his brain crunched the numbers and made a bet. As it happened, that bet bit him in the butt. But, for good or for ill, it wasn't a bad bet—just a wrong one.

This is the problem with the guesswork that underlies our cognitive system. When it works well (and, as we've seen, overall it works better than anything else around), it makes us fast, efficient thinkers capable of remarkable intellectual feats. But, as with so many systems, the strengths of inductive reasoning are also its weaknesses. For every way that induction serves us admirably, it also creates a series of predictable biases in the way we think.

It was Donald Leka's misfortune to illustrate one of these inductive biases: leaping to conclusions. Actually, as I noted above, leaping to conclusions is what we always do in inductive reasoning, but we generally only call it that when the process fails us—that is, when we leap to *wrong* conclusions. In those instances, our habit of relying on meager evidence, normally so clever, suddenly looks foolish (and makes us look foolish, too). That's bad enough, but Don's story also showcases a more specific and disturbing aspect of this bias. Since the whole point of inductive reasoning is to draw sweeping assumptions based on limited evidence, it is an outstanding machine for generating stereotypes. Think about the magnitude of the extrapolation involved in going from "This swan is white" to "All swans are white." In context, it seems unproblematic, but now try this: "This Muslim is a terrorist"; "All Muslims are terrorists." Suddenly, induction doesn't seem so benign.

If the stereotypes we generate based on small amounts of evidence could be overturned by equally small amounts of counterevidence, this particular feature of inductive reasoning wouldn't be terribly worrisome. A counterexample or two would give the lie to false and pernicious generalizations, and we would amend or reject our beliefs accordingly. But this is the paradox of inductive reasoning: although small amounts of evidence are sufficient to make us draw conclusions, they are seldom sufficient to make us revise them.

Consider, for instance, a second story, this one told to me by a woman named Elizabeth O'Donovan. Once, many years ago, Elizabeth got into an argument with a friend about whether Orion is a winter constellation. (Because of the annual rotation of the earth around the sun, most constellations are visible only at certain times of the year.) Elizabeth emphatically insisted that it was not. "The embarrassing part," she told me, "is that at the time that I was doing all this insisting, my friend and I were standing in a parking lot in December and I had just pointed to the sky and said, 'That's weird. Orion shouldn't be out now; it's a *summer* constellation.'"

You might think that gazing directly at evidence that contradicted her claim would have given Elizabeth pause, but it did not. Instead, the argument escalated until she bet her friend that he was wrong. The loser, they agreed, would take the winner out to dinner once a week for four weeks. "I was so damn determined," she recalled, "that I figured it was some sort of crazy astronomical phenomenon. My logic was something like, 'Well, everyone knows that every fifty-two years, Orion appears for eighteen months straight.'" As we'll see later, this kind of tortured theorizing is typical of the crisis that ensues when new evidence challenges an entrenched theory. It's also a decent indicator that you are about to lose a bet. (For the record, Orion is visible in the night sky from roughly October through March, in both the northern and southern hemispheres. Elizabeth treated her friend to four weeks of fried chicken.)

Elizabeth's story illustrates another of our inductive biases. This one is famous enough to have earned its own separate name in the psychological literature: confirmation bias. As you might guess, confirmation bias is the tendency to give more weight to evidence that confirms our beliefs than to evidence that challenges them. On the face of it, this sounds irrational (and sometimes looks it, as Elizabeth unwittingly demonstrated). In fact, though, confirmation bias is often entirely sensible. We hold our beliefs for a reason, after all—specifically, because we've already encountered other, earlier evidence that suggests that they are true. And, although this, too, can seem pigheaded, it's smart to put more stock in that earlier evidence than in whatever counterevidence we come across later. Remember how our beliefs are probabilistic? Probability theory tells us that the more common something is—long-necked giraffes, white swans, subject-verb-object sentences—the earlier and more often we will encounter it. As a result, it makes sense to treat early evidence preferentially.

Still, however defensible confirmation bias might be, it deals another blow to our ideal thinker. That's the admirable soul we met earlier in this chapter, the one who gathers as much evidence as possible and assesses it neutrally before reaching a conclusion. We already saw inductive reasoning upend the first half of this ideal. We don't gather the maximum possible evidence in order to reach a conclusion; we reach the maximum possible conclusion based on the barest minimum of evidence. Now it turns out that inductive reasoning upends the second half as well. We don't assess evidence neutrally; we assess it in light of whatever theories we've already formed on the basis of whatever other, earlier evidence we have encountered.

This idea was given its most influential treatment by Thomas Kuhn, the historian and philosopher of science, in his 1962 work *The Structure of Scientific Revolutions*. Before Kuhn, scientists were generally regarded as the apotheosis of the above-mentioned ideal thinker. These epistemologically prudent souls were thought to opt for logic over guesswork, reject verification (looking for white swans) in favor of falsification (looking for black swans), test their hypotheses extensively, collect and analyze evidence neutrally, and only then arrive at their theories. Kuhn challenged this notion, arguing that—among other problems with this model—it is impossible to do science in the absence of a preexisting theory.

Kuhn didn't mean this as a criticism, or at least not only as a criticism. Without some kind of belief system in place, he posited, we wouldn't even know what kinds of questions to ask, let alone how to make sense of the answers. Far from freeing us up to regard the evidence neutrally, the absence of theories would render us unable to figure out what even counted as evidence, or what it should be counted as evidence *for*. Kuhn's great insight was that preexisting theories are necessary to the kind of inquiry that is the very essence of science. And the history of the field bears this out: science is full of examples of how faith in a theory has led people to the evidence, rather than evidence leading them to the theory. In the early nineteenth century, for instance, astronomers were puzzled by perturbations in the orbit of Uranus that seemed to contradict Newtonian mechanics. Because they weren't prepared to jettison Newton, they posited the existence of an unknown planet whose gravitational pull was affecting Uranus's path, and calculated that planet's necessary orbit around the sun. Guided by this work, later astronomers with better telescopes took a second look at the sky and, sure enough, discovered Neptune—less than one degree away from where the theorists had predicted it would be.*

The discovery of Neptune is a crystalline illustration of Kuhn's point that theories represent the beginning of science as much as its endpoint. Theories tell us what questions to ask ("Why is Uranus's orbit out of whack?"), what kind of answers to look for ("Something really big must be exerting a gravitational pull on it.") and where to find them ("According to Newtonian calculations, that big thing must be over there."). They also tell us what *not* to look for and what questions *not* to ask, which is why those astronomers didn't bother looking for a giant intergalactic battleship warping Uranus's orbit instead. These are invaluable directives, prerequisite to doing science—or, for that matter, to doing much of anything. As Alan

---

* This story about Neptune presents something of a challenge to my earlier claim that tortured theorizing is often a sign of being on the losing end of a bet. Specifically, it suggests that tortured theories only seem tortured when they turn out to be wrong. If Neptune didn't exist, explaining away deviations in Uranus's orbit by positing a giant undiscovered planet in the outer reaches of the solar system would seem like a pretty desperate move. Or consider a still unresolved example: physicists currently think that 96 percent of all the matter and energy in the universe is invisible—so-called dark matter and dark energy. The virtue of this highly counterintuitive (not to say cockamamie) proposal is that it makes sense of scientific findings that would otherwise call into question the theory of gravity. This is a classic example of extremely strong prior beliefs (we *really* believe in gravity) trumping extremely strong counterevidence. It remains to be seen whether the dark-matter theory will ultimately seem as foolish as proposing that Orion loiters in the sky every fifty-two years or as prescient as predicting the existence of Neptune.

Greenspan pointed out, during a moment in his congressional testimony when he seemed to be coming under fire for merely possessing a political ideology, "An ideology is a conceptual framework, the way people deal with reality. Everyone has one. You have to. To exist, you need an ideology."

Greenspan was right. To exist, to deal with reality, we need a conceptual framework: theories that tell us which questions to ask and which ones not to, where to look and where not to bother. When that framework serves us well—when, say, it spares us the effort of asking what other kinds of long things a giraffe might possess, or taking seriously the proposition that behind a certain shaded rectangle we might encounter a certain naked movie star—we call it brilliant, and call it inductive reasoning. When it serves us poorly, we call it idiotic, and call it confirmation bias. As Elizabeth O'Donovan demonstrated, the effect of that bias—of viewing all evidence in light of the theories we already hold—is that we sometimes view the evidence very strangely indeed.

Actually, Elizabeth showed us only one of the many faces of confirmation bias. To see another one in action, consider a different story about astronomy, this one borrowed from Kuhn. In the West, until the mid-fifteenth century, the heavens were thought to be immutable. This theory was part of a belief system that reigned far beyond the borders of science; the idea that the heavens were eternal and unchanging (in contrast to the inconsistency and impermanence of life on earth) was a cornerstone of pre-modern Christianity. But then Copernicus came along with his idea about the earth revolving around the sun, and the Church went reeling, and suddenly much of astronomy was up for grabs. In the fifty years immediately following the Copernican revolution, Western astronomers began to observe changes in the heavens they had failed to notice for centuries: new stars appearing, others disappearing, sunspots flaring and fading out. In China, meanwhile, where the sky overhead was identical but the ideology on the ground was different, astronomers had been recording such phenomena for at least 500 years. These early Western astronomers did Elizabeth O'Donovan one better. Instead of failing to believe the counterevidence, they literally failed to see it.

Sometimes, by contrast, we see the counterevidence just fine—but, thanks to confirmation bias, we decide that it has no bearing on the validity of our beliefs. In logic, this tendency is known, rather charmingly, as the No True Scotsman fallacy. Let's say you believe that no Scotsman puts sugar in his porridge. I protest that my uncle, Angus McGregor of Glasgow, puts sugar in his porridge every day. "Aye," you reply, "but no *true* Scotsman puts sugar in his porridge." So much for my counterevidence—and so much the better for your belief. This is an evergreen rhetorical trick, especially in religion and politics. As everyone knows, no true Christian supports legalized abortion (or opposes it), no true follower of the Qur'an supports suicide bombings (or opposes them), no true Democrat supported the Iraq War (or opposed it) . . . et cetera.

The Iraq War also provides a nice example of another form of confirmation bias. At a point when conditions on the ground were plainly deteriorating, then-President George W. Bush argued otherwise by, in the words of the journalist George Packer, "interpreting increased violence in Iraq as a token of the enemy's frustration with American success." Sometimes, as Bush showed, we look straight at the counterevidence yet conclude that it supports our beliefs instead. The NASA higher-ups responsible for the space shuttle *Columbia*—which disintegrated upon reentry in 2003, killing all seven astronauts onboard—demonstrated this as well: before the disaster, they consistently claimed that previous damage to the space shuttle was proof of the aircraft's strength rather than evidence of a fatal design flaw. More generally, we all demonstrate it every time we insist that "the exception proves the rule." Think about the claim this adage is making: that a piece of *acknowledged* counterevidence weighs in favor of the hypothesis it appears to weigh against.

The final form of confirmation bias I want to introduce is by far the most pervasive—and, partly for that reason, by far the most troubling. On the face of it, though, it seems like the most benign, because it requires no active shenanigans on our part—no refusal to believe the evidence, like Elizabeth O'Donovan, no dismissal of its relevance, like the stubborn Scotsman, no co-opting of it, like George Bush. Instead, this form of confirmation bias is entirely passive: we simply fail to look for any information that could contradict our beliefs. The sixteenth-century scientist, philosopher, and statesman

Francis Bacon called this failure "the greatest impediment and aberration of the human understanding," and it's easy to see why. As we know, only the black swans can tell us anything definitive about our beliefs—and yet, we persistently fail to seek them out.

Two of my favorite examples of this form of confirmation bias come from the wonderfully evidence-resistant realm of early anatomy and physiology. The first is the traditional Judeo-Christian belief that women had one more rib than men (Adam having furnished one for the making of Eve). This belief somehow survived until 1543, when the Flemish anatomist Andreas Vesalius finally showed otherwise—by, you know, counting. The second includes just about every claim ever made by Pliny the Elder, a Roman scientist and author who lived in the first century AD. Pliny was, arguably, the most influential misinformed man in history, a veritable Johnny Appleseed of bad ideas. Consider his thoughts on menstruation, as recorded in his supposed masterpiece, the scientific omnibus *Naturalis Historia*:

> On the approach of a woman in this state, milk will become sour, seeds which are touched by her become sterile, grafts wither away, garden plants are parched up, and the fruit will fall from the tree beneath which she sits. Her very look, even, will dim the brightness of mirrors, blunt the edge of steel, and take away the polish from ivory. A swarm of bees, if looked upon by her, will die immediately; . . . while dogs which may have tasted of the matter so discharged are seized with madness, and their bite is venomous and incurable.

Surely it wouldn't have been hard to run a quick experiment on that one. And yet, until the stirrings of the Scientific Revolution, no one thought to go looking for evidence that might contradict the prevailing medical beliefs of 1,500 years.

As perverse as they may seem, these many forms of creatively dodging the counterevidence represent a backhanded tribute to its importance. However much we ignore, deny, distort, or misconstrue it, evidence continues to matter to us, enormously. In fact, we ignore, deny, distort, and misconstrue evidence *because* it matters to us. We know that it is the coin of the epistemological realm: that if we expect our beliefs to seem credible, we will have to furnish their grounds. In a sense, this is the positive side of the 'Cuz It's True Constraint. If we think we hold our beliefs because they comport with the evidence, we must also think that we will revise them when new evidence arises. As a consequence, every proposition, no matter how much we might initially resist it, must have an evidentiary threshold somewhere, a line beyond which disbelief passes over into belief. If you show up on my doorstep with a spaceship and a small green friend and we all fly off to Pluto together, I will commence believing in UFOs. Closer to home, we see evidentiary thresholds being crossed all the time. That's how belief in geocentrism—once the most radical of conjectures—came to be taken for granted, and how a global consensus is emerging on climate change, and how Elizabeth O'Donovan eventually accepted that Orion is a winter constellation.

But we also see evidentiary thresholds *not* being crossed—sometimes for centuries, as in the case of Pliny's medical theories. As powerful as confirmation bias is, it cannot fully account for this: for the persistence and duration with which we sometimes fail to accept evidence that could alter our theories. Another factor is the claim, implicit or explicit in many belief systems, that attending to counterevidence can be dangerous—to your health or family or nation, to your moral fiber or your mortal soul. (As a European Communist once said in response to the question of whether he had read any of the criticisms of Communism, "A man does not sip a bottle of cyanide just to find out what it tastes like.") Confirmation bias is also bolstered by the fact that looking for counterevidence often requires time, energy, learning, liberty, and sufficient social capital to weather the suspicion and derision of defenders of the status quo. If the dominant theory works to your detriment, odds are those are resources you don't possess. (Imagine the average medieval woman trying to take on Pliny.) And if the dominant theory works to your advantage, or at least leaves you unscathed—well, why bother challenging it?

As all this suggests, our relationship to evidence is seldom purely a cognitive one. Vilifying menstruating women, bolstering anti-Muslim stereotypes, murdering innocent citizens of Salem: plainly, evidence is almost invariably a political, social, and moral issue as well. To take a particularly stark example, consider the case of Albert Speer, minister of armaments and war production during the Third Reich, close friend to Adolf Hitler, and the highest-ranking Nazi official ever to express remorse for his actions. In his memoir, *Inside the Third Reich*, Speer candidly addressed his failure to look for evidence of what was happening around him. "I did not query [a friend who told him not to visit Auschwitz], I did not query Himmler, I did not query Hitler," he wrote. "I did not speak with personal friends. I did not investigate—for I did not want to know what was happening there . . . for fear of discovering something which might have made me turn away from my course. I had closed my eyes."

Judge William Stoughton of Salem, Massachusetts, became complicit in injustice and murder by accepting evidence he should have ignored. Albert Speer became complicit by ignoring evidence he should have accepted. Together, they show us some of the gravest possible consequences of mismanaging the data around us—and the vital importance of learning to manage it better. It is possible to do this: like the U.S. legal system, we as individuals can develop a fairer and more consistent relationship to evidence over time. By indirection, Speer himself shows us how to begin. *I did not query*, he wrote. *I did not speak. I did not investigate. I closed my eyes.* These are sins of omission, sins of passivity; and they suggest, correctly, that if we want to improve our relationship to evidence, we must take a more active role in how we think—must, in a sense, take the reins of our own minds.

To do this, we must query and speak and investigate and open our eyes. Specifically, and crucially, we must learn to actively combat our inductive biases: to deliberately seek out evidence that challenges our beliefs, and to take seriously such evidence when we come across it. One person who recognized the value of doing this was Charles Darwin. In his autobiography, he recalled that, "I had, during many years, followed a golden rule, namely, that whenever a published fact, a new observation or thought came across me, which was opposed to my general results, to make a memorandum of it without fail and at once; for I had found by experience that such facts and thoughts were far more apt to escape from the memory than favorable ones."

You don't need to be one of history's greatest scientists to combat your inductive biases. Remembering to attend to counterevidence isn't difficult; it is simply a habit of mind. But, like all habits of mind, it requires conscious cultivation. Without that, the first evidence we encounter will remain the last word on the truth. That's why, as we are about to see, so many of our strongest beliefs are determined by mere accidents of fate: where we were born, what our parents believed, what other information shaped us from our earliest days. Once that initial evidence takes hold, we are off and running. No matter how skewed or scanty it may be, it will form the basis for all our future beliefs. Inductive reasoning guarantees as much. And it guarantees, too, that we will find plenty of data to support us, and precious little to contradict us. And that, in turn, all but guarantees that our theories will be very, very difficult to fell.

7.

Our Society

Our faith is faith in some one else's faith, and in
the greatest matters this is most the case.
—WILLIAM JAMES, "THE WILL TO BELIEVE"

Here is Switzerland—that bastion of political stability, military neutrality, excellent chocolate, and hyper-accurate clocks—and here is a startling fact about it. Although it is one of the world's oldest and most established democracies, women there were not allowed to vote until 1971.

By the standards of other democratic nations, this is, needless to say, stunningly retrograde. Women were enfranchised in New Zealand in 1893, in Finland in 1906, in Austria, Germany, Great Britain, Hungary, and Poland in 1918, and in the United States in 1920. Even France and Italy, although rather late to the party themselves, extended the vote to women by the end of the Second World War. Within a few years, Argentina, Japan, Mexico, and Pakistan had followed suit. By 1971, Switzerland was one of just a tiny handful of nations where women remained disenfranchised; the others included Bangladesh, Bahrain, Jordan, Kuwait, Samoa, and Iraq.

Unlike those countries, Switzerland has long been a world leader with respect to other global benchmarks: per capita income and employment, political stability and personal liberties, healthcare, education, and literacy (including for girls and women), and overall quality of life. How, then, did it come to be an island of dissent on the issue of women's suffrage? More broadly, how does membership in a community—whether it is as large as a nation or as small as a neighborhood—influence our beliefs about the world? And why does sharing a belief with others sometimes make us virtually immune to outside opinion that we are wrong?

Switzerland didn't start off seeming particularly exceptional on the issue of women's rights. As in most developed nations, the struggle for suffrage there began in the late 1800s and gained momentum after the turn of the century. But somewhere along the line, while suffragists elsewhere were chalking up a steady stream of victories, Switzerland started drifting away from the emerging Western consensus on the political equality of women. This was evident as early as 1929, when the prominent U.S. suffragist Carrie Chapman Catt chided her friends across the Atlantic for being "behind the times." She could not understand, she said, "why the men and the women of Switzerland do not follow the example of all the rest of the world."

Catt, who died in 1947, would be left wondering for the rest of her days. A proposal for women's suffrage didn't even make it onto the national ballot in Switzerland until 1959, thirty years after her remarks, and it was soundly defeated—67 percent to 31 percent. There was, however, a glimmer of hope amid that trouncing: for the first time, a Swiss canton—Vaud, in the southwest part of the country—extended local voting rights to its female citizens. Within a few years, other cantons (there are twenty-six in all) began to follow suit.

This was a welcome development for suffragists, but also one that led to a certain amount of absurdity. In Switzerland, the cantons determine who can vote in local and cantonal elections, while the federal government decides who can vote on national initiatives and referendums. That power-sharing arrangement worked just fine until significant discrepancies started to develop between national and cantonal voting rights—such that, for instance, Lise Girardin, who became the first female mayor of Geneva in 1968, was allowed to run the nation's second largest city but not allowed to vote in national elections.

The same year that Girardin took office, another event galvanized the long-suffering Swiss suffrage movement. For the first time, Switzerland indicated its willingness to sign the eighteen-year-old European Convention on Human Rights—but only if the nation was granted an exemption from those sections that extended political rights to women. Outrage over this proposed caveat led suffragists to organize the March on Bern, one of the very few large-scale national protests in the history of the Swiss suffrage movement.

Whether because of the momentum created by the Human Rights Convention kerfuffle, because of the increasingly untenable disparity between cantonal and federal voting rights, or simply because of the times—even famously neutral, isolationist Switzerland wasn't immune to the social revolutions taking place around the world in the 1960s and '70s—the days of an all-male Swiss electorate were numbered. On February 7, 1971, the matter was put to vote again, and this time, the men of Switzerland decided that their female compatriots deserved the ballot. The final tally was 66 percent in favor to 34 percent against—a near-exact reversal of the outcome in 1959.

But the story doesn't end there. Communities come in all sizes, and if the collective national community of Switzerland decided in 1971 that it was wrong to exclude women from the vote, the same could not be said of all the smaller communities that together comprise the nation. After the federal referendum passed, most of the cantons that still barred women from voting at the local and cantonal levels amended their laws as well. But two cantons held out. One of these was Appenzell Ausserrhoden, whose male citizens didn't extend the vote to women until 1989. The other was Appenzell Innerrhoden, whose male citizens *never* did so. Women there gained the right to vote only when the Swiss Supreme Court finally forced the issue—ironically, to comply with a federal Equal Rights Amendment that was by then on the books. That was in 1990. On average across the

A 1968 poster opposing women's right to vote in Switzerland. The text above the image reads "Leave us out of it!" The text below says "Women's Suffrage No."

globe, the women of any given nation have had to wait forty-seven years longer for the right to vote than their male compatriots. In Switzerland, where male citizens began gathering in town squares for public balloting in 1291, universal suffrage took exactly seven centuries.*

Today in the developed world, the idea that women should be allowed

---

* Even by a far more conservative estimate, dating only to the establishment of Switzerland's modern federal constitution in 1848, the nation smashes the global average at 143 years. The only women in the world who waited longer for the right to vote than those of the Appenzells were those of Kazakhstan (1992) and Kuwait (2005), and the black women of South Africa (1994). Then there are the women of Saudi Arabia, who are *still* waiting.

to vote is about as uncontroversial a political claim as you can make. The fact that resistance to it lingered for so long anywhere in the West—let alone in prosperous, educated, democratic Switzerland—serves as a striking reminder that even those beliefs we take to be self-evident can vary astonishingly from one community to the next. That, in turn, raises a troubling question about the very nature of belief. All of us like to think that our ideas about the world are, if not necessarily right, at least fundamentally striving toward rightness. What does it mean, then, that those ideas so often shift not with the available evidence but, like language or currency or speed limits, with the mere crossing of a border?

In 1267, a quarter-century before those first members of the Swiss confederacy began casting their ballots, the English philosopher and friar Roger Bacon sent Pope Clement IV a book about error. Actually, the book was about nearly everything (appropriately titled *Opus Majus*, its subject matter ranged from theology and philosophy to linguistics, optics, and the manufacture of gunpowder), but it opened with a discussion about why people get things wrong. To Bacon's mind, all error could be chalked up to just four problems, which he called (rather charmingly, to English speakers) *offendicula*: impediments or obstacles to truth. One of those obstacles was a kind of thirteenth-century version of Modern Jackass: the tendency to cover up one's own ignorance with the pretense of knowledge. Another was the persuasive power of authority. A third was blind adherence to custom, and the last was the influence of popular opinion.

I have been writing, up until now, as if both our beliefs and our errors were the products of individual minds interacting independently with the external world—through perception, inductive reasoning, and so forth. But of Roger Bacon's four *offendicula*, three pertain unambiguously not to cognitive processes but to social ones: to the riot of wrongness that can ensue when a whole bunch of minds get together. This assessment of why we make mistakes was echoed, three hundred-odd years later, by Francis Bacon (something of a spiritual heir to Roger, but otherwise no relation). For Francis Bacon, too, there were four major sources of human error, which he called the four idols. The idol of the Tribe roughly corresponds to the terrain I covered in the last three chapters: universal, species-wide cognitive habits that can lead us into error. The idol of the Cave refers to chauvinism—the tendency to distrust or dismiss all peoples and beliefs foreign to our own clan. The idol of the Marketplace is analogous to what the earlier Bacon called the influence of public opinion, and includes the potentially misleading effects of language and rhetoric. The last idol, that of the Theater, concerns false doctrine that are propagated by religious, scientific, or philosophical authorities, and that are so basic to a society's worldview that they are no longer questioned.

Like the earlier Bacon, then, the later one saw most errors as stemming from collective social forces rather than individual cognitive ones. This is a recurring theme in the history of wrongness. Or, more precisely, it is a recurring *question* in the history of wrongness: whether we are more error-prone when we follow the masses or strike out on our own. I think of this as the Fifty Million Frenchmen question, after the expression "fifty million Frenchmen can't be wrong." The saying comes from a 1927 hit song that poked fun at American prudery:

> *All of our fashions come from gay Par-ee*
> *And if they come above the knee*
> *Fifty million Frenchmen can't be wrong. . . .*
> *If they prefer to see their women dressed*
> *With more or less of less and less,*
> *Fifty million Frenchmen can't be wrong. . . .*
> *And when we brag about our liberty*
> *And they laugh at you and me*
> *Fifty million Frenchmen can't be wrong.*

In short, if everybody's doing it, it must be a good idea. This is a notion that has received considerable support well outside the domain of pop songs. The Cornell psychologist and behavioral economist Thomas Gilovich has observed that, "Other things being equal, the greater the number of people who believe something, the more likely it is to be true."

And the legal scholar Cass Sunstein has pointed out that, "Conformity of this kind is not stupid or senseless," since "the decisions of other people convey information about what really should be done." The financial writer James Surowiecki calls this notion "social proof"—the idea that "if lots of people are doing something or believe something, there must be a good reason why."*

The other side of the Fifty Million Frenchmen coin is the one your mother loves: if all your friends were jumping off the roof, would you jump, too? This injunction not to be a lemming—to think for oneself instead of following the masses—was the point Roger Bacon and Francis Bacon were trying to make as well. (Two esteemed Englishmen and your mother can't be wrong.) Some philosophers, including John Locke and David Hume, have formalized this idea, arguing that secondhand information, no matter how compelling or pervasive, never constitutes sufficient grounds for knowledge. According to these thinkers, we can only claim to know something if we ourselves have directly observed or experienced it.

Thinking for oneself is, beyond a doubt, a laudable goal. But there are three problems with the idea that it is a good way to ward off error. The first is that the glorification of independent thought can easily become a refuge for holders of utterly oddball beliefs. You can dismiss any quantity of informed and intelligent adversaries if you choose to regard them as victims of a collective, crowd-driven madness, while casting yourself as the lone voice of truth. The second problem is that (as we have seen), our own direct observations and experiences are not necessarily more trustwor-

---

* To be clear, Gilovich, Surowiecki, and Sunstein all acknowledge serious limitations to this follow-the-crowd logic. Among other problems, Gilovich points out, we tend to assume that most rational people believe what we believe, so our sense of the consensus of the crowd might itself be in error. Surowiecki believes strongly in the wisdom of crowds—he is the author of a 2004 book by that name—but only if their decisions reflect the aggregation of many independently developed beliefs, rather than the belief of a few people snowballing into the belief of the masses. Sunstein, meanwhile, acknowledges the potential utility of conformity largely as a preamble to exposing its dangers, and especially its political dangers—which is the central theme of his own book, *Why Societies Need Dissent.*

thy than secondhand knowledge. If Captain Robert Bartlett, the man who spotted the glaciers of Iceland from 350 miles away, had trusted his own senses over his nautical charts—a clear case of firsthand versus second-hand information—he would have come to the wrong conclusion about his whereabouts.

The last and most significant problem with the idea that we should al-ways think for ourselves is that, bluntly put, we can't. Every one of us is pro-foundly dependent on other people's minds—so profoundly that if we took seriously the charge to think for ourselves, we would have to relinquish our faith in the vast majority of the things we think we know. In his *Confessions*, Augustine wrote that,

> I began to realize that I believed countless things which I had never seen or which had taken place when I was not there to see—so many events in the history of the world, so many facts about places and towns which I had never seen, and so much that I believed on the word of friends or doctors or various other people. Unless we took these things on trust, we should accom-plish absolutely nothing in this life.

And that, mind you, was 1,600 years ago, before the mad proliferation of data and ideas that began in the Age of Exploration, sped up during the Industrial Revolution, and hit warp speed with the advent of modern infor-mation technology. Today, each of us takes vast quantities of information on faith, in ways both ancient and new. That's what we're doing every time we read a newspaper, board an airplane, look something up on Wikipedia, vaccinate our children (or don't), and assume that our parents really are our parents (which, as Augustine went on to note, is the consummate example of a fact that most of us take for granted yet none of us know firsthand).

Even specialists and experts rely on other people's knowledge constantly—far more than you might imagine, and possibly enough to make you nervous. My sister-in-law, for instance, recently had the experience of watching her doctor Google the correct dosage of a medicine she was about to prescribe. Or take the example of Leonard Susskind, who is a professor of theoretical physics at Stanford University, a member of the National Academy of Sciences, and one of the founders of string theory. All of that makes him about as expert as you can get in the domain of science, yet here he is on one of its fundamental principles: "If I were to flip a coin a million times, I'd be damn sure I wasn't going to get all heads," he once wrote. "I'm not a betting man, but I'd be so sure that I'd bet my life or my soul on it. . . . I'm absolutely certain that the laws of large numbers—probability theory—will work and protect me. All of science is based on it." And yet, he concluded, "I can't prove it, and I don't really know why it works."

In other words, one of the world's leading scientists is obliged to take on faith one of the most basic precepts of his own field. Presumably, Susskind is even more at sea when it comes to matters *outside* his domain—whether salty foods really increase your blood pressure, say, or whether turnips really grow best in loamy soil. And what's true for him is true for all of us. The vast majority of our beliefs are really beliefs once removed. Our faith that we are right is faith that someone else is right.

This reliance on other people's knowledge—those around us as well as those who came before us—is, on balance, a very good thing. Life is short, and most of us don't want to spend any more of it than absolutely necessary trying to independently verify the facts about turnips. Relying on other people to do that work buys us all a lot of time. It also buys us, in essence, many billions of prosthetic brains. Thanks to other people's knowledge, I know a bit about what Thomas Jefferson was like in person, how it feels to climb Mount Everest, and what kind of creatures live in the depths of the Mariana Trench. Depending on secondhand information makes our lives both much more efficient and much more interesting than they would otherwise be.

That said, this dependence raises an important question about the nature of belief. The world around us positively bristles with secondhand sources, from the White House press secretary to *The Weekly World News*, from Tom and Ray Magliozzi to Rabbi Moses ben Nachman (1194–1270). Obviously, we don't believe all such sources indiscriminately. So how do we determine which ones to trust? One option—the one that harks back to the ideal thinker of the last chapter—would be to consciously evaluate each source on the basis of multiple rational criteria: whether and how often it has proved trustworthy in the past; whether it has a transparent and seemingly sound method for assessing the information it promulgates; whether it appears to be impartial or biased with respect to that information; and whether other people (especially authorities in the field) regard it as reliable.

All of us do engage in this kind of deliberate and thorough source evaluation from time to time. And, as an ideal of intellectual inquiry, we both teach it to and expect it from other people, especially students, scholars, and professionals in data-driven fields. In our day-to-day life, however, departure from this ideal process is the norm. Instead of trusting a piece of information because we have vetted its source, we trust a source, and therefore accept its information. The philosopher Avishai Margalit put this nicely. "It is not the case that I am caught in a web of beliefs," he wrote. ". . . Rather, I am caught in a network of witnesses." Our relationships to these "witnesses"—the people and institutions that attest to the truth of various beliefs—predate and determine our reaction to whatever information they supply. As Margalit said, "my belief *in* [one of these witnesses] is prior to my belief *that* (what she says is true)."

Belief *in* is prior: however far this might be from our sense of how we should form our ideas about the world, it is the first principle of how we actually do so. All of us are caught in Margalit's "networks of witnesses"— not just in one but in many, and not just from time to time but all the time, from the moment we are born until the day we die. As countless commentators have observed, this lends to our beliefs an element of the arbitrary. Montaigne, for instance, remarked that people "are swept [into a belief]— either by the custom of their country or by their parental upbringing, or by chance—as by a tempest, without judgment or choice, indeed most often before the age of discretion."* This claim is at once obvious and irksome, not least because it is directly at odds with the 'Cuz It's True Constraint. If we think we believe our beliefs based on the facts, we aren't likely to appre-

---

* A case in point: the single best predictor of someone's political ideology is their parents' political ideology.

ciate the alternative theory that we actually believe them because we were born in Tuscaloosa instead of Dubai.

This relationship between communities and beliefs is a two-way street. If we often form our beliefs on the basis of our communities, we also form our communities on the basis of our beliefs. There may be no better contemporary example of this than the Internet, which has enabled far-flung strangers to form confederacies around their common convictions, whatever those may be. But people have been bonding together on the basis of belief since long before search engines made it so easy. Ancient Epicureans, Orthodox Jews, socialists, suffragists, indie rockers in skinny jeans: all of them, like all of us, sought out (and, when possible, settled among) the likeminded.

Sociologists call this predilection "homophily": the tendency to like people who are like us. Homophily isn't necessarily the kind of thing we explicitly espouse. Here in the United States, with our ethos of melting-pot multiculturalism, two-thirds of us claim to want to share a community with those whose beliefs and backgrounds differ from our own. In reality, though, most of us live around people who look, earn, worship, and vote a whole lot like we do. (As the *Washington Post* pointed out after the 2008 presidential election, "Nearly half of all Americans live in 'landslide counties' where Democrats or Republicans regularly win in a rout"—just one example of our tendency to hang out with our own.) Whether we spend so much time with these people because we agree with them, or agree with them because we spend so much time with them, the crucial point remains the same. We do not just hold a belief; we hold a membership in a community of believers.

That membership confers on us some very significant advantages. Some of these are practical, as I've already noted. Since communal beliefs are familiar, established, and supported (socially if not factually), hewing to them is both comfortable and efficient. It is also remunerative: typically, the goods a community has on offer—from professional opportunities to political power—are awarded to those who share its beliefs and withheld from those who don't. But the most important advantages we gain from membership in a community are the emotional ones: the comfort, pleasure, and security of being surrounded by people who agree with and understand us. Taken together with more practical and material factors, these psychological benefits provide a powerful incentive to keep faith with those around us. And keep faith we do—even, as we are about to see, when doing so leads us into error, folly, and travesty.

In the 1950s, the social psychologist Solomon Asch conducted what has become one of the most famous experiments in the history of his field. Asch brought groups of five to eight people into a classroom and showed them two flashcards at a time—one with a single vertical line on it, the other with three vertical lines. He then asked the people to tell him, one at a time and out loud, which line on the second card was the same length as the line on the first card.

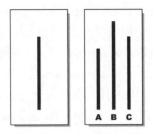

As you can see from the above images, this is not a terribly challenging task. Young children can do it correctly, and in control experiments designed to determine baseline success rates, Asch's subjects sailed through the flashcards without any difficulty.

In the actual experiment, however, there was a hitch: only one of the people in the room was really a subject. The others were working for Asch ("stooges," in psych-experiment parlance), and, per his instructions, after the first few flashcards, they all began to give the same wrong answer. The consequences for the lone authentic subject were striking. Three-quarters of them gave the wrong answer at least once, and one-quarter gave the wrong answer for half or more of the flashcards. On average, the subjects' error rate rose from under 1 percent when acting independently to almost 37 percent when influenced by the group.

The Asch line studies tend to make people queasy, and with good reason. None of us like to think that we are unduly influenced by peer pressure, and all of us want to believe that we call things as we see them, regardless of what those around us say. So it is disturbing to imagine that we so readily forsake the evidence of our own senses just to go along with a group. Even more disturbing, though, is the possibility that we do this unconsciously. That possibility was suggested by Gregory Berns, a psychiatrist and neuroscientist at Emory University, who conducted a modified version of the Asch studies in 2005. Berns got roughly the same results as Asch (the wrong answers given by his stooges held sway 41 percent of the time), but his subjects participated from within functional magnetic resonance imaging machines, devices that measure activity in the brain. As the subjects were giving their wrong answers, those measurements showed increased activity in the part of the brain responsible for spatial awareness, but not in the parts responsible for higher-level cognition, such as conscious decision-making and conflict-resolution. Berns concluded that his subjects *were* calling it like they saw it. They weren't knowingly suppressing a correct answer to conform with the judgment of the group. Instead, the judgment of the group actually changed how they saw the lines.

The Asch studies and their recent high-tech replication provide a particularly stark example of a universal phenomenon: like pre-Copernican Western astronomers, we see things as those around us see them. In fact, as these studies show, we do so even when the people around us aren't neighbors or relatives or friends, but just an ad hoc community of strangers. And we do so even when this "community" is tiny; in subsequent studies, Asch found that the social-conformity effect kicked in with the use of just three fake subjects. Moreover, we do so even when the judgment in question concerns a straightforward matter of fact, such as the comparative length of a series of lines. How much more susceptible to peer pressure must we be, then, when it comes from large groups of people with whom we share a place, a history, and a culture—and when it is brought to bear on far more complicated and ambiguous evidence? In other words, how much more must our real communities influence our real beliefs?

To answer this question, I want to return to the Appenzells, the two cantons in Switzerland where women couldn't vote until 1989 and 1990. To understand these two cantons in specific, you have to understand something about the cantons in general, which is that their independence is a sacrosanct pillar of Swiss political culture—a kind of state's rights sentiment on steroids. There's a joke in Switzerland that illustrates the point: a German kid, an American kid, and a Swiss kid are sitting around talking about how babies are made. The German kid claims that they are brought to their parents by storks. The American kid describes the mechanics of sex. Then the Swiss kid pipes up and says, "In Switzerland, it varies by canton."

The point is that in Switzerland, virtually *everything* varies by canton. One of these variables is communication. The country recognizes four national languages—German, French, Italian, and Romansch—and the differences between and loyalties within these language groups and their associated cultures run deep. (If Switzerland has an analogue to America's red state/blue state divide, it is between the country's German-speaking population, which is more conservative and isolationist, and its French-speaking population, which is more liberal and internationalist.) Another variable is geography. The more mountainous southern cantons have smaller populations and heavily agrarian economies, while the northern cantons are more populous and urbanized. Then there is religion. The country is almost evenly split between Catholics and Protestants—and, in 1847, it almost *did* split between them, when a civil war broke out between the predominantly Catholic and predominantly Protestant cantons.

This Protestant/Catholic divide also created Appenzell Innerrhoden and Appenzell Ausserrhoden. The two cantons were one until 1597, at which point they separated along religious lines. Today, Innerrhoden is largely Catholic, Ausserrhoden largely Protestant. Otherwise, though, the two are very similar. Both are tiny, rural, mountainous, sparsely populated, and almost entirely German-speaking. And, as you might infer from the suffrage situation, both are deeply conservative. The extremely apt motto of the tourist department for Appenzellerland—the collective name for the two cantons—is "As If Time Had Stood Still."

Until recently, voting practices ranked high among the frozen-in-amber aspects of life in the Appenzells. Beginning at least as early as the 1300s, voting there was conducted through an institution known as the *Landsgemeinde*, possibly the oldest continuous form of direct democracy on earth. On voting days, every eligible male citizen gathered in an appointed town square, bearing either a sword or a bayonet. These weapons, often handed down from father to son for generations on end, served as a kind of voter-registration card; no other proof of citizenship was necessary—or, for that matter, admissible. (To this day in Innerrhoden, where the practice persists, women must present official voting cards, while men need only bring their swords.) Voting was conducted openly, via voice vote or a show of hands. There were no ballot boxes, no electronic voting machines, and most assuredly no women.

How did the men of the Appenzells defend this exclusion? To some extent—and especially during the early years of the battle over women's suffrage—they relied on the same arguments that were used all over the world: that political participation rendered women unfeminine ("there is nothing so unpleasant as a superintellectual woman," opined one Swiss antisuffragist); that most Swiss women didn't really want the vote anyway (because "they can influence their men and are happy with their condition"); that the domestic sphere would be destroyed if women were "forced" into the public one; that Switzerland had been at peace for over a hundred years, stayed out of two world wars, and cultivated immense prosperity, all without women voting—so best not to fix what wasn't broken; that politics is a man's business and women could not be trusted to safeguard the interests of the nation.

All these arguments, however, paled in comparison to the strongest, most enduring, and most uniquely Swiss objection to women's suffrage: that it would annihilate the all-male tradition of the *Landsgemeinde* and everything it stood for. Ironically, one of the things it stood for was Switzerland's unusually long and rich relationship to democracy. The feeling among antisuffragists, said Lee Ann Banaszak, a political science professor at Pennsylvania State University who studied the Swiss suffrage movement, was that "there was this unique political and historical institution that was very important, that represented the origins of direct democracy, and that would be destroyed by giving women the right to vote." Antisuffragists even commissioned studies showing that the town squares where voting was traditionally held were not large enough to accommodate the entire adult population—meaning that either the *Landsgemeinde* had to go, or male-only suffrage had to stay.

But the *Landsgemeinde* represented something else, too. In Switzerland, the right to vote had always been linked with military service (hence the swords and bayonets)—and, like the military, the *Landsgemeinde* fostered both a no-girls-allowed clubhouse mentality and a distinctly masculine sense of honor and duty. "By the 1960s, communal voting was one of the last strongholds for men," said Regina Wecker, a professor of women's history in Basel. "It's not just that you vote; it's that you go there, you vote, and afterwards you go to the pub. So what was involved was their entire sense of community, their entire sense of who they were and the influence they held." Letting women vote threatened to undermine all that—terminating centuries of tradition, destroying community bonds, and robbing men and women alike of their unique place in society. Or so the argument went: women's suffrage would obliterate the very characteristics that made Appenzellerland unique.

From the vantage point of our own era and culture, in which opposition to women's suffrage strikes most people as Paleolithic*, it's tempting to mock the antisuffrage Appenzellerites, in the boys-and-their-toys tradition of justified feminist disgust. This is, after all, a group of people who passionately believed that the right to vote was contingent on the possession, passed down from father to son, of a . . . well, let's call it a sword. I'll talk more about this temptation toward mockery at the end of this chapter—about our instinct to despise and differentiate ourselves from the likes of these antisuffragists. For the moment, though, I want to focus instead on something we have in common with them. This isn't their belief in the political inferiority of women (which I trust most readers will find

---

* But not everyone. Here's the right-wing gadfly Ann Coulter: "If we took away women's right to vote, we'd never have to worry about another Democrat president. It's kind of a pipe dream, it's a personal fantasy of mine, but I don't think it's going to happen."

risible), nor their desire to honor their community's history and traditions (which I trust most readers will find reasonable). It is, instead, a problem that bedevils all of us as members of communities of believers. I call this problem our disagreement deficit, and it comes in four parts.

Boiled down to their barest essence (we will unboil them in a moment), these parts are as follows. First, our communities expose us to disproportionate support for our own ideas. Second, they shield us from the disagreement of outsiders. Third, they cause us to disregard whatever outside disagreement we do encounter. Finally, they quash the development of disagreement from within. These factors create a kind of societal counterpart to cognition's confirmation bias, and they provoke the same problem. Whatever the other virtues of our communities, they are dangerously effective at bolstering our conviction that we are right and shielding us from the possibility that we are wrong.

Of the four parts of our disagreement deficit, the first is the most self-explanatory. Since, as we have seen, communities often either form around or foster shared beliefs, they leave us overexposed to people who second our opinions. (Consider that, in 1959, when women's suffrage was increasingly the global norm, opposition to it in Innerrhoden was running at upwards of 95 percent.) Inevitably, this constant and disproportionate affirmation of our own convictions makes them seem both more warranted and more widely held than they really are. This is our disagreement deficit, inverted: an agreement surplus.

The flip side of all that affirmation—and the second reason for our disagreement deficit—is that we are underexposed to sources that challenge our ideas. All of us believe in getting second opinions when it comes to medical issues, but when it comes to most other matters, we are perfectly content to stick with the opinion we already have. As Thomas Gilovich observed, religious fundamentalists generally don't read Darwin in their free time. Likewise, most of us are supremely unmotivated to educate ourselves about beliefs with which we disagree.

This underexposure is easy to maintain, since most of us don't spend much time with people whose belief systems differ dramatically from our own. Moreover, even when we do spend time with such people, we seldom discuss our differences. We talk about the weather, not about climate change; about our recent vacation, not our recent abortion. We can hardly be blamed for this behavior, since it is widely socially endorsed: I'm calling it part of our disagreement deficit, but most people just call it good manners. "Try to do and say those things only which will be agreeable to others," advised Emily Post, that doyenne of American etiquette.

However apt this advice might be for socially awkward dinner guests, it does nothing to help alert us to possible flaws in our belief systems. For that, we're better off taking some not-very-mannerly advice from a not-very-mannerly source: the magician and comedian Penn Jillette, who would have appalled the genteel Post, and who once dismissed most conventional etiquette as "bullshit" on his TV show of that name. In an interview for AskMen.com, Jillette attacked the notion that "shutting up about what you believe is showing tolerance to other people." On the contrary, he said, "I believe shutting up about what you believe is a way to stay close-minded, a way not to be busted. If you have some crazy thought and keep it in your head, there is much less chance that someone will say, 'what are you, fucking nuts?'" In other words, he argued, "One of the quickest ways to find out if you are wrong is to state what you believe."

Jillette might be right, but it is Post and her many progeny in the politeness business who rule the day. Most of us hesitate to state our beliefs directly to those who disagree, and, conversely, to openly disagree with other people's beliefs. A friend of mine—who is not known for her retiring personality when she is among her own—confessed to me that she has all but given up on confronting people with whom she disagrees. "No matter how important an issue is to me, and how scary it is to think that the vast majority of Americans disagree with me on it—even in those cases where my life could be much the worse because of that disagreement—I still, 99.9 percent of the time, don't argue with people who disagree with me," she said.

Not everyone feels this way, of course. Evangelists, for instance, regard it as their bounden duty to share their own beliefs and correct the errors of others. And, too, there are the Jerry Springers of the world, unafraid to (as Jillette might say) call bullshit on everything that runs counter to their own high-pitched convictions. But my friend's suspicion that it is impossible to change other people's minds is widespread. And it is not unfounded, which brings us to the third reason for our disagreement deficit: even when we do encounter outside challenges to our beliefs, we usually disregard them. In fact, much as we tend to automatically accept information from people we trust, we tend to automatically reject information from unfamiliar or disagreeable sources.

The antisuffragists of the Appenzells are a case in point. As women's suffrage became more established in Switzerland and more common the world over, outside pressure increased on the cantons to extend the vote to women. But the Appenzellerites remained unmoved—precisely *because* this pressure came from outside. As Banaszak wrote in a book comparing the Swiss and American suffrage movements, Swiss opponents of suffrage regarded women's voting rights as an "unwanted reform" that "was being forced upon them by the national government, politicians, the press, and foreign influences." In fact, if outside pressure moved the men of Appenzell at all, it moved them toward a *more* extreme position. Banaszak quotes a suffragist who recalled meeting a man from the Appenzells who was inclined to support women's suffrage until "he was at the *Landsgemeinde* and saw the ring of people, people from outside Appenzell, who screamed out so loud [in protest] that the members had to ask for silence."* Far from making us reevaluate our beliefs, external opposition—especially opposition that we perceive as threatening or insulting—tends to make us dig our heels in even more.

This leads to something of a damned-if-you-do, damned-if-you-don't predicament—because, as it turns out, *not* being exposed to external op-

---

* This man's reaction is an example of what psychologists call the insult effect. Studies have shown that if you and another person are debating the merits of a particular idea and the other person suddenly insults you, you will instantly retreat further into your own position, and your conviction that the other person is wrong will intensify. This seems like a natural reaction—but, of course, your interlocutor's manners have nothing to do with how right or wrong he is. (On the other hand, his manners might have a lot to do with whether or not you want to be a member of his community.) This suggests an annoying but immovable fact of life: sometimes, disagreeable people are right.

position can also make us grow more adamant about our beliefs. This is the infamous phenomenon known as groupthink. In 1972, the psychologist Irving Janis defined groupthink as, "a mode of thinking that people engage in when they are deeply involved in a cohesive in-group, when the members' strivings for unanimity override their motivation to realistically appraise alternative courses of action." Groupthink most commonly affects homogenous, close-knit communities that are overly insulated from internal and external criticism, and that perceive themselves as different from or under attack by outsiders. Its symptoms include censorship of dissent, rejection or rationalization of criticisms, the conviction of moral superiority, and the demonization of those who hold opposing beliefs. It typically leads to the incomplete or inaccurate assessment of information, the failure to seriously consider other possible options, a tendency to make rash decisions, and the refusal to reevaluate or alter those decisions once they've been made.

Shall I even bother naming names? Janis cited as victims of groupthink the Kennedy Administration during the Bay of Pigs disaster and the Johnson Administration in Vietnam, and plenty of readers are no doubt mentally adding the latest Bush Administration and its prosecution of the Iraq War. Plainly, the consequences of groupthink can be catastrophic. But even the mere existence of the phenomenon is troubling. It seems that participation in communities of believers—which, as I've already noted, is both inevitable, pleasurable, and psychologically indispensable—can drive us toward a degree of conviction, and a degree of extremity, that we might not otherwise feel. It's as if our own inner world is oddly more capacious than the outer one, able to accommodate a degree of ambiguity that is all too often foreclosed by the boosterism of our cohort or the skepticism of outsiders. This suggests that our communities can be dangerous for our intellectual and moral health. And that, in turn, suggests that we all live, perpetually, on the horns of a dilemma—because if it is intellectually and morally corrosive to always think with others, it is also (as we have seen) impossible to always think for ourselves.

It is *not* impossible, however, to deliberately stave off the dangers of groupthink. Irving Janis proposed a list of ways to do so, including explicitly encouraging disagreement, assigning someone the role of devil's advocate, and actively seeking outside input. Many people cite President Kennedy's handling of the Cuban Missile Crisis as a successful effort to counteract groupthink (it seems he learned something from the Bay of Pigs), and others see reason for optimism in President Obama's stated commitment to "vigorous debate inside the White House." My favorite example, however, comes from the Talmud, the rabbinical writings that serve as a commentary on the Torah and the basis of Orthodox Judaism. According to these writings, if there is a unanimous guilty verdict in a death penalty case, the defendant must be allowed to go free—a provision intended to ensure that, in matters so serious that someone's life is on the line, at least one person has prevented groupthink by providing a dissenting opinion.

Groupthink arises from the parts of our disagreement deficit that I've already introduced: disproportionate exposure to support for our beliefs, underexposure to the opposition, and a tendency to discount that opposition even if we do encounter it. But it also hints at the fourth and final part: the suppression of doubt or differences of opinion within a community. Sometimes, this suppression is subtle, or even self-imposed—just an instinctive shying away from anything that could disturb a group to which we are loyal, or disrupt the material and psychological infrastructure of our lives. This kind of self-censorship almost certainly played a role in the widespread opposition to women's suffrage in the Appenzells. Not only did 95 percent of male citizens there vote against the initial suffrage referendum, they did so publicly, by a show of hands. Think about trying to raise your own hand when 95 percent of your neighbors aren't raising their own—and then think about the Asch line studies.

Sometimes, though, the suppression of dissent within a community is deliberate and overt. As Joseph Jastrow observed in *The Story of Human Error*, group conformity has long been enforced through ostracism, exile, and violence. "The laboratory is a latecomer on the human scene," he wrote. "The scepter, the battlefield, the arena, the mob, tribunals for heresy, the stake, are far older as moulding instruments of belief, and more direct and effective." His point was the old familiar one: might makes right. In countless communities, historically as well as today, the accuracy of a belief is essentially established by fiat,* and community members are dissuaded from dissent by the threat of force. This kind of suasion was not a factor in the battle over suffrage in the Appenzells. To see it in its full-blown form, we need to make a brief layover in a very different part of the globe.

In 1990, an Afghan man named Abdul Rahman converted to Christianity. Such conversions are extremely rare in Afghanistan—the country is 99 percent Islamic—but Rahman had been working for a Catholic charity that provided medical assistance to refugees, and he came to believe in the religion of his colleagues. In the aftermath of his conversion, Rahman's life as he had known it collapsed around him. His wife, who remained a devout Muslim, divorced him on the grounds that he was an infidel. He lost the ensuing custody battle over his two daughters for the same reason. His parents disowned him, stating that, "Because he has converted from Islam to another religion we don't want him in our house."

All that was bad enough. But then, in 2006, Rahman was arrested by the Afghan police on charges of apostasy and imprisoned. In accordance with the Hanafi school of sharia law, the prosecutors asked for the death penalty. One of them, Abdul Wasi, said that Rahman "should be cut off and removed from the rest of Muslim society and should be killed." The Afghan attorney general seconded that opinion, urging that the prisoner be hanged. Only after tremendous international pressure was brought to bear on the case was Rahman released from prison. Under threat of extrajudicial (if not judicial) death, he was granted asylum by Italy and fled

---

* One notorious example of this is lysenkoism, the practice of establishing scientific truths via political diktat. It was named for Trofim Denisovich Lysenko, a national agriculture director in the former Soviet Union whose erroneous theories about agriculture, biology, and heritability enjoyed the imprimatur of Stalin and therefore reigned supreme in the Soviet Union from the late 1930s until 1964. At Lysenko's urging, the state famously decreed genetics "a bourgeois pseudoscience," and many legitimate scientists were sent to labor camps or executed.

his native country. Banished from his home, cut off from his loved ones, and condemned to wander among strangers, Abdul Rahman, the Muslim-turned-Christian, became, in essence, a *juif errant*.

Rahman's case is extreme by any standards. But being criticized, ostracized, and threatened, suffering the loss of family, friends, property, and opportunity—these are all-too-common consequences of breaking with the prevailing beliefs of our communities. Even Rahman's exile, while particularly explicit, isn't particularly unusual. Given that each of our beliefs represents a kind of membership card to a group of believers, it's not surprising that relinquishing the belief often involves relinquishing access to the group—or, at the very least, severely diminishing our status and welcome within it. (Reducing the sting slightly is the fact that the feeling is often mutual. Once a belief ceases to be attractive to us, those who hold it sometimes become notably less appealing as well.)

Rahman's case also illustrates another important point about the relationship between beliefs and communities. What really gets you into trouble with a community isn't holding a belief it scorns; it is abandoning a belief it cherishes. However difficult life might be for non-Muslims living in Afghanistan, the Afghan judiciary is not in the habit of sentencing born-and-bred Christians to death. It was Abdul Rahman's rejection of Islam, not his embrace of Christianity per se, that landed him in so much hot water.

Given everything we've seen so far about how communities work, this makes sense. While insular groups are relatively immune to outside opinion, they are highly dependent on reinforcement of their belief system from within. As a result, internal dissent, unlike outside opposition, can be deeply destabilizing. Consider one of the striking findings of the Asch line studies: if just one of the fake subjects begins giving the right answers, all the real subjects start doing so as well. Seen from one angle, this finding is heartening, since it suggests that a single person speaking freely suffices to break the stranglehold of conformity—like the little boy pointing out that the emperor has no clothes. Seen from a different angle, however, it suggests that a lone dissident can destroy the cohesiveness of an entire community. From this latter perspective, doubt and dissent represent a kind of contagion, capable of spreading and destroying the health of the communal body. Accordingly, many communities act quickly to cure, quarantine, or expel (or, in extreme cases, eliminate) any nonconformists among them.

If a single person breaking ranks on a single belief can threaten the cohesion of an entire community, it can also—and perhaps even more alarmingly—threaten the entire nature of believing. This is the point I gestured toward at the beginning of this chapter: if our beliefs can change when we cross a border (or meet a Catholic aid worker), then truth comes to seem like nothing more than a local perspective. That's disturbing, because the whole point of truth is that it is supposed to be universal. Shahnawaz Farooqui, a Muslim journalist and commentator who supported the death penalty for Abdul Rahman, put the matter plainly. "He will have to be executed," Farooqui said, because "if somebody at one point affirms the truth and then rejects it or denies it, it would jeopardize the whole paradigm of truth."

Farooqui was right—not about Rahman and the death penalty, but about the fact that affirming and later rejecting a belief jeopardizes the whole paradigm of truth. As I argue throughout this book, our mistakes disturb us in part because they call into question not just our confidence in a single belief, but our confidence in the entire act of believing. When we come to see one of our own past beliefs as false, we also glimpse, for a moment, the persistent structural possibility of error: our minds, the world, the gap between them—the whole unsettling shebang. As important and life-altering (and even gratifying) as this revelation can be, it runs contrary to what I've described here as one of the chief functions of a community: to buttress our sense that we are right, and protect us from constantly contending with the possibility that we are wrong.

Small wonder that such revelations are so unwelcome within communities of believers, and bring down so much trouble on the individual member who abandons his or her faith. When we realize that we were wrong about a private belief, the chief thing we stand to lose is our pride. But when we share a belief with others, the stakes of rejecting it escalate astronomically. They include, as we've seen, the practical and emotional advantages of conforming with a community. But they also include the community itself—the trust, esteem, companionship, and love of the people we know best. Even more gravely, they include the stability and familiarity of our identities (for instance, as a devout Muslim), and our faith in the very existence of truth. Short of life and limb (which are occasionally on the line as well), the price of being wrong could scarcely be higher, and the experience could scarcely be more destabilizing.

Given these stakes, it makes sense that we are inclined to keep faith with those around us, to insist on the accuracy of our shared convictions, and to condemn those who reject or betray them. Left unchecked, however, this kind of rigid community loyalty is not benign. As the examples in this chapter and the course of history both show, blind adherence to our communities can produce results so appalling that it's easy to respond with undiluted moral revulsion. And yet, while I don't want to discourage anyone from being appalled by injustice, moral revulsion takes us only so far. No one plans to wind up on the wrong side of history, after all—yet very few of us ever pause to ask ourselves whether, this time, we might not be the good guys. So the question, for my purposes, isn't whether the communities in these examples perpetrated moral wrongs. They did. The question is how they managed, while doing so, to feel so unshakably right. And it is also this: Can you and I be certain that we would have acted differently?

All of us would like to think so, of course. But then, 100 percent of us would also like to think we would have been among the 25 percent of Asch subjects who kept on giving the right answers even in the face of a group consensus to the contrary. I think of this as the French Resistance fantasy. We would all like to believe that, had we lived in France during World War II, we would have been among those heroic souls fighting the Nazi occupation and helping ferry the persecuted to safety. The reality, though, is that only about 2 percent of French citizens actively participated in the Resistance. Maybe you and I would have been among them, but the odds are not on our side. None of us can say for sure that we would have acted differently from the silent masses of occupied France. For that matter, none of us can say for sure how we would have acted if we had been a German citizen of the same era—or a male citizen of the Appenzells in 1971, or a devout Muslim in the Afghanistan of today. Just as disturbing, and more important, we also can't be sure that some of the beliefs we hold today won't appear grievously unjust in the future. This is error-blindness as a moral problem: we can't always know, today, which of our current beliefs will someday come to seem ethically indefensible—to us, or to history. As we've seen, the bonds of a community are just too powerful, and the aperture of its lens too narrow, for any of us to know with certainty that we are acting more freely and seeing more clearly than those whom history has now condemned as wrong.

That isn't to say that a certain stubborn liberty of mind is beyond us. None of us are automatons, after all, and, outside of science fiction, not even the strictest community can fully brainwash us. Granted, our friends, families, churches, neighbors, and nations have a powerful—indeed an incomparable—influence on us. But beliefs, like mules and centaurs, are fundamentally hybrid creatures: we experience them half in public society, half in the private heart. In the best outcome, these two domains keep each other in check. The people around us prevent us from believing things that are (as Penn Jillette put it) "fucking nuts," while our own inner voice keeps rising up and breaking the surface tension that could otherwise turn a community into a bubble.

Keep that balance intact, and all of us can experience the pleasures of communal life without fear of sacrificing our autonomy (to say nothing of our soul). Throw all the weight to one side or the other, though, and you unleash either the danger of an individual unrestrained by society, or the far greater danger of a society unrestrained by its individuals. To keep this balance, we must understand what can foil it. This is where I want to turn now: to the attractions of certainty, and the temptations that can convert a group of like-minded individuals into a community of zealots.

8.

The Allure of Certainty

Properly speaking, there is no certainty; there
are only people who are certain.
—CHARLES RENOUVIER, *ESSAIS DE CRITIQUE GÉNÉRALE*

The trouble began, as it so often does, with taxes. In AD 6, the Roman
Empire, ramping up its policy of territorial expansion and control, decided
to impose a tariff on the Jews of the province of Judaea, in what is now
Israel and the West Bank. By then, the local Jews had been living under a
capricious and often cruel Roman rule for seventy years, so the tax issue
was hardly their only grievance. Still, it rankled, and the question of what
to do about it caused a schism in the community. The majority heeded the
counsel of the high priest Joazar and reluctantly agreed to pay up in the
interest of keeping the peace. But a handful, led by one Judas of Galilee,
rebelled. Disgusted by what he saw as Joazar's complicity with Roman rule,
Judas vowed to establish a new sect of Jews whose members, in the words of

the first-century Jewish historian Josephus, "have an inviolable attachment
to liberty, and say that God is to be their only Ruler and Lord."*

That sounds like an honorable attitude. And a courageous one: Judas and
his followers, a small and marginalized minority, took on one of history's
most formidable imperial states. As such, they seem like good candidates
for hero status in the eyes of their fellow Jews, ancient and modern—and
some people view them that way. But to Josephus, and to many others before
and since, they were little better than villains and murderers. Judas's sect
practiced a scorched-earth policy (including against other Jews, to deprive
them of food and shelter and thereby force them to join the sectarian fight),
advocated the outright murder not only of Romans but also of Jewish "col-
laborators" (essentially, anyone with less single-minded politics than their
own), and contributed to the destruction of Jerusalem and the ferocity of
Roman reprisals through their own extreme violence and unwillingness to
negotiate. Josephus records a characteristic raid—the sacking of the Jewish
enclave of Ein-Gedi, where the able-bodied men apparently fled, and, "As
for such that could not run away, being women and children, they slew of
them above seven hundred." The historian sums up the sect and its legacy
this way:

> All sorts of misfortunes also sprang from these men, and the na-
> tion was infected with this doctrine to an incredible degree; one
> violent war came upon us after another, and we lost our friends
> which used to alleviate our pains; there were also very great rob-
> beries and murder of our principal men. . . . Such a change was
> made, as added a mighty weight toward bringing all to destruc-
> tion, which these men occasioned by their thus conspiring to-
> gether; for Judas and Sadduc [another leader of the rebellion],
> who excited a fourth philosophic sect among us, and had a great

---

* Josephus is not an unproblematic source, since he is variously accused of being an
apologist for the Romans and an apologist for the Jews. Still, his writings constitute
the most extensive extant account of Judas of Galilee and his followers, and even those
historians with different interpretations of this era of Jewish life generally take him as
their point of departure.

many followers therein, filled our civil government with tumults
at present, and laid the foundations of our future miseries.

Who were the members of this "fourth philosophic sect," in all their
unphilosophical brutality? These were the original, capital-Z Zealots. History doesn't record the fate of Judas, but most of the other Zealots perished
in the first Jewish-Roman war, which began in AD 66 and ended four years
later, with the destruction of the temple in Jerusalem and the defeat of the
Jews. A small band of survivors retreated to a fort at Masada, near the Dead
Sea, where they held off a Roman siege for three years. When the Romans
finally breached the fort, they discovered that its 960 inhabitants had organized a mass self-slaughter, murdering one another (suicide being forbidden
in Hebrew law) rather than letting themselves be captured or killed by the
Romans.[†]

As the generic use of their name suggests, the legacy of the Zealots
was not ideological but methodological. Murdering in the name of faith,
religious or otherwise, was hardly unheard of before they came along, but
they clarified and epitomized it as a practice. In the two millennia since the
last of Judas of Galilee's Zealots perished, a thousand lowercase zealots have
kept that legacy alive—meaning, they have killed in its name. These latter-day zealots have hailed from many different backgrounds and held many
different beliefs. At heart, though, and paradoxically, they have all shared
a single conviction: that they and they alone are in possession of the truth.
(The very word "zealot" comes from a Greek root meaning to be jealous of
the truth—to guard it as your own.) What zealots have in common, then,
is the absolute conviction that they are right. In fact, of all the symbolic
ones and zeros that extremists use to write their ideological binary codes—
us/them, same/different, good/evil—the fundamental one is right/wrong.
Zealotry demands a complete rejection of the possibility of error.

The conviction that we cannot possibly be wrong: this is certainty.

---

† The Masada holdouts might actually have been Sicarii, a splinter group of the Zealots
that was even more zealous. Josephus distinguishes between the two, but inconsistently,
and other reports are conflicting.

We've seen a lot of this conviction already, in the form of people who are sure they can see, or sure of what they *do* see (mountain chains, pregnant women), or sure of what they believe or predict or recall. Most of the time, this garden-variety certainty seems far removed from zealotry—and in a sense, it is. There's a very big difference between, say, insisting that you are right about Orion and, say, murdering the Protestants, Muslims, Jews, bigamists, blasphemers, sodomites, and witches who are defiling your country. Not everyone who is filled with passionate certitude is Torquemada.

In another sense, though, certainty and zealotry are not far removed from each other at all. We got a glimpse of the close association between them, briefly, in the form of the Evil Assumption. If I believe unshakably in the rightness of my own convictions, it follows that those who hold opposing views are denying the truth and luring others into falsehood. From there, it is a short step to thinking that I am morally entitled—or even morally obliged—to silence such people any way I can, including through conversion, coercion, and, if necessary, murder. It is such a short step, in fact, that history is rife with instances where absolute convictions fomented and rationalized violence. We typically associate these spasms of ideologically motivated bloodshed with certain institutions: extremist religions (the Crusades, the Inquisition), superiority-minded racial or ethnic clans (the Rwandan genocide, the Third Reich), and totalitarian states (Stalinism, the Khmer Rouge).* But institutions are not suprahuman entities, manipulating people to serve their own ends. Institutions *have* no ends. Top to bottom, they are conceived, created, and maintained by human beings. The certainty they exploit is the certainty—or the longing for it—already present inside each of us.

Zealotry, in other words, begins at home. The certainty that we some-

---

* I am not trying to suggest a moral equivalence among these events, or between an enslaved minority fighting to liberate its people (e.g., the original Zealots) and a ruling class fighting to promulgate its own power (e.g., the Third Reich). The roots of violent conflict are invariably complex, manifold, and, above all, specific; and differences between the strength of various zealous groups and the merits of their causes are, of course, salient. However, I am interested here not in how these groups differ but in what they have in common: an unshakable sense of rightness.

times see channeled toward malevolent ends is not, in its essence, different from the flare of righteous anger that causes each of us to think, mid-argument, that it is only the other person who is irrational, unyielding, and wrong. We might not see ourselves in the marauding Zealots that laid waste to Ein-Gedi. We might never—let us hope we do not—use violence to impose our worldview on other people. But we, too, are jealous of the truth.

This unshakable conviction of rightness represents the logical outcome of everything we've read about so far. Our sense of certainty is kindled by the feeling of knowing—that inner sensation that something just *is*, with all of the solidity and self-evidence suggested by that most basic of verbs. Viewed in some lights, in fact, the idea of knowledge and the idea of certainty seem indistinguishable. But to most of us, certainty suggests something bigger and more forceful than knowledge. The great American satirist Ambrose Bierce defined it as "being mistaken at the top of one's voice," and it is this shouted-from-the-rooftops quality that makes certainty distinctive. Compared to the feeling of knowing (which is, by definition, a feeling, an inner state), certainty seems both amped up and externalized. It is, we might say, a more public, action-oriented analogue to knowledge.

The feeling of knowing, then, is less a synonym for certainty than a precondition for it. And we have encountered other preconditions as well. There are our sensory perceptions, so immediate and convincing that they seem beyond dispute. There is the logical necessity, captured by the 'Cuz It's True Constraint, of thinking that our beliefs are grounded in the facts. There are the biases we bring to bear when we assess the evidence for and against those beliefs. And there is the fact that our convictions and our communities are mutually reinforcing, so that we can't question our beliefs without running the risk of losing the support, status, and sense of identity that comes with belonging to a particular society.

All of these factors conduce to the condition of certainty—even as they should caution us against it. We have seen, after all, that knowledge is a bankrupt category and that the feeling of knowing is not a reliable indicator of accuracy. We have seen that our senses can fail us, our minds mislead us, our communities blind us. And we have seen, too, that certainty can be a moral catastrophe waiting to happen. Moreover, we often recoil from the certainty of others even when they aren't using it to excuse injustice or violence. The certainty of those with whom we disagree—whether the disagreement concerns who should run the country or who should run the dishwasher—never looks justified to us, and frequently looks odious. As often as not, we regard it as a sign of excessive emotional attachment to an idea, or an indicator of a narrow, fearful, or stubborn frame of mind. By contrast, we experience our own certainty as simply a side-effect of our rightness, justifiable because our cause is just. And, remarkably, despite our generally supple, imaginative, extrapolation-happy minds, we cannot transpose this scene. We cannot imagine, or do not care, that our own certainty, when seen from the outside, must look just as unbecoming and ill-grounded as the certainty we abhor in others.

This is one of the most defining and dangerous characteristics of certainty: it is toxic to a shift in a perspective. If imagination is what enables us to conceive of and enjoy stories other than our own, and if empathy is the act of taking other people's stories seriously, certainty deadens or destroys both qualities. When we are caught up in our own convictions, other people's stories—which is to say, other people—cease to matter to us. This happens on the scale of history (a specific person's story is always irrelevant to zealots, unless it serves the ends of the group), but it also happens to each of us as individuals. If you doubt it, listen to yourself the next time you argue with a family member. Leaving behind our more thoughtful and generous selves, we become smug, or patronizing, or scornful, or downright bellicose. And that's when we are fighting with people we love.

So certainty is lethal to two of our most redeeming and humane qualities, imagination and empathy. It is ridiculed by philosophers as intellectually indefensible. (Voltaire called it "absurd," and Bertrand Russell disparaged it as "an intellectual vice.") It is widely excoriated as (in the words of the writer Will Durant) "murderous." When we ourselves observe it in others, we find it laughable at best, despicable at worst. This is a singularly ugly portrait. So why do we continue to find certainty so attractive?

• • •

Imagine for a moment that a man is hiking in the Alps when he suddenly finds his progress blocked by a narrow but terrifyingly deep crevasse. There's no safe passage around it, and he cannot retreat the way he came. The question, then, isn't what the man should do; his only option is to leap over the chasm. The question is how he should feel about doing it.

This hypothetical scenario was devised by William James to help us think about the merits of certainty. While most of his fellow philosophers were criticizing it as intellectually untenable or morally repugnant or both, James decided to come to its defense. Or rather, to its partial defense: he, too, worried about the potential moral consequences of certainty—but, ever the pragmatist, he argued that it had also some distinct practical advantages. However intellectually honorable doubt might be, he pointed out, it would clearly serve our hypothetical hiker poorly. The better option would be for him to believe absolutely in his ability to leap over the crevasse.*

James meant by this that shaky ground should not always deter us from unshakable faith. There are countless instances when our own lives or the larger world have been changed for the better by a passionate conviction: that you can lower your cholesterol or get into medical school or secure a better future for your children; that polio can be eradicated or that the wilderness can be protected or that people with disabilities should not be prevented

---

* One implication of James's argument is that doubt, like certainty, can be dangerous in sufficiently large doses. There's a nice illustration of this in the realm of mental health. William Hirstein, the psychologist who studied confabulation, described it as "pathological certainty": no matter how wild confabulators' beliefs might be, they cannot be shaken. Hirstein saw a counterpoint to confabulation in obsessive compulsive disorder, which he called "pathological doubt." Unlike confabulators, people with OCD want to "raise [the] standards of certainty to absurdly high levels." Thus your partner reassuring you that he locked the door before coming upstairs is not sufficient proof that your door is really locked; nor, for that matter, is the fact that you yourself locked it five minutes ago. Doubt keeps creeping back in, even where it has no rightful or useful place. The psychiatrist Thomas Szasz didn't write about confabulation, but he, too, saw unshakable conviction and chronic uncertainty as the two poles of mental illness. "Doubt is to certainty," he wrote, "as neurosis is to psychosis. The neurotic is in doubt and has fears about persons and things; the psychotic has convictions and makes claims about them."

from rich and full participation in public life. As James put it, sometimes unswerving beliefs "help to *make* the truth which they declare."

In these situations, certainty is the best choice because doubt is a bad one—counterproductive at best, dangerous at worst. But there are also occasions where certainty is the best option because doubt isn't really an option at all. This was the (again, partial) defense of certainty offered by the philosopher Ludwig Wittgenstein. In the face of those of his colleagues who believed that certainty was intrinsically absurd, Wittgenstein argued that, sometimes, it is *un*certainty that doesn't make any sense. If we want to get through life in a functional fashion, he noted, we have no choice but to treat some of our beliefs as absolutely certain. These beliefs serve as a kind of bedrock on which to build the rest of our worldview; instead of questioning them, we use them to ask and answer all our *other* questions. "At the foundation of well-founded belief," Wittgenstein wrote, "lies belief that is not founded." Not ill-founded, mind you: just not founded at all.*

As an example of such a belief, Wittgenstein takes his conviction that he has two hands. This was the most extreme example he could have chosen, for the same reason that anosognosia is the most extreme example of error: because beliefs about our bodies are essentially immune to doubt. For this and other bedrock beliefs, he argued, we literally *can't* provide any convincing grounds, because the belief itself is "as certain as anything that I could produce in evidence for it." If someone were to ask him how many hands he had, Wittgenstein pointed out, "I should not make sure by looking. If I were to have any doubt of it, then I don't know why I should trust my eyes. For why shouldn't I test my *eyes* by looking to find out whether I see my two hands?" In this case and many others like it, he argued, it is doubt that is the absurdity, and certainty that is the only reasonable option.

---

* My favorite description of this unfounded-belief conundrum comes not from Wittgenstein but (in second- or third-hand fashion) from the anthropologist Clifford Geertz. In his book *The Interpretation of Cultures*, Geertz tells us of "an Indian story—at least, I heard it as an Indian story—about an Englishman who, having been told that the world rested on a platform which rested on the back of an elephant which rested in turn on the back of a turtle, asked . . . what did the turtle rest on? Another turtle. And that turtle? 'Ah, Sahib, after that it is turtles all the way down.'"

Wittgenstein, then, defended certainty on the grounds that it is sometimes logically necessary—that without being sure of some things, we can't even begin to think about everything else. (This is an echo, in a deeper register, of Kuhn's point that we can't make sense of the world without theories.) James, meanwhile, defended certainty on the grounds that it is sometimes an aid to action, necessary to our survival and success. Each of these defenses points to a third, which is that certainty is evolutionarily advantageous. As I said earlier, taking the time to interrogate a belief requires more cognitive resources—and, potentially, poses a greater risk—than simply accepting it. For this reason, William Hirstein (the author of *Brain Fiction*) calls doubt "a cognitive luxury," one that "occurs only in highly developed nervous systems."

Hirstein has a point; you will be hard-pressed to find a skeptical mollusk. And what goes for our collective evolutionary past also goes for our individual developmental trajectory—which is why you will also be hard-pressed to find a skeptical one-year-old. "The child learns by believing the adult," Wittgenstein observed. "Doubt comes *after* belief." It also comes in different forms and stages. It's one thing to doubt the existence of Santa Claus, another thing to doubt the accuracy of a news story, and a third thing to doubt the accuracy of a news story you yourself wrote. How adept we are at these different degrees of doubt depends on a variety of factors, including how emotionally capable we are of tolerating uncertainty (more on that in a moment) and how much we have been exposed to and explicitly trained in skeptical inquiry. Doubt, it seems, is a skill—and one that, as we saw earlier, needs to be learned and honed. Credulity, by contrast, appears to be something very like an instinct.

So doubt post-dates belief, both in the long haul of evolution and in the shorter haul of our own emotional and intellectual development. And we can shrink the time frame even further: doubt also seems to come after belief in many individual instances in which we process information about the world. That, at any rate, was the finding of the psychologist Daniel Gilbert and his colleagues, in a 1990 study designed to test an assertion by the Dutch philosopher Baruch Spinoza. Spinoza claimed that when we encounter a new piece of information, we automatically accept it as true, and only reject it as false (if we do so at all) through a separate and subsequent process. This claim ran counter to a more intuitive and—at least according to Descartes— more optimal model of cognition, in which we first weigh the likelihood that a new piece of information is true, and then accept or reject it accordingly. To borrow Gilbert's example (because who wouldn't?), consider the following sentence: "armadillos may be lured from a thicket with soft cheese." If Spinoza is right, then merely by reading this sentence, you are also, however fleetingly, believing it. In this model, belief is our default cognitive setting, while doubt or disbelief requires a second, super-added act.

All of us have experienced something like what Spinoza was getting at. As Gilbert and his colleagues point out, if I'm driving along and I suddenly see a dachshund in the middle of the road, I will swerve my car long before I can decide whether the proposition at hand ("there is a dachshund in the middle of the road") is true or false. One could take matters a step further and suppose that I would also swerve my car if I saw a *unicorn* in the middle of the road—even though, if I took the time to contemplate the situation, I would surely conclude that unicorns do not exist, in the middle of the road or anywhere else. In fact, most of us really have swerved in response to imaginary entities. Not long ago I was walking under a scaffolding in Manhattan, when in a flash I found myself jumping aside and covering my head with my arms. Some fluctuation in the light or a trick of my peripheral vision or— who knows?—a random misfiring of my synapses had created the false but alarming impression that a section of the scaffolding was falling toward me. This wasn't true, thankfully, but I acted as if it were—for very good reasons, and ones that underscore the evolutionary utility of certainty.

In a practical sense, then, it's clear that we sometimes behave as if a proposition is true before we have had a chance to evaluate it. Gilbert and his colleagues wanted to find out if this is only how we behave, or if it is actually how we believe. They reasoned that if disbelieving a proposition consists of not one process but two—initially accepting and only subsequently rejecting it—then people should be more likely to believe untrue things if they are interrupted immediately after exposure to them. And that's exactly what they found. In a series of experiments, subjects who were distracted immediately after learning new information were more likely to believe that false statements were true, but not more likely to believe that true statements were false. It was as if merely creating a mental image of a statement (the armadillo creeping toward the camembert) was sufficient to make the subjects believe it—another instance of confusing the ideas in our mind with realities about the world.

Aside from scoring a point for Spinoza, this research sheds some light on the cognitive basis for why certainty comes so much easier to us than doubt. But if this is a neurological truth, it is also, and more self-evidently, an emotional one. Certainty might be a practical, logical, and evolutionary necessity, but the simplest truth about it is that it feels good. It gives us the comforting illusion that our environment is stable and knowable, and that therefore we are safe within it. Just as important, it makes us feel informed, intelligent, and powerful. When we are certain, we are lords of our maps: the outer limits of our knowledge and the outer limits of the world are one and the same.

Seen in this light, our dislike of doubt is a kind of emotional agoraphobia. Uncertainty leaves us stranded in a universe that is too big, too open, too ill-defined. Even Voltaire, the one who dismissed certainty as absurd, acknowledged in the same breath that doubt is "uncomfortable." The word is understated yet oddly precise: the open space of doubt leaves us ill at ease, unable to relax or feel secure. Where certainty reassures us with answers, doubt confronts us with questions, not only about our future but also about our past: about the decisions we made, the beliefs we held, the people and groups to whom we offered our allegiance, the very way we lived our lives. To make matters worse, facing our own private uncertainty can also compel us to face the existence of uncertainty in general—the unconsoling fact that nothing in the world can be perfectly known by any mere mortal, and that therefore we can't shield ourselves and our loved ones from error, accident, and disaster.

No wonder we gravitate toward certainty instead. It's not that we are oblivious to its intellectual and moral dangers; it's that those dangers seem pretty abstract when compared with the immediate practical, emotional, and existential perils of doubt. In fact, just as our love of being right is best understood as a fear of being wrong, our attraction to certainty is best understood as an aversion to uncertainty. To explore that aversion, I want to turn now to three representatives of the domain of chronic doubt: Hamlet, the famously indecisive prince of the Danes; John Kerry, the Democratic presidential candidate who rescued the term "waffle" from the breakfast table; and that most baffling and maddening figure of modern American politics, the Undecided Voter.

Appropriately enough, the world's most famous play about doubt opens with a question. The setting is Denmark, the time is shortly after the death of the king (Hamlet's father) and the question that reverberates across the stage manages to be at once banal and chilling: *"Who's there?"* Who is there, is among others, the dead king's ghost, who wants to have one last talk with his son. When Hamlet appears, the ghost explains that he, the king, did not die a natural death but was murdered by his own brother, Claudius, who has since married Hamlet's widowed mother and assumed the throne. The ghost implores Hamlet to avenge this murder by killing Claudius. This Hamlet does—but only after agonizing over the matter for five long acts, and only with, literally, his dying breath. By then, the majority of the other significant characters are dead, too, including Hamlet's mother and (by his own doing) three of his friends—all lives that might have been spared if Hamlet's "native hue of resolution" had not been "sicklied o'er with the pale cast of thought."

So much has been made of Hamlet's indecisiveness—even seventh graders routinely write term papers on the topic—that it is widely regarded as his defining trait. But this wasn't always the case. As the critic Harold Jenkins has observed, for at least the first 150 years of his literary life, Hamlet was generally viewed as "vigorous, bold and heroic"—a victim of his circumstances, not his psyche. But then, in the eighteenth century, the writer James Boswell remarked on "that irresolution which forms so marked a part of [Hamlet's] character," and the description stuck. Over the next hundred years, and with help from additional commentary by the likes of Goethe and Coleridge, the Hamlet we know today was born: a man so paralyzed by indecision that he is unable to take action.

If it's true that every generation gets the Hamlet it deserves, it would be interesting to figure out why eighteenth-century British theatergoers suddenly required such a paralyzed and doubt-ridden prince. What was it in the political and cultural climate of the moment that suddenly made action and conviction, thought and doubt such transfixing issues? Whatever it was, it is with us still—just as Boswell's characterization of Hamlet has yet to be convincingly supplanted by any other. The prince who lives in our modern consciousness, the one who fascinates us and drives us crazy, is the man of (in Coleridge's words) "everlasting broodings."

In this now-standard reading, doubt is Hamlet's tragic flaw, responsible for both his inner anguish and the external calamities of the play. But there's something strange about this interpretation of *Hamlet*, and of Hamlet. For starters, the prince tries to kill Claudius two acts earlier than he succeeds. That he accidentally kills Claudius's trusted counselor Polonius instead is a failure of execution, not a failure of conviction. Nor did Hamlet hesitate to arrange for the murder of his two school friends, Rosencrantz and Guildenstern, when he learned that they were spying on him—hardly the action of the man one critic deemed "Prince Pussyfoot."

Still, Hamlet *does* struggle with doubt. Even if he is more a man of action than we generally allow, he is also clearly a man of contemplation—alive to contradiction and complexity, and troubled by the possibility of error. We know that he believes that our powers of reflection are not meant to "fust in us unus'd," and we watch him bring those powers to bear not only on the question of whether to murder his uncle but also on the merits of ending his own life ("to be, or not to be"), and on the meaning of life and afterlife more generally.

Clearly, then, that the capacity to doubt is part of Hamlet's disposition. What is less clear is why that characteristic has struck so many critics as such a profound defect. It's not as if the prince dillydallies for fourteen scenes over whether to order the BLT or the chicken salad. This is someone who has been asked to commit murder. And not just any murder, but one that is both a regicide and a virtual parricide: the deliberate assassination of a man who is at once his sovereign, his uncle, his stepfather, and his mother's husband. One assumes that any reasonable person would be given pause by such a situation. (And such was the interpretation of Hamlet pre-Boswell: that of a reasonable man in an unreasonable position).

As if this ethical, political, and familial predicament weren't enough, Hamlet also has another problem on his hands. This one is evidentiary: he has no firsthand knowledge of the killing he's been asked to avenge. Put yourself in his shoes for a moment. You have been commanded to commit a terrible crime—by a *ghost*. What if it was a mendacious ghost? What if it wants you to take an innocent man's life for its own inscrutable and possibly devious purposes? What if your senses deceived you and there was no ghost at all? If we reviled the prosecutors of the Salem witch trials for their blithe acceptance of spectral evidence, surely we should commend Hamlet for his skepticism about the same. Surely, in other words, his doubt is commensurate with the genuine uncertainty of his situation, and with the magnitude and gravity of the action he is contemplating.

Why, then, does Hamlet's doubt strike us as so problematic? Shouldn't we encourage—in fact, demand—serious deliberation before the taking of anyone's life? Furthermore, do we really believe that, had the prince slain his uncle in Act One, everyone would have lived happily ever after? And if so, what are we thinking? Very little in literature or life supports the notion that crimes of passion produce happy endings, or that hasty actions yield fruitful returns, or that hot-blooded world leaders excel at restoring and maintaining the peace.* So why do we persist in feeling that doubt is Hamlet's problem, and that a greater degree of certainty would be the solution?

---

* Shakespeare's own work notably fails to support this conclusion. The two most anguished men in his oeuvre (and possibly in all of literary history) are Prince Hamlet and King Lear—and if you think the former was destroyed by doubt, you should see what certainty did to the latter. Like *Hamlet*, *Lear* ends in a bloodbath, with the king, all three of his daughters, and most of the other major characters dead. Here, though, the agent of tragedy is Lear's unshakable conviction and the haste with which he puts it into action. As leadership styles go, his more closely resembles the off-with-their-heads! recklessness of the Queen of Hearts than the contemplativeness of the Prince of the Danes. For Lear, as the critic Maynard Mack put it, "action comes as naturally as breathing and twice as quick." This swiftness of action is what was so wanting in Hamlet—and, to hear the critics talk, so wanted—yet Lear shows us that such conviction can easily be as deadly as doubt.

One answer to this question lies not in Hamlet's character but in his station. No one cares whether, say, Reynaldo, the servant to Polonius, is a figure of towering certainty or trembling doubt—but Hamlet is a prince, and we do care, deeply, about the conviction of our leaders (even, apparently, our fictional ones). And not without reason. For starters, we recognize that the practical merits of certainty are particularly useful to politicians, who must make dozens of consequential decisions while the rest of us are just trying to figure out our Friday night plans. Hesitate over each of them for five acts, and your ship of state is going to list alarmingly.

But practicality alone can't explain why we find certainty so desirable in our leaders, and doubt so intolerable. On the contrary: pure pragmatism would dictate that we embrace a measure of doubt in the political sphere, since even the most cursory acquaintance with history shows us that immovable certainty can be a disastrous quality in a leader. Obviously, though, pure pragmatism is not what we are dealing with. In politics as everywhere, it is joined by (and often trumped by) emotion. And emotionally, as we have already seen, our allegiances lie strongly with certainty.

When I mentioned this earlier, I was talking about our *own* certainty and doubt—about how it feels safe and pleasurable to be steadfast in our convictions. But we also find other people's certainty deeply attractive. We have all experienced this pull, in ways both large and small. I have a pretty decent sense of direction, but I've been known to follow a friend along entirely the wrong road (and entirely without thinking about it), simply because she strode down it with such confidence. Likewise, we tend to follow the highly assured down figurative roads of all kinds, without necessarily questioning where they (or we) are going. As with our own certainty, so too with theirs: we mistake it for a sign that they are right.

Like most of the behaviors that can lead us into error, following a confident leader is not intrinsically irrational. Much of the time, in fact, it creates a perfectly sensible distribution of labor. The leaders in a group are spared the hassle of having too many cooks in the kitchen—a relief for them, since, even as they embody certainty, they also yearn for it right along with the rest of us. (A choice example: frustrated by the on-the-one-hand, on-the-other-hand advice of his monetary advisors, Harry Truman once jokingly threatened to appoint a one-armed economist.) Meanwhile, we followers are relieved of the burden of decision making, not to mention freed up to focus on other things.

Better still, some of our own doubt is alleviated by following a confident leader—because, as it happens, other people's certainty makes *us* feel certain. As social psychologists can tell you, both doubt and certainty are as contagious as the common cold: all else being equal, our own confidence increases around people who radiate assurance, and our own doubts flare up around the hesitant. It's no surprise, then, that in politics (as in business, the military, and the sixth-grade student council), we typically anoint the ultraconfident to lead us. William Hirstein even suggests that, when it comes to those in power, we often feel that "an answer that is possibly (or even probably) wrong is better than none at all." Translation: we are more alarmed by leaders who waver than by those who screw up.*

This brings us, of course, to John Kerry. Specifically, it brings us to the 2004 election, which pitted Kerry against then-incumbent George W. Bush—truly one of history's finer examples of a contest between a man who wavered and a man who screwed up. On the one side was Kerry, who fought a war he subsequently repudiated and funded a war he previously denounced— two reasons, although not the only two, that the right painted him as a tergiversator. On the other side was Bush, who framed complex geopolitical issues in black and white and brooked no challenges to his opinions—two reasons, although not the only two, that the left painted him as autocratic and dangerously unsophisticated. In a sense, the infamous polarization of the 2004 electorate could be boiled down to this: voters who were disquieted by changes of mind versus voters who were disquieted by impermeable conviction.

---

* This is true not just in politics but in any realm that requires swift, frequent, and firm decision making. Take sports: in a *New York Times* article on umpiring, the writer Joseph Berger observed that, "With baseballs flying at speeds faster than cars on a highway, umpires sometimes make mistakes—what referee hasn't? But they must remain unflinching. Admit you're wrong and chaos—or, worse, ridicule—can ensue." Berger quotes one umpire who notes that, "A good official always comes strong with his calls. He's always able to sell it, even if he realizes he's made a mistake."

Accusing your opponent of changing his mind is, I will grant, a standard move in the playbook of American politics. But in John Kerry's case, that accusation *was* the playbook. It wasn't just his altered stances on Vietnam and Iraq that attracted criticism. Kerry's detractors also charged him with vacillating on the death penalty, welfare reform, social security, gay marriage, affirmative action, the Patriot Act, and No Child Left Behind, among others. To give you a sense of the tenor of the election season, William Safire, the "On Language" columnist for the *New York Times Magazine*, took on the phrases "wishy-washy," "waffle," and "flip-flop," all between March and October of 2004.[†] Jay Leno proposed two possible slogans for the Kerry campaign: "A mind is a terrible thing to make up," and "Undecided voters—I'm just like you!" During the Republican Convention, delegates took to doing a kind of side-to-side stadium wave whenever Kerry's name was mentioned: a visual waffle (or call it a waver). For ten bucks, you could purchase a pair of actual flip-flops—the footwear, I mean—with Kerry's face on them. Or you could sport anti-Kerry campaign buttons featuring pictures of waffles or of Heinz ketchup bottles—the latter being an oblique reference to his wife, Teresa Heinz Kerry, and a direct reference to his supposed indecisiveness: "57 positions on every issue."

Some of the allegations of waffling leveled against Kerry were bogus—such as the suggestion that serving in Vietnam is incompatible with viewing it as a moral and political disaster. Others were legitimate—such as the claim that he changed his mind on mandatory minimum sentences not out of a principled reconsideration of the issues but because of standard "tough on crime" political pressure. But the validity (or lack thereof) of these charges isn't the point. It never was. In our political culture, whether or not a leader has good reasons for changing his mind is generally less important than the fact that he changed it in the first place.

---

† Safire would want me to point out that these terms are not interchangeable. Accusing someone of flip-flopping (changing positions on an issue) is not the same as accusing him of waffling (being indecisive) or of being wishy-washy (seeming weak). Still, these terms are often deployed together in service of a larger accusation: that their target has too many thoughts and too few convictions.

Take John Kerry's much-ridiculed assertion that he was for the Iraq War before he was against it. Now, there is a case to be made that this was a perfectly legitimate political trajectory to traverse. Almost all of us know people who underwent a comparable change of heart. And many of us *are* such people: of the 76 percent of Americans who supported the war at its outset in 2003, fully half had withdrawn that support by 2007. In the intervening years, after all, new information had become available to the public, the on-the-ground situation in Iraq had changed, and the credibility of the Bush Administration had waned. The hope that we were bringing a better life to the Iraqi people had grown increasingly difficult to sustain. And the cost of the war—in literal dollars, human lives, and America's diminished moral status in the international community—had far exceeded anything anyone could have imagined on the day in 2003 that Bush declared "Mission Accomplished." Surely, then, this was a situation that merited the high-minded if somewhat sneering riposte of John Maynard Keynes: "When the facts change, I change my mind. What do you do, sir?"

Keynes's policy is a good one. But, like Kerry's U-turns, it is at odds with an enduring and troubling feature of our political culture. In politics, staying the course is admired (and changing direction is denigrated) *intrinsically*—that is, without regard to where the course itself might lead. As the late renowned military historian Barbara Tuchman observed, "to recognize error, to cut losses, to alter course, is the most repugnant option in government." This is Hamlet all over again: we notice the uncertainty, hesitations, and reversals without noticing (or caring) what inspired them. No matter how merited doubt and admissions of error might be, we loathe them in our political leaders, and associate them—inaccurately, but indissolubly—with weakness.

Before some readers take umbrage, let me acknowledge that this is an excessively broad use of the word "we." It's true that the allure of certainty is potent and, in one form or another, near-universal. And it's also true that, in the mass marketplace of attraction, the crowds tend to form around those who exude conviction. But it doesn't follow that all of us admire certainty and abhor doubt (or that any of us have a straightforward relationship to either of them). On the contrary, and as the Bush-Kerry contest suggests, some people are rendered as acutely uncomfortable by ardent conviction as others are by indecision.

Still, even the doubt-tolerant have their breaking point. Public opinion might have been divided about George Bush and John Kerry in 2004, and about John McCain and Barack Obama in 2008, but on one issue, at least, we enjoyed almost complete unanimity: we all despised the undecided voter. Even the treatment the far left and far right accorded to their respective nemeses seemed positively respectful compared to the hatred, contempt, and mockery aimed at the undecideds. Two examples, both culled from the 2008 election, will suffice to illustrate the point. On the *Daily Show*, Jon Stewart presented a pie chart that divided undecided voters into four equally unflattering categories: "attention seekers; racist Democrats; the chronically insecure; and the stupid." A few weeks later, the humorist David Sedaris wrote what became an instantly famous *New Yorker* article in which he imagined the following situation transpiring on an airplane. "The flight attendant comes down the aisle with her food cart and, eventually, parks it beside my seat. 'Can I interest you in the chicken?' she asks. 'Or would you prefer the platter of shit with bits of broken glass in it?' To be undecided in this election," Sedaris wrote, "is to pause for a moment and then ask how the chicken is cooked."

This is the undecided voter in the popular consciousness: needy, insecure, ideologically unpalatable, moronic, and incapable of choosing between chicken and shit—i.e., a chickenshit. Just what is it, exactly, that gets us so worked up about these people? One possibility—a reasonable and, I think, partially accurate one—is that we fear and despise uncertainty in the electorate for the same reason we fear and despise it in the elected. If we rely on our political leaders to make important decisions every day, we rely on our fellow voters to make a particularly important decision at the polls, and we are appalled and alarmed by those who seem unable to do so. And, although these indecisive voters don't have the same kind of power as the president, they do have a power disproportionate to their numbers. Part of what gets us riled up, then, is the sense that the entire electoral process, and our own political future, is held hostage by the tiny fraction of voters who can't make up their minds.

Still, something tells me that even if we ameliorated this problem—say, by abolishing the electoral college, which would significantly diminish the influence of undecided voters—we would still react to such people with outrage and scorn. After all, if the only thing we cared about was the outcome of the election, we should get far more worked up about the millions of voters who flatly disagree with us than about the slim percentage that isn't sure. Instead, when push comes to shove, we generally have more fellow-feeling for our political opponents. Those people might want the plate of shit, but at least they agree with us on this much: some things are so important that everyone should take a definite stand on them.

This is why undecided voters drive us crazy. They think hard about something that most of us don't have to think about at all. Confronted by a choice that we find patently obvious, they are unsure what to believe, and so they hesitate, vacillate, wait for more information. In other contexts, such actions seem reasonable, even laudable. In fact, they comport pretty closely with the ideal thinker I introduced back in our discussion of evidence. This isn't to say that the average undecided voter represents some kind of optimal philosopher-citizen whom we should all seek to emulate. (For starters, as we saw earlier, that ideal thinker isn't so ideal in the first place.) What these voters *do* represent, however, are possibilities the rest of us often foreclose: the ability to experience uncertainty about even hugely important beliefs; the ability to wonder, right up until the moment that the die is cast, if we might be wrong.

If the undecided voter has a strong suit, that is it: she knows that she could be wrong. If the rest of us have a strong suit, it is that we care, passionately, about our beliefs. As conflicting as these two strengths might initially seem, they can, in theory, be reconciled. The psychologist Rollo May once wrote about the "seeming contradiction that *we must be fully committed, but we must also be aware at the same time that we might possibly be wrong.*" Note that this is not an argument for centrism, or for abandoning the courage of our convictions. May's point was precisely that we can retain our convictions—and our conviction—while jettisoning the barricade of certainty that surrounds them. Our commitment to an idea, he concluded, "is healthiest when it is not *without* doubt, but *in spite of* doubt."

Most of us do not want to be doctrinaire. Most of us do not want to be zealots. And yet it is bitterly hard to put May's maxim into practice. Even with the best of intentions, we are often unable to relinquish certainty about our beliefs. One obstacle to doing so is the feeling of being right, shored up as it is by everything from our sensory impressions to our social relations to the structure of human cognition. But a second and paradoxical obstacle is our fear of being wrong. True, certainty cannot protect us from error, any more than shouting a belief can make it true. But it can and does shield us, at least temporarily, from facing our fallibility.

The psychologist Leon Festinger documented this protective effect of certainty in the 1950s, in the study that gave us the now-famous term "cognitive dissonance." Along with several colleagues and hired observers, Festinger infiltrated a group of people who believed in the doomsday prophecies of a suburban housewife named (actually, pseudonymed) Marian Keech. Keech claimed that she was in touch with a Jesuslike figure from outer space who sent her messages about alien visits, spaceship landings, and the impending destruction of the world by flood. When none of these prophecies came to pass, Festinger found, the staunchest believers in the group grew *more* fervent in their faith, not less.*

The beliefs held by Keech and her cohort were unusual. But their behavior when those beliefs were disproved was not. Whether you believe in flying saucers or the free market or just about anything else, you are (if you are human) prone to using certainty to avoid facing up to the fact that

---

* As Festinger described it, cognitive dissonance is the uncomfortable feeling that results from simultaneously holding two contradictory ideas. This dissonance can arise from a conflict between a belief and its disconfirmation ("the spaceship will land on Tuesday," "no spaceship landed on Tuesday"), or between a belief and a behavior ("smoking is bad for you"; "I'm on my second pack of the day"). Festinger proposed that there are two ways to ameliorate this uncomfortable feeling. The most direct way is to change your mind or your actions, but this can be difficult if you are heavily invested in the disproved belief or heavily dependent on the contraindicated behavior. The other option—more contorted, but sometimes more comfortable—is to convince yourself and others that the false belief isn't really false, or that the harmful behavior isn't all that harmful. This is why heightened adamancy and evangelism are not uncommon in the face of disconfirmed beliefs—as we will soon see.

you could be wrong. That's why, when we feel ourselves losing ground in a fight, we often grow more rather than less adamant about our claims—not because we are so sure that we are right, but because we fear that we are not. Remember the Warner Brothers coyote, the one who runs off the cliff but doesn't fall until he looks down? Certainty is our way of not looking down.

All of which begs the question: What's so scary down there, anyway? Like most fears, our fear of wrongness is half real, half spectral. It's not exactly true that there is nothing to fear but fear itself, since wrongness really can have clifflike consequences for our lives. But it *is* true that the fear of wrongness does nothing but hurt us. It makes it harder to avoid errors (you can't skirt a cliff you can't see), and harder to forgive ourselves and others for making them. For everyone involved, then, looking closely at the experience of wrongness is far better than refusing to look at all. So this is where we are headed now: over the cliff, if you will—to find out how it feels to fall, and what awaits us at the bottom.

PART III

THE EXPERIENCE OF ERROR

9.

Being Wrong

Now that my ladder's gone
I must lie down where all the ladders start
In the foul rag and bone shop of the heart.
—W. B. Yeats,
"The Circus Animals' Desertion"

So far, this book has been about how we get things wrong—about how our senses, our minds, and our allegiances can all lead us into error. The chapters to come are about what happens once we recognize those errors: about how we react when our convictions collapse out from under us, and how we are changed by that experience. These sections of the book describe, respectively, the "before" and "after" stages of wrongness.

This chapter is about something different. It is about what happens *during* wrongness—about the moment when the feeling of being right seroconverts to the feeling of being wrong. Psychologically as well as structurally, this moment forms the central experience of error. It is here that some part of our past self gives up the ghost, and some part of the person we will become begins to stir. As that suggests, this moment is crucial to our moral and intellectual development. It is crucial to why we fear and despise error. It is crucial to helping us understand and move beyond those emotions. And it is almost impossible to describe.

I gestured toward this difficulty in Chapter One, when I noted that we can't talk about error in the first person present tense. The moment in which we can logically say "I am wrong" simply doesn't exist; in becoming aware that a belief is false, we simultaneously cease to believe it. Still, *something* has to transpire between thinking that we are right and knowing that we were wrong. Yet the nature of that "something" is remarkably elusive. For the most part, our beliefs change either too quickly or too slowly to isolate the actual encounter with error.

Consider slow belief change first. Many of our beliefs simply erode over time, eventually vanishing altogether or reconfiguring beyond recognition without ever passing through an obvious crisis. A broad range of beliefs can succumb to this kind of tectonic drift, from the trivial (belief that you look great in bellbottoms) to the momentous (belief in God). By its very nature, this kind of long, gradual change is extremely difficult to track. Who can say when mountains become meadows, or glaciers become grassland? The comparable human changes happen on a far smaller time scale, but they can be almost as hard to perceive. A friend says: "It's like I skip from the part where I'm very strident about a particular point of view to the cocktail party ten years later where I'm wittily mocking my former stridency. I guess there has to be a process in there, a gradual letting-go—first of stridency, then of the point of view altogether. But I don't have the experience in present time of admitting to wrongness."

When it comes to observing imperceptibly slow natural processes— flowers blooming, weather systems forming, stars moving across the sky— we rely on time-lapse photography. If we wanted to isolate the wrongness implicit in our own gradual changes, we would need a kind of internal equivalent to that—which, as it happens, we have. Unfortunately, it is called memory, and as we have seen, it is notoriously unreliable. Moreover, it is most unreliable precisely with respect to accurately recalling past beliefs. This effect is widely documented. For instance, in 1973, the psychologist Greg Markus asked over 3,000 people to rate their stances (along one of those seven-point "strongly disagree / strongly agree" scales) on a range of social issues, including affirmative action, the legalization of marijuana, and equal rights for women. A decade later, he asked these same people to assess their positions again—and also to recall how they had felt about the issues a decade earlier. Across the board, these "what I used to think" ratings far more closely reflected the subjects' current beliefs than those they had actually held in 1973. Here, it wasn't just the wrongness that disappeared from the process of belief change. It was the change itself.

This is the kind of revisionist political history that George Orwell described—and decried—in *1984*. The novel's protagonist, Winston Smith, works in the Records Department of the Ministry of Truth, changing the facts and forecasts in old newspaper articles to bring them in line with present-day realities. These changes help create the illusion of absolute infallibility, which in turn helps maintain absolute power: Winston is a servant (and ultimately a victim) of a fascist state. Of course, the fact that our memories can serve the same function as a dystopian Ministry of Truth doesn't mean that we are all protofascists. Unlike the deliberate distortions imagined by Orwell, our own constant revising of memory is largely unconscious, and usually innocuous. But as with the Records Department, our memories often serve the quasi-magical function of causing our mistakes to quietly disappear.

One person who has seen this happen is Philip Tetlock. Tetlock is a psychology professor and political scientist who has conducted longitudinal studies of the accuracy of political forecasts by so-called experts—academics, pundits, policy wonks, and the like. As a matter of course, Tetlock would get back in touch with his subjects after the events they had predicted did or did not come to pass. In doing so, he discovered that these experts systematically misremembered their forecasts, believing them to have been far more accurate than his records showed. This, Tetlock said, created "a methodological nuisance: it is hard to ask someone why they got it wrong when they think they got it right." This could be said of the rest of us, too.

In updating the past to accord with the present, we eliminate the necessity (and the possibility) of confronting our mistakes. If we think we've always believed what we believe right now, there is no friction, no change, no error, and above all no uncomfortably different past self to account for.

If gradual belief change protects us from the experience of error by attenuating it virtually out of existence, sudden belief change does the opposite: it condenses that experience almost to the vanishing point. In these abrupt belief changes, the revelation that we were wrong is simultaneously a revelation of a new truth. Here, our experience of error is like one of those particles in high-energy physics that is so short-lived and unstable that it flashes into and out of existence at virtually the same time. For the most part, physicists can detect the presence of such particles (or rather, the *past* presence of such particles) only indirectly, by observing a change in the amount of matter and energy in a closed system. The same goes for our high-speed errors. We vault over the actual experience of wrongness so quickly that the only evidence that we erred is that something inside us has changed.

This tendency to skip straight from Right A to Right B illuminates an important fact about how we change our beliefs—and also how we *don't* change them. Here is Thomas Kuhn, the philosopher of science, describing the way scientists react when their pet theories are unraveling: "What scientists never do when confronted by even severe and prolonged anomalies," Kuhn wrote, ". . . . [is] renounce the paradigm that led them into crisis." Instead, he concluded, "A scientific theory is declared invalid only if an alternate candidate is available to take its place." That is, scientific theories very seldom collapse under the weight of their own inadequacy. They topple only when a new and seemingly better belief turns up to replace it.

As with scientists, so too with the rest of us. Sometimes in life we find ourselves between jobs, and sometimes we find ourselves between lovers, and sometimes we find ourselves between homes. But we almost never find ourselves between theories. Rather than assess a belief on its own merits, we choose *among* beliefs, clinging to our current ones until something better comes along. There's nothing intrinsically wrong with this strategy—in fact, it might be the only truly viable one*—but it does narrow the moment of wrongness to mere nanoseconds. We are absolutely right about something up until the very instant that, lo and behold, we are absolutely right about something else.

Occasionally, though we stumble. There we are, trying to leapfrog from before to after, from the solid ground of Right A to the solid ground of Right B, and instead we fall into the chasm between them. This is the terrain of pure wrongness—the abyss we find ourselves in when a belief of ours has fallen apart and we have nothing on hand to replace it. This is not an easy or a comfortable place. It is not (despite my general enthusiasm for error and my effort to rehabilitate its reputation) a place I suggest you spend much time. The condition of having been wrong about something might irk us or confuse us or deflate our ego. But the condition of *being* wrong—of being stuck in real-time wrongness with no obvious way out—absolutely levels us.

Fortunately, we don't get stuck in this place of pure wrongness very often. And we don't get stuck there via the collapse of small or medium-size beliefs. We get stuck there when we are really wrong about really big things—beliefs so important and far-reaching that we can neither easily replace them nor easily live without them. If our trivial beliefs sometimes burst as lightly as bubbles—just a quick pop of surprise and they're gone—these gigantic beliefs collapse like stars, leaving only us and a black hole behind. If you mortgaged your family's future on your faith in Bernie Madoff; if you hitched your whole wagon to a doctrine or a deity you no longer believe in; if you were wrong about someone you loved and the kind of life you thought the two of you would live together; if you have betrayed your own principles in any of the countless dark ways we can surprise ourselves over the course of a lifetime: if any of this or anything like this has happened to you, then you have suffered in the space of pure wrongness.

---

* As Kuhn observed, "All historically significant theories have agreed with the facts, but only more or less. There is no more precise answer to the question whether or how well an individual theory fits the facts. But . . . [i]t makes a great deal of sense to ask which of two actual and competing theories fits the facts *better*." Kuhn was talking about formal scientific theories, but the same generally goes for lay beliefs as well.

One person who knows all about this space is Anita Wilson.* When I met Anita, she was a thirty-one-year-old special-education teacher living in New York City. Talking to her, it occurred to me that she must excel at her job. She struck me as calm, empathetic, sane, and kind, and I liked her immediately. But the road she had taken to all these places—to her career, to New York, to serenity and happiness—was both tortuous and torturous.

When Anita was eight years old, her family moved from Chicago to the central valley of California and went from being, in her words, "average, church-going Christians" to "crazy evangelicals." As a child and young adult, Anita's faith was deep and sincere. She spent her free time handing out religious tracts to strangers and participating in the various youth programs run by her church. She worried that her friends back in Chicago would go to hell. For that matter, she worried that *she* would go to hell. "I remember very clearly thinking that I wouldn't live past thirty because the Rapture would come by then," she told me. "And I can remember having moments of terror: What if it came and they took my mom but not me? I'd get concerned about whether I was really saved: Did I really, really believe that Jesus existed? But I pushed it aside, because to not believe meant that I would go to hell—and I definitely *did* believe in that."

Anita was a talented artist, and when she was twenty, she was accepted into art school in New York. Surprisingly, her parents let her go. ("I think they worried that if they opposed it, they'd lose me entirely," she recalled. "I also think they figured I'd be back in six months.") Shortly before she was to leave, a fellow church member—one who had been beloved by the congregation and had served as a kind of older sister and second mother to Anita—was killed in a car accident. For Anita, it opened up the first conscious fissure in her faith. "Here was a woman who embodied the essence of what Jesus was trying to teach. And she finally had everything she wanted: a husband, three young children—she was thirty when she died. I was really sad and really angry, and I remember in church there was all this singing and clapping, and no room at all for grief. Everyone was like, 'Oh, now she is where she's supposed to be.' That's the first time I can remember thinking: this is bullshit."

---

* At her request, I have changed her name and some of her biographical details.

Anita went ahead and moved to New York, where she met a man who was, for lack of a better term, a practicing atheist. Like other people's belief, his nonbelief shaped his ethics and his understanding of the world—and also his community, since his family and many of his friends were similarly nonreligious. Improbably or otherwise, Anita and the man fell in love. Through dating him, she came to reject the evangelical Christianity of her upbringing and adopt his worldview instead. As dramatic as that transition might seem, it was, she recalled, "relatively easy. I had the support of all these people who didn't believe in God, and they were smart and sophisticated. And it was so refreshing to be around people who were actually curious about the world and unafraid to ask questions."

Then Anita and her boyfriend broke up—and here is where her story of wrongness really begins. In meeting the atheist and his community, she had encountered a whole different belief system than the one she had grown up with. Faced with two different and incompatible theories about the world—an almost Kuhnian conflict of paradigms—she chose his. But when the relationship fell apart, the support structure that had made that choice both tenable and desirable collapsed as well, and it took the belief system with it. By then, though, it was too late to return to the faith of her family. It had sprung too many holes, was too much at odds with both the world she saw around her and the voice she heard within her. A thousand years before her birth, al-Ghazali, the Persian philosopher, meditated on precisely this problem. Of the irreversibility of breaking with past beliefs, he wrote, "There can be no desire to return to servile conformism once it has been abandoned, since a prerequisite for being a servile conformist is that one does not know [oneself] to be such." But when someone recognizes his former beliefs as false, al-Ghazali continued, "the glass of his servile conformism is shattered—an irreparable fragmentation and a mess which cannot be mended by patching and piecing together." Instead, he concluded, "it can only be melted by fire and newly reshaped."[†]

---

† A different and somewhat less acerbic translation of this passage renders "servile conformism" as "blind belief." In either case, al-Ghazali's argument is essentially a restatement of the 'Cuz It's True Constraint. Once we come to feel that we believed something

Melted by fire: that is the crucial phrase. Raised to be afraid of a literal hell, Anita suddenly found herself plunged into a figurative one instead. After the breakup, she said, "I plummeted into a pit of awfulness." She no longer believed in her childhood religion, but she had no idea how to live without it, and she had no idea what to believe instead. Without meaning to, she had broken with one conviction—one really enormous, important, all-encompassing conviction—without having a replacement belief at the ready: the preconditions for pure wrongness. And that is where she found herself. Not just wrong about Christianity, not just wrong about atheism, not just wrong in the past. Just—wrong. Wrong right now, wrong in this moment and still wrong in the next.

What is it like, this normally elusive space of unresolved, ongoing wrongness? "The first word that comes to mind," Anita told me, "is terror. Chronic terror. And I mean, day in and day out. I remember having this revelation at one point that I could be totally, viscerally terrified *and* do my laundry." Lending credence to the notion that wrongness can be indistinguishable from madness, she said, "I know this sounds extreme, but I got about as close to insane as you can get. When you're talking about religion, you're talking about your whole understanding of the world. And when you start to question that, when the certainty starts to slide, you face inner chaos—an absolutely bitter battle for your life. It was just so massively disorienting. I had no idea who I was, what I believed, what I didn't believe. I felt like a toddler lost in the middle of Manhattan."

A tiny child alone in one of the most overwhelming places on earth: I've thought about this image often while working on this book—and, for that matter, while going about my life. What keeps me coming back to it is the way that it captures so much of the otherwise fugitive experience of wrongness. There is the sudden awareness of the immensity of the world, and of our own extreme smallness, vulnerability, and confusion within it. There is the utterly primal nature of our emotional response in such situations: panic, anguish, rage. There is the fear that we don't have the ability

---

for reasons other than the truth of that belief, we have all but destroyed our ability to keep believing it.

or resources to find our way again in the world. And, somewhere in the mix, there is also the wronged and outraged and grieving sense that we shouldn't be there in the first place—that some cruel or careless being, more powerful than we are, has abandoned us to our fate. (And how much worse that feeling must be when what you've lost is your faith in God, whose job is precisely to be the grown-up for grown-ups: *Our Father, who art in heaven*.)

Anita's image of the lost child also captures another part of the experience of pure wrongness. In the face of radical error, it isn't just the world that suddenly seems uncertain, unknown, and new; it is also the self. Thus James Sully, that original wrongologist, wrote in 1881 that, "any great transformation of our environment may lead to a partial confusion with respect to self. For not only do great and violent changes in our surroundings beget profound changes in our feelings and ideas, but since the idea of self is under one of its aspects essentially that of a relation to not-self, any great revolution in the one term, will confuse the recognition of the other." Eighty years later, the sociologist Helen Merrell Lynd made virtually the same point. "As trust in oneself and in the outer world develop together," she wrote, "so doubt of oneself and of the outer world are also intermeshed." Anita understood all this: she described her own experience of breaking with her past as, in part, "an intense mourning of identity."

When we are stuck inside the space of error, then, we are lost twice over: once in the world, and again in ourselves. As painful as that sounds, it can also be redemptive. This, too, is suggested by the image of the toddler alone in New York. Drastic error makes us young again, in both the hardest and the best of ways. I've already touched on the hard ways: we grow small and scared, sacrifice some of our self-knowledge, lose our sense of where we belong in the world. Still, put a kid in the middle of Times Square, and, lost or not, sooner or later he'll look up in awe. Likewise, most of us eventually manage to look up from the despair of wrongness and feel something of a child's wonder at the vastness and mystery of the world. Eventually, too, we get our act together and go explore that big new space—the one outside us, but also the one within us. In fact, perhaps the chief thing we learn from being wrong is how much growing up we still have to do. "The time after my boyfriend and I broke up was incredibly dark, black, bleak," Anita Wilson recalled. "But ultimately it was also this kind of fantastic experience of searching and learning. Before then, I was always immersed in someone else's identity. Now, I really feel like me. It sounds like such a cliché, but I really did have to go to this terrifying place of losing myself in order to truly find myself."

This is the thing about fully experiencing wrongness. It strips us of all our theories, including our theories about ourselves. This isn't fun while it's happening—it leaves us feeling flayed, laid bare to the bone and the world—but it does make possible that rarest of occurrences: real change. As we'll see toward the end of this book, if we could somehow observe the moment of error every time it happens—slow it down and expand it when we normally condense it to mere instants, speed it up and compress it when we attenuate it to years or decades—change is what we would see at its core every time. This helps explain our dislike of error, since most of us are at least somewhat averse to change. And it also explains why the place of pure wrongness is so hard, so heated, so full of emotional drama. It is, in essence, a psychological construction site, all pits and wrecking balls and cranes: the place where we destroy and rebuild ourselves, where all the ground gives way, and all the ladders start.

So we can suffer inside the experience of error, or hurdle over it, or dilute it with time. One way or another, though, the outcome is the same: we move from belief to disbelief. Given what we've seen so far about how much we dislike being wrong and how many forces conspire to make us feel right, it's something of a miracle that we ever manage to make this transition. And yet, with reasonable frequency, we *do* make it: somehow, something manages to nudge us out of our sublime confidence that we are right and into the realization that we were wrong. One of the fundamental challenges of wrongology is to figure out what that something is, and how it works—and why, very often, it doesn't.

We know one thing for sure: mere exposure to the idea that we are in error is seldom sufficient to budge us. As we saw earlier, we receive information that we are wrong fairly frequently—and, almost as frequently, we cheerily disregard it. Recently, for example, while spending some time in Oregon, my home away from home, I took a break from work to go for a bike ride. My destination was a certain alpine lake, and, along the way, I chatted briefly with a somewhat crotchety older man who had been fly-fishing in a nearby river. He asked where I was headed, and when I answered, he told me that I was on the wrong road. I thanked him pleasantly and continued on my way. I figured he thought I should be on the main thoroughfare, which would have gotten me to my destination faster, while I was opting for a more scenic and roundabout route. I also suspected him of trying to steer me, a young female cyclist, toward an easier option, since the road I had chosen was steep and challenging.

Eight miles later, when I rounded a corner and dead-ended into barbed wire and private property, I realized the guy had simply told me the facts. I had taken a wrong turn, and the road I was on wasn't going to get me anywhere near a lake. I could have saved myself sixteen miles of fairly arduous alpine cycling if I had bothered to have a longer conversation with him, or to take him a bit more seriously. And quite possibly I would have done so—if, say, he had been a little friendlier, or a fellow cyclist, or someone I recognized from town, or a woman.

Whatever might have made me pay more attention to this man, in other words, had nothing at all to do with how right he was. This is, unfortunately, a universal truth. Sometimes people succeed in showing us our errors and sometimes they fail, but only rarely does that success or failure hinge on the accuracy of their information. Instead, as we saw in our discussion of community, it has almost everything to do with the interpersonal forces at work: trust or mistrust, attraction or repulsion, identification or alienation. It's no surprise, then, that other people's input is often insufficient to make us recognize our mistakes.

Here, though, is something more surprising. Although I finally admitted my own error on the basis of a barbed-wire fence, we are often equally reluctant to accept the suggestion that we are wrong when it comes to us from the physical world—a far more impartial and therefore (one might imagine) far more palatable source of feedback. These red flags in our environment are, in essence, a kind of forcing function—the engineer's term of art for features of the physical world that alert us to the fact that we are making a mistake. If you've just emerged from the grocery store and are trying to get into a black Ford F–150 that happens to be someone else's black Ford F–150, the key will not turn in the lock—one of a great many car-related forcing functions that have long been standard protocol in the automotive industry.

Forcing functions are, on the whole, quite effective. But they can't stop you from, say, jiggling your key in the lock, twisting it almost to the breaking point, taking it out, looking at it, inserting it upside down, and finally giving up and heading over to try the passenger door—at which point, you note the presence of an unfamiliar diaper bag and the absence of your coffee mug, and the light dawns. As this example suggests, environmental feedback is not all that different from human feedback: it can draw attention to our errors, but it cannot force us to acknowledge them.* The fact is, with the exception of our own minds, no power on earth has the consistent and absolute ability to convince us that we are wrong. However much we might be prompted by cues from other people or our environment, the choice to face up to error is ultimately ours alone.

Why can we do this sometimes but not others? For one thing, as we saw earlier, it's a lot harder to let go of a belief if we don't have a new one to replace it. For another, as Leon Festinger observed in his study of cognitive dissonance, it's a lot harder if we are heavily invested in that belief—if, to borrow a term from economics, we have accrued significant sunk costs. Traditionally, sunk costs refer to money that is already spent and can't be recovered. Let's say you shelled out five grand for a used car, and three weeks later it got a flat tire. When you take it to the mechanic, he tells you that you need

---

* For another example of ignoring input from our physical environment, consider my sister, who is one of those otherwise brilliant people who, for some reason, can't find her way out of a paper bag. (I can recall her getting lost in a restaurant and a shoe store, and I strongly suspect that she could become disoriented in a mid-sized airplane.) Once, after returning from a meeting in her own building, she rounded a corner expecting to come across the door to her office, but instead found herself facing a corridor with a window at the end. That's a pretty straightforward example of our environment giving us information that we are wrong—but, my sister said, "the first thing that came to mind wasn't, *I'm lost.* It was, *Who put that window there?*" As always, the possibility that we ourselves have fucked up is the hypothesis of last resort.

both rear tires replaced and the alignment adjusted. Bang: you've just added 250 bucks to your ticket price. A month later, the clutch gives out. You get it fixed—for a cool $900—but pretty soon you start having trouble with the ignition. Turns out you need the fuel pump repaired. There goes another $350. Now you've spent $1,500 to keep your $5,000 lemon running.

So should you ditch the car and buy another one, or should you hope for the best and stick with the one you've got? An economist would say that, whatever you decide, you shouldn't factor in the $6,500 you've already spent. That's your sunk cost, and since the money is gone either way, a rational actor would ignore it. But human beings are famously bad at ignoring sunk costs, because we are not really rational actors. We are *quasi*-rational actors, in whom reason is forever sharing the stage with ego and hope and stubbornness and loathing and loyalty. The upshot is that we are woefully bad at cutting our losses—and not just when it comes to money. We are also seduced by the sunk costs of our actions: think about those mountain climbers who keep making their way up Everest when conditions clearly dictate that they should turn around. And, of course, we are seduced by the sunk costs of our beliefs.

These belief investments can be very light—the sliver of ego we stake on a friendly bet—or they can be the figurative equivalent of our life's savings. Take Anita Wilson's one-time belief in the literal truth of the Bible. Just for starters, her sunk costs included her trust in her parents, her standing in and connections to her community, her public identity, her private sense of self, and, arguably, twenty years of her life. That's a formidable list, and we haven't even gotten to innumerable ancillary beliefs (such as the merits of evolutionary theory and the morality of abortion), or to not-so-ancillary ideas about the nature and meaning of life. Does the world and everything in it exist for a divine purpose? Is a loving God watching over me? Will I be saved on Judgment Day? Will there *be* a Judgment Day? Fundamentally: am I, in the biggest of big pictures, safe, smart, worthy, righteous, right? To have a belief that answers all these questions is to be sunk into it at a psychological cost considerably beyond calculation.

The problem is that, as with the feeling of rightness, our investment in a belief (or conversely, our indifference to it) has no necessary relationship to its truth. No amount of sunk costs can make an erroneous belief accurate, just as fixing the flat on a junky car can't make it un-junky. But our sunk costs *do* have a keen relationship to our loyalty. The more we spend on a belief, the harder it is to extricate ourselves from it. As Anita put it, "there's a continuum of things you can be wrong about, and some of them are bearable, and some of them are not. I can't really accept the possibility that I'm wrong about hell now. But you know, in part that's because if I'm wrong about that one, I'm fucked."

This brings us back to the main point: given the power of sunk costs and our capacity to ignore negative feedback about our beliefs, it's a wonder any of us *ever* manages to acknowledge that we were wrong. That we sometimes do so is a testament to the human mind—but to what part of it is anybody's guess. If it is hard to isolate the moment of pure error, it is even harder to isolate what's going on inside us when we do or don't face up to our mistakes. We can surmise from our own experience, however, that it has a lot to do with context. Or rather, with *contexts*: with what is going on both around us and within us.

What's going on around us comes down to two questions. The first is how much we are sheltered from or exposed to challenges to our beliefs. When we claim that people who disagree with us "live in a bubble," we mean that their environment is not forcing them (or enabling them) to face the flaws in their beliefs. The second is whether the people around us make it easy or hard to accept our errors. The cult members studied by Leon Festinger faced public ridicule when their prophecies (some of which had been printed in the local newspaper) failed to come true. As Festinger pointed out, that ridicule was not merely mean-spirited but also, as we saw with the Swiss antisuffragists, counterproductive. "The jeering of nonbelievers," he wrote, "simply makes it far more difficult for the adherents to withdraw from the movement and admit that they were wrong." However much we might enjoy crowing at other people's errors, it gives those people little reason to change their minds and consider sharing our beliefs instead.*

---

* In a 2008 post to the blog she writes for *The Atlantic*, Megan McArdle, the magazine's business and economics editor, chided her fellow opponents to the Iraq War for falling

If the workings of this outer context are relatively straightforward, the workings of the inner one are hopelessly complex. Like all dynamic systems, our inner universes are governed by a kind of chaos theory: sensitive in unpredictable ways to minor fluctuations, easily perturbed, oftentimes seemingly random. In such a system, it's hard to explain why humility and humor sometimes win out over pride and touchiness, and even tougher to predict the outcome in advance. As a consequence, our ability to own up to our mistakes will always be partway mysterious—determined, as much as anything, by our moment-to-moment mood.

But if our attitude toward error is sometimes a product of the time of day, it is also a product of our time of life. Acknowledging our mistakes is an intellectual and (especially) an emotional skill, and as such it evolves in tandem with our cognitive and psychological development. For instance, the intolerance we routinely impute to adolescents and the wisdom we often ascribe to the elderly are, in part, reflections of different developmental stages in our relationship to wrongness. The hallmark of teenagers is that they think they know everything, and are therefore happy to point out other people's errors—but woe betide the adult who tries to suggest that the kids could be wrong. (These teenage tendencies can help as well as hinder the process of belief change. When I asked Anita Wilson how she had been able to change her mind about something as fundamental as her faith, she said that it was partly about age: "The one thing I had going for me was that I was still basically a teenager, so disagreeing with my parents was natural.")[†]

_____

into this trap. "With every 'I told you so' and demand that they apologize to you, personally, for the sin of being wrong, you are hardening the hawks against the possibility of changing their minds," she wrote. "I know you may feel that you cannot be happy until they apologize, admit that they were wrong, that they were stupid, that everything they ever believed about war was in error. They know it too. Indeed, after all the sniping, many people will refuse to say they are wrong because it would make you happy. They don't want to make you happy. Frankly, you haven't given them any reason to."

† Teenagers make for an interesting case study in the annals of error, since their relationship to wrongness amounts to the familiar one with the volume turned all the way up. Regardless of age, almost all of us are far more alert to other people's errors than to our own. But young adults are the unsurpassed masters of this asymmetry,

By contrast, the wisdom we perceive in the elderly often stems from their hard-earned knowledge that *no one* knows everything. In the long haul, they recognize, all of us screw up, misunderstand ideas, misjudge situations, underestimate other people, overestimate ourselves—and all of this over and over again. In this respect, their sagacity is a form of humility, one that enables a less rigid relationship to the world. (Sadly, the developmental curve sometimes comes full circle. The other cliché about old age, that it makes people cantankerous and set in their ways, is also a product of cognitive development—or rather, of cognitive degeneration. Thus the elderly can sometimes come to seem a lot like adolescents: hawklike in their keenness for other people's shortcomings, steadfast in defense of their own rightness.)

Our capacity to acknowledge error, then, has something to do with where we are in life, both immediately and overall. But it has nearly everything to do with *who* we are in life. It would be easy to observe that people who are arrogant, obstinate, and close minded have difficulty admitting error, whereas those who are more humble, curious, and open to change fare better. But there's something unsatisfying about this. For one thing, as I've already noted, all of us contain an admixture of these elements. For another, this explanation verges on the circular: saying that people who are stubborn and narrow-minded can't admit to being wrong sounds a lot like saying that people who can't admit to being wrong can't admit to being wrong. It's true enough, but it doesn't tell us *why* each of us feels about error the particular way we do.

---

often combining a positively savage disdain for the perceived errors of others with a sublime confidence in their own rightness. I say this with affection, and even admiration. Sometimes the world needs the unblinking conviction of youth: Joan of Arc was a teenager (although not quite in the modern sense), Bob Dylan was in his early twenties when he forged the de facto soundtrack of the civil rights movement, and many of the organizers of and participants in the democratic revolutions of the twentieth and twenty-first centuries have been high school and college students. But I also say it with a twinge of rueful identification, and with belated apologies to my parents—and I'm not alone. Almost every adult I talked to about this book made wry acknowledgment of the blistering intensity of their teenage beliefs—beliefs that, in most cases, they softened or simply rejected later in life. It only underscores the main point to observe that teenagers generally regard these later admissions of error as hopeless acts of selling out.

A better answer was suggested by Irna Gadd, a psychoanalyst in New York. "Our capacity to tolerate error," Gadd said, "depends on our capacity to tolerate emotion." Most of our mistakes are nowhere near as emotionally leveling as the pure wrongness experienced by Anita Wilson, but virtually all of them require us to feel *something*: a wash of dismay, a moment of foolishness, guilt over our dismissive treatment of someone else who turned out to be right—I could go on. (And I will in the next chapters, where we'll look more closely at the range of emotions that wrongness can provoke.) It is the presentiment of these feelings, and the recoil from them, that renders us so defensive in the face of possible error. In this respect, the experience of pure wrongness, although rare, is the telling one: our resistance to error is, in no small part, a resistance to being left alone with too few certainties and too many emotions.

For some people, this experience is essentially unbearable. When I spoke with Anita Wilson, I asked whether her parents (with whom she remains close) had questioned their faith at all after she renounced it. "Quietly, behind the scenes, my mom can bend a little," she told me. "But my father is more rigid. He once said to me, 'If I don't believe that every word in the Bible is true, I don't know what I believe.' And I'm like: come on. There are all kinds of passages in the Bible that can't be literally true, there are things that can't be true if other things are true, and there are things my dad plainly doesn't believe—about menstruating women and so forth. But he has to hold on to that certainty. Without it, his whole world would fall apart. He'd go insane. I honestly don't know that he's strong enough to handle it."

All of us know people like this—people whose rigidity serves to protect a certain inner fragility, who cannot bend precisely because they are at risk of breaking. For that matter, all of us *are* people like this sometimes. No matter how psychologically resilient we may be, facing up to our own errors time and again is tough. And sometimes we just can't. Sometimes we are too exhausted or too sad or too far out of our element to risk feeling worse (or even just feeling *more*), and so instead we wax stubborn, or defensive, or downright mean. The irony, of course, is that none of these feelings are all that great, either—and nor do they engender particularly comforting interactions with others. True, we will have succeeded in pulling up the drawbridge, manning the battlements, and skirting a confrontation with our fallibility. But we will also have succeeded (if that is the word) at creating conflict with another person—not infrequently, with someone we love. And, too, we will have succeeded in stranding ourselves inside the particular and unpleasant kind of loneliness occasioned by one's own poor behavior.

Then there is the other, less obvious problem with failing to face up to wrongness: we miss out on the wrongness itself. If the ability to admit that we are wrong depends on the ability to tolerate emotion, it is because being wrong, like grieving or falling in love, is fundamentally an emotional experience. Such experiences can be agonizing, but the corny truism about them is true: if you haven't experienced them, you haven't fully lived. As with love and loss, so too with error. Sure, it can hurt you, but the only way to protect yourself from that potential is by closing yourself off to new experiences and other people. And to do that is to throw your life out with the bathwater.

Happily, we don't need to do this. If our ability to accept error is mercurial and mysterious, we do know this much: it is also mutable. Like all abilities, it comes from inside us, and as such it is ours to cultivate or neglect. For the most part, we opt for neglect, which is why the typical relationship to error is characterized by distance and defensiveness. But if you have ever tried those out in a real relationship (meaning, with a human being), you know that they are the short road to disaster. The only way to counter them is to *act* counter to them: to substitute openness for defensiveness and intimacy for distance. I said earlier that this is not a self-help book, since (for reasons both practical and philosophical) my primary goal isn't to help us avoid error. But when it comes to the opposite task—*not* avoiding error— we can use all the help we can get. The aim of the rest of this book, then, is to get closer to error: close enough to examine other people's real-life experiences of it, and, in the end, close enough to live with our own.

10.

How Wrong?

Once you have missed the first buttonhole
you'll never manage to button up.
—Johann Wolfgang von Goethe

On the morning of October 22, 1844, a group of people gathered to await the end of the world. They met in homes, in churches, and in outdoor revival meetings, primarily in New York and New England but also throughout the United States and Canada, and as far away as England, Australia, and South America. Nobody knows how numerous they were. Some scholars put the number at 25,000 and some put it at over a million, while most believe it was in the hundreds of thousands. Whatever the figure, the assembled group was too large to be dismissed as a cult and too diverse to be described as a sect. The believers included Baptists, Methodists, Episcopalians, Lutherans, and members of various other Christian denominations, plus a handful of unaffiliated former atheists. They also included an almost perfect cross section of mid-nineteenth-century society. Sociologists often argue that apocalyptic creeds appeal primarily to the poor and the disenfranchised—those for whom the afterlife promises more than life itself has ever offered. But on that day in 1844, judges, lawyers and doctors, farmers and factory workers and freed slaves, the educated and the ignorant, the wealthy and the impoverished: all of them gathered as one to await the Rapture.

What this otherwise diverse group of people had in common was faith in the teachings of one William Miller, a do-it-yourself preacher who had analyzed the Bible and determined the date of the Second Coming. Miller was born in Massachusetts in 1782, the eldest of sixteen children and the grandson of a Baptist minister. When he was four, his family moved to upstate New York, where the nationwide religious revival that would become known as the Second Great Awakening was just beginning to stir. In later years, the part of the state near Miller's home would be called the Burned-Over District, because it was so ablaze with religious conviction that there was scarcely anyone left to convert.

The time, the place, and the lineage suggest an auspicious beginning for a future religious leader—but as a young man, Miller renounced his faith in Christianity. He was troubled, he later wrote, by "inconsistencies and contradictions in the Bible," and at the suggestion of some friends in Vermont, where he had recently moved with his new wife, he began reading Voltaire, Hume, and Thomas Paine. All three thinkers rejected the authority of religious doctrine in favor of independent rational thought, and Miller grew to share their convictions.

Then came the War of 1812. Many a man has reunited with God on the battlefield, and Miller was one of them. As captain of the Thirtieth Infantry, Miller fought in the Battle of Plattsburgh, where outnumbered American troops defeated the British and helped turn the course of the war. To Miller, the improbable victory was evidence of the hand of God: "so surprising a result against such odds, did seem to me like the work of a mightier power than man." Or so he wrote later. But it's hard not to wonder if what really got to Miller was the close encounter with mortality. He had long worried that rationalism, for all its virtues, was "inseparably connected with, and did tend to, the denial of a future existence [i.e., life after death]"—a shortcoming that must have seemed more acute after witnessing the ravages of battle. (And, too, after losing his father and sister, both of whom died around the time of the war.) Rather than accept the possibility of annihilation, Miller wrote, "I should prefer the heaven and hell of the Scriptures, and take my chance respecting them." Thus did the wayward Baptist return to the Bible.

Yet the contradictions in Christianity that had vexed Miller in the past vexed him still. In 1816, a friend from his Voltaire days challenged him to reconcile those contradictions or abandon the Bible altogether, and Miller took up the gauntlet. For the next several years, he dedicated himself to creating a system, consisting of fourteen rules, intended to render all of scripture internally consistent. He would forever after advertise this system as simple and infallible, but an outsider could be forgiven for struggling to discern these qualities. (Rule #8: "Figures always have a figurative meaning . . . such as mountains, meaning governments; beasts, meaning kingdoms, waters, meaning people." Rule #10: "Figures sometimes have two or more different significations, as day is used in a figurative sense to represent three different periods of time. 1. Indefinite. 2. Definite, a day for a year. 3. Day for a thousand years." Rule #11: "How to know when a word is used figuratively. If it makes good sense as it stands, and does no violence to the simple laws of nature, then it must be understood literally; if not, figuratively.") It was these rules of interpretation that led Miller to conclude that the end of the world was at hand. Thus was it written in the Bible, and thus must it be.

Plenty of people draw their own dramatic conclusions about the fate of the earth—or, for that matter, about perpetual motion, the health risks of microwaves, and what really happened at Waco—but very few achieve international stature and throngs of followers. In all probability, Miller would have spent his days preaching about the Advent in obscurity if he hadn't chanced to team up with one Joshua Himes. Himes was Rasputin, Warren Buffet, Karl Rove, and William Randolph Hearst rolled into one: a canny advisor, a formidable fundraiser, a brilliant politician, and a public relations genius. The two met in 1839, when Miller, who had been a low-key figure on the itinerant-preacher circuit for some years, was modestly describing his doctrine to a small crowd in Exeter, New Hampshire. Himes came to believe in the tiny Millerite movement, and then to transform it. He promptly launched two newspapers, *Signs of the Times* and *The Midnight Cry*, which soon achieved a combined weekly circulation of 60,000. (Other papers would follow.) He issued millions of copies of pamphlets, hymnbooks, and illustrated posters explaining the timeline of the end of the world, and then established book depots around the country to make these publications available. He pushed Miller to take his message beyond small towns and farming communities and into the big cities of the Eastern Seaboard. At the same time, he ordered the construction of a giant tent to house massive Millerite revival meetings in rural areas. He focused on recruiting other ministers (some 400, by his own estimate) rather than just congregation members, in order to amplify the impact of each new convert. Then he developed a preaching schedule for each of them so punishing that it makes American presidential campaigns look like a walk in the park. These efforts, combined with a zeitgeist that was particularly conducive to religious fervor, quickly turned Millerism into a household word.

At first, Millerite doctrine did not specify the exact date of the Second Coming. Its timing was contingent on the fulfillment of a series of other prophecies, arcane in their details, and Millerites argued among themselves at length about whether those prophecies had already come to pass. Miller himself had long held only that the Rapture would probably occur "about the year 1843"; when pressed, he finally stated that he thought the world would end sometime between March 21, 1843, and March 21, 1844. When the latter date passed without incident, Miller's followers began to be anxious, but also to believe the Judgment Day must be increasingly near at hand. (Recall Leon Festinger, who found that failed prophecies often lead to an upsurge in faith.) Ultimately it was not Miller but one of his adherents, the preacher Samuel Snow, who proposed the date of October 22 and presented the calculations to justify it.

Perhaps because of the climate of anxiety and expectation, Snow's suggestion caught on like wildfire. In short order, Advent in October became an article of faith among rank-and-file Millerites. Whether because they

A lecture chart used by William Miller, detailing 2,520 years of fulfilled prophecies expected to culminate in 1843, Miller's original forecast for the date of the Second Coming.

were irked by Snow's presumption or chastened by the failure of their earlier predictions, Miller, Himes, and other movement higher-ups were slower to jump on the bandwagon. Miller himself wrote that he was not convinced "until about two or three weeks previous to the 22d of October, when seeing [that faith in Snow's date] had obtained such prevalence . . . I was persuaded that it was a work of God." (Fifty million Millerites can't be wrong.) By the beginning of the fateful month, there was near unanimity among the devout: the long-awaited Rapture was almost upon them.

Whatever else may be said of Miller, Himes, and their followers, it bears observing that in the vast majority of cases, their faith was sincere. In keeping with the ethos of the time, the sincerity of that faith can be measured in works—or, sometimes, in the eschewal of work. Many Millerites declined to plant their fields in 1844, believing that the world would end before winter arrived. Of those who had planted in the spring, many left their crops to rot at harvest time, acknowledging before God that soon neither the righteous nor the damned would require earthly sustenance. Cattle and other farm animals were slaughtered to feed the hungry. Believers settled their worldly debts and gave the remainder of their money and property away, often to help their poorer brethren pay their bills.* Himes closed down his newspapers at the beginning of October, in anticipation of a time when journalism—that most worldly of professions—would be very much beside the point. In the final days before the expected end-time, families abandoned their homes and moved into churches, fields, and other communal places of worship to await judgment among the devout. This, then, was how the dawn of October 22 found the Millerites: hopeful, frightened, joyous, estranged from all but their fellow believers, in many cases newly homeless and penniless—and ready, deeply ready, to meet their maker.

We know what happens next, of course. The sun rises. The sun sets. The Messiah does not appear. The world fails to end. These events (or, more aptly, these non-events) are known to historians as the Great Disappointment. To modern ears, the word "disappointment" sounds strangely under-

---

* Others apparently spent their money in different ways. The opening "Talk of the Town" in the very first edition of *The New Yorker* (dated February 17, 1925) is about the Millerite movement, then a mere three generations in the past. In its now-familiar arch voice, the column noted that, "Two or three hundred thousand of our great-grandparents bought white ascension robes for the event. . . . Muslin for ascension robes could be bought by the bolt, or in the latest Parisian models."

stated, but the Millerites themselves used it again and again to cover a broad and terrible swath of emotional terrain: shock, confusion, humiliation, despair, grief. A significant number of them left behind written accounts of that day, and many of these are eloquent in expressing that anguish. One such chronicler, a man named Washington Morse, averred that the "disappointment to the Advent believers . . . can find a parallel only in the sorrow of the disciples at the crucifixion [sic] of their Lord." To another, Hiram Edson, "it seemed that the loss of all earthly friends could have been no comparison. We wept, and wept, till the day dawn." And a third, Luther Boutelle, described how "unspeakably sad [were] the faithful and longing ones. Still in the cold world! No deliverance—the Lord not come! . . . All were silent, save to inquire, 'where are we?' and 'what next?'"

What next, indeed? What do you do when you arise one morning certain that you will see your savior's face and be taken into heaven by nightfall, only to have the next day dawn on a world wholly, dismally unchanged? What do you do about the unwelcome restoration of the day-to-day obligations of terrestrial life—crops to salvage, stores to tend, children to feed, the I-told-you-so's of your neighbors to face?

As a practical matter, attending to these exigencies must have been the first order of business for the beleaguered Millerites. Philosophically, though, they faced another pressing issue. We know—and, for the most part, they could not help but know, too—that Millerite doctrine had been wrong. But *how* wrong? This question dogs almost every significant mistake we make. In the aftermath of our errors, our first task is always to establish their scope and nature. Where, precisely, did we go astray? Which wrong road did we take? And exactly how far down it did we travel?

These questions present us with both an intellectual and an emotional challenge. Figuring out where we went wrong can be genuinely puzzling—the conceptual equivalent of trying to retrace your steps in a dark woods. But facing up to the true scope and nature of our errors is also (and more self-evidently) psychologically demanding. Crucially, these two challenges are inseparable: if we can't do the emotional work of fully accepting our mistakes, we can't do the conceptual work of figuring out where, how, and why we made them. (That's one reason why defensiveness is so bad for problem solving and progress of all kinds: in relationships, in business, in creative and intellectual pursuits.) Later in this chapter, we'll look more closely at our regrettable tendency to flub the first challenge—to excuse or minimize our errors, and to cling as hard as we can, for as long as we can, to whatever shard of rightness remains. First, though, we need to understand the stakes of these challenges. That is, we need to understand why our answer to the "how wrong?" question matters so very much.

Consider what happened when the Millerites found themselves confronting this question. After their Adventist predictions failed to materialize, they floated countless competing theories for what had gone wrong. If, as we saw in the last chapter, Anita Wilson found herself adrift in a sea of wrongness without a single theory to her name, the Millerites had the opposite problem. They were positively inundated with theories—too many to fully evaluate, too many even to track.* A year and a half after the Great Disappointment, one former believer, Enoch Jacobs, exclaimed, "O what an ocean of contradictory theories is that upon which the multitudes have been floating for the last eighteen months. Do you not long for rest from these conflicting elements?"

This manic proliferation of new theories in the aftermath of major error is common. In fact, Thomas Kuhn, the historian of science, argued that the periods between the breakdown of one belief system and the entrenchment of a new one are *always* characterized by an explosion of competing hypotheses. Each of those hypotheses represents a different answer to the "how wrong?" question: we construct our new theories based largely on what we think was wrong with the old ones. By determining where we went astray in the past, in other words, we also determine where we will wind up in the future.

As that suggests, the way we answer the "how wrong?" question also dictates which of our beliefs we must discard and which ones we can continue to endorse. Beliefs, after all, do not exist in isolation from one an-

---

* Actually, Anita's problem and the Millerites' problem amounted to the same thing. Having no theory at all and having too many theories both suggest that you are in the middle of a crisis of knowledge.

other. Sometimes they are bound together by logic: if you believe that God created the world and all its contents in seven days, you must also believe that evolutionary biology is wrong. Alternatively, sometimes they have no necessary relationship to each other but are experienced (and enforced) as interrelated within a given community. Either way, the point is that our beliefs come in bundles. That makes it hard to remove or replace one without affecting the others—and it gets harder as the belief in question gets more central. In this respect, beliefs are like the beams in a building or the words in a sentence: you can't eliminate one and expect the fundamental soundness or fundamental meaning of the overall system to remain unchanged. As a result, being wrong sometimes triggers a cascade of transformations so extensive that the belief system that emerges afterward bears almost no resemblance to its predecessor.

My friend Mark experienced a common version of this ideological domino effect when he realized that he was gay. "In order to come out," he explained, "I needed to reject a lot of what I had believed up till then"—what he had believed about gay people, that is. Because Mark had been raised Catholic, a lot of those beliefs came from the Church. Questioning its teachings on homosexuality led him to question (and in many cases reject) other Catholic teachings as well. "I was surprised," he told me, "to find that in the process [of coming out], I needed to toss out a lot of other beliefs, beliefs about things that had nothing to do with being gay."

But of course—and here's where things get interesting—Mark *didn't* need to toss out all those beliefs. For every person like him, there is someone else who rejected the Catholic Church's position on homosexuality but continued to embrace its other teachings. Mark answered the "how wrong?" question one way (pretty far toward the direction of "totally wrong," as it happens), but other people in virtually the same boat have answered it differently. That's the thing about the "how wrong?" question: almost no matter what we were wrong about, we can find countless different ways to take the measure of our mistakes.

Take the Millerites. All of them faced the task of unraveling a single, shared error to its point of origin. Where, exactly, had they gone wrong? At one end of the range of possible answers lies the flat disavowal of error. This is the realm of denial, where mistakes come only in size zero. You might think that every Millerite would have had to acknowledge at least some degree of error after the Great Disappointment—the continued existence of the planet being, after all, the forcing function par excellence. But no: displaying their powers of imagination and defying our own, the truly diehard among the Millerites declined to admit that they had been wrong in any respect. Instead, in a somewhat dazzling act of revisionist theology, they claimed that Christ really *had* returned to earth—by entering the hearts of his followers, who now dwelt with him in (terrestrial) paradise.

If denial demarcates one extreme end of the range of possible answers to "how wrong?", the other end is defined by acceptance. But acceptance is a trickier, more elastic condition than denial. There is a limit to how small our errors can get, and that limit is nonexistence. But there isn't necessarily a limit to how *large* they can get.* Of those Millerites who generally accepted that they had been wrong, some abandoned belief in God altogether. Others simply parted ways with organized religion. Still others repudiated only the teachings of William Miller. As this suggests, even sincere acknowledgment of error comes in many sizes, each with radically different implications for the person who has erred.

I'll talk more about denial and acceptance in the next chapter, since they represent two especially important aspects of our relationship to error. For now, though, I want to focus on the messy middle of our "how wrong?" responses. These responses are characterized neither by full acceptance nor by flat denial, but rather by downplaying, hedging, backpedaling, justifying, or otherwise minimizing the scope of our mistakes. You don't need me to tell you that this kind of minimization is exceedingly common. Remember

---

* In theory, the outer limit of wrongness would be the condition of being wrong about absolutely everything. A computer scientist named Keunwoo Lee has given us a name for this hypothetical state: fractal wrongness. Lee defines fractal wrongness as "being wrong at every conceivable scale of resolution." Thus if I'm fractally wrong, I'm wrong about all of my overarching beliefs, wrong about the people who corroborate those beliefs, wrong about the facts I think support those beliefs, wrong about the beliefs that stem from those beliefs . . . et cetera. As a condition, fractal wrongness is, thankfully, unattainable. As an insult, however, it is incomparable.

the situation I described in the last chapter, where we stand outside some-one else's car, persistently trying to open it with our own key? I cribbed that example from the psychologist Donald Norman's *The Design of Everyday Things*, an indictment of poorly conceived objects—from door handles to nuclear reactors—and how we discover and correct the mistakes they cause us to make. Norman writes that, in every situation he has studied, "the error correction [process] seems to start at the lowest possible level and slowly works its way higher." That is, we tend to suspect that something is wrong with the key or that something is wrong with the lock long before we suspect that we've got the wrong car—or that we only imagined having a car in the first place, or that while we were shopping aliens came down from space and injected Martian superglue into our locks. Although Nor-man is essentially an error-studies specialist, and as such focuses primar-ily on mechanical and procedural errors rather than beliefs, I suspect that his observation holds across the board: we all incline toward conservatism when it comes to determining the size of our mistakes.

We've already seen that a certain amount of conservatism in the face of challenges to our worldview is both normal and defensible. Just as it is rarely to our advantage to contemplate the possibility that a giraffe had a long flight from Kenya, it is rarely to our advantage to contemplate the pos-sibility that our car door has been glued shut by aliens. Sometimes, though, this conservatism, which begins as a smart cognitive strategy, winds up looking like a desperate emotional one. In those situations, as we are about to see—and as the Millerites were kind enough to demonstrate for us—we are not so much honestly trying to size up our errors as frantically trying to downsize them.

The morning after the Great Disappointment, Hiram Edson had a vision. Edson is the man I quoted earlier as saying that the events of October 22, 1844, were a harder blow than the loss of all earthly friends, so you can imagine how he was feeling on October 23. Contemplating the potential scale of the previous day's mistake, he wrote, "My advent experience has been the richest and brightest of all my Christian experience. If this had proved a failure, what was the rest of my Christian experience worth? Has the Bible proved a failure? Is there no God—no heaven—no golden home city—no paradise? Is all this but a cunningly devised fable? Is there no reality to our fondest hopes and expectations of these things?"

In an effort to shake these grim thoughts, or at least do some good in the world, Edson set out from his home to try to comfort his fellow Millerites. But no sooner had he started on his way than (as he later reported) "Heaven seemed open to my view, and I saw distinctly, and clearly, that instead of our High Priest coming out of the Most Holy of the heavenly sanctuary to come to this earth . . . that he for the first time entered on that day the second apartment of that sanctuary; and that he had a work to perform in the Most Holy before coming to this earth." Rather than signaling the Second Coming, Edson concluded, October 22 marked the day that Christ had assumed his place in the holiest compartment of the heavens, from whence he would begin judging conditions on earth in preparation for his return.

This doctrine, formulated by Edson more or less on the spot, is known as Investigative Judgment. It was formalized by two other Millerites, Ellen White and her husband James White, who together founded the Seventh-Day Adventists on its basis. In effect, the Adventists substituted an unfalsifiable celestial event for a falsifiable (and falsified) earthly one—a bit of theological legerdemain that allowed the new sect to flourish. Today, Seventh-Day Adventists claim 15 million members in some 200 countries. The orthodox among them continue to believe that Christ has been engaged in judging the souls on earth since 1844, and that when that work is done, Armageddon will be upon us.

To those devout Seventh-Day Adventists, Hiram Edson's vision was a message from God. Other readers, though, might have a different interpretation. Those who are inclined toward generosity might think that Edson's vision was much like the kind of vision blind Hannah had. Just as she "saw" a notebook and a nicely tanned doctor, he "saw" his Savior in the second compartment of heaven. For those with this turn of mind, Edson was essentially confabulating: like Hannah, he generated a sincere but ungrounded explanation for his error. Less generous-minded readers, meanwhile, might question that sincerity, and see Edson's vision as simply an elaborate—and, as fate would have it, world-altering—way of saving face.

Few of us change the course of history when we make excuses for being wrong. But all of us occasionally seek to save face when our beliefs turn out to have been "cunningly devised fables." Instead of simply acknowledging our mistakes, we point fingers, append caveats, call attention to mitigating factors, protest that there were extenuating circumstances, and so on. And like Edson, we are remarkably creative—visionary, you might even say—in how we accomplish this. In a sense, though, "creative" is exactly the wrong word for this kind of behavior—since, in the end, such tactics are largely destructive. True, these defensive maneuvers protect us from experiencing the uncomfortable emotions we associate with wrongness. But, like all acts of defensiveness, they also produce friction between people, stymie collaboration and creativity, make us seem rigid and insecure, and (as I suggested above) prevent us from engaging in the kind of clear-eyed assessment of our mistakes that can help us make different and better decisions in the future. In other words, these strategies for deflecting responsibility for our errors stand in the way of a better, more productive relationship to wrongness. I call these strategies the Wrong Buts (as in, "I was wrong, but . . ."), and I will call on the Millerites to illustrate them—since, in their efforts to account for their shared error, they did us the favor of employing almost all of them.*

Consider, for example, the time-frame defense, or what we might call "I was wrong, but wait until next year." The gist of this excuse is that I am right but the world is running behind schedule; however mistaken my beliefs might look at this moment, they will be borne out eventually. This was the explicit argument of many Millerites, who, in the words of one scholar of the movement, "continued to set times [for the Advent] for the next seven years. Some earmarked the end for October 23 at 6:00 PM, others for Oc-

---

* For those with an appetite for more recent real-life excuses for error, Philip Tetlock, the psychology professor and political scientist, provides a concise, informative, and often funny catalog of the Wrong Buts (although not by that name) in his book, *Expert Political Judgment.*

tober 24. There were high expectations for exactly a year after the Great Disappointment on October 22, 1845, with 1846, 1847, and the seven-year point of 1851 also heating up the millenarianism." While Hiram Edson had claimed that Miller had been right about the date but wrong about its significance, these other Millerites claimed that they had been right about the impending end of the world but just a bit off on the timing. In essence, they downgraded a crisis of faith to an arithmetic mistake.

The time-frame defense is a perennial favorite among political analysts, stock-market watchers, and anyone else who has ever tried to forecast the future (which is all of us). George W. Bush availed himself of it in 2006, when he claimed—in response to opinion polls indicating that 70 percent of Americans disapproved of his handling of the Iraq War—that he would be vindicated by "the long march of history." As that line suggests, one implication of the time-frame defense is that, however wrong I seem, I am actually *more* right than those who currently look it: I am a visionary, able to see the lay of the land from a more distant and loftier (i.e., Godlike) perspective. The trouble with the time-frame defense is that, while it is almost always available, it is very often ludicrous. By its logic, the journalist who infamously reported the death of Mark Twain thirteen years early was prophetically right.

A second and similarly popular Wrong But maneuver is the near-miss defense. Here the claim is not that our prediction will come to pass eventually, but rather that it *almost* came to pass. ("I was wrong, but only by a little.") This was, in essence, Hiram Edson's claim: Christ might not have come down to earth—but, hey, he had entered the most holy compartment of heaven. The near-miss defense can also take the form of claiming that, but for some trifling incident (heavy rain in New Hampshire on voting day, a tractor-trailer causing a traffic jam on the interstate, a butterfly flapping its wings in Brazil), my forecast would have been absolutely correct. Boiled down to its indisputably true but patently absurd essence, the argument of the near-miss defense is that if I hadn't been wrong, I would have been right.

A variation on the near-miss defense is the out-of-left-field defense. The claim here is that I was on track to being absolutely right when—bang!—

some bizarre and unforeseeable event derailed the natural course of things and rendered me unexpectedly wrong. One problem with this excuse is that just about any event can be defined as unforeseeable if you yourself failed to foresee it. Another problem is that it presumes that, absent this left-field factor, the outcome would have been exactly as you predicted. As Philip Tetlock writes, "It is almost as though [people who invoke the out-of-left-field defense] are telling us 'Of course, I know what would have happened. I just got back from a trip in my alternative-universe teleportation device and can assure you that events there dovetailed perfectly with my preconceptions.'"

Unlike the other Wrong Buts, the out-of-left-field excuse was not of much use to the Millerites, who could hardly go around claiming that God's Almighty Plan had been unexpectedly derailed. (For God, one assumes, there is no left field.) But they could and did avail themselves of one of the most popular Wrong Buts of all time: blaming other people. ("I was wrong, but it's your fault.") In this defense, we essentially outsource our errors. Sure, we screwed up, but only in trusting a source that turned out to be unreliable, or following a leader who turned out to be dishonest or deluded.

It's hard to know what to make of this defense, since it is always simultaneously reasonable and unreasonable. The situation of the rank-and-file Millerites makes this clear. Inevitably, after the Great Disappointment, many of them blamed Miller for leading them astray. But whatever other forces the Millerite masses might have been subject to, they were not coerced. (In fact, they could not have been, since profound faith is, in the end, a necessarily private commitment.) Nor could they fairly claim to have been kept in the dark, either. Millerism wasn't one of those religious sects based on secret arcana known only unto high priests; broad dissemination of its tenets and the calculations used to justify them was both the means and the message of the movement. Nor, finally, had the Millerites been defrauded. William Miller was no Bernie Madoff, and his followers, unlike Madoff's clients, hadn't been intentionally deceived. They had simply placed their faith in an expert who turned out to be wrong. In that respect, they deserve our sympathy, at least up to a point. As we've seen, all societies function on the basis of distributed expertise, and all of us rely on others in areas where our own knowledge falls short. Still, those of us in free countries choose our leaders, and we have the obligation to do so with care. Our own and our society's fortunes stand or fall on our ability to do so. Witness Millerism: it became a giant, history-making debacle not because Miller himself was wrong, but because so many others were wrong to trust him.

That said, Miller *was* wrong. And he admitted it, too—in some ways, as we'll soon see, more thoroughly and gracefully than most of his followers. Still, he couldn't resist availing himself of a fifth and final Wrong But, one I call the "better safe than sorry" defense. When we employ the near-miss and out-of-left-field defenses, we claim that we were wrong but almost right. When we employ the time-frame defense, we claim that we seem wrong but will be proved right eventually. Miller, for his part, claimed that he had been wrong but that he had made the right mistake. Better to cry wolf and be wrong, he argued, than to remain silent and eaten. "I feel even now more satisfaction in having warned my fellow men than I should feel, were I conscious that I had believed them in danger, and not raised my voice," Miller wrote. "How keen would have been my regret, had I refrained to present what in my soul I believed to be truth, and the result had proved that souls must perish through my neglect!" Having done his level best to spare his fellow believers from mortal danger, Miller declined to express any regret over his error. "I therefore cannot censure myself," he concluded "for having conscientiously performed what I believed to be my duty."*

---

* The most famous defense of the Better Safe Than Sorry excuse was offered by the seventeenth-century philosopher and mathematician Blaise Pascal, in what is now known as Pascal's wager. Pascal pointed out that, if you must be wrong about God, you are much better off believing he exists and being wrong than believing he doesn't exist and being wrong. Thus the wager: even if you think the odds are a gazillion to one against the existence of God, you should still throw your lot in on his side. It's hard to argue with this logic *qua* logic; the wager draws on the same kind of decision theory that is still used today to minimize risk and maximize gain in a wide range of fields. But for most people, it is a profoundly unsatisfactory defense of faith, since a calculated belief seems like no kind of belief at all. Even the very language of the wager seems off: surely, our meditations on the meaning of life, not to mention the fate of our mortal soul, shouldn't sound quite so much like the Preakness. Then there's the bothersome problem that, if an omniscient God did exist, he would surely see straight

. . .

Sometimes, of course, we *do* choose the right mistake. Sometimes other people lead us astray. Sometimes our predictions almost come to pass, sometimes they are derailed by unforeseeable circumstances, and sometimes they really are vindicated by history. In short, none of the excuses we use to account for our errors is intrinsically unfounded. The trouble is, we almost never use these excuses—or rather, their opposite number, the all-but-unheard-of Right Buts—when things go our way. We don't protest that we were right but only by the slimmest of margins, we don't chalk up our rightness to a flukish outside event, and we don't earnestly explain that, however right we look now, we will inevitably be proved wrong in the future. Nor do we accept the Wrong Buts as valid when our adversaries use them. As is so often the case when it comes to error, we wield these defenses in woefully lopsided fashion.

And we also wield them far too often. As I said at the beginning of this book, we are exceptionally bad at saying "I was wrong"—or at least, we are bad at leaving it at that. For most of us, it's tough not to tack that "but" onto *every* admission of error. (Try saying an unadorned "I was wrong"—the full stop at the end, the silence afterward—and you'll see how unfamiliar and uncomfortable it feels.) In part, this reflects our dislike of sitting with our wrongness any longer than necessary, since the "but" helps hasten us away from our errors. But it also reflects our urge to explain everything in the world—an urge that extends, emphatically, to our own mistakes. This desire to account for why we were wrong is not a bad thing. In fact, the frenetic theorizing that occurs in the aftermath of error represents one of the *better* things about being wrong: proof positive that our fallibility drives us to think and rethink, to be creative and to create.

Still, there's a fine line between explaining our mistakes and explain-

---

through these Pascalian calculations. As William James noted, "if we were ourselves in the place of the deity, we should probably take particular pleasure in cutting off believers of this pattern from their infinite reward." Here again, the 'Cuz It's True Constraint holds sway: we are supposed to think we hold our beliefs because they are true, not because we stand to gain by them.

ing them away. Not infrequently, we start out trying to answer the "how wrong?" question in all sincerity and end up taking refuge in the Wrong Buts. Upon retracing our steps to discover where we erred, we find that the path we took still feels both sensible and defensible, and we start making excuses almost despite ourselves. (We've all had the experience of saying, "Look, I'm not trying to justify what happened, I just want to explain it"— only to realize, in very short order, that we are justifying left and right.) Here, too, wrongness reveals its fugitive nature: it's as if, once we can explain a mistake, it ceases to feel like one. Even when we know that we were wrong, we can sometimes go on feeling—and insisting—that we were almost right, or that we were wrong for good reasons, or simply, wishfully, that we weren't actually so wrong after all.

There may be no better demonstration of this conflict between feeling our wrongness and feeling our rightness than William Miller's own response to the Great Disappointment. We know about this response in some detail, because Miller left behind *An Apology and Defense*. The title alone reflects the two impulses I just described, and the contents blend near-complete accountability with wonderfully resolute faith in his faith. "As all men are responsible to the community for the sentiments they may promulgate," Miller wrote, "the public has a right to expect from me, a candid statement in reference to my disappointment in not realizing the Advent of Christ in AD 1843–4, which I had confidently believed." That candid statement is swiftly forthcoming: "For we were certainly disappointed," he continued. "We expected the personal coming of Christ at that time; and now to contend that we were not mistaken, is dishonest. We should never be ashamed to frankly confess all our errors."

True to his word, Miller declined to paper over those errors with any of the elaborate explanations that were so fashionable among some of his followers. "I have no confidence," he confessed, "in any of the new theories that have grown out of that movement, viz., that Christ then came as the Bridegroom, that the door of mercy was closed, that there is no salvation for sinners, that the seventh trumpet then sounded, or that it was a fulfillment of prophecy in any sense." Few other popular leaders—whether political or religious, in our time, in Miller's time, or in any time—have been so thoroughgoing and unvarnished in acknowledging their mistakes.

The most striking part of Miller's *Apology*, however, is not the admission of error but the persistence of belief. In contrast to the grieving and soul-searching recorded by other Millerites, there is no weeping here, no wondering, no dark nights of doubting and despair. For good or ill, William Miller had that rare faith that runs so deep that no amount of adversity—and no amount of counterevidence—could dislodge it. Although he declined to side with those of his former acolytes who immediately began recalculating the date of the Apocalypse, he firmly believed that it was coming, and soon. (In fact, he speculated that God might have planned the delay so that more people would have time to study the Bible and save their souls—the Great Disappointment as a kind of spiritual snooze button.) Undaunted by the events of October 22, he looked around him and perceived that, "The signs of the times thicken on every hand; and the prophetic periods I think must certainly have brought us into the neighborhood of the event." He ends his *Apology* with an exhortation to his readers: "You my brethren, who are called by the name of Christ, will you not examine the Scriptures respecting the nearness of the advent?" For these, he wrote—one hundred and sixty-five years ago—"are emphatically the last days."

11.

Denial and Acceptance

"I should not like to be wrong," said Poirot.
"It is not—how do you say?—my *métier*."
—AGATHA CHRISTIE, *THE MURDER OF ROGER ACKROYD*

On July 29, 1985, Penny Beerntsen and her husband Tom left work early and went to the beach. Their ten-year-old son was playing at a friend's house that day, but their eleven-year-old daughter came with them. The family lived in southeast Wisconsin, and the beach they chose was in a state park on the shores of Lake Michigan. It was a beautiful midsummer day, and toward the afternoon, Penny decided to go for a run. She jogged north along the water for three miles, then turned and headed back in the direction of her husband and daughter. When she was about a mile away from them, she glanced down at her watch; it was ten minutes before four o'clock. When she looked up again, a man was emerging from the sand dunes that rose up behind the beach.

An instant, like an atom, can sometimes split, explosively. Penny knew right away what the man wanted, and, in a flash decision, she made for the lake. She realized too late that the water was only slowing her down; by the time she got back to the shore, the man had caught up with her. When he wrapped his arm in a chokehold around her neck, two thoughts went through her mind. "I remember them very specifically," Penny told me. "The first was that I needed to stay calm. And the second was, 'I need to get a real good look at this guy, so that if I survive this, I can identify him.'"

The man dragged Penny into the sand dunes, told her he had a knife, and demanded that she have sex with him. She resisted, first by talking about her family—her two young children, her husband who would come looking for her soon—and then by fighting back. The two were face to face, and, Penny said, "I remember thinking that I needed to draw some blood, to leave some marks on him, and I tried to scratch his face. But whenever I would reach for him, he would straighten his arms, which were longer than mine. And then he started to strangle me." The man did this three or four times, each time waiting until Penny began to black out and then asking if she was ready to have sex. When she refused and continued to fight back, he became enraged and started slamming her head into the ground, until, finally, she lost consciousness.

When she came to, the man was gone. She was naked and her hands were covered in blood. Her vision was blurred, and her speech was impaired, like that of a stroke victim. She began crawling toward the beach on her knees and wrists, keeping her palms away from the sand in case the blood on them belonged to her assailant and could be used as evidence against him. When she got to the water's edge she called for help. A young couple on the beach spotted her, wrapped her in a towel, and, holding her up between them, started walking her back toward where her family had been.

About an hour had elapsed since Penny had looked at her watch and, in the meantime, her husband had grown concerned. Certain that something was very wrong, Tom Beerntsen called his mother and had her come pick up his daughter, then called the police, and then set off looking for Penny. Partway up the beach he found her—bloody, disoriented, staggering along between strangers. He picked her up and ran back to a waiting ambulance, which rushed her to the nearest emergency room. By the time they got there, the police had already arrived. When the medical staff took a break from stitching cuts and taking x-rays and conducting the rape protocol, a sheriff's deputy asked Penny if she had gotten a look at her attacker. By this time her speech had come back. "Yes," she said, "I sure did."

The word "witness" derives (obviously enough when you think about it, although I for one never had) from the word "wit." Today we mostly use "wit" to describe a sharp sense of humor, but before that it referred to the mind—the meaning we invoke when we talk about keeping our wits about us. And before that, back when the word "witness" came into use, "wit" simply meant "knowledge." We occasionally hear shades of that meaning today, too, which is why doing something unwittingly means doing it unknowingly.

A witness, then, is one who knows. This is an etymological fact, but also, and more profoundly, a psychological one. As we have seen, we take it for granted that we are authorities about events that we ourselves beheld or experienced. Like Wittgenstein's two hands, the things we see with our own two eyes do not seem open to debate. We treat our life experiences, like our mathematical axioms, as givens—not as things that require verification, but as the foundation on which we build the rest of our knowledge of the world.

This use of private experience as a warranty of truth is elevated and formalized in the domain of the law. (And in my own domain. Journalists rely heavily on first-person reports to lend immediacy and legitimacy to their stories: hence all those bystanders providing "eyewitness accounts" on the evening news.) Eyewitness testimony is among the oldest forms of legal evidence, and by far the most compelling. In fact, only within the last twenty years or so has another kind of evidence emerged to challenge its authority: DNA testing.

DNA tests are not infallible. Any process controlled by human beings can be derailed by human error, and genetic testing is no exception. Biological material can be lost, mislabeled, or contaminated; lazy or incompetent technicians can bungle the tests; unscrupulous investigators can skew the results. But, given a system of checks and balances to detect and prevent these problems, DNA testing is the closest thing the legal system has to a silver bullet. It is relatively simple, totally replicable, has a very slim margin of error, and—unlike blood-typing and other earlier scientific evidence—it provides a virtually one-to-one match between the biological sample and the person from whom it came. (This is, after all, the same technology we trust to establish paternity and to ensure safe matches in organ donation.) It has been called, not without cause, a "revelation machine."[*]

The introduction of DNA testing into the judicial system has created something of a standoff between one of the oldest and one of the newest forms of evidence. As judges and juries grow more educated about DNA, the science is starting to prevail, and it seems certain to win out in the long run. But eyewitness testimony remains powerful, and, in those cases where no DNA sample is available, it carries the day. Of all the kinds of evidence presented in court—physical evidence, biological evidence, character evidence, expert testimony, written documents—a confident eyewitness remains the single most powerful predictor of a jury's final verdict. Nowhere is our faith in the accuracy of our own experience more explicit than in the courts, and nowhere is it more consequential.

Yet consider what happens when we actually bear witness. In 1902, a heated argument between two students in a college classroom turned violent. One of the students pulled a gun on the other, the professor leapt in to try to prevent disaster, and, in the ensuing chaos, a shot was fired. This was in the days before school shootings were all too common, but even by those bygone standards, this one was particularly unusual: it was fake. The whole thing was choreographed by one Franz von Liszt, a professor of criminology at the University of Berlin. After the putative gunman was led away, the shaken students were asked to provide individual accounts of what had happened, giving as much detail as possible. Liszt then compared

---

[*] As long as the sample isn't contaminated, the error rate for DNA testing is estimated at roughly one in a million. Under the testing procedures used by the FBI, the odds of two unrelated people matching the same DNA sample are one in 100 billion. Since the total population of the planet is under nine billion, DNA evidence can reasonably be regarded as conclusive.

their accounts to the actual script of the event, which the actors had followed to the letter.

The results of this study were disturbing then, and they remain so today. The best eyewitnesses got more than 25 percent of the facts wrong. The worst erred 80 percent of the time. As another professor who had observed the experiment wrote, "Words were put into the mouths of men who had been silent spectators during the whole short episode; actions were attributed to the chief participants of which not the slightest trace existed; and essential parts of the tragi-comedy were completely eliminated from the memory of a number of witnesses."

In staging the first empirical study of eyewitness accuracy, Liszt made a dramatic contribution to both psychology and criminology. (And to pedagogy, since variations on his experiment are now staples of introductory psychology courses.) His study has been replicated countless times over the last hundred years, with no measurable improvement in eyewitness accuracy. Yet these experiments have had virtually no impact on our intuitive faith in firsthand accounts, and scarcely more on their legal standing.

Still, they underscore an important fact, one that has cropped up in different guises throughout this book: the sheer persuasiveness of first-person experience is not a good indicator of its fidelity to the truth. It's as if we forget, when we are under the spell of that experience, about the other possible meaning of "first person." Taken in a different context—in literature—it means almost the opposite of unassailable authority. It means limited omniscience. It means unreliability. It means subjectivity. It means, quite simply, one person's story.

After Penny Beerntsen was transferred from the emergency room to the main hospital, a police artist came to her bedside and, in the presence of the sheriff, made a drawing based on her description of her assailant. "Immediately after he was finished," she recalled, "I asked if they had a suspect in mind, and I was told yes." The sheriff had nine photos with him, and he placed them on Penny's bedside table and asked if any of the men looked like her attacker. Penny looked over the mug shots and picked out a man named Steven Avery. By the time she went to sleep that night, Avery was in custody.

Penny was discharged from the hospital the next day. Late the following night, she received an obscene phone call from someone who seemed to know the details of the attack—nothing he couldn't have gleaned from the newspaper accounts, but still sufficient to alarm her. The next morning she contacted the sheriff's department to report the call, and the department decided to conduct a live lineup to make sure they had the right man behind bars. "There were eight men on the other side of the one-way glass," Penny said. "I was trying to look at each one carefully, like I had with the pictures, and when I came to Steve I had a real visceral reaction. I started to shake, I could feel the color drain from my face, I could feel the hair stand up on the back of my neck." Penny chose Avery from the lineup. She would identify him once more, on December 9, 1985, when the trial started and she declared in front of the court that she was "absolutely sure" that he was her assailant. The trial lasted one week. At the end of it, Steven Avery was convicted of sexual assault and attempted murder and sentenced to thirty-two years in prison. At the time, he was twenty-three years old.

The trial brought Penny some closure, but, as she tried to return to normal life, she found that she was often angry—not usefully angry, she felt, but unpredictably and uncontrollably so: at her husband, at her kids, at herself. Then, early in 1987, she learned that a nearby university was hosting a talk on restorative justice. An alternative model of criminal justice, restorative justice focuses on the impact of crimes on individuals and communities rather than on the state, and works to bring about accountability, compensation, and reconciliation. Penny attended the talk, and something clicked. She left before it was over and, in the dead of winter, put on a pair of cross-country skis, went to the beach where she'd been assaulted, and had a private reckoning. "I remember saying—just to myself, you know—'Steve, you don't have power over me anymore.' And I remember feeling like a huge weight had lifted." She came back, got trained in restorative justice and victim-offender mediation, and began working in the Wisconsin prisons.

"A lot of my healing took place inside maximum-security prisons," she told me. "The first time I went there, I thought I was going to see a bunch of monsters who somehow were different from the rest of us. But what I discovered was that at some point in our lives we are all victims, and at other points we are all offenders. Even if our offense doesn't land us in prison, we all hurt other people." As a volunteer, Penny served on panels designed to convey to inmates the effects of violent crime on its victims. Her goal wasn't to make the inmates feel remorse for its own sake; it was to help them accept responsibility for their actions and do something meaningful with the rest of their lives. "None of us can take back what we've done in the past," she said. "So the first thing I'd always tell them is that the most meaningful apology is how you live the rest of your life." But if the past can't be changed, it also can't be denied—and so, in panel after panel, Penny talked about the importance of admitting mistakes.

While Penny was working in the prison system, Steven Avery was working to get out of it. After the guilty verdict—he had pled innocent—his family started a Steven Avery Defense Fund. His lawyers challenged the conviction, but it was upheld by the appellate court. The defense appealed that ruling, too, but the Wisconsin Supreme Court declined to hear the case. For a long time after that, it seemed as if Avery had run out of options. In 1985, DNA testing was all but unheard of in the United States; the only physical evidence presented in the original trial was a hair found on Penny's shirt, which the prosecution claimed was microscopically (not genetically) consistent with Avery's. But as the years passed, the forensic use of DNA became more common, and in 1996, Avery successfully petitioned the court to reexamine the biological material in the case. Using technology that would be considered primitive today, a crime lab tested fingernail scrapings taken from Penny in the hospital and found three different samples of DNA. One belonged to her, another was ambiguous, and the last didn't correspond to Penny or Avery. A judge ruled that the findings were inconclusive, and Avery remained behind bars.

The appeals and hearings were hard on Penny, primarily because they kept dragging the assault back into the foreground of her life. From time to time, though, she was also given pause by the sheer doggedness of Avery and his family. "I'd been working with inmates, after all," she recalled, "and I'd seen that at some point most of them just gave up their appeals. So I remember wondering, why is this guy so persistent?" Then, in 2001, she learned that the Wisconsin Innocence Project—part of a national organization that uses DNA evidence to overturn wrongful convictions—had agreed to take Avery's case. Penny's initial reaction was anger: "I just felt like, here we go again, this is never going to end. And if this DNA doesn't exonerate him or is inconclusive, two years down the road is there going to be another hearing?" But she was also shaken. "I remember going through the thought process of: you know, they probably don't take every case that crosses their desk. So why did they agree to take his?"

Individual actors can move quickly—in the fraction of a second it takes to glance down at a watch or rush toward the water. But systems are often unimaginably slow. In the Avery case, there were delays because of legal issues and delays because of technical issues. There were delays because someone was busy, because someone was on vacation, because newer cases took priority. The months stretched into a year, and then into two, and then into two and a half. Meanwhile, Avery sat in jail, and Penny went about her life—raising her kids, running the candy and ice cream shop she and her husband owned, working in the prisons. Then one day, in the spring of 2003, she opened the door to her house and saw her husband pull into the driveway, followed by her lawyer. When Tom Beerntsen stepped out of his car, he was ashen. Penny took one look at him and understood immediately. "Oh my God," she said. "It wasn't him."

Most victims of violent crimes who have misidentified their assailants—a small and terrible fraternity—have tremendous difficulty accepting their mistake. In 1991, a man named Glen Woodall was released from prison in West Virginia after serving four years of two life sentences for two rapes he did not commit. In Woodall's case, the workings of justice had gone particularly awry. It was bad enough that the victims, who had barely been able to see their masked attacker, had been hypnotized to "enhance" their memory, a practice dismissed by most legal professionals as manipulative and unreliable. Far worse, though, was this: the conviction hinged on an act of scientific fraud. The man responsible for blood work at the West

Virginia crime lab had simply faked the results. Woodall was exonerated by DNA testing and awarded a million-dollar settlement by the state—itself a remarkable acknowledgment of error, since people who have been wrongfully convicted seldom receive significant compensation for their ordeal. Coverage of the case filled the local newspapers and airwaves. Discussion of what had gone wrong dominated the state legislature. Multiple investigative committees were formed. Nonetheless, on the day that Woodall left prison, one of the two victims ran up to the van that was transporting him and, weeping and banging on the door, prevented it from being opened. Despite the discredited scientist, the massive public outcry, the legislative hearings, and the DNA, she remained convinced that Woodall was the attacker she had never seen.

This woman's response was unusual in that it was exceptionally public—and, in a sense, exceptionally brave. But enduring belief in the guilt of the exonerated is common among those who have faced similar situations. It's easy to understand why, and impossible not to sympathize. To go through your own terrible ordeal only to learn that you have played a starring role in someone else's terrible ordeal; to see somebody as the perpetrator of an atrocity only to find out that he is, like you, a victim; to assign all of your rage and terror and pain to the wrong person; to have whatever "closure" you may have reached be wrenched open again—who among us is confident that we could face all this with acceptance and grace? Indeed, who could be expected to? It is far more likely that we would face it awkwardly and in agony; far easier to choose, through denial, not to face it at all.

Denial has a bad reputation. We are quick to sneer at it, to regard it as the last, sorry refuge of those who are too immature, insecure, or pigheaded to face the truth. But, as we see in the story of the rape victim who tried to stop Glen Woodall's ride to freedom, denying our mistakes is sometimes an understandable reaction, one that deserves sympathy rather than censure. Denial is not, after all, a response to the facts. It is a response to the feelings those facts evoke—and sometimes, those feelings are simply too much to bear.

This understanding of denial, like so many of our current ideas about human nature, was originally formulated by Freud. Freud defined denial as the refusal to recognize the existence or truth of unwelcome facts, and classified it among the defense mechanisms we unconsciously employ to protect ourselves from anxiety or distress. With various minor emendations, this has been the standard definition ever since. Since 1969, when the Swiss psychiatrist Elisabeth Kübler-Ross included denial in her now-canonic description of the five stages of grief, it has been widely recognized as a normal—even a prototypical—initial response to trauma. Kübler-Ross developed her model based primarily on how people react to being diagnosed with a terminal disease, but it has since been recognized as equally applicable to a wide range of other unwelcome shocks: the death of a loved one, debilitating illness or injury, divorce, loss of one's job, and so on.

If you don't have any direct experience with this kind of trauma-induced denial, it's easy to assume that it is less a deep psychological reaction and more a surface rhetorical reflex: *this can't be happening to me, you must have the wrong person, there's got to be some kind of mistake here.* In reality, though, the denial reaction to trauma is profound and potent. To take a particularly mind-boggling example: at least 20 percent of seriously ill people who are told that they are near death actually *forget* the news within a few days—a form of denial so extreme that it involves not simply rejecting but entirely obliterating unwanted information.

As Kübler-Ross found, this denial reaction is healthy. (At least at first; eventually, of course, the sick must move beyond denial if they want to cope with their illness, and the bereaved must move beyond it to cope with their loss.) It is a natural reaction to fear and grief, and it serves to soften a blow that would otherwise be too sudden and severe to tolerate. When it comes to the kind of denial people express in the face of devastating news, we generally recognize this protective function, and, accordingly, we respond with compassion. But what about the other kind of denial—the intransigent, infuriating, ostrichlike refusal to acknowledge one's mistakes?

Here's the thing: that other kind of denial is *not* another kind of denial. With error as with disaster, we screen out unwelcome information to protect ourselves from discomfort, anxiety, and trauma. Denial is still a defense mechanism, but in this case, it defends us against the experience of being wrong. We've already seen that that experience can provoke intense and often painful emotions. And we've seen, too, that our beliefs are inextricable from our identities, our communities, and our overall sense of security and happiness. No wonder, then, that any major assault on our beliefs represents a trauma in its own right—one that can arouse denial just as swiftly as any other upsetting event.

I should clarify that I'm talking here about the kind of denial of error that is sincere and subconscious, not the kind that is conscious and cynical. We all engage in the conscious version from time to time—for example, when we keep pressing a point in an argument even after we've realized that we are wrong. This is a mild example of conscious denial; we know that we're wrong, but we can't quite summon the wherewithal to face it. But stronger examples abound, most notoriously in the arena of politics, which is to denial what a greenhouse is to an orchid: it grows uncommonly big and colorful there.* When FDR was campaigning for his first term, he made a speech in Pittsburgh in which he promised, like so many candidates before and after, that under no circumstances would he raise taxes. A few years later, securely ensconced in the White House and facing a wildly out-of-balance budget, he realized he would have to bite the bullet and renege on his earlier pledge. When he asked his speechwriter, Sam Rosenman, how he should handle the reversal, Rosenman reportedly replied, "Deny you have ever been in Pittsburgh."

Rosenman's advice was given in jest, if it was given at all. Still, it captures the imperative of denial perfectly: remove yourself as far as possible from any association with error. It also suggests a basic truth about conscious denial, which is that it involves conscious deceit. Likewise, unconscious denial involves unconscious deceit—but in this case, the chief person we deceive is

---

* The sincere form of denial flourishes in politics, too. To quote the historian Barbara Tuchman: "Wooden-headedness, the source of self-deception, is a factor that plays a remarkably large role in government. It consists in assessing a situation in terms of preconceived fixed notions while ignoring or rejecting any contrary signs. It is acting according to wish while not allowing oneself to be deflected by the facts. It is epitomized in a historian's statement about Phillip II of Spain, the surpassing wooden-head of all sovereigns: 'No experience of the failure of his policy could shake his belief in its essential excellence.'"

ourself. That's why sincere denial is also known as self-deception; it entails keeping a truth from ourselves that we cannot bear to know.

How we are able to perpetrate a deception against ourselves is a long-standing mystery of psychology and philosophy. To understand what's so tricky about it, imagine that a couple of your acquaintance, Roger and Anna, are experiencing relationship difficulties: Anna is having an affair, Roger is in complete denial about it. Anna routinely comes home at ten or eleven at night ("working late at the office," she tells Roger) and goes away alone on weekends ("visiting old friends"). She spends inordinate amounts of time on the phone, and, when he accidentally walks in on her, jumps guiltily, changes tone, wraps up the conversation immediately, and reports that she was talking to her mother. When Roger goes to use their computer one day, Anna's email account is open and he glimpses a line of an email (not to him) that reads, "Darling, when can I see you again?"—a question he dismisses as an affectionate inquiry to a friend. You and other well-meaning friends gently try to put him on his guard. But, despite ample evidence that he should be nervous, Roger is certain that Anna would never cheat on him.

From an outside perspective—yours, say—it's easy to see that Roger is in denial about Anna. His faith in her fidelity, while touching, is simply wrong. It's also easy to see how Anna could deceive him (even if she doesn't seem to be doing a very good job of it). Her boyfriend doesn't have any direct access to her inner world, after all, and she is free to keep her real feelings, desires, and actions to herself if she chooses. But it is much harder to understand how Roger could deceive himself. To protect himself from information about Anna's affair, he must know enough to avoid it—enough to not read the rest of that email, not ask too many questions about her weekend, and not surprise her at the office late one night with takeout food and flowers. But if he knows enough about what's going on to carefully avoid it, how can he simultaneously *not* know it? As Sartre wrote, to be self-deceived, "I have to know this truth very precisely in order to hide it from myself the more carefully." To be in denial, then—to not know things that, given the available evidence, we *should* know—we must be both the deceiver *and* the deceived.

How does the human mind manage this? Most observers have suggested that it can do so only by dividing itself. Plato, Aristotle, Augustine, and Freud (among many others) all made sense of denial by proposing separate, semiautonomous, and semi-warring parts of the self: the mind against the will, the mind against the soul, the conscious against the unconscious, the split ego against itself. These descriptions of the self in conflict are fascinating, but in the end, they don't shed much light on the conundrum of self-deception. As the philosopher Sissela Bok has pointed out, the idea of a partitioned self is only a metaphor. It's easy to forget this, because it is an unusually good metaphor—so good that, somewhere along the line, it started to seem like a literal description of how we function. But notwithstanding its hold on our imagination, the idea of a divided self remains an analogy, not an explanation. Our brains are not actually duplex apartments occupied by feuding neighbors, and how we bring about the complicated act of deceiving ourselves remains a mystery.

One of the chief reasons this mystery matters is that it bears on the moral status of denial. If our mind is figuratively divided against itself, with one part oblivious to its errors and the other part actively working to keep things that way, who bears the responsibility for being wrong? Just one part of ourselves—and if so, which one? Or is our whole self somehow to blame, despite being deeply and genuinely in the dark? Or can we not be held responsible for our errors at all when we are in denial? Are we, in those moments, simply victims twice over—once of some hidden part of ourselves, and once of the trauma that made us turn from the truth in the first place?

These questions all add up to the same ethical dilemma: should we or should we not be held accountable for refusing to admit that we are wrong? So far, I've presented the case for compassion in the face of denial, on the grounds that it is a natural reaction to trauma. But it doesn't take much to throw that case into serious question. What about people who deny that the Holocaust occurred? What about former South African President Thabo Mbeki, who, in defiance of the scientific consensus, insisted that AIDS is not caused by HIV and cannot be controlled with antiretroviral medication—a denial that contributed to the deaths of an estimated 320,000 South Africans, the mass orphaning of children, and widespread economic crisis?

More broadly, what happens when the refusal to acknowledge error is so extreme—and the consequences of that refusal so grave—that compassion starts to seem like an inadequate, ingenuous, or even dangerous response?

Peter Neufeld is the codirector and one of the two founders of the Innocence Project, the organization I mentioned earlier that uses DNA evidence to overturn wrongful convictions. In addition to trying to free innocent people from prison, he and his colleagues work to improve criminal justice procedures so that fewer mistaken incarcerations occur in the first place. What with these two mandates, Neufeld spends a lot of time telling people that they are wrong, or that the way they do their work is unjust and dangerously error-prone. As you might imagine, dealing with denial is a de facto part of his job description.

When I met Neufeld in his offices in Lower Manhattan, one of the first things he did was walk me through the many different stages of denial he routinely encounters. He was quick to point out that not everyone goes through all these stages, or even through any of them: many people working in law enforcement support the work of the Innocence Project and cooperate fully in its efforts to free the wrongfully convicted. But some don't, and the depth and scope of their denial can be staggering. That denial begins, Neufeld says, with a resistance to even seeking out the truth: a denial-prone prosecutor will simply oppose the Innocence Project's request for DNA testing—even though prosecutors themselves use genetic tests all the time to get convictions. (While many states grant their prisoners at least some access to DNA testing, the U.S. Supreme Court ruled in 2009 that convicts don't have a guaranteed right to such tests.) As a result, Neufeld and his colleagues spend thousands of hours and hundreds of thousands of dollars simply trying to get permission to conduct DNA tests.

Sooner or later, though, a judge will usually approve the request for genetic testing. You might imagine that if the results exonerate the convict, that would be that—but instead, Neufeld told me, prosecutors will often argue that the testing process must have been flawed and insist on redoing it. When those results also clear the convict, an intractable prosecutor will switch gears, concocting a new theory about how the crime was committed that renders the DNA evidence irrelevant. That strategy seldom impresses judges, and at this stage of the game, most of them will order that the convict be exonerated and freed.

The matter doesn't necessarily end there, though, because judges can't stop prosecutors from deciding to retry a case. "We'll be leaving the courtroom after an exoneration," Neufeld says, "and the prosecutor will say, 'we still think your client is guilty, and we're going to retry him.'" Months go by, "and then finally the prosecutor comes back and says, 'we're agreeing to dismiss the charges, not because your client is innocent, but because with the passage of time it's too difficult to get the witnesses.' Or, 'we don't want to put the victim through the hardship of having to testify again after she got closure.'" Such prosecutors give up the case, but not their conviction that they are correct. To the bitter end and beyond, Neufeld says, "There's a whole category of prosecutors and detectives who still say 'I can't tell you how, I can't give you a logical explanation, but there's no doubt in my mind that your guy is guilty.'"

To show you these stages of denial in action, I need to introduce you to Michael McGrath, the former attorney general of Montana. In 1987, a particularly horrific assault occurred in the city of Billings: late one night, an intruder climbed through the bedroom window of an eight-year-old girl and raped her multiple times. The perpetrator, who left behind semen and pubic hair in the girl's underwear, was unknown to the victim, and she was able to describe him only in very general terms (blond hair, pale skin, acne). Based on that description, an artist generated a sketch, and a police officer mentioned that it looked like someone he'd busted the week before—a kid who had been fighting with another student in the high school parking lot. That kid was named Jimmy Ray Bromgard, and in short order he was arrested, convicted (on the basis of the girl's testimony and a state forensic expert who claimed that Bromgard's hair matched those found at the crime scene), and sentenced to forty years in prison.

In 2000, the Innocence Project took up the case, tested the semen, and determined that it couldn't have come from Bromgard. Enter Attorney General Michael McGrath. McGrath accepted the DNA results, but he proposed a novel explanation for them. Maybe, he suggested, Jimmy Bromgard is a chimera. In Greek mythology, a chimera is a monster of mixed origins: part lion, part snake, part goat. In modern biology, a chimera is the result of the death, in utero, of one of two non-identical twins, and the subsequent blending of two types of DNA in the surviving individual. Chimerism in humans is extremely rare; a total of thirty cases have been reported, anywhere, ever. Nonetheless, McGrath insisted that Bromgard be subjected to more testing, until his blood, semen, and saliva all proved genetically identical, and unrelated to the material found at the crime scene.

Then things got ugly. The Innocence Project sent the pubic hairs to the FBI to be retested, and those didn't match either—even though Montana's own forensic scientist, Arnold Melnikoff, had testified in court that, based on microscopic analysis, the odds of the hairs coming from anyone other than Bromgard were one in 10,000. The DNA mismatch sounded alarm bells throughout Montana, since Melnikoff was no less than head of the state crime lab, and, in that capacity, had testified in hundreds of other cases. When other forensic scientists reviewed his work in the Bromgard case, they concluded that Melnikoff's testimony "contains egregious misstatements not only of the science of forensic hair examination but also of genetics and statistics. . . . His testimony is completely contrary to generally accepted scientific principles." Bromgard was freed after almost fifteen years in prison, and he sued the state of Montana over his wrongful conviction.

As part of that lawsuit, Peter Neufeld deposed Michael McGrath—a deposition that turned out to be an unparalleled case study of denial. (It took place at a law firm on a street called South Last Chance Gully. Dickens couldn't have done better.) In fact, the deposition turns out to be a case study of many of the themes in this book: the rejection of counterevidence, the spinning of wildly elaborate hypotheses to protect our core beliefs, the use of asymmetric standards of logic and reason, and, above all, the prioritization of our own sense of rightness over truth, fairness, honor, and just about any other value you care to name.

McGrath entered the deposition with one unshakable conviction: that Jimmy Ray Bromgard was still the prime suspect in the Billings rape. Maybe, the attorney general proposed, Bromgard raped the little girl but left no bio-logical evidence behind, and the semen and hair in her underwear had come from somewhere else. Like where, asked Neufeld—and here's where things get so disturbing and bizarre that it's worth quoting from the transcript at some length:

McGRATH: The semen could have come from multiple different sources.

NEUFELD: Why don't you tell me what those multiple sources are.

McGRATH: It's potentially possible that [the victim] was sexually ac-tive with somebody else.

The victim, you will recall, was eight years old.

McGRATH: [Or] it's possible that her sister was sexually active with somebody else.

The victim's sister was eleven at the time of the rape.

McGRATH: It's possible that a third person could have been in the room. It's possible. It's possible that the father could have left that stain in a myriad of different ways.

NEUFELD: What other different ways?

McGRATH: He could have masturbated in that room in those un-derwear. . . . The father and the mother could have had sex in that room in that bed, or somehow transferred a stain to those underwear. . . . [The father] could have had a wet dream; could have been sleeping in that bed; he could have had an incestual relationship with one of the daughters.

So we have four possibilities: the eight-year-old was sexually active; her eleven-year-old sister was sexually active while wearing her sister's under-pants; a third party was in the room (even though the victim had testified to a single intruder); or the father had deposited the semen in one perverse way or another. Neufeld, clearly somewhat nonplussed, concedes that all these scenarios are hypothetically possible—but, he says:

NEUFELD: You have no basis to believe that happened here, do you?

McGRATH: Other than I was a prosecutor for eighteen years, and I've been in the criminal justice system for twenty-five years. I think it's a very definite possibility.

NEUFELD: That's the sole source of it?

McGRATH: Which is a pretty significant source.

Moving from the biological evidence to the eyewitness testimony, Neufeld and the attorney general discuss the child's identification of her assailant:

McGRATH: I thought it was quite significant identification testimony.

NEUFELD: You thought that when a victim says on direct examination that, "I was 60 to 65 percent sure," and then when asked by the prosecutor, "Putting aside the percentages, how sure are you that it's Jimmy Ray Bromgard?," and she says, "Not very sure," you consider that to be very powerful ID testimony?

McGRATH: Yes.

I could go on—the deposition runs to 249 pages, most of them sounding much like this—but I won't. If McGrath's testimony weren't so horrifying—if the rape of a child, the reputation of her father, and the freedom of an innocent man weren't on the line—it would verge on the comedic, sheerly by virtue of its absurdity. If there's any saving grace to this kind of extreme denial, it is that, as Neufeld put it, "when other people look at this stuff, they go, 'oh my God, this guy is crazy.'" And they did. Jimmy Ray Bromgard settled his case against the state of Montana for $3.5 million. Michael McGrath moved, unsuccessfully, to have the deposition sealed from the public.

What's scariest about this story is that it isn't particularly unusual. Neufeld told me countless others much like it. There was the crime-lab worker in a rape and murder case who continued to think that Neufeld's client was guilty, even though the DNA had excluded him and implicated another man. "I said, 'What do you mean?'" Neufeld asked. "'What scientific evidence is there that he did it? What *non*-scientific evidence is there that he did it?' And she said, 'I know he did it. When I testified at his trial, I saw murder in his eyes.'" Or take the story of Calvin Johnson, an African-American honors student and star athlete, arrested in 1983 for raping a white woman, a crime he did not commit. When conventional (not genetic) analysis of the pubic hairs recovered from the crime scene showed that they didn't match Johnson's hair, the district attorney in the case proposed that they came not from the perpetrator but from a public restroom or the laundromat where the victim washed her sheets and clothes. That was the moment, Johnson later recalled, when he realized, "He doesn't care about me, about my life. He just wants to get a conviction." In that, he succeeded: Johnson served almost sixteen years of a life sentence before being exonerated by DNA.

These lab workers, prosecutors, and attorneys general are not the victims of the crimes they investigate and prosecute. They haven't been subjected to the trauma of violence and violation, nor to the secondary traumas of the legal and media circuses that so often follow. They are, supposedly, professionals. Moreover, as Neufeld notes, they are professionals who "rely on logic to make a living, who are part of a system that is predicated on the use of evidence and reason to see that justice is done." So, to be blunt: What on earth is their problem?

The most obvious and least sympathy-inducing answer is that their careers are on the line. "Prosecutors' reputations are made on these big cases," Neufeld said, and they can be unmade there as well. But another, less contemptible motive for their denial is that these people, too, are protecting themselves from trauma. "It's very difficult for anyone to admit, 'Okay, yes, I played a role in convicting an innocent man, of depriving him of his liberty, or God forbid, his life,'" Neufeld said. As nightmares go, the one suffered by the prosecutor in a wrongful conviction is nothing compared to the ones suffered by the victim and the wrongfully accused. But it is a nightmare nonetheless, a recipe for sleepless nights and shattered faith in your work, your judgment, your moral worth. Even when our errors are comparatively anodyne, the experience of being wrong tends to challenge our faith that we are basically good, honest, smart, reliable people. Involvement in a wrongful conviction magnifies that problem a thousand-fold, both because the consequence of the error is so grave and because people who have signed on to serve the cause of justice generally see themselves, not unreasonably, as being on the side of the angels.

If anyone ever had cause to believe that she was on the side of the angels, surely it was Penny Beerntsen. In the aftermath of her assault, she summoned the strength not just to rebuild her own life, but to help other people repair their lives as well—and not just any other people, but convicts, including some who easily could have been her attacker. Likewise, if anyone ever had cause to be convinced that she was right, that was Penny, too. From the first moments of her attack, she focused on being able to accurately identify her assailant. Even as he beat and strangled her, she forced herself to memorize his features. Afterward, injured, traumatized, and unable to walk, she crawled to the shore on her wrists to preserve the blood on her hands as evidence.

In a sense, then, Penny Beerntsen was primed for denial. She had survived the kind of trauma that makes it an appropriate and even a necessary reaction. Through her conduct both during and after the assault, she had earned (insofar as any of us ever can) the right to feel righteous, and the right to feel right. When the DNA results exonerated Steven Avery, she easily could have turned her back on them. Like so many people who wind up involved in wrongful convictions, she could have remained unmoved by the evidence. She could have continued to insist on Avery's guilt, and on her own rightness. She could have done all of this. But she didn't.

Maybe it was her personality: conscientious, empathetic, sensitive to injustice. Maybe it was her years of working in the prisons, of learning to see the inmates as people and helping them face their own wrongdoings. Maybe it was the fact that she trusted the science. Probably it was some of all this. At any rate, when Penny Beerntsen's lawyer and her husband broke the news about Steven Avery's innocence, she instantly accepted that she had been wrong. And, just as instantly, she plummeted into one of the darkest periods of her life. "This might sound unbelievable," Penny told me, "but I really feel this way: the day I learned I had identified the wrong person was much worse than the day I was assaulted. My first thought was, 'I don't deserve to live.'"

Penny's sense of horror and responsibility was twofold. The first, obvious, part was that she had helped send a man to prison for eighteen years for a crime he didn't commit. But a second wave of guilt set in later, when she learned the identity of her actual assailant. As happens in roughly 40 percent of wrongful convictions, the DNA results not only exonerated the original suspect but identified the real criminal—in this case, a man named Gregory Allen, who by then was serving time for the rape of another woman. That assault had been exceptionally brutal—it had earned Allen sixty years in prison—and, Penny learned, the authorities suspected him of committing eight to ten other rapes in the years between Penny's attack and Allen's 1996 incarceration. "I thought about those women all the time," Penny told me. "Oh my God, how their lives had been changed because of a mistake I'd made."

In the months and years after Penny acknowledged her error, she would learn a great deal about how it had come about. First there was the fallibility of perception and memory. "Everyone made a big deal about how I had identified Steven three times," she said—once in the photos she was shown in the hospital, once in the live lineup, and once in court. "But I know now that what the memory experts say is true: you get one shot at it. As soon as I picked out a photo, that became my mental image of my rapist. From that moment on, that's the face I was remembering, not the face of the man who attacked me on the beach."

More disturbingly, Penny learned about the many ways the sheriff's department had poorly served her, Avery, and the cause of justice more generally. They had reinforced her photo selection by telling her that Avery was the suspect they'd had in mind. They had coached her to conceal any doubts she might have harbored. (The first time the district attorney asked her how sure she was about the identification, she'd said 90 percent. His reply, according to her: "When you're on the stand, you better say one hundred.") They had admitted conventional hair analysis as evidence in the case, even though the procedure is widely regarded as worthless.*

Most egregiously, though, the sheriff's department had failed to follow up on other leads. One week after Avery was arrested, the local police department had called Penny to tell her they had a different suspect in mind—one who looked a lot like Avery and had been showing increasing signs of violence. The cops had been tailing him for two weeks, but had been too busy on the day of the assault to track his movements. When Penny relayed this information to the sheriff's department, she said, "I was told, 'Don't talk to the police department, it will only confuse you. We'll look into this.' Which I felt was patronizing—like my little female mind couldn't handle the facts." She later learned, from a report by the Wisconsin attorney general on Avery's wrongful conviction, that a police detective had gone to the sheriff to ask if he was considering the additional suspect. The sheriff had replied, "We've got our guy," and declined to investigate the other man. That man was Gregory Allen.

At the time that she learned of Avery's innocence, though, Penny knew almost none of this. She blamed herself, and set about trying to understand how she could have been so wrong about something so important. DNA exonerations tend to be high profile, and Avery's image appeared in the papers and on television almost every day in the weeks after the news broke. "I remember trying to study his face. I would pick up the local paper and look at the picture and even though intellectually I understood, 'this is not the man who hurt you,' on an emotional level I still had that visceral reaction. There was still fear there—I would still shake, the hair on the back of my neck would still stand up—because for so many years, the face I saw in my flashbacks and in my nightmares was his."

Remarkably, Penny didn't let her fear deter her from making contact

---

* In the 1970s, at the request of a federal oversight agency, ninety forensic laboratories analyzed five different hair samples each. On average for the five samples, the analysts correctly matched the hair to its donor 50, 28, 54, 68, and 56 percent of the time. They might as well have flipped coins.

with Avery. Almost immediately after the exoneration, she wrote him a letter, in which she apologized as best as she could for her mistake. "When I
testified in court," she wrote, "I honestly believed you were my assailant. I
was wrong. I cannot ask for, nor do I deserve, your forgiveness. I can only
say to you, in deepest humility, how sorry I am." She also offered to answer,
in person, any questions he or his family might have, a standard step in
victim-offender mediation. In doing so, she made it clear that, this time,
she viewed herself as the offender and Avery as the victim.

Five months later, Penny, Avery, and their respective lawyers met together for the first time outside a criminal court. "I don't think I've ever
been so nervous in my life," she recalled. "I could hear my heart beat. But
when Steve came in the room and I stood up and went over and extended
my hand, he gave me this hearty, hearty handshake." Avery is quiet and
somewhat learning disabled, and Penny did most of the talking. But she
knew he had expressed compassion for her in the past—on the day he was
released from prison, he told the media, "I don't blame the victim; this isn't
her fault"—and she felt that he listened to her with sympathy. When the
meeting ended, she went over to him and asked if she could give him a hug.
Without answering, he swept her into a bear hug, and, she recalled, "I said
to him, so only he could hear me, 'Steve, I'm so sorry.' And he said, 'It's okay,
Penny, it's over.' That was the most grace-filled thing anyone's ever said to
me in my life."

But, of course, it wasn't over. In many ways, Penny was just starting to
come to terms with what had happened. She became friends with the lawyers at the Innocence Project—the people toward whom she had initially
felt so much anger—and began to learn more about cases like her own. Before Avery's exoneration, she said, "I remember watching some cop special
on TV about a wrongful conviction and thinking, 'oh, come on, how often
does that really happen?'" Now, she says, she looks at the system differently.
"I really believe that 99.9 percent of police would never intentionally target
the wrong person, but there can be such a huge amount of tunnel vision."
She knows, because she experienced it herself. "When people would say,
'Couldn't Steven be innocent?,' I would immediately remind myself of all
the evidence that seemed to point to his guilt. I fixated on anything that

seemed to affirm that I'd picked the right person." This is confirmation bias at work, and Penny experienced another form of it as well: ignoring or misconstruing any evidence that challenged her belief in Avery's guilt. At the trial, sixteen separate witnesses had testified that Avery had been at work on the day of the rape, but Penny dismissed their stories as too similar to each other to be believable—an outstanding example of interpreting the evidence against your theory as evidence *for* your theory instead.

As she learned more about the factors that contribute to wrongful convictions, Penny came to understand, intellectually, how her own mistake could have happened. Emotionally, though, she remained tormented by it. She never forgot that Avery had been confined to prison from the ages of twenty-three to forty-one—the prime of anyone's life—and she never stopped feeling enormously, oppressively responsible. Finally, she decided to act on the maxim she had always shared with the inmates: the ultimate apology is how you live the rest of your life. Through her friends at the Innocence Project, she began reaching out to other victims who had misidentified their assailants.

One day, she found herself on the phone with a woman who had just learned that the man imprisoned for raping her was innocent. The woman wasn't in denial, but she was undone by shock and distress. Penny told her that what had happened wasn't her fault—that it was the job of the police, not the victim, to investigate crimes thoroughly and fairly. She reminded the woman that she had done her best under traumatic circumstances. She acknowledged that the woman couldn't undo her error or give the exonerated man back his missing years of freedom, but pointed out that never forgiving herself wouldn't benefit either of them. "And that's when the light dawned," Penny told me. "I suddenly realized, Oh my God, I would never judge this woman the way I judge myself. It helped me, finally, to come to grips with it—with the fact that making a horrible mistake does not make me, or anyone, a horrible person."

The story of Penny Beerntsen and Steven Avery, already a tragic and complicated one, has a terrible coda. In March of 2007, less than four years after he was released from prison, Avery was arrested, tried, and convicted for the 2005 murder of Teresa Halbach, a 25-year-old Wisconsin woman. It is the first and only time in the history of the Innocence Project that an exoneree has gone on to commit a violent crime.

When I first learned of the conviction, I thought I would leave Penny's story out of this book. This was, above all, an emotional reaction: I didn't want to write about the murder, I didn't want anyone close to the victim to have to face additional media coverage, and I didn't want to reduce Halbach's entire life and death to an epilogue in someone else's story. But it was also a political reaction. I believe in the work of the Innocence Project, and I worried that drawing attention to Avery's radically atypical story would bolster the already-widespread conviction that there are no innocent people behind bars.*

In part, though, my reaction was professional. The horrifying plot twist makes Penny's story a difficult and controversial one to tell, and it was tempting to avoid the whole morass. There are, after all, other victims who have misidentified their assailants and faced up to their mistakes—not many, it's true, but some. As a journalist, I couldn't help but recognize that those people's experiences would make better stories—where by "better," I mean, of course, simpler: simpler narratively, and simpler ethically.

But the more I thought about using a different story, the more troubled I became. The world isn't a simple place (narratively or, God knows, ethically) and the prospect of trying to pretend that it is—in order to write a chapter about *denial*—soon became untenably absurd. I knew that part of this chapter was going to be about the potentially insidious attraction, for prosecutors and victims alike, of simple stories (good guys, bad guys, morally satisfying conclusions), and about the way this attraction can lead

---

* Defenders of this position don't deny that a prisoner could be innocent of a specific crime; instead, they challenge the person's overall innocence, his or her moral worth. As they see it, anyone who gets caught in the dragnet of the law must be a bad egg, already or soon to be guilty of *something*, so that society is better off keeping such people locked up—due process and DNA be damned. For a thorough debunking of this argument, I strongly recommend Peter Neufeld, Barry Scheck, and Jim Dwyer's *Actual Innocence.*

us into error, including in situations where lives are on the line. Yet there I was yielding to that same attraction myself, edging quietly away from unwelcome and complicated truths.

In the end, I decided to take my cue from Penny. Even in the midst of her triple nightmare—the assault, the misidentification, the murder—she managed to resist the urge to simplify the complexity around her. "There are people who now firmly believe that the DNA was wrong, that Steve was my assailant," Penny told me. "The sheriff's deputy, the former deputy, tons of people have said it: that I was duped, that the DNA was either fudged or erroneous. A lot of people are having a hard time accepting now that the DNA was accurate." But she herself nurtures no such illusions. She understands the science, and she knows that it not only exonerated Avery but implicated another man—one who looked similar, lived in the same area, was known by the police to be dangerous, and is currently serving time in jail for a DNA-based conviction in another rape.

Nor did Penny believe what some other people were saying: that Avery had been framed for Halbach's murder, that local law enforcement officers were taking revenge for the way the wrongful conviction had made them look bad. Penny knew, from her own trial, that Avery had a history of cruelty to animals, and had once run a neighbor off the road and pointed a rifle at her, backing off only when he realized that her infant daughter was also in the car. During the years Avery was in prison, these facts had almost comforted Penny, serving to assure her that she had accused the right man. After his exoneration, she had somehow elided them. But when he was accused of Halbach's murder, they came back to her, and this time, she didn't look away. Although he was innocent of her rape, Penny knew that Avery was a troubled and a violence-prone man.

For Penny, then, denial was never an option. Or at least, that is how she tells it. And yet, as we have seen, denial is *always* an option, and an attractive one. It serves to shield us from pain, humiliation, guilt, and change—such a basic and forceful imperative that, even at its most egregious, denial is relatively easy to understand. In fact, it is acceptance that is often the greater mystery. If we shake our heads at people like Attorney General Michael McGrath and call him crazy, we shake our heads at people like Penny

Beerntsen with something like awe. True, admiring other people's ability to face their mistakes isn't the same as facing our own. But it is a start. It reminds us that, as seen from the outside, denying error looks irrational, irresponsible, and ugly, while admitting it looks like courage, and like honor, and like grace.

And sometimes, too, it looks extremely hard. For Penny, refusing to resort to denial means living with immensely complicated and contradictory realities: with her suffering but also her error; with Avery's suffering but also his atrocity. She had felt warmly toward him, moved by his ordeal and blessed by his compassion toward her in the face of it. When he was accused of Halbach's murder, she was, she said, "flabbergasted." She wondered how she could have been so wrong yet again, this time about Avery as a person. And she thought, too, about her own uncontrollable anger after the rape, and tried to fathom the kind of rage that might accumulate during almost two decades of wrongful imprisonment. To her already doubled sense of responsibility—for Avery's lost years, for the other women who had suffered at the hands of Gregory Allen—she now had to add a third, of almost inconceivable gravity: "If I had identified the correct person, would Teresa Halbach be alive today?"

As Penny knows, that question is unanswerable. Nobody can say what the course of history would have been if her life and Avery's had never intersected. And she knows, too, that she will have to find a way to live without that answer, and without the answer to many other questions about why the prosecution of her assault went so terribly awry.

This is what makes Penny's story so remarkable: she is able to live both with *and* without the truth. That is exactly what overcoming denial calls on us to do. Sometimes in life we won't know the answers, and sometimes we will know them but not like them. Our minds, no matter how miraculous, are still limited. Our hearts, no matter how generous, can't always keep us from hurting other people. In other words, denial isn't just about refusing to accept the difficult, complicated, messy *external* world. Nor is acceptance just about accepting the facts. It is also, and most importantly, about accepting ourselves.

12.

Heartbreak

You fight your superficiality, your shallowness, so as to try to come at people without unreal expectations, without an overload of bias or hope or arrogance, as untanklike as you can be . . . and yet you never fail to get them wrong. You might as well have the brain of a tank. You get them wrong before you meet them: you get them wrong while you're with them and then you get home to tell somebody else about the meeting and you get them all wrong again. Since the same generally goes for them with you, the whole thing is really a dazzling illusion empty of all perception, an astonishing farce of misperception. And yet what are we to do about this terribly significant business of other people, which gets bled of the significance we think it has and takes on a significance that is ludicrous, so ill equipped are we all to envision one another's interior workings and invisible aims? . . . The fact remains that getting people right is not what living is all about anyway. It's getting them wrong that is living, getting them wrong and wrong and wrong and then, on careful reconsideration, getting them wrong again. That's how we know we are alive: we're wrong.

—PHILLIP ROTH, *AMERICAN PASTORAL*

Raoul Felder is a divorce lawyer. Specifically, he is a celebrity divorce lawyer, with the adjective "celebrity" modifying the man, his clients, and his clients' exes: think Elizabeth Taylor, Martin Scorcese, Mike Tyson, 50 Cent. If you are wronged in love and very rich, very famous, or very both, Felder is your go-to guy.

Probably you should try to get rich, famous, and divorced just to go sit in Felder's waiting room. Back in the pre–9/11 era, when Rudy Giuliani (also a client) was busy cleaning out the triple-X storefronts of Times Square like they were the caves of Tora Bora, Felder stopped by a recently condemned smut shop and scavenged a few items. You can admire one of them in his waiting room: the "Love Tester," a five-foot-tall, Coney Island-worthy contraption that promises to measure your sex appeal on its love-o-meter (zero to uncontrollable). Or you can rest your eyes on another Felder find: a food vending machine from some long-extinct automat of the type that was omnipresent in New York in the 1930s and '40s. This one offers, in art deco lettering, Hot Dishes. Or you can just look at the walls, which are hung with innumerable framed magazine covers featuring Felder himself. "Dr. Estranged Love," reads one. Another—from *Vanity Fair*, appropriately— features the famed lawyer astride a life-sized plastic tiger.

Sitting in Felder's waiting room, surrounded by its peculiar blend of kitsch, irony, self-aggrandizement, and smut, you realize something. It isn't just marriages that come here to die. It's the *idea* of marriage. All of our noble notions about the beauty and durability of love, the romance, the wedding cake, the rings, the vows: all of that is either sent up or taken down by the waiting room's collected campiness. True, every divorce hints at the possibility that our notion of love is suffering from a fatal flaw. Still, not every divorce lawyer turns that fact into a fashion statement. Felder, however, has styled his office as a particularly garish graveyard for the dream of true love. Likewise, he has styled himself as love's particularly over-the-top undertaker—which explains what I was doing in his waiting room. Lacking the fame, the money, and the marriage, I wasn't there to get a divorce. I was there to talk to Felder about why people are so wrong, so often, about love.

Wrongness and love: when I sat down to write this book, I was determined to avoid creating what I thought of as the wrongology slideshow. You know: here we are being wrong at the beach, here we are being wrong in Paris, here's my nephew being wrong in kindergarten. That's why this book isn't built around chapters like "wrongness and science" and "wrongness and politics." Both of those domains (and plenty more) are rich with examples of screwing up. But to approach the subject of error that way seemed to risk compiling an encyclopedia rather than writing a book.

From the beginning, though, wrongness and love struck me as a different story. Specifically, it struck me as *the* story. Of all the things we like to be right about, none is so important to us as being right about other people. This imperative reaches a kind of urgent apotheosis in matters of love. But to understand why, we need to start much earlier—before the age of consent, before our first crush, even before the dawn of complete consciousness. Like our desire for nourishment and security (and, as we'll see, closely related to them), our desire to get other people right begins to develop the moment we enter this world.

Trickily, however, it begins in reverse: as young children, we need other people to get *us* right. Our very survival depends on our caretakers understanding and meeting our needs—first and foremost for physical comfort and safety, and secondarily (but scarcely less crucially) for emotional reassurance and closeness. As we get older, we improve the odds of getting those needs met by turning our emerging intellects to the task of understanding other people. "One of our earliest and most important developmental challenges is to learn to interpret the emotional tone of a moment correctly," observes the analyst Irna Gadd. When we get it right, we are rewarded: our needs are met, our desires are fulfilled, we are folded into the circle of bright, considerate, good-to-be-around beings. Misinterpret, and—depending on our family environment—the negative feedback can be swift. We don't get what we want or need, we are ignored or corrected, we irritate or enrage a parent or sibling or caretaker. In the end, we are left feeling publicly humiliated or privately ashamed—or simply, deeply alone.

It makes sense, then, that we care so much about getting other people right.* And it makes sense, too, that, overall, we are astonishingly good at it. The phone rings and you pick it up and your mother says hi, and you know—from a thousand miles away, with only one syllable to work with—that something is wrong. An expression flickers across a stranger's face and you have a very good chance of correctly deducing his feelings. You and a friend sit through a particularly ludicrous meeting together and carefully avoid catching each other's eyes, because if you did, you would each know so much about what was going on in the other's mind that you would both laugh out loud. These acts of instant interpersonal comprehension are among the most mundane facts of life; we experience them dozens of times a day, mostly without noticing. Yet they are among the most extraordinary of human abilities. To understand someone else, to fathom what's going on in her world, to see into her mind and heart: if at first this is what makes staying alive possible, ultimately, it is what makes life worthwhile.

As that suggests, our need to be "gotten" by other people, so critical in early childhood, doesn't fade as we age. "People frequently walk into my office and they want to know: Are you married? Do you have children? Are you divorced? Are you gay? Are you a New Yorker? Are both of your parents alive?" Gadd says. "What they're really asking is: Will you understand me?" (Take note of this assumption that we need to have shared backgrounds and experiences in order to really understand each other; we'll return to it shortly.) When that kind of comprehension is not forthcoming, we take it hard. Think about how distressing it is to feel misunderstood, and how frustrating it is when someone believes something about you—

---

* Of course, we also want to be right about other people because they supply so many of the rest of our convictions. Recall Avishai Margalit's point that we exist within a web of witnesses, not a web of beliefs. Or recall the Millerites: if we are wrong about our preacher, we risk being wrong about our whole cosmology.

that you're irresponsible or can't handle commitment or don't pull your weight at work—that you think is untrue. Conversely, there are few things more gratifying than the feeling that someone deeply understands us. In fact, as we are about to see, this feeling of being "gotten" is the sine qua non of our most important relationships, and the very hallmark of being in love.

Pity poor Charles Swann. In the first volume of Proust's *In Search of Lost Time*, we watch him fall helplessly, haplessly, stupidly in love with a woman named Odette de Crecy. Bad choice: Odette is greedy, pretentious, vulgar, unpredictable, and cruel. And that's just her personality. There's also her CV to consider: an early stint in a whorehouse, a later career as a courtesan, at least one lesbian affair, multiple orgies, and rumors of anonymous sex in the woodsier parts of the Bois de Boulogne. (If you've never read Proust and this doesn't make you reconsider, I don't know what will.) From the get-go, it's clear to everyone except Charles that she consorts with him for love of his money and status, not for love of the man himself.

But no matter: our hero is besotted. However badly he is treated, he remains, the narrator notes, "always prepared to believe what he hoped for"— that Odette is worthy of his love, and that she cares for him as passionately as he cares for her. He endures not only her vapidity and infidelity, but also the company of her insipid, ignorant, preening friends. And by endures, I mean *endures*: Charles Swann's love affair lasts ten years (and 200 pages), culminating in marriage and the birth of a daughter, before Odette de Crecy leaves him for another man of greater means and Charles comes to his senses. The story ends with him exclaiming, "To think that I wasted years of my life, that I wanted to die, that I felt my deepest love, for a woman who did not appeal to me, who was not my type!"

Being wrong about love: Scarlett O'Hara did it in *Gone with the Wind*, Pip did it in *Great Expectations*, Cécile did it in *Dangerous Liaisons*, I did it in 1999, and at some point or another, you've probably done it, too. One reason this is an enduring theme of literature is that it is, alas, an enduring theme of life.* But another reason is that it hinges on a great (maybe *the* great) psychological story. We are born into this world profoundly alone, our strange, unbounded minds trapped in our ordinary, earthwormy bodies—the condition that led Nietzsche to refer to us, wonderingly, as "hybrids of plants and of ghosts." We spend our lives trying to overcome this fundamental separation, but we can never entirely surmount it. Try as we might, we can't gain direct access to other people's inner worlds—to their thoughts and feelings, their private histories, their secret desires, their deepest beliefs. Nor can we grant them direct access to our own. As wonderfully, joyfully close as we can be to other people, there always remains, between us and them, an enduring margin of mystery. And, just as the gap between us and everything else means that we can be wrong about facts, memories, convictions, and predictions, it means that we can be wrong about one another.

That said, there's something a bit weird about drawing an equivalence among these kinds of wrongness. Our beliefs about human beings somehow feel fundamentally different than our beliefs about, say, God, or the global financial system, or whether it's better to take the Long Island Expressway or the Triborough Bridge in rush hour. The difference begins here: when I try to understand another person, my mind is trying to make sense of another mind. That means I'm forging a belief about something that—at least in some very basic sense—I *am*. However much individual people might differ from one another in certain respects, we all share roughly the same mental structures and aptitudes: a human sensory system and nervous system, a human consciousness and a human unconscious. As a result, we have at our disposal different tools for understanding (and misunderstanding) one another than we have for trying to make sense of other things.

One of these tools, an indispensable one, is communication. Unlike the Triborough Bridge or the global financial system, human beings can just

---

* As the title "Heartbreak" suggests, this chapter is largely about the kind of wrongness involved in becoming disillusioned with or being left by a lover. But there are other and better ways to be wrong about love, too. Consider one of the world's most popular story lines, as featured in (among about a gazillion others) *When Harry Met Sally* and *Pride and Prejudice*: boy meets girl; boy and girl hate each other; boy and girl fall madly in love.

tell each other about ourselves. Sure, words might mark our separation from the absolute essence of things (as Locke argued), but they also bring us closer together. Thanks to language, we can talk about our internal states, and we have a rich and reliable vocabulary with which to do so. Not that this vocabulary, or communication more generally, is *perfectly* reliable: my communications require your interpretations, and, as with other interpretative processes, this one can go awry. Maybe I'm deliberately trying to deceive you. Maybe I'm so lacking in self-awareness that my reports about myself are not to be trusted. Or maybe you and I just have different understandings of linguistically identical statements. To me, "I'm really stressed out" might mean "ask me how I'm doing"; to you, it might mean "please leave me alone." Still, notwithstanding these potential pitfalls, this ability to communicate about our thoughts and feelings is one of the more necessary and remarkable—and definitional—aspects of being human.

Another of our unique tools for understanding one another is extrapolation. That is, we can make inferences about other people's internal states based on familiarity with our own. The specific instances of this kind of extrapolation can seem trivial: "You're worried because your miniature schnauzer went missing? I understand, because I have a dachshund, and I'd be devastated if anything happened to him." Yet even those two sentences imply a shared understanding of attachment, love, anxiety, heartbreak, and hope. For a silly example, that's a decent-sized swath of our emotional landscape. As that suggests, without the ability to extrapolate based on our own emotions and experiences, we would be completely lost when it came to the task of understanding other people. Ask yourself: If we didn't possess such similar minds, would we have any hope of understanding one another?

That is the question the contemporary American philosopher Thomas Nagel pondered in a famous essay called, "What Is It Like to Be a Bat?" The main thrust of Nagel's essay doesn't concern us here (it was about the age-old philosophical conundrum known as the mind-body problem), and you could be forgiven for wondering how *any* of it could possibly apply. Unless you have a thing for vampires, meditations on the nature of bats will seem irrelevant to interpersonal understanding, romantic love, and why we care about being right about other people. As it turns out, though, how Nagel thought about bats can teach us something about how we think about each other.

Nagel began by pointing out that bats are mammals, and as such almost certainly have some kind of conscious awareness, just like dogs and dolphins and you and me. So there must be some inner experience of bathood; it must be "like" something to be a bat, whereas it is presumably not like anything at all to be an amoeba or a sound wave or a stone. But exactly what it is like to be a bat, Nagel argued, we will never know. The difference between their kind of consciousness and ours is simply too vast. (As Nagel put it, "anyone who has spent some time in an enclosed space with an excited bat knows what it is to encounter a fundamentally *alien* form of life.") Just for starters, consider the issue of perception. Bats live in the same world as we do (and sometimes in the same house), yet that world must look unimaginably different when filtered through their sensory system than through our own. We humans can try to imagine the world as rendered by sonar, just as we can try to imagine flying around in the dark, dining on insects, and spending our days sleeping upside down in the attic. As Nagel noted, however, this exercise "tells me only what it would be like for *me* to behave as a bat behaves. But that is not the question. I want to know what it is like for a *bat* to be a bat." Alas, that is something we cannot know. The only way to know what it's like to be a bat is to—duh—be a bat.

This problem does not begin and end with bats. For example, Nagel noted that it is equally beyond his powers to fully grasp the inner world of someone who has been deaf and blind from birth. Nor, presumably, is it possible for that person to fully imagine the inner lives of the rest of us, saturated as they are with sight and sound. This is where reasoning about one another by analogy runs up against its limits: the more different you and I are, the less we will be able to identify with each other, and the more difficult it will be to understand each other. If we can't see ourselves in another person at all—if his beliefs and background and reactions and emotions conflict too radically with our own—we often just withdraw the assumption that he is like us in any important way. That kind of dehumanization generally leads nowhere good. As Nagel suggested in his essay, denying the reality or value of experiences just because we ourselves can't comprehend them verges on—and certainly creates the preconditions for—cruelty.* In fact, this was the point of his essay: our failure to understand another being's inner reality doesn't make that reality any less real, or any less valuable to that being.

When it comes to humans and bats, this failure of comprehension is inevitable. But not so with humans and other humans, as Nagel took pains to point out. However odd your neighbor may be, however unpredictable your boss, however inscrutable your daughter's strangely silent new boyfriend, none of them are "fundamentally alien" life-forms. As human beings, we are all equipped with roughly the same tools for understanding one another: vision, not sonar; ambulation, not flight; human consciousness and not some other kind. The struggle to achieve this understanding, even across very different backgrounds and experiences, forms the heart of many religious and moral teachings, and amounts to some of the most important and honorable work that we can do.

But such work is not always easy. Even if you are nothing like a bat and a great deal like me, there's still an insurmountable difference between the way I understand you and the way I understand myself. I might understand you by *analogy* to myself, but I cannot understand you *as* a self. A self, by definition, can only be understood as such from the inside. That understanding isn't necessarily accurate; as we'll see in the next chapter, self-knowledge, too, can fail us. But it is very different from understanding someone from the outside, which is the only way I can understand other people.

This fundamental difference in perspective has an important practical corollary. Because we know other people only from the outside, we assume

---

* Our very morality is grounded in this paradox of identification. The most basic and universal ethical precept, the golden rule—"do unto others as you would have them do unto you"—suggests that we can treat other people right only by reference to our own likes, dislikes, needs, hopes, and fears. Accordingly, one effective way to undermine the golden rule is to claim that other people aren't like us, and therefore don't share our same needs. Thus apologists for slavery argued that African-Americans were not intellectually advanced enough to benefit from liberty, nor emotionally sensitive enough to grieve the destruction of family and community ties.

they *can* be known from the outside; we think we can understand people reasonably well based solely on their words and deeds. At the same time, because we know ourselves from the inside, we think we can *only* be known from the inside.* Each of us lives, day in and day out, with an intricate internal reality: with the fluctuations of our moods, the complexity of our emotions, the ongoing committee meeting in our brain, the things we think but never say out loud. As a consequence, it's easy to feel that no one can grasp our true nature without access to this rich and dynamic inner world.

One mundane but striking example of this comes from a study conducted by Emily Pronin, the Stanford psychologist, with three of her colleagues. In the study, subjects were given word fragments (such as "_ _ N N E R" and "B _ _ T" and "C H E _ _") and told to complete them with the first word that came to mind. Afterward, they were asked to explain, in writing, what they thought their responses revealed about their interests, motivations, and overall disposition. Then they were given the responses chosen by another participant and asked what that person's answers revealed about his or her character. (For half the participants, the order was reversed: they evaluated someone else's word choices first and then did the task themselves.) As the chart on the next page shows, the discrepancy between these assessments is both gaping and funny. For instance, the same person who characterized her own choice of words as "happenstance" and felt that they revealed nothing about her inferred the following from another person's choices: "I think this girl is on her period . . . I also think that she either feels she or someone else is in a dishonest sexual relationship."

---

* This asymmetry can take a toll on relationships of all sorts. Psychological studies have shown that people in shared living situations generally think they do more chores than their housemates, that people in relationships tend to think they try harder than their partner to resolve conjugal issues, and that each of the colleagues collaborating on a project typically thinks he or she is pulling more weight than everyone else. Granted, sometimes there's a genuine disparity between one person's work and another's. But at least as often, the hour I spent scrubbing the scum from the bathroom tiles (or talking about intimacy issues with my therapist, or drawing up a five-year budget for the project proposal) is just particularly real to me, whereas whatever work you might have done remains an abstraction—at worst unnoticed and at best fleetingly appreciated, but certainly not minutely calibrated in terms of time and energy expended.

ANALYSIS OF OWN COMPLETIONS	ANALYSIS OF OTHER PARTICIPANT'S COMPLETIONS
A. "I'm almost convinced that these are not at all revealing."	A. "He doesn't seem to read too much, since the natural (to me) completion of B _ _ K would be 'book,' **BEAK** seems rather random, and might indicate deliberate unfocus of mind."
B. "I don't agree with these word-stem completions as a measure of my personality."	B. "I get the feeling that whoever did this is pretty vain, but basically a nice guy."
C. "These word completions don't seem to reveal much about me at all . . . random completions."	C. "The person seems goal-oriented and thinks about competitive settings."
D. "Some of the words I wrote seem to be the antithesis of how I view the world. For instance, I hope that I am not always concerned about being **STRONG,** the **BEST,** or a **WINNER.**"	D. "I have a feeling that the individual in question may be tired very often in his or her life. In addition, I think that he or she might be interested in having close personal interactions with someone of the opposite sex. The person may also enjoy playing games."
E. "I don't really think that my word completions reveal that much about me . . . occurred as a result of happenstance."	E. "I think this girl is on her period . . . I also think that she either feels she or someone else is in a dishonest sexual relationship, according to the words **WHORE, SLOT** (similar to slut), **CHEAT** . . ."
F. "I think word completions are limited in this ability [to reveal anything about the subject]."	F. "He seems to focus on competition and winning. This person could be an athlete or someone who is very competitive."
G. "For nearly every word-stem, only one possible solution came to mind."	G. "If I had to guess, I'd say that this subject is a nature-lover type."

Some of the responses from a word-fragment experiment conducted by the psychologists Emily Pronin, Justin Kruger, Kenneth Savitsky, and Lee Ross. Each letter indicates a specific participant: answer "A" in column one was provided by the same person as answer "A" in column two, and so forth.

One thing this study demonstrates is our aptitude, amply illustrated elsewhere in this book, for making sweeping and specific inferences on the basis of extremely scanty information. But it also reveals the striking difference between our sense of how justly we can make those inferences about others and how justly they can be made about us. It's as if we regard other people as psychological crystals, with everything important refracted to the visible surface, while regarding ourselves as psychological icebergs, with the majority of what matters submerged and invisible.

This is, for one thing, a methodological problem: we think we can know other people based on criteria we reject for ourselves. But it is also, and more pressingly, an emotional problem. When Pronin and her colleagues wrote up the word-fragment study for *The Journal of Personality and Social Psychology*, they called their paper, "You Don't Know Me, But I Know You"—a title that sounds at first like a taunt, and then resolves into a lament. If I am only truly knowable from the inside, no one but me can truly know me. This isolation within ourselves can be mitigated (by intimacy with other people), and it can be dodged (by not thinking about it), but it cannot be eradicated. It is, as I stated at the start of this chapter, the fundamental condition of our existence. There is a story (which is so lovely that I hope it's true, although I haven't been able to verify it) that someone once asked the South African writer J. M. Coetzee to name his favorite novel. Coetzee replied that it was Daniel Defoe's *Robinson Crusoe*—because, he explained, the story of a man alone on an island is the only story there is.

Crusoe named his small island Despair, and the choice was apt. Despair—the deep, existential kind—stems from the awareness that we are each marooned on the island of our self, that we will live and die there alone. We are cut off from all the other islands, no matter how numerous and nearby they appear; we cannot swim across the straits, or swap our island for a different one, or even know for sure that the other ones exist outside the spell of our own senses. Certainly we cannot know the particulars of life on those islands—the full inner experience of our mother or our best friend or our sweetheart or our child. There is, between us and them—between us and everything—an irremediable rift.

We have met this rift over and over in this book. It is the same one that keeps us separated from and fated only to speculate about the rest of the universe; the same one whose existence leaves us vulnerable to error. I've said that the sudden recognition of this rift is the essence of the experience of wrongness. But now it turns out that recognizing this rift can also be the essence of the experience of despair. Encountering it, we are reminded that we are alone on our islands, cut off from one another and from the essential truths of the world. Our errors and our existential angst spring from a common source.

Seen in this light, it's no wonder we despise being wrong. It reminds us, however obliquely, of this rift between us and the world: of the limits—*all* the limits—of being human. And it's no wonder, either, that most of us work so assiduously to dodge this rift in our daily lives. We go to our jobs, stop by the bar on our way home, hang out with our friends, raise our kids— because these things are the stuff of life, to be sure, but also because they are strategies for keeping the terror of isolation in check. Søren Kierkeg-aard, that existentialist before there was existentialism, compared us in this respect to those early American pioneers who banged on their pots and pans all night long, hoping to keep the wolves at bay.

Keeping wolves at bay is a start. But of all our ways of dealing with this rift, our favorite by far is the one that promises to eliminate it entirely— to transform our desert island into a tropical paradise, our fundamental separation into ecstatic union. This strategy is our last, best hope for escap-ing the loneliness of existence and giving despair the slip. I am talking, of course, about love.

What happens in Plato's *Symposium* is this: a bunch of guys go to a party, get drunk, and sit around bullshitting about love. (Don't be fooled by today's healthcare symposiums and technology symposiums and workplace-safety symposiums. In ancient Greek, the word specifically referred to a drinking bash.) Of the seven soliloquies supposedly delivered that night, two have achieved immortality. The first is the famous "origins of love" speech that Plato attributes to the great comic playwright Aristophanes. Putting words into Aristophanes' mouth (and tongue into cheek), Plato has him explain that the first human beings were each made up of two men, two women, or a man and a woman—doubled creatures of such extraordinary cleverness and courage that they dared to plot against the gods. Zeus, angered by this hubris, split these original humans in half, leaving them and all their descendents to spend much of their lives searching for their missing counterparts. That is why, Aristophanes tells us, "the precise expression of the [lover's] desire . . . [is] that he should melt into his beloved, and that henceforth they should be one being instead of two." Love, he concludes, "is simply the name for the desire and pursuit of the whole."

If you've read *The Symposium*, you know that Plato plays Aristophanes largely for laughs. As it turns out, though, the playwright's idea of love was not so different from the philosopher's—which is to say, from Platonic love, the other enduring legacy of that imaginary dinner party. These days, we mostly use the term "Platonic love" in contradistinction to the carnal kind. But Plato meant something more than that. To him, the highest form of love was intellectual—the love of one mind for another. That love, he claimed, brought us back in touch with cosmic truths, those we understood intuitively before our souls took on their imperfect, incarnate forms and we were wrenched out of oneness with the universe. For Plato as for Aristophanes, love restored us to a lost wholeness.

Fast-forward 2,500 years. The global population has ballooned from 100 million to 7 billion. Untold numbers of ideas, books, boozy dinner parties, love affairs, languages, religions, cities, cultures, and nations have flourished on and faded from the earth. Ancient Greece lies in ruins. No-fault divorce is turning forty. Lesbian wedding announcements appear in the *New York Times*. And yet, somehow, our understanding of love has changed almost not at all. Across the ages from Plato's day to our own, up and down the cultural registers from lowbrow to high, the notion of love as the union of souls persists. It was alive and well in that Yorkshire manor named Wuthering Heights, where Catherine declared of Heathcliff that, "whatever our souls are made of, his and mine are the same." It wafted out of every radio in America in 1988, when Phil Collins topped the charts singing about "two hearts living in just one mind." It survives, hoary yet somehow holding its own, when we speak of our "soul mates" and our "better halves." And it lives on, too, in our loftiest literary traditions. Here is Shakespeare, half stern, half imploring, in the opening lines of one of his most famous sonnets: *Let me not to the marriage of true minds / Admit impediments.*

The marriage of minds: the insistent message here is that love does not begin with the heart (or points south). It begins from the neck up, with the search for a communion of consciousnesses. We want love to save us from our isolation, from the fundamental and sometimes frightening solitude of being human. Shakespeare continues:

> Love's not Time's fool, though rosy lips and cheeks
> Within his bending sickle's compass come;
> Love alters not with his brief hours and weeks,
> But bears it out even to the edge of doom.

In other words, the body must succumb to Time (with a capital T; the Grim Reaper in street clothes), but Time succumbs to Love. Shakespeare, who didn't want to admit any impediment to true love, didn't want to admit any end to it, either. To solve our existential despair problem, love must endure until, as we say, death do us part. Better still, it must trump even death. Shakespeare saw it halting at "the edge of doom," but others allege that love carries us completely beyond the reach of the reaper. I give you, again, Phil Collins: "together forever till the end of time." Grant us undying love and eternal life, and we'll all be just fine.

All this business about commingled souls, about a communion that predates time and postdates death—this is not just the stuff of sonnets and pop songs. We actually *feel* this way. The couples counselor Harville Hendrix has written that the entire experience of falling in love can be distilled down to just four characteristic emotions. The first, he says, is a feeling of recognition—the thing that makes you say to your newfound love (the quotes are his), "I know we've just met, but somehow I feel as though I already know you." The second is a feeling of timelessness: "Even though we've only been seeing each other for a short time, I can't remember when I didn't know you." The third is a feeling of reunification: "When I'm with you, I no longer feel alone; I feel whole, complete." The fourth is a feeling of necessity: "I can't live without you." This is Aristophanes all over again. We speak of our partners as if they were a long-lost part of our selves—and, accordingly, we are certain that they will be with us forever. We know they will never cheat on us. We know that we will never cheat on them. We say that we have never felt so understood; we say that nothing has ever felt so right.

What is remarkable about this idea of love is how deeply entrenched it is—in our hearts as well as our culture—even as it utterly fails to correspond to reality. We fall out of love left and right. We question whether we were really in it in the first place. We cheat and are cheated on. We leave and are left. We come to believe that we never truly knew our lover after all. We look back on our passion in the chilly dawn of disenchantment—in the after-afterglow—and are so baffled by our conduct that we chalk it up to something like temporary insanity.

In short, we are wrong about love routinely. There's even a case to be made that love *is* error, or at least is likely to lead us there. Sherlock Holmes, that literary embodiment of our much-admired if lately discredited ideal thinker, "never spoke of the softer passions, save with a gibe and a sneer." Love, for him, was "grit in a sensitive instrument" that would inevitably lead into error. In this same spirit, we routinely speak of love as being blind—meaning that it makes *us* blind, unable to perceive the truth about our beloved. Eros and Cupid, the Greek and Roman gods of love, are frequently depicted as blindfolded, and Atē, the Greek goddess of infatuation, is sometimes referred to as the blind goddess. (According to myth, Atē scorned the surface of the earth, preferring to walk around on the top of men's heads: infatuation crushing reason.) Similarly, we speak of finding our lover "intoxicating," of being "besotted" and "drunk on love." And we speak of the "madness of love" (per Socrates) or being "crazy in love" (per Beyoncé). All these locutions suggest that love, like wrongness, is an altered state—and, accordingly, that our representation of our loved one is likely to be at least somewhat askew.

In small doses, this is an accusation most of us can accept. We understand that we are not the most objective judges of our loved ones, since, by definition, loving someone requires relinquishing our claim to objectivity.

"The fellow who kisses the mole on his mistress' neck, the lover who is delighted with the growth on his dove's nose, the father who calls his son's crossed eyes gleaming—what, I ask, can this be except pure folly?" inquires Erasmus. "You agree that this is folly three and four times over; but it is this same folly that makes our friendships and keeps them after they are made." When it comes to our loved ones, being a little wrong in the right direction is the name of the game.

Still, being a little wrong in the right direction is one thing, and being massively wrong in the wrong direction is something else entirely. When we are colossally wrong about love, it feels like nothing we've ever experienced—and yet, structurally, such errors are similar to mistakes about any other major belief. For starters, they often come about for the same kinds of reasons. We are swayed by the conventions and prejudices of our communities, we draw swift and sweeping conclusions based on scanty evidence (there's an armada of psychological research showing that we form strong and often lasting impressions of other people within the first sixty seconds of meeting them—in fact, often within the first *two* seconds), and we are reluctant to change or revise those conclusions once we have formed them.* None of this prevents us from thinking that we are keen observers of our fellow humans, of course. As the seventeenth-century French writer François de La Rochefoucauld observed, "Everyone complains about their memory; no one complains about their judgment."

If the reasons we err in love are familiar, so too is the trajectory those errors follow. When we are in love, we can't imagine that we will ever be out of it—a kind of error-blindness of the heart. If we leave our lover, that illusion often switches: we can't quite believe that we were ever really in it. (Recall Charles Swann, expressing his wonder, sorrow, and scorn that he should have behaved so absurdly for a woman "who did not appeal to him.") If we are the one who is left (and sometimes even when we are the one who

---

* As Thomas Gilovich has pointed out, this is particularly true of negative first impressions, since the negativity serves as a deterrent to seeking out additional evidence. If I think you are an inconsiderate blowhard, I'm likely to avoid your company, thereby limiting my chances of ever coming across any evidence to the contrary.

did the leaving), we reel from the shock of losing the organizing principle of our current life and the template for our future. And we often treat our lovers as we treat our theories, rejecting one that isn't quite working only when we have a new one to replace it. That's part of why so many people have affairs by way of ending their relationships, or rocket into a "rebound relationship" after a difficult breakup.

Structurally, then, errors of love are similar to errors in general. Emotionally, however, they are in a league of their own: astounding, enduring, miserable, incomprehensible. True, certain other large-scale errors can rival or even dwarf them; we've gotten a taste of that in recent chapters. But relatively few of us will undergo, for example, the traumatic and total abandonment of a deeply held religious belief, or the wrongful identification of an assailant. By contrast, the vast majority of us will get our hearts seriously broken, quite possibly more than once. And when we do, we will experience not one but two kinds of wrongness about love. The first is a specific error about a specific person—the loss of faith in a relationship, whether it ended because our partner left us or because we grew disillusioned. But, as I've suggested, we will also find that we were wrong about love in a more general way: that we embraced an account of it that is manifestly implausible. The specific error might be the one that breaks our heart, but the general one noticeably compounds the heartache. A lover who is part of our very soul can't be wrong for us, nor can we be wrong about her. A love that is eternal cannot end. And yet it does, and there we are—mired in a misery made all the more extreme by virtue of being unthinkable.

We can't do much about the specific error—the one in which we turn out to be wrong about (or wronged by) someone we once deeply loved. (In fact, this is a good example of a kind of error we can't eliminate and shouldn't want to.) But what about the general error? Why do we embrace a narrative of love that makes the demise of our relationships that much more shocking, humiliating, and painful? There are, after all, less romantic and more realistic narratives of love available to us: the cool biochemical one, say, where the only heroes are hormones; the implacable evolutionary one, where the communion of souls is supplanted by the transmission of genes; or just a slightly more world-weary one, where love is rewarding and worth it, but nonetheless unpredictable and possibly impermanent—Shakespeare's wandering bark rather than his fixèd mark. Any of these would, at the very least, help brace us for the blow of love's end.

But at what price? Let go of the romantic notion of love, and we also relinquish the protection it purports to offer us against loneliness and despair. Love can't bridge the gap between us and the world if it is, itself, evidence of that gap—just another fallible human theory, about ourselves, about the people we love, about the intimate "us" of a relationship. Whatever the cost, then, we must think of love as wholly removed from the earthly, imperfect realm of theory-making. Like the love of Aristophanes' conjoined couples before they angered the gods, like the love of Adam and Eve before they were exiled from the Garden of Eden, we want our own love to predate and transcend the gap between us and the world.

In some ways, this strategy seems doomed to fail. As anyone who has experienced it knows, heartbreak socks us not only with the temporary loneliness of lost love, but also with the enduring loneliness of being alive. When we are in its grip, the lesser crisis of heartbreak is not terribly distinguishable from the greater crisis of existential despair. And yet there is a method to the madness. The idea of transcendent love can't save us from all suffering, but it *can* save us from perpetual suffering. It makes our moments of disconnect from the universe seem isolated and astounding, rather than ongoing and inevitable. And that, in turn, helps us dismiss such moments as aberrations and forge the necessary amnesia to carry on with our lives.

That should sound familiar, because our overall relationship to error follows the same pattern. As I noted at the beginning of this book, we take rightness to be our steady state, while experiencing error as an isolated incident, no matter how many times it has happened to us. This might be a pragmatic choice—just a strategy for getting through the day with a minimum of hassle—but it is also emotionally alluring. Constantly reckoning with the possibility that we are wrong requires remaining aware of the chasm between us and the universe. It compels us to acknowledge that we can't know with certainty the truth about each other or the world, beyond the certainty that, in the deepest and most final sense, we are alone. That explains why we work so hard to dodge reminders of our fallibility, and why we weather so uneasily even our relatively trivial mistakes. And it helps explain, too, why being wrong about love is so particularly intolerable. Love as the unifier of souls, the conqueror of time and death, transcendent, infallible, enduring: now that's something we can't afford to be wrong about. "If this be error and upon me proved," Shakespeare concludes, "I never writ, nor no man ever loved."*

Lovely, lovely—but turn the page. In the next four sonnets in this series, we learn that Shakespeare (or at least his narrator) has betrayed his love: "What wretched errors hath my heart committed!" Here is perhaps history's greatest chronicler of timeless and transcendent love, yet he knew as well as anyone about its failures. But since he declined, on balance, to "admit impediment," the time has come to return to someone who harbors no such scruples.

The excesses of Raoul Felder's workplace do not stop at the waiting room. His office, size huge, is a tchotchke museum: globes, plaques, baseball caps, photographs of the rich and famous, toys, newspaper clippings, the odd Picasso original. His desk is so big you could land a small personal aircraft on it, yet so cluttered with curios I had trouble finding a spot for my three-inch tape recorder. Nor is his penchant for indiscriminate collection and display limited to décor. In under ninety minutes with me, he quoted Yeats, Kissinger, Newton, Santayana, Churchill (twice), *Casablanca*, T. S. Eliot,

---

* I've been writing about love of other people as a balm for our existential wounds, but love of God fulfills this need as well. Arguably, it fulfills it even better, since healing that wound is the explicit premise and promise of most of the world's major religions. Through God's love—our love of God, God's love for us—we will find both unity and eternal life. Like the language of romantic love, the language of religion reflects this hope. We say that we are one with God; that when we walk with God, we never walk alone; that God will never forsake us; that God has entered our hearts. (Sometimes, in fact, the language of religion explicitly borrows from the language of romance: we speak of Jesus as the bridegroom, of people as married to God or the church.) It follows that (as we've seen) concluding that we were wrong about God can feel like heartbreak. Here, too, what is so devastating is not merely the error itself, nor even the loss of faith, but the vast existential chasm that opens at our feet.

Kipling, and a taxi driver in Berlin. He could charge by the aphorism and still make a killing. But not for him any dulcet quotes about the marriage of true minds, et cetera. Felder's specialty is the dissolution of the bonds of love, and his speech is accordingly acid. You wouldn't go to him for romantic inspiration, and you wouldn't go to him for marriage counseling. But you *would* go to him, as I did, for a vivid picture of what it looks like when our sentimental notion of love collapses.

People walk into his office, Felder says, with two predominant emotions. First, they feel deeply wronged. "If your lumber wasn't delivered on time and you had to sue for it, it's not a great moral cause," Felder says. "But when people come in here, you'd think they were talking about the decline of Western Civilization, or Genghis Kahn pillaging villages, rather than some little thing that happened on the third floor on Park Ave." Second, they feel incredibly righteous. "People come in here saying, 'You can't believe what happened to me; you've never heard anything like this before'"—although Felder has heard it *all* before. "And then," he continues, "you get this story where she's blameless and he's a jerk, or, if it's the guy, he's Prince Charming and she's the Wicked Witch of the West. When you finally get both people in the same room, it's like they're talking about two different marriages. But each person believes passionately in the truth of what they're saying."

In Felder's view, his clients' egos can't tolerate anything short of this absolute rightness. "People don't want to believe they're wrong about anything," he says, "but particularly not about love. For starters, it's supposed to be our wisest decision. It's not; it's probably the stupidest. What other important choice do we make on the basis of hormones? But anyway, it's definitely the most momentous. Given the present state of civil law, marriage is probably the biggest financial deal you'll ever make, and obviously it's one of your biggest personal decisions."

Given those stakes, Felder says, "it's a terrible shock when you have to accept your own fallibility." (This is all the more true, he notes, for his A-list clients, the ones who are accustomed to authority and control. "People believe in their own infallibility in a ratio that's consistent with their power in life," he says. "As you get higher, you get more and more people around you saying you're right, and you get less and less used to being contradicted or being wrong.") Even if you can accept your fallibility in general, the specific crisis of a failed marriage is a stunningly hard pill to swallow. "With divorce, you're losing a validation of yourself. It's like: 'I trusted this girl, I told her my innermost secrets and this was going to be my companion through life and I made a mistake, I'm no judge of people.' That's got to shake you on a pretty deep level."

At least, it has to shake you if you face it. But many of us don't. Instead, as with so many of our mistakes, we opt for denial. Even as our relationship is disintegrating around us, we refuse to accept that our beliefs about it and our dreams for the future were flawed. Our beloved is merely sowing his wild oats, or sorting out her intimacy issues, or suffering from a midlife crisis; sooner or later, we say, she'll come back to her senses, and back to us. Or we accept that the relationship is over—maybe we even end it ourselves— but we deny that we were complicit in its demise. "You're not the person I fell in love with," we allege—as if only our lover's inconstancy, whether literal or figurative, is to blame. "People can't get to the point where they act like vulnerable human beings, so instead they write off their exes," Felder says. "It's not, 'okay, maybe I was wrong here.' It's 'I was right, and she behaved aberrationally.'"

To Felder—admittedly the most jaded of observers—this urge to dodge our own responsibility when love goes wrong is so intense it verges on the murderous. Most people won't articulate it, he says, "but they wish that their ex or their soon-to-be ex would just die. I've had a few of them actually come out and say it: 'Why don't you just go and die somewhere?' But I think they all feel that way. Anger, humiliation, the sense of having been deceived—the veneer of civilization comes off very easily in these situations."

For those of us who get along with our exes just fine, this claim might sound as over-the-top as Felder's furnishings. But even if it characterizes only a particularly extreme subset of cases, the degree of antipathy he describes is troubling. And even if many marriages end amicably (or at least non-homicidally), they still end—close to 40 percent of them, these days.*

---

* The oft-reported 50 percent divorce rate in the United States comes from a faulty calculation method and is not correct. The actual divorce rate is significantly lower—and,

That's a lot of wrongness about love. After all, most of these people started out smitten. As Felder put it, "Nobody in the history of the world ever got married and said, 'This is going to last 30 minutes and then we're going to get divorced.'" So how did all these people go from romance and wedding bells—a veritable idyll of rightness—to concluding that their erstwhile soul mate was wrong for them?

This is not a question divorce lawyers can answer; their job begins when relationships end. To understand why relationships founder in the first place, we need to turn elsewhere—to a caretaker rather than an undertaker of romantic love. We've already met one such person in passing: Harville Hendrix, a marriage counselor of more than thirty years' standing, head of a therapist training and certification program, and author of three bestselling books on relationships. If Felder is a celebrity divorce lawyer, Hendrix is something of a celebrity psychologist; this is the guy Oprah called the "marriage whisperer."

When I spoke with Hendrix, he started out by noting that we initially experience romantic love in a way that would make our poets and pop singers proud. "In the early stages of love, you actually do experience a kind of merger of consciousness," he said. "People who are falling in love seem to kind of fuse together for a while." Unsurprisingly, this fused phase corresponds to the rosiest time in the life of most couples. Eventually, though, some cracks start to appear—both in the feeling of unity and in the couple's contentment. "At some point you differentiate," Hendrix said. "You say, 'I am me and not you, and this is what I think and not that.'" These areas of divergences can be trivial—"'Actually, I don't really enjoy that kind of movie,' or 'I really like butter pecan ice cream better than vanilla, even though it was fun to eat it with you sometimes,'" to borrow Hendrix's examples—or they can be more substantive: different religious beliefs, different ideas about raising children, different sexual desires, different attitudes about money. In a sense, though, the nature of these differences doesn't

---

apparently, declining. That's the good news. The bad news is that it's still high (usually calculated between 36 and 40 percent), and astronomically so for second and third marriages: 60 percent and 73 percent, respectively.

matter that much, Hendrix says. It's their mere existence that presents a problem: "The power struggle that happens after the romantic phase is always triggered by something showing up in the relationship that you had denied or overlooked, or that the other person had withheld."

It's not that either partner had lied, Hendrix said—although people often accuse one another of doing so. Instead, he continued, "There's a kind of collusion in romantic love not to breach reality. So when two different realities finally do enter the picture, there's a real competition for who has the truth. You get a kind of turf war: 'I'm right'; 'no, I'm right.' 'No, I didn't'; 'yes you did.' People get anxious, because suddenly they feel that their vision of the world is under attack. And then they resort to anger, which is the attempt to get someone else to surrender their reality so you don't have to surrender yours."

This is the thing about intimate relationships: we sign up to share our lives with someone else, and sooner or later we realize that we are also living with another person's reality. But we don't particularly *want* to live with our partner's reality. We just want him or her to second our own. The failure to do so constitutes a betrayal of a tacit contract—a commitment to affirm our vision of the world. This is the person whose job is to understand us perfectly and share our worldview down to its last particular (or so we think, consciously or otherwise), and his or her failure to do so is both maddening and threatening.

We also fight so much inside our intimate relationships because it is there that our core convictions are most vulnerable to challenge. Remember the difference between how communities react to internal versus external dissent? When strangers disagree with us, we can choose to ignore, dismiss, or denigrate them, without any immediate or obvious consequences for our own happiness. But when our loved ones disagree with us, we don't have such an easy out. We can feel their realities encroaching on our own, and we have to deal with the discomfort of conflicting theories and the distressing possibility that we might need to be vulnerable, give ground, be mistaken. Of course, we can ignore, dismiss, or denigrate our loved ones, too—and many people do—but the result is miserable for everyone involved.

The other and better option, Hendrix says, is to accept our partner's reality alongside our own. "People have to learn to listen and listen and listen and listen until they finally get it that their partner has their own inner world—that you like apples and your partner likes oranges and that it's okay to like oranges. One of my axioms is that if you want to be in a relationship, you have to get it that you live with another person. That person isn't you. She's not merged with you. She's not your picture of who she is. She doesn't live inside your mind. She doesn't know what you're thinking, and you don't know what she's thinking. So you have to back off and move from reactivity to curiosity. You have to ask questions. You have to listen."

That sounds pretty basic, but it is harder to pull off than you might think. After I talked to Hendrix, I shared some of his remarks with a good friend who was going through a difficult time with his girlfriend. He wrote back, gratefully and wryly, to say that he found the passage comforting—because he felt it justified his own position in his relationship. "Hearing him say that there are two sides to every story makes you say, 'if only my partner realized there are two sides to every story . . .'—a statement to which the conclusion is something like, 'then she would realize that I'm right.'" My friend understood, of course, that Hendrix's advice applied to him, too. Still, he said, he couldn't help but feel like: wow, my girlfriend really needs to read this.

Well, surprise, surprise. Our attachment to our own sense of rightness runs deep, and our capacity to protect it from assault is cunning and fierce. It is hard, excruciatingly hard, to let go of the conviction that our own ideas, attitudes, and ways of living are the best ones. And yet, ironically, it's mainly relinquishing this attachment to rightness that is difficult and uncomfortable—not, generally speaking, what happens afterward. This provides a crucial clue about the origins of our desire to be right. It isn't that we care so fiercely about the substance of our claims. It is that we care about feeling affirmed, respected, and loved.

The conflation of these things—wanting to be right with wanting to be valued—helps explain why disagreements within intimate relationships can feel not just like betrayal, but like rejection. That's one reason why silly squabbles over the dishes sometimes blow up into epic battles about whether our partner listens to us, understands us, and cares for us. The moral here is obvious: we can learn to live with disagreement and error as long as we feel esteemed and loved. That conclusion has suggested itself over and over throughout this book. We saw it in the deepest cognitive sense in our discussion of inductive reasoning, where it became clear that getting things wrong doesn't mean that something is wrong with us. And we saw it in the deepest emotional sense in the chapter on denial and acceptance, when Penny Beerntsen realized that making a horrible mistake did not make her—and does not make anyone—a horrible person.

So we should be able to be wrong from time to time, and be at peace with other people's occasional wrongness, and still love and be loved. That's so basic as to be banal, and yet it runs counter to our prevailing model of romantic love. There is no room for divergence, disagreement, or error in the starry-eyed, soul-mate version of love articulated by Aristophanes et al. To accommodate those eventualities—and we had better accommodate them, since we can be damn sure they are coming—we need a more capacious model of love. In this model, love is not predicated on sharing each other's world as we might share a soul. It is predicated, instead, on sharing it as we might share a story.

This analogy is not accidental. What is true of a story is true of love: for either one to work, you'd better be good at talking and good at listening. Likewise, if stories only succeed when we consent to suspend disbelief, relationships require of us something similar: the ability to let go of our own worldview long enough to be intrigued and moved by someone else's. This is storybook love in a whole different sense of the phrase. It is not about living idyllically in our similarities, but about living peacefully and pleasurably in our differences. It is not bestowed from beyond the normal human realm but struggled for and gained, slowly and with effort. And it is not about unchanging love. It is about letting love change us.

13.

Transformation

> It is all too common for caterpillars to become butterflies
> and then maintain that in their youth they had been little butterflies.
> —G. E. VAILLANT, *ADAPTATION TO LIFE*

On April 4, 1968, the day that Martin Luther King Jr., was killed, Claiborne Paul Ellis threw a party. At the time, Ellis owned and operated a gas station in Durham, North Carolina—and, on the side, ran the Durham branch of the Ku Klux Klan. When the local radio station announced the assassination, he let out a whoop and began calling his fellow Klansmen, inviting them over to celebrate King's death. "We just had a real party at the service station," he would later tell the famed journalist Studs Terkel, "really rejoicin' 'cause that sonofabitch was dead."

C. P. Ellis, as everyone called him, grew up poor and uneducated in North Carolina at a time when white supremacy was rampant there. By the 1960s, there were 112 Klan chapters in the state, which together boasted some eight or nine thousand members; according to federal investigators and the Anti-Defamation League, it was the most active and best-run branch of the KKK in the nation. The state's future and famously racist senator, Jesse Helms, was then providing weekly news commentaries on TV and radio stations in Raleigh—platforms he routinely used to denounce Martin Luther King and the civil rights movement as hell-bent on the destruction of America, and to expound on the "purely scientific" evidence that black people were inferior to whites.

For Ellis—whose father had been abusive and alcoholic, who had dropped out of school in the eighth grade, who married at seventeen, who worked every day of his life yet could barely afford to clothe his three children, the last of them born blind and developmentally disabled—white supremacy made a difficult existence a little more tolerable. The Klan gave Ellis an explanation for why his life was so hard (because of black people), and it gave him a community. He thrived within it and quickly began rising through its ranks, culminating in his appointment as Exalted Cyclops—i.e., head honcho—of the Durham Klavern. Pretty soon, the white power structure in town knew who Ellis was and began working with him, albeit behind closed doors. (As Ellis told Terkel, "councilmen would call me up: 'The Blacks are comin' up tonight and makin' outrageous demands. How about some of you people showin' up and have a little balance?'") Thanks to the Klan, and for the first time he could remember, Ellis was enjoying some measure of confidence, respect, and power.

Then something happened: the course of C. P. Ellis's life intersected, in a small but significant way, with the course of history. In 1970, the federal government funneled $75 million to North Carolina to desegregate its schools. That money should have been unnecessary—sixteen years earlier, the Supreme Court had declared, in *Brown v. Board of Education*, that school segregation was unconstitutional—but the state's schools were still a legal, racial, and educational disaster. The federal funds were divvied up, and $80,000 was earmarked for a series of workshops to persuade Durham's citizens to cooperate in integration.

For the organizers of those workshops, the first order of business was to identify the city's most important leaders and convince them to participate.

One of the people charged with doing so was a man named Joe Becton, at the time the director of the Durham Human Relations Commission. Becton realized that the city's poor, white, anti-integration citizens could derail the process if they weren't invited to participate, and he decided that the best person to represent them was the leader of the local KKK. Ellis's initial response to the invitation was unequivocal: "I don't intend to associate with a bunch of niggers." But Becton kept after him—insisting, in essence, that Ellis's constituents needed a spokesperson—and eventually Ellis gave in.

Meanwhile, across town, the organizers were recruiting another community leader, an African-American woman named Ann Atwater. If Ellis was to be the spokesperson for some of Durham's most impoverished and disenfranchised white citizens, Atwater would represent its most impoverished and disenfranchised blacks. Atwater's life, like Ellis's, had been hard; she had her first child at sixteen, to a husband who left her soon after, and her work as a nanny and housecleaner never brought in enough income to lift her and her family out of poverty. Like Ellis, she was angry about her plight, and, like him, she poured that anger into activism—organizing housing protests against unscrupulous landlords, educating welfare recipients about their rights, planning sit-ins and rallies to protest racial and economic injustice, and, in general, serving as the de facto mayor of Hayti, the poor black neighborhood of Durham.

Ellis had crossed paths with Atwater before the workshops and had not been favorably impressed. Here he is describing his feelings about her to Studs Terkel: "How I hated—pardon the expression, I don't use it now—how I just hated that black nigger. Big, fat, heavy woman. She'd pull about eight demonstrations, and first thing you know they had two, three blacks at the checkout counter." Predictably, their encounter at the first meeting to plan the integration workshops did not go well. According to the journalist Osha Davidson, who chronicled the relationship between C. P. Ellis and Ann Atwater in his 1996 book *Best of Enemies*, Ellis got the ball rolling by losing his temper over the very premise of the workshops: that racism was a problem in the schools. "If we didn't have niggers in the schools, we wouldn't *have* any problems," he shouted. "The problem here today is *niggers*." Atwater, never a particularly retiring soul herself, responded in kind: "The problem is that we have stupid white crackers like C. P. Ellis in Durham!"

It was not an auspicious beginning—but it was, at least, an informative one. Bill Riddick, the man charged with running the workshops, saw immediately that Ellis and Atwater were the two people in the room with the power to either salvage or sabotage his efforts, and he decided that his most pressing task was to get the two of them to work together. Not being a man to do things by half measures, Riddick asked them to co-chair the desegregation workshops.

Across the board, the initial reaction was horror. The African-American community and its allies were outraged: Who in his right mind would invite a KKK leader to chair a committee on desegregation? Ellis, meanwhile, was almost equally appalled. As he later told Davidson, his first thought was, "ain't no way I can work with that gal!" Still, his resistance was tempered by two factors. The first was that the Klan had accustomed him to positions of leadership, and the idea of playing a role in a larger, city-wide process appealed to him. The second and more surprising factor was that Ellis had privately accepted that segregation was a lost cause. He knew about the Supreme Court decision, he had seen what had happened in other states, and he had concluded that the Klan was powerless to stop this particular train in its tracks. There wasn't much he could do, he decided, except (in Davidson's words), "help make desegregation less painful for white children"—including his own. To do that, he would need to accept Bill Riddick's invitation. When he learned that Ann Atwater had said yes, he followed suit.

Like the first planning meeting, the first meeting of the committee co-chairs was disastrous. It took place in a café in downtown Durham, and Ellis spent much of it pacing around the restaurant, unwilling to sit down in a public establishment with black people. When he finally did take a seat, he refused to talk to Atwater directly, speaking instead through Riddick, who'd come along to facilitate the meeting. When Atwater, Ellis, and Riddick parted ways afterward, it was deeply unclear to all three of them how the supposed committee co-chairs would ever work together.

Then, a few nights later, the phone rang in Ellis's apartment. "You keep working with those niggers and you gonna get yourself shot," the person on the other end of the line said before hanging up. It wasn't the first nasty phone call Ellis had received since becoming involved with the desegregation committee; after he had agreed to serve as co-chair, people had called up accusing him of being a race traitor and asking him "what the fuck you doing working with niggers?" But it was the first explicit death threat, and, after getting it, Ellis made a decision. Instead of putting the phone back in its cradle, he called Atwater and said he wanted to try to make the program work.

Shortly after that, Ellis and Atwater found themselves alone in an auditorium where one of the workshops had just ended. The two of them, not normally given to intimate conversation, somehow started talking about their own children's educational experiences. As it happened, Ellis's son and Atwater's daughter both attended Durham's Hillside High, the most racially and economically plagued school in the district. As Atwater described her concerns as a parent—the difficulty of convincing her children that being poorer than their classmates didn't mean that they were lesser; the humiliation and pain of not being able to provide for them as well as she wanted to; the struggle to keep them from feeling ashamed of their background—Ellis felt a jolt of recognition. Atwater's struggles as a parent were his struggles, too. To both Atwater's shock and his own, he began to cry: for himself and his children, but also—astonishingly—for her children, too, and for Atwater herself.

Ellis later told Studs Terkel that in that moment in the auditorium, his relationship to Atwater changed—to Atwater and, by extension, to everything. For the first time, he looked at her and saw another human being. "I began to see, here we are, two people from the far ends of the fence, havin' identical problems, except her bein' black and me bein' white," he recalled. "From that moment on, I tell ya, that gal and I worked together good. I begin to love the girl, really."

When Anita Wilson started to question her faith in God, her life got a lot more miserable before it got better. When astronomers started discovering inconsistencies in Aristotelian theory, their understanding of the universe got a lot more confusing before it got clearer. When you redo your kitchen top to bottom—from the wiring in the walls down to the crud under the sink—things look a lot messier before they look nicer. For C. P. Ellis, life didn't get better when he first started questioning his racial ideology. It got messy, confusing, and miserable. He had nightmares in which his father, a Klansman in his own time, was alive again and walking toward him, yet seemed unable to recognize him. When the nightmares didn't wake him, the death threats did. Worse still, his children, like him, became the objects of threats and taunts—a particularly painful consequence, since his children were the reason Ellis had gotten involved in the workshops in the first place.

But the transformation that was taking place inside Ellis now felt as inexorable as the larger societal changes that had made integration seem inevitable. As a kid from the wrong side of the tracks, Ellis had always been sensitive to poverty, and even before his experience with Atwater, he had registered, reluctantly, the economic sufferings of Durham's African-Americans. "I'd look at a black person walkin' down the street," Ellis told Terkel, "and the guy'd have ragged shoes or his clothes would be worn. That began to do somethin' to me inside."

The workshops turned that faint whisper from Ellis's conscience into a steady series of questions, and then into disconcerting answers. Black people were not the problem, he realized: not his problem, not Durham's problem, not America's problem. For the most part, the African-Americans he met during the workshops lived in substandard housing, sent their kids to substandard schools, and worked substandard jobs (often two or three of them at a time) for substandard pay, if they were lucky enough to work at all. In other words, they were like him, with one crucial difference: *he* was *their* problem. Davidson put it well: "What, [Ellis] wondered, had the Klan actually accomplished for white working people with the endless meetings and bitter fights against desegregation? *Not a damned thing*, he thought. All it had done was to make a miserable existence a little more miserable for poor and uneducated blacks."

Before the series of integration workshops was over, Ellis went to the local Ku Klux Klan chapter and turned in his keys. Beginning to end, the workshops had lasted only ten days. From the moment Joe Becton first invited him to participate to the moment Ellis found himself standing up to speak at the closing ceremony, only a handful of weeks had elapsed. It was the merest fraction of his forty-four years, a stunningly small amount of time in which to turn around an entire life. And yet, he told the assembled crowd, "Something . . . has happened to me." He paused a long time before continuing. "I think it's for the best." A lot of people, Ellis said, had told him that his participation in the program had cost him his standing among conservative whites—the power brokers of his community, and for that matter of the country. "That may be true," Ellis acknowledged. "But I have done what I thought was right."

C. P. Ellis died in 2005. From shortly after he left the Klan in 1970 until 1994, he worked as an organizer for the International Union of Operating Engineers. After he retired, he was asked about his greatest professional accomplishment. Without hesitating, he declared that it had been helping forty low-income African-American women negotiate the right to take Martin Luther King Day as a paid holiday—the first contract in the city of Durham to honor the great civil rights leader's memory.

The story of C. P. Ellis, unique in its details, is familiar in its broad contours. It is a classic conversion story, and conversion stories are one of the classic Western narratives about the self. Think of Saul (later Paul), the zealous Pharisee and tormenter of Christians, finding God in a bolt of lightning on the road to Damascus. Or think of Augustine, the one-time Manichean—the Gnostic religion that was, at the time, one of the world's most important faiths—who committed himself to Christianity after hearing a voice in his garden commanding him to read the Bible. What makes conversion stories distinctive in the annals of wrongness is that they don't just involve repudiating a past belief in order to believe something else. Instead, they involve a wholesale change in identity. In these stories, the experience of being wrong challenges and transforms our very sense of self.

I've argued throughout this book that error in general startles, troubles, and sometimes delights us by showing us that the world isn't as we imagined it to be. But the errors featured in conversion stories show us that we aren't always as we imagine *ourselves* to be, either. In the abstract, we all understand that this can happen—that the self, like the world, is perfectly capable of surprising us. But when it comes to our own notably non-abstract selves, we tend to operate under the assumption that we know who we are, and that we will be the same person tomorrow as we are today. One of the most formidable powers of wrongness is to challenge this assumption. Because it can entail renouncing central aspects of the person we always thought we were and becoming someone we never imagined we would be, the experience of error shows us our own self as both occluded and in flux. As we'll see, sometimes we welcome this vision of selfhood and sometimes we reject it—but either way, much of error's emotional force comes from its capacity to unsettle our idea of who we are.

That capacity is particularly evident in the story of C. P. Ellis, but to some extent all errors—even trifling ones—have the potential to disrupt our sense of self. For instance, in the course of working on this book, a stranger who had gotten word of its subject matter wrote to tell me about an exceedingly twenty-first-century bet he had lost. It concerned, of all things, the number of carbohydrates in a jar of pickles. Now, this bet is notable primarily for its triviality; I could have stared at my computer for a very long time before generating a comparably absurd and inconsequential instance of error. Nonetheless, the carbohydrate issue managed to become contentious—enough so that a debate ensued and a wager was placed; enough so that, years later, the loser of that wager vividly remembered his error.

The pickle-jar man is named Jonathan, and he turned out to have fairly keen insight into why such a silly quarrel stung at the time, and why that sting had so much staying power. "I wasn't attached to the conclusion," he explained, "only to the quality of being able to accurately recall information, and perhaps to the quality of being a person who knows information." In other words, this entirely insignificant issue managed to implicate both Jonathan's memory and his intelligence—two aspects of our identity we all prize. These, mind you, were the stakes in a confrontation over an unimportant matter of fact, not over a principle or a worldview. Jonathan didn't spend weeks or months or years reasoning his way toward his erroneous belief about pickles. Nor did he learn it from his family and community, or derive it from any deep-seated convictions. He just read the label wrong. Nonetheless, his mistake sent a tremor—however slight and short-lived— through his sense of who he was.

This is the claim I made back in Chapter One: our errors represent a moment of alienation from ourselves. Obviously, though, some errors precipitate an alienation more extreme and enduring than others. To go from being a Grand Cyclops of the Ku Klux Klan to a labor organizer working with African-American union members is to alter almost beyond recognition how you and others perceive yourself. We've passed near the borders of this terrain before. I have talked elsewhere about the relationship between belief and identity, and we've seen people grapple with the impact of their errors on their sense of who they are—from Abdul Rahman's conversion to Christianity to Anita Wilson's "intense mourning of identity."

If changing our minds about certain overarching beliefs—beliefs about faith, family, politics, and so forth—can significantly upset our sense of self, so can changing our minds about our own minds. In fact, this is the most obvious way the experience of being wrong can affect our identity: we can conclude that we were mistaken about who we thought we were. After all, our sense of self, like our sense of everything else in the world, is comprised of a bunch of beliefs—and, like all beliefs, these can be in error. All of us have held ideas about ourselves that have either collapsed abruptly or fallen by the wayside over time. We thought we didn't want kids, we thought we'd grow up to be a doctor, we thought we couldn't be happy living in L.A., we thought we'd never succumb to depression or develop an addiction or begin an affair. For all of us, our own private history—like the history of science, like the history of humankind—is littered with discarded theories.

To get a sense of how easily we can be wrong about ourselves, consider the phenomenon of buyer's remorse. In essence, buyer's remorse is our failure to accurately predict our own needs, desires, beliefs, and emotions— not thirty years hence about, say, the most contested political issue of our time, but three days hence about, say, orange suede cowboy boots. We generally reserve the term "buyer's remorse" for literal acts of consumption, but its basic trajectory—crave something; acquire it; regret it—applies far more broadly. We can have gastrointestinal buyer's remorse (as when that lactose-intolerant friend decides to order a milkshake); libidinal buyer's remorse (as in the morning after an ill-advised one-night stand); romantic buyer's remorse (wherein you surgically remove the "Amy + Patrick" tattoo from your shoulder); and ideological buyer's remorse (about what you buy into, rather than what you buy).

If we only experienced buyer's remorse about impulsive decisions, it would not bear very deeply on wrongness. The issue at hand wouldn't be fallibility so much as impetuousness—a failure to check in with ourselves before taking action. In reality, though, we are just as likely (if not more so) to regret choices that we deliberated over at great length. The problem in buyer's remorse, then, isn't that we don't ask ourselves the right questions about what we'll want in the future. The problem is that we don't know ourselves well enough, or remain static for long enough, to consistently come up with the right answer.

This problem isn't limited to the future—to our aptitude (or lack thereof) for forecasting our emotions and convictions. As we've seen, we don't always accurately recall what we felt or believed in the past either. What's more, sometimes we can't even accurately survey our internal landscape in the present. That's why blind Hannah could be wrong about whether she could see, and why a bunch of shoppers could be wrong about why they liked a particular pair of pantyhose. Whether we are reflecting on our past, contemplating our present, or predicting our future, our understanding of our self can turn out to be in error.

Like wrongness itself, this idea that we can misunderstand ourselves arouses deeply conflicting feelings. Though we all accept in the abstract that we don't know ourselves perfectly, we reliably resist the suggestion that we are wrong right now about some specific aspect of our self-understanding. And with reason. I have argued that error springs from a gap between our mental representation of something and the thing itself. But what happens when that something is us? To agree that we can be wrong about ourselves, we must accept the perplexing proposition that there is a gap between what is being represented (our mind) and what is doing the representing (also our mind).*

In many ways, we *do* accept that there are things the mind doesn't know about itself. Thanks to Freud, we now call this domain of obscurity the unconscious, but we've known about it since long before his time. Augustine (who, as the subject of his own conversion experience, had reason to wonder how it is possible to get ourselves wrong) grappled with the problem of imperfect self-knowledge with characteristic insight. The mind, he wrote, "is a vast, immeasurable sanctuary. Who can plumb its depths?" Not him, he admitted—but, he realized, that suggested a strange paradox. "Although it is part of my nature, I cannot understand all that I am. This means, then, that the mind is too narrow to contain itself entirely. But where is that part of it which it does not itself contain? Is it somewhere outside itself and not within it? How, then, can it be part of it, if it is not contained in it?"

The brain is wider than the sky, wrote Emily Dickinson, that other great philosopher-saint of selfhood. But, as Augustine observed, it is also wider than *itself*. We exceed our own boundaries; we are more and other than we know ourselves to be. This abundance and mysteriousness, this overflowing potential for who-knows-what—these are some of the most thrilling and necessary qualities of the self. Still, there's no question that they can also be frightening. If it is hard to accept inexplicability and unpredictability in the world around us, it can be even harder to accept those elements within us. Identifying and understanding the causes of our own behavior, knowing and accounting for who we are, and predicting how we will think, feel, and act in the future are matters of real urgency to us. We want to be right about

---

* Sometimes, of course, there *isn't* a gap between our self-knowledge and our self. If you believe that you are depressed, you are depressed; if you believe that you feel good, you feel good. Likewise, if you believe that you're in love, you're in love—even if, like Charles Swann, you later come to regard that belief as madness. After all, what other, better test for depression or happiness or infatuation could there be? Unlike in external matters (whether the breeze is hot or cold, whether the meeting is Tuesday or Wednesday), there is sometimes no truth about the self beyond the one we create. In these cases, who we think we are is, for all intents and purposes, who we are.

ourselves for the same reason we want to be right about the world: because it enables us to feel grounded, confident, safe—even sane.

This need to be right about ourselves—past, present, and future—is what drives our yearning for perfect self-knowledge. And it also drives our yearning for something else: perfect self-consistency. As with complete self-knowledge, we know, in theory, that an unchanging self is not part of the bargain of being human. In fact, sometimes we enthusiastically embrace our mutability. Witness the self-help section of any bookstore, where positive change is promised in glorious abundance. Or head to a different aisle and check out the memoirs, many of which are, in essence, contemporary conversion narratives—accounts of sweeping, identity-altering wrongness. The gang member turned youth pastor, the druggy turned yogi, the captain of industry turned stay-at-home dad: these are the literary descendents (albeit in some cases very distant ones) of Augustine's *Confessions*. Similarly, if you leave the bookstore and turn on the TV, you can watch just about any facet of someone's life—physique, fashion, family dynamics—undergo a dramatic conversion courtesy of a reality series. It's no accident that these shows and self-help books and transformation memoirs often achieve soaring popularity, just as it's no accident that the stories of Paul and Augustine are central to the Western canon—and that the men themselves were canonized. We thrill to stories of life-altering change, we long to believe that such change is possible, and we *do* believe that it can redeem us.*

What is strange about this enthusiasm for radical transformation is that it coexists with a deep resistance to surrendering any part of our current self, and an equally deep suspicion of substantive change in other people. However much we might admire those who are able to reassess their beliefs,

---

* This isn't to say that radical change always represents an improvement. From the perspective of the convert, the transformation must always be for the better, but to an outsider, conversion experiences don't necessarily balance the moral checkbook. Osha Davidson tells the story of the U.S. Senator Tom Watson, who was born in Georgia in 1856 and spent the early part of his career opposing racial injustice, supporting voting rights for African-American men, and trying to unite the labor and agrarian classes across race lines. By the end of his life, Watson had become a white supremacist who railed against blacks, Jews, and Catholics, and was much admired by the KKK.

admit to errors, and transform their lives, we are also wary of those who change too much (recall John Kerry), dubious about whether real change is even possible (*a leopard doesn't change its spots*, we say; and *you can't teach an old dog new tricks*), and convinced that there is something virtuous about maintaining a consistent identity. In a kind of fourth-century indictment of flip-floppers, Augustine wrote of his "complete certainty" that "what remains constant is better than that which is changeable"—people very much included.

Most of us are at peace with the fact that some elements of our identities *aren't* constant, that things like our skills and priorities (to say nothing of our bodies) inevitably change over time. But not so when it comes to other aspects of the self. These include our personality ("I am conscientious," "I have a temper," "I am shy"), our basic talents and deficits ("I'm good with numbers," "I have a short attention span"), and certain core beliefs, both about ourselves ("I'm someone my friends can rely on") and about the universe at large ("there is a God," "education is important," "it's a dog-eat-dog world"). The essential elements of our character, our native aptitudes and shortcomings, our grounding moral and intellectual principles, our ways of relating to ourselves, to others, and to the world: these are the things that give each of us our "I." And, like Augustine, we by and large believe that this central "I" should remain fixed, a kind of ground floor to support the integrity of the entire structure.

But then along comes error and challenges all of this—the idea that we know who we are, as well as the idea that we *are* who we are. We've already seen that the category of knowledge can't accommodate the possibility of being wrong, and it turns out that this is true of self-knowledge, too. If we conceive of the self as a consistent and knowable entity, it is hard to imagine how we could ever get ourselves wrong. In fact, hewing too closely to this model of the self can force us to dismiss both the possibility of error and the possibility of change—even in cases where, to an outside observer, both seem blatantly evident.

Consider the case of Whittaker Chambers. In 1925, Chambers, then a promising young undergraduate at Columbia University, dropped out of college and joined the Communist Party. For the remainder of his twenties and most of his thirties, Chambers was a committed atheist, an impassioned Communist—and, for five years, a Soviet spy. Then, in 1938, he broke with the party, found God, and turned virulently anti-Communist. Ten years later, he testified before the House Un-American Activities Committee and, subsequently, in one of the most famous trials of the twentieth century: the federal case against Alger Hiss, Chambers's former friend and alleged fellow spy.

If Chambers's faith in Communism was so profound that it led him to betray his country and risk his life, his break with it was equally absolute. He didn't turn away from the Party so much as turn *on* it, denouncing it as "evil, absolute evil." Here was a man whose deepest ideological and theological convictions, whose very actions and identity had changed perhaps as drastically as anyone's can in one lifetime. And yet, he would write in his autobiography, *Witness*, "I cannot say I changed." Instead, he continued: "There tore through me a transformation with the force of a river which, dammed up and diverted for a lifetime, bursts its way back to its true channel. I became what I was. I ceased to be what I was not."

Instead of changing, Chambers felt, he had simply resumed his true identity. This claim is a common feature of conversion narratives. Indeed, the very word "conversion" comes from a Latin verb that means not to change but to return. Thus, converts to Islam are sometimes called "reverts," and many other religious traditions describe new members of the faith as "coming home" or "returning to the flock." One of Chambers's fellow Communists, the French writer André Gide, captured this idea of returning to a fixed if hidden self nicely when he "declared that he had always been a Communist at heart, without knowing it, even when he had been most Christian." (Gide, too, would eventually grow disillusioned with Communism.)

The implausibility of this claim—that we have always been the exact opposite of who we once seemed to be—reflects the difficulty we get ourselves into when we decline to acknowledge that we can change. We hear that difficulty in Whittaker Chambers's impossible grammar: "I became what I was." And we hear it, too, in Augustine's strikingly contorted description of his life before finding God: "for I had placed myself behind my own back," he wrote, "refusing to see myself." And yet, as implausible as this idea sounds, it is a cornerstone of both popular and professional psychology. We commonly invoke it in daily life, as when we suggest that the most homophobic guy in town is himself homosexual deep down, or when we accuse people of "protesting too much"—that is, of disagreeing so stridently with a belief that they must secretly or subconsciously agree with it.

This folk notion was elevated to the status of a formal theory by the psychologist Carl Jung, who argued that our conscious and unconscious beliefs exist in opposition to each other. The more vociferously someone defends a belief, Jung held, the more we can be sure that he is defending it primarily against his own internal doubts, which will someday surge into consciousness and force a polar shift in perspective. According to Jung, this was especially true of the most dogmatic beliefs—which, by rendering all conscious doubt impermissible, must be all the more subconsciously resisted, and thus all the more unstable. (The obvious and important implication of this argument is that the more we can accommodate ambivalence, counterevidence, and doubt, the more stable our beliefs and identities will be.)

The idea that we possess a true self serves a hugely important psychological purpose. If we have an essential and unchanging identity, one we are destined to discover sooner or later, then the beliefs we hold, the choices we make, the person we become—none of this happens by chance. Instead, the entire course of our lives is inevitable, dictated by the certainty that our real self will eventually surface. Writing about his decision to testify against Alger Hiss, Whittaker Chambers declared that, "it was for this that my whole life had been lived. For this I had been a Communist, for this I had ceased to be a Communist. For this the tranquil strengthening years had been granted to me. This challenge was the terrible meaning of my whole life." In this narrative, even Chambers's false self—the devoted Communist—had to exist for a while in order to serve the greater purpose of his true self, the crusading anti-Communist.

This narrative is appealing for the same reason that it is problematic: within it, we can do no wrong. Our false beliefs were foreordained, our apparent errors occurred strictly in the service of a larger truth. This idea is made explicit in the religious affirmation that "God makes no mistakes":

even the seeming trials and blunders of our lives are part of a larger plan.* As that implies, stories starring a true self are teleological; we end up exactly where we are meant to be. This, too, is both an attraction and a weakness of the idea of an essential self. It suggests that our lives are deterministic, that yesterday's convictions—which we thought we chose based on their intellectual, emotional, or spiritual merits—were merely a trap into which we were lured for the benefit of some predetermined future self. Whatever meaning or worth our past might have had on its own terms is effectively written out of existence.

Even more problematically, the idea of a true self suggests that we will never undergo momentous upheaval again. How could we? Having finally discovered who we really are and have always been, there is no further transformation available to us. If the self is constantly changing, then we can constantly feel our way forward, constantly become someone new—but if each of us possesses a fixed essence, then we can only return to it. Accordingly, our past departure from that essential self can only be a single and inexplicable aberration, associated as often as not with betrayal, transgression, and sin. (Recall Chambers denouncing Communism, his erstwhile faith, as "evil, absolute evil.")

Singular, aberrational, transgressive, evil: we've seen this constellation of ideas before. This is the pessimistic model of wrongness, in which error is an unwelcome anomaly, a mark of our exile from the sacred realm of truth. Helpfully, this reminds us that we have another model for making sense of wrongness as well—one that casts a different light not only on

---

* There is a secular version of this idea, too; I call it "friends don't let friends be wrong." This is what happens when you try to tell a friend about a mistake you made, and she hastens to assure you that it really wasn't a mistake—that you did the best you could in the moment, or that you learned from it and so it was "for the best" or "meant to be." Of course, sometimes we *did* do the best we could, and sometimes do learn from our mistakes. But this doesn't mean they weren't mistakes. A mistake is a mistake whether we make it for a dumb reason or a smart one, whether it has a bad outcome or a good one. If we decree that mistakes aren't really mistakes when they arise from a positive process (doing our best) or result in a positive outcome (learning something), we reinforce the notion that wrongness is intrinsically negative.

our errors but also on ourselves. Here, wrongness is a natural and ongoing process, and we are not deformed but transformed by it. "The bud disappears when the blossom breaks through," wrote the German philosopher G. W. F. Hegel, "and we might say that the former is refuted by the latter; in the same way when the fruit comes, the blossom may be explained to be a false form of the plant's existence." But, of course, we *don't* say this of organic entities like buds and blossoms and fruit. And we need not say it about ourselves, either. In the optimistic model of wrongness, error is not a sign that our past selves were failures and falsehoods. Instead, it is one of those forces, like sap and sunlight, that imperceptibly helps another organic entity—us human beings—to grow up.

When you were a little kid, you were fabulously wrong about things all the time. In large part, this was because you suffered from a serious information deficit: the quantity of even extremely basic facts that eluded you was staggering. To take just one example, you didn't know much about your own body. Developmental psychologists have shown that children under four have no idea what brains do, and think that dolls are as likely to possess them as humans. Similarly, children under seven can typically name only three things found inside the body (blood, bones, and the heart) and are drastically wide of the mark when it comes to the nature and function of other internal organs. (One psychologist quotes a child as saying that lungs "are for your hair. Without them you couldn't have hair.") Likewise, most kids under eight think that boys can become girls and girls can become boys simply by changing their hairstyle and clothing.

The issue here isn't that kids aren't smart, or that they aren't generating sophisticated theories about human biology and everything else in the world. In both cases, they are. (As you might recall from Chapter Five, all of us begin theorizing about the world before we're out of diapers.) The issue, instead, is that children suffer from a shortage of data—and not just about their bodies, but about everything: people, objects, language, culture, politics, the laws that govern the physical world. Sometimes they haven't stumbled across the necessary information yet, and sometimes they haven't reached a developmental stage where they can grasp it. And sometimes, too, information is deliberately withheld from them—which explains why children are often particularly wrong about things like the mechanics of sex and reproduction, the identity of their biological parents, and how (or even that) a family member has died.*

Compounding the problem of insufficient information is the problem of bad information. Children believe in things like Santa Claus and the tooth fairy not because they are particularly credulous but for the same reasons the rest of us believe our beliefs. Their information about these phenomena comes from trusted sources (typically, their parents) and is often supported by physical evidence (cookie crumbs by the chimney, quarters under the pillow). It isn't the kids' fault that the evidence is fabricated and that their sources mislead them. Nor is it their fault that their primary community, outside of their family, generally consists of other children, who tend to be equally ill-informed. Given what we saw earlier about the influence of community on beliefs, you can imagine (or simply recall) how readily bad information spreads around lunchrooms and playgrounds. A friend captures this funny state of childhood belief systems nicely when he recollects that, "At some point in elementary school someone told me—and I believed—that chocolate milk was made from milk that had blood in it, but I didn't believe that in order to have children, my parents took off their clothes and had sex."

Eventually, kids grow up and learn the truth about sex and death and chocolate milk. In the interim, though, they live in a world rich with wrong-

---

* Death and reproduction are particularly common areas of confusion and error for kids, partly because so much information about these subjects is kept from them, and partly because even for adults, it's tough to fathom how we get existence from nonexistence, or, conversely, nonexistence from existence. The developmental psychologist Susan Carey tells the story of a child who, when asked to explain reproduction, "gravely explained that to create a baby, parents first buy a duck, which then turns into a rabbit, which then turns into a baby." When queried further (by, one imagines, some very puzzled researchers), the child claimed that he had learned this from a book—as it turns out, one that eschewed a description of sexual intercourse in favor of talking about bunnies and ducklings.

ness. I choose the adjective "rich" deliberately. To be sure, childhood errors, like errors more generally, can sometimes be humiliating or traumatizing. Most of us have some early memories of excruciating mistakes (multiple people told me they could still recall their embarrassment at grabbing onto a parent for comfort in a crowded place, only to look up and realize that the "parent" was a stranger), and some children are routinely chided for being wrong. (Chided, or worse: to be "corrected" can mean, among other things, to be subjected to corporal punishment.)

On the whole, though, being wrong when we're very young is less a series of isolated incidents (as we regard it in adulthood) than a constant process—inextricable from learning, inextricable from growing up. Forming theories about the world, testing them, and figuring out where they went wrong is the very stuff of childhood. In fact it is, literally, child's play. Scientists, parents, and educators all agree that kids play to figure out the workings of the world. What looks, to an adult, like a game of blocks or a stint in the sandbox is really one giant, joyful science experiment. Moreover, recent work in developmental psychology suggests that error might play the same role in the lives of children as it does in the lives of scientists—inspiring them to sit up and take notice, generate new theories, and try to understand what is going on around them. Being wrong, in other words, appears to be a key means by which kids learn, and one associated as much as anything with absorption, excitement, novelty, and fun.†

As we get older, the learning curve decelerates, and all these things drop off exponentially. We make fewer mistakes, function more efficiently, and come to share with other adults certain baseline beliefs about the world. But we also spend much less of our time in anything remotely akin to exploration, learning, and play. The pleasurable mistakes of childhood disrupt our lives less often, partly because the world is less novel to us, and partly because we don't seek out whatever novelty remains—or at least we don't

---

† In claiming that error is essentially a mechanism for learning, I'm not trying to make the opposite claim: that learning is essentially contingent on error. We do learn from our mistakes, but we also learn in a wide variety of other ways: through imitation, intervention, practice, and explicit instruction, to name just a few.

do so with the same zeal (and the same institutional support: classrooms, afterschool programs, summer camps) as children.

There are exceptions, of course. Long after we have left behind the error-rich kingdom of childhood, we find ways to put ourselves in the path of wrongness in order to grow and change. Take the example of travel. Like children, travelers explore the unknown—where, also like children, they routinely make linguistic errors, violate social codes, and get lost, literally and otherwise. This is why every traveler has his or her share of stories about being egregiously wrong: the farther afield you venture, the more you set yourself up for confusion, surprise, and the violation of your beliefs. If we could journey far enough—if, say, we could visit a distant planet subject to different physical constraints and populated by alien life forms—one assumes that we would be even more ignorant, wonderstruck, and error-prone than kids.

The desire to experience this kind of wrongness is seldom the explicit reason people engage in recreational travel, and it's certainly not the *only* reason. (We also set out to visit friends, brush up on our Portuguese, see the Great Barrier Reef.) But it is often the implicit one. Sometimes, we *want* to be the toddler in Times Square. We travel to feel like a kid again: because we hope to experience the world as new, and because we believe the best way to learn about it is to play in it. In traveling (as in other kinds of adventures that we'll encounter in the last chapter), we embrace the possibility of being wrong not out of necessity, but because it changes our lives for the better.

We need not necessarily venture abroad to have these kinds of willing experiences of error. Sometimes, the unknown places we visit are the unknown places inside of us. Psychotherapy, for instance, is explicitly premised on the notion that we can change by exploring the parts of ourselves that have been hidden from conscious awareness—in particular, by coming to understand our own habitual delusions and mistakes. The psychologist Ronnie Janoff-Bulman has suggested that therapeutic interventions "can all be considered attempts to get the client to question and change old assumptions and construals of reality." Likewise, the psychoanalyst Heinz Hartmann noted that "a great part of psychoanalysis can be described as a theory of self-deceptions"—how and why we get ourselves wrong, and how uncovering those errors can change us.

We venture inward, then, for the same reasons we venture out: to fill in the unknown places on the map and correct our misperceptions about what's going on there. In the process, we get to know ourselves better—but, ideally, we also get better selves. The goal of therapy, after all, isn't just to help us understand why we feel and act as we do. It's also to help us *change* the way we feel and act: to foster a set of beliefs that is less rigid, more functional, and more forgiving, toward ourselves as well as those around us. The same could be said of all the other practices, from prayer to twelve-step programs to Buddhist meditation, that push us to accept our fallibility. Like therapy, and for that matter like travel, these practices help us weather challenges to our worldview with patience, curiosity, and understanding.

This is one of the most powerful ways being wrong can transform us: it can help us become more compassionate people. Being right might be fun but, as we've seen, it has a tendency to bring out the worst in us. By contrast, being wrong is often the farthest thing in the world from fun—and yet, in the end, it has the potential to bring out the best in us. Or rather: to change us for the better. When I asked Anita Wilson how she thought her experience of wrongness had affected her, she said, "I'm a much kinder person than I used to be."

A friend of mine expressed a similar sentiment. "Here's my story, which I bet is the story of many women," she told me. "I was brought up Catholic and always believed that having an abortion was wrong. I felt at the time that it was the only thing I believed in one hundred percent—it was wrong and I would never have one. Then I got pregnant and even though I was married, it just was not our time and I had an abortion. I had to work on it but I came to believe that I was not a murderer, just a regular person going through life." The experience of having to reevaluate her own belief system, she concluded, "helped me in not being so judgmental."

Ultimately, then, we are transformed by error through accepting it. To be judgmental, we must feel sure that we know right from wrong, and that we ourselves would never confuse the two. But the experience of erring shows us otherwise. It reminds us that, having been wrong in the past, we could easily be wrong again—and not just in the abstract but right now, here in the middle of this argument about pickles or constellations or crumb cake. At the same time, it reminds us to treat other people with compassion, to honor them in their possible rightness as well as their inevitable, occasional wrongness. Instead of taking their errors as a sign that they are ignorant or idiotic or evil, we can look to our own lives and reach the opposite conclusion: that they are, like us, just human.

One person who was able to do this was C. P. Ellis. During the televised broadcast of the 1988 Democratic Convention, Ellis told Studs Terkel, "the cameras zoomed in on one Klansman. He was saying, 'I hope Jesse Jackson gets AIDS and dies.' I felt sympathy for him. That's the way my old friends used to think. Me, too." At first, this is a startling statement. Inside mainstream America, we seldom hear (or want to hear) anyone express compassion for white supremacists. But Ellis wasn't endorsing this man's opinion. By 1988, he had been out of the Klan for eighteen years. He was simply expressing sympathy, in all the telling double meaning of the word: a sense of fellow-feeling, coupled with a sense of pity. Remember Whittaker Chambers, who, after renouncing Communism, claimed that he had "ceased to be what I was not"? At the heart of Chambers's story of error and transformation is the statement: *that was not truly me*. At the heart of Ellis's story of error and transformation is the statement: *that was me*.

It takes courage to leave our past selves behind. But it takes even more to carry some token of them with us as we go: to accept that we have erred, recognize that we have changed, remember with compassion our caterpillar past. As difficult as this can be, the dividends are worth it. "The main interest in life and work," said Foucault, "is to become someone else that you were not in the beginning." Such transformations don't only come about through wrongness, of course—but wrongness is always an opportunity for such transformations. Recall what I said earlier: if we could freeze the frame on each of our mistakes, what we would see in the center every time would be change.

The scale of that change varies widely, but in the end it knows no limits. Our errors can alter our beliefs, our relationships, ourselves. In a sense, they can even change our whole world. We can find ourselves living—

uncomfortably, frighteningly, thrillingly—in a place where we can experience things we could never have experienced before. "They say the older you get, the harder it is for you to change," C. P. Ellis said. "That's not necessarily true. Since I changed, I've set down and listened to tapes of Martin Luther King. I listen to it and tears come to my eyes, 'cause I know what he's sayin' now. I know what's happenin'."

PART IV

EMBRACING ERROR

14.

The Paradox of Error

I was of three minds,
Like a tree
In which there are three blackbirds.
—Wallace Stevens,
"13 Ways of Looking at a Blackbird"

One day in the summer of 2008, just before the July Fourth holidays, a patient was wheeled into an operating room at Beth Israel Deaconess Medical Center in Boston. BIDMC is one of the top medical institutions in the nation, and a teaching hospital for Harvard Medical School. Its staff sees some quarter of a million people every year and performs almost 175 surgeries each week. This particular one unfolded much as most surgeries do. The patient was anesthetized, the area to be operated on was prepped, and the initial incision was made. When the surgeon had completed his work, the patient was wheeled into a recovery room, still unconscious. When she awoke, she looked down at herself, looked up at her doctor, and asked why the wrong side of her body was in bandages.

Much of this book has been devoted to bringing to light the good side of error: the lessons we can learn from it, the ways it can change us, its connection to our intelligence, imagination, and humanity. But there is no good side to medical error. If, like this patient, you someday wake up in a hospital to discover that a surgeon has operated on the wrong part of your body, you will not pause to reflect on all the ways you can learn and grow through error. You will not feel curiosity or openness, and you will not feel gratitude—unless it is gratitude for having survived. According to the Institute of Medicine, between 690,000 and 748,000 patients are affected by medical errors in the United States every year, and between 44,000 and 98,000 die from them. Even the lowball estimate makes medical mistakes the eighth leading cause of death in the nation—worse than breast cancer, AIDS, and motor vehicle accidents. It also makes medicine far more error prone, and more dangerously so, than most other high-risk fields. For commercial aviation to take the same toll in the United States as medical errors do, a sold-out 747 would have to crash every three days, killing everyone on board.

These statistics are disturbing. Almost more troubling, though, is the medical profession's traditional response to them, which has largely involved evasion, obfuscation, minimization, defensiveness, and denial. This isn't true of every individual healthcare provider, of course, but it has long characterized the overall ethos within the culture of medicine. In her 2005 book on medical error, *After Harm*, the bioethicist Nancy Berlinger described the way this ethos is perpetuated. "Observing more senior physicians, students learn that their mentors and supervisors believe in, practice and reward the concealment of errors," Berlinger wrote. "They learn how to talk about unanticipated outcomes until a 'mistake' morphs into a 'complication.' Above all, they learn not to tell the patient anything." She goes on to describe "the depth of physicians' resistance to disclosure and the lengths to which some will go to justify the habit of nondisclosure—it was only a technical error, things just happen, the patient won't understand, the patient does not need to know." In keeping with this assessment, a 2002 survey of doctors' attitudes found that honest disclosure is "so far from the norm as to be 'uncommon.'"*

If so, what happened at Beth Israel Deaconess Medical Center was uncommon. The instant the patient drew attention to the mistake, the surgeon realized what had happened, explained it as thoroughly as possible, and—although the act must have felt woefully inadequate—apologized. He then contacted the chief of his department and Paul Levy, the hospital's CEO, and told them about the situation. Reviewing the case, Levy and other BIDMC higher-ups decided that the mistake was serious enough that both the hospital and the community it served deserved to know what had happened. In very short order, they emailed the entire hospital staff—some 5,000 people—and sent a press release about the incident to local media outlets.

Needless to say, this uncommon reaction didn't come out of nowhere. In January 2008, six months before the botched surgery, Levy, his board, and his staff made a kind of New Year's Resolution: by January 1, 2012, they would eliminate all preventable medical harm. Although most hospitals seek to reduce error, BIDMC is one of the very few in the nation to establish such a specific and audacious goal.

Early on in this book, I observed that one of the recurring questions about error is whether it is basically eradicable or basically inevitable. As a

---

* To excuse their defensiveness and silence, doctors often point to the threat of being sued. But such fears might be largely unfounded. For starters, thirty-five states have now passed "I'm sorry" laws, which prevent physicians' apologies from being used against them in malpractice suits. Moreover, evidence suggests that openly disclosing and apologizing for errors might actually *decrease* the likelihood of being sued. In 1987, after facing a couple of high-profile, high-cost malpractice suits, the Veterans Affairs Medical Center in Lexington, Kentucky, became the first hospital in the nation to implement an apologize-and-disclose policy for medical error. In the thirty-plus years since then, the hospital has gone to court only three times. Over that same period, its legal fees have dropped dramatically, and its average per-patient settlement has been $16,000; the nationwide average for similar hospitals is $98,000. These statistics aren't surprising when you consider a few others—for instance, that 40 percent of medical-error victims say that a full explanation and apology would have prevented them from seeking legal action.

philosophical matter, this question is important, since (as I suggested earlier) the way we answer it says a lot about how we feel about being wrong. As a practical matter, it's clear that the answer lies somewhere in between: many kinds of error can and should be curtailed, very few can be done away with entirely, and some we shouldn't even want to get rid of. What is both philosophically *and* practically interesting about this question, however, is the paradox that lurks at its heart: if you want to try to eradicate error, you have to start by assuming that it is inevitable.

The patient-safety initiative at Beth Israel Deaconess Medical Center illustrates this paradox. The first thing the hospital did in pursuit of its goal of eliminating error was to launch a comprehensive investigation of "all the differing ways patients get hurt," as Kenneth Sands, the senior vice president of healthcare quality, told a *Boston Globe* reporter at the time. The hospital also began publishing its medical error data publically, on its website, in deliberately frank terms. And hospital administrators committed themselves to, in the words of the initial resolution, "continually monitoring all preventable and non-preventable occurrences of harm." All this explains why the reaction to the wrong-side surgery was so fast, sweeping, and open. "Our view," Paul Levy told me, "is that if you don't acknowledge that mistakes occurred, you'll never eliminate the likelihood that they'll occur again."

Levy's principle can be generalized. If you really want to be right (or at least improve the odds of being right), you have to start by acknowledging your fallibility, deliberately seeking out your mistakes, and figuring out what caused you to make them. This truth has long been recognized in domains where being right is not just a zingy little ego boost but a matter of real urgency: in transportation, industrial design, food and drug safety, nuclear energy, and so forth. When they are at their best, such domains have a productive obsession with error. They try to imagine every possible reason a mistake could occur, they prevent as many of them as possible, and they conduct exhaustive postmortems on the ones that slip through. By embracing error as inevitable, these industries are better able to anticipate mistakes, prevent them, and respond appropriately when those prevention efforts fail.

Among high-risk fields, commercial aviation currently sets the standard for error management. As often happens, the airline industry's commitment to curtailing error grew out of a mistake of unprecedented and tragic proportions. In 1977, two Boeing 747s collided at the Tenerife airport in the Canary Islands, killing close to 600 people—then and now, the worst accident in aviation history. When safety officials investigated, they found that the collision was caused by a concatenation of errors, individually minor but collectively catastrophic. The airline industry responded by establishing strict protocols for every aspect of aviation—from how runways should be labeled to what phrases air traffic controllers and pilots can use to communicate with each other. These protocols succeeded in reducing significant commercial aviation accidents in the United States from 0.178 per million flight hours in 1998 to 0.104 per million flight hours in 2007.

Another well-known example of corporate efforts to prevent error is the quality-control process known as Six Sigma. Six Sigma was pioneered at Motorola in 1986 and is now used by the majority of Fortune 500 companies, plus countless smaller businesses. The protocol's name comes from statistics: the Greek letter sigma (σ) indicates the amount of standard deviation from a given norm. In this case, all deviation is assumed to be undesirable—an error in a manufacturing process or in its end product. A company that has achieved Six Sigma experiences just 3.4 such errors per million opportunities to err, a laudably low failure rate (or, framed positively, a 99.9997 percent success rate). To get a sense of what this means, consider that a company that ships 300,000 packages per year with a 99 percent success rate sends 3,000 packages to the wrong place. If that same company achieved Six Sigma, only a single package would go astray.

There are countless variations on Six Sigma in use today (and the program itself is a variation on many earlier quality-control measures), but they all share certain basic principles and protocols. Chief among these are a reliance on hard data and, as the name implies, a phobia of deviation. Traditionally, many companies evaluate their success based on how well they do *on average*—whether it takes an average of three days to deliver that package, say, or whether the brake pads you manufacture are an average of three-eighths of an inch thick. But the trouble with averages is that they can conceal many potential lapses and mistakes. If it takes an average of three days for your packages to reach their destination, some could be arriving in nine hours, others in two and a half weeks. If some of your brake pads are a half-inch thick and some are a quarter-inch thick, they might not fit with your other components, or they might not pass safety standards, or they might be rejected by the auto manufacturers you supply. With Six Sigma, then, the goal isn't to improve the average per se, but to reduce the deviation from that average. To do this, Six Sigma analysts make use of a procedure that is usually encapsulated as "define, measure, analyze, improve, control." In essence, that procedure involves isolating and assessing every single variable pertaining to a given process. Then analysts begin adjusting those variables to achieve and maintain the optimal outcome in terms of a company's final product, customer satisfaction, and bottom line.*

All of these error-prevention techniques—from Six Sigma to the innovations of the airline industry to the efforts at Beth Israel—have three key elements in common. The first, as I've indicated, is acceptance of the likelihood of error. That's why officials at BIDMC set about trying to determine "all the differing ways patients get hurt." And it's why Six Sigma analysts systematically imagine the failure of every component of a product or process, the likely implications of that failure, and the best ways to stave it off (a technique borrowed from an early quality-control measure known as Failure Mode and Effects Analysis). In fact, even as Six Sigma aims for near perfection, it also strives to build into companies and processes a "tolerance for failure." That is, it seeks to foster both awareness of the possibility of screw-ups and strong risk-management strategies, so that any error that does occur will be a "safe failure."

The second element these error-prevention strategies have in common is openness. Perhaps the most dramatic difference between Paul Levy's handling of his hospital's wrong-side surgery and more conventional reactions

---

* Remember how I argued, earlier in this book, that we associate error with deviation from normal or desirable conditions—and, by extension, with evil and sin? Six Sigma presents both an unusually explicit and an unusually benign—in fact, beneficial—example of this set of associations. Among Six Sigma aficionados, deviation is not only taken to represent an error but also routinely referred to as (these are actual quotes) "the enemy" and "evil."

to medical error was its extreme transparency. The hospital went as far as it could toward widespread and detailed acknowledgment of the error without compromising the privacy of the patient. As that suggests, this openness wasn't done on behalf of the patient, as a kind of bigger, showier apology. (The hospital *was* open with the patient, and did apologize, but such apologies should transpire only between the medical team, the appropriate hospital administrators, the patient, and the patient's family.) It's more accurate to say that it was done on behalf of *future* patients. The point of the very public admission of error was to ensure that everyone in the hospital learned as much as possible from it, to remind staff members to follow the error-prevention protocols already in place, and to generate as many new ideas as possible for preventing future problems. A similar recognition of the importance of openness spurred the airline industry to create a culture in which crew and ground members are encouraged (and in some cases even required) to report mistakes and are protected from punishment and litigation if they do so. Likewise, GE, one of the early Six Sigma adopters, claims that to eliminate error, it has "opened our culture to ideas from everyone, everywhere, decimated the bureaucracy and made boundaryless behavior a reflexive, natural part of our culture."[†]

The final element that all error-deterrent systems have in common is a reliance on verifiable data—what Six Sigma analysts call "management by fact" rather than by "opinions and assumptions." One of the great mysteries of what went awry in the wrong-side surgery at BIDMC was that, as Kenneth Sands put it, "for whatever reason, [the surgeon] simply felt that

---

† Another interesting example of the use of transparency to curtail error comes from the open-source movement. Originally developed within computer science, the movement grew out of the belief that the more visible the workings of any given system, the more rapidly errors and shortcomings would be detected and corrected, and the better and more robust that system would be. Although still quite young, open source has already had path-breaking successes in domains as different as operating systems, encyclopedias, and the way academic papers are reviewed. (Not to mention the Internet, which was developed almost entirely through an open-source process.) While conventional operation and design processes tend to be closed and centralized, the open-source movement, like every deliberate effort to understand and prevent error, emphasizes transparency, inclusivity, and democratization.

he was on the correct side" of the patient. "Whatever reason" and "simply feeling" are precisely the kinds of cues that error-proofing processes seek to override. That's why these processes place so much emphasis on verifying even small, seemingly straightforward aspects of the procedure in question. Think about the last time you locked your keys in your car because you assumed you'd tossed them into your bag as usual: we know from our own experience that one way we err is through the failure of tasks that are so obvious or automated that we seldom bother to double-check them.

Relying on hard data, committing to open and democratic communication, acknowledging fallibility: these are the central tenets of any system that aims to protect us from error. They are also markedly different from how we normally think—from our often hasty and asymmetric treatment of evidence, from the cloistering effects of insular communities, and from our instinctive recourse to defensiveness and denial. In fact, the whole reason these error-proofing techniques exist is to exert a counterweight on our steady state. Jettison those techniques, leave us to our own devices, and—as we have seen—we will unreflectively assume that we are right and will investigate for error only after something has gone patently awry.

If you are GE, or Motorola, or American Airlines, you have a very good reason to invest in these error-prevention strategies. Without them, you will risk endangering lives, incurring damning publicity, inviting legal action, and losing money, clients, and possibly your entire business. For corporations, in other words, paying attention to error pays. Between 1986 and 2006, Motorola reported savings of more than $17 billion thanks to Six Sigma. Likewise, when the University of Michigan medical system implemented an apologize-and-explain program, their annual legal fees dropped from $3 million to $1 million. On a national level, the savings to be gained are similarly significant: according to the Institute of Medicine, medical mistakes cost the United States between $17 billion and $29 billion annually. (That's why preventing medical errors is widely regarded as a way to offset some of the skyrocketing costs of healthcare.) And that's not even including those expenses that are difficult or impossible to quantify, from company reputation to customer satisfaction—to say nothing of customer lives.

If it behooves companies in such material and moral ways to accept their fallibility and own up to their mistakes, surely the same goes for each of us as individuals—and for all of us as communities, cultures, and nations. We've already gotten a good look at the obstacles to doing so: at the difficulty of recognizing the limits of our knowledge, the allure of certainty, and the defensiveness and denial we often resort to in the aftermath of our mistakes. And yet, despite all that, sometimes we *are* able to embrace uncertainty and error—and not just in domains where life, limb, and finance demand it, but in the tussle and clamor of everyday life.

One of the first words all of us learn is: no. Sure, "daddy" or "mama" or "more" or "up" might edge it out, but the capacity for negation and refusal comes to us very, very early—typically within the first twelve to eighteen months of life. It is soon followed (or, less often, preceded) by "yes," and, for a while, that's the kind of world we live in: a black-and-white, yes-and-no universe. Psychologists call this developmental stage "splitting."* Right around the age of five, though, something interesting happens: we learn the word "maybe." This first tentative foray marks the beginning of our ability to acknowledge, quantify, and talk about uncertainty. As such, it also marks a major step toward learning—like the corporations and hospitals we just saw—to incorporate the possibility of error into our lives.

From that first "maybe," our language blossoms outward into both a glossary and a grammar of doubt. I've claimed elsewhere in this book that we are drawn to adamancy, that we treat our theories like facts and are made uncomfortable by ambiguity and error. All that is true. But it's also true that, circumstances permitting, we are not only able to express uncertainty but are extraordinarily creative and resourceful in how we do so. This creativity begins with words (*perhaps, probably, hypothetically, doubtful,*

---

* People with borderline personality disorder are sometimes described as being stuck in this stage, because they continue to regard the world as a place of absolutes. The disorder is characterized by, among other things, an overpowering need to be right and a corresponding inability to accept the possibility of error, or the potential validity of multiple viewpoints.

debatable, sometimes, occasionally, conceivably), and extends to entire grammatical functions. The conditional tense—coulda, shoulda, woulda—excels at the expression of regret and uncertainty. The subjunctive, not a tense but (appropriately) a mood, connotes doubt, improbability, and false beliefs; its prevailing atmosphere is one of ambiguity. The subjunctive has largely disappeared from English, lingering only in grammatical niceties like, "If that *were* true, I would be the first to admit it." In Romance languages, though, it is alive and well—the default idiom of dreams, hopes, suppositions, counterfactual situations, and disbelief.

From these linguistic building blocks, we construct countless verbal strategies for accommodating uncertainty and error. Among these: we suggest ("off the top of my head"), we survey ("what's your take on this?"), we generalize ("roughly speaking"), we qualify ("I tend to agree"), we hedge our bets ("to the best of my knowledge"), we wager ("I'd say there's a sixty–forty chance"), and we cover our tracks ("don't quote me on this"). Also, in strange and fascinating fashion, we multiply ourselves to make room for competing beliefs. So, for instance, we say "I'm of two minds," as if entertaining two contradictory hypotheses required becoming two different people—an idea that comports with the notion that belief and identity are inextricable. Similarly, we say "on the third hand," as if our attraction to binaries were built into our very bodies, so that venturing beyond them required a phantom limb. In this parallel universe of two minds and three hands, there are many possible right and wrong (or right-ish and wrong-ish) answers. We use these expressions to stake out the range of available positions on an issue before taking a stand—or to indicate that uncertainty itself is our stand.

Consciously or otherwise, we also use these linguistic strategies to influence our audience. If being contradicted or facing other people's categorical pronouncements tends to make listeners stubborn, defensive, and inclined to disagree, open expressions of uncertainty can be remarkably disarming. To take a trivial but common example, I once sat in on a graduate seminar in which a student prefaced a remark by saying, "I might be going out on a limb here." Before that moment, the class had been contentious; the prevailing ethos seemed to be a kind of academic one-upmanship, in which the point was to undermine all previous observations. After this student's comment, though, the room seemed to relax. Because she took it upon herself to acknowledge the provisionality of her idea, her classmates were able to contemplate its potential merit instead of rushing to invalidate it.

These kinds of disarming, self-deprecating comments ("this could be wrong, but . . ." "maybe I'm off the mark here . . .") are generally considered more typical of the speech patterns of women than men. Not coincidentally, they are often criticized as overly timid and self-sabotaging. But I'm not sure that's the whole story. Awareness of one's own qualms, attention to contradiction, acceptance of the possibility of error: these strike me as signs of sophisticated thinking, far preferable in many contexts to the confident bulldozer of unmodified assertions. Philip Tetlock, too, defends these and similar speech patterns (or rather, the mental habits they reflect), describing them, admiringly, as "self-subversive thinking." That is, they let us function as our own intellectual sparring partner, thereby honing—or puncturing—our beliefs. They also help us do greater justice to complex topics and make it possible to have riskier thoughts. At the same time, by moving away from decree and toward inquiry, they set the stage for more open and interesting conversations. Perhaps the most striking and paradoxical effect of the graduate student's out-on-a-limb caveat was that, even as it presented her idea as potentially erroneous, it caused her classmates to take that idea more seriously: it inspired her listeners to actually listen.

That's important, because, as Harville Hendrix observed, listening is one of the best ways we can make room in our lives for our own fallibility. You might imagine that it would be one of the easiest ways, too—certainly easier than technical approaches like Six Sigma—but in fact, as we saw earlier, it is surprisingly hard. At least, it is hard to listen closely, sincerely, and for any length of time. This is true even when listening carefully really matters. For instance, studies have shown that, on average, doctors interrupt their patients eighteen seconds after they have started explaining the reason for their visit. Trained to assemble a clinical picture as rapidly as possible, doctors often start homing in on a diagnosis almost before the patient has begun describing his condition. This is frustrating for the interrupted patient and worrisome for the rest of us: nobody wants to be treated this way by a doctor, and nobody believes it can lead to optimal medical outcomes. Yet given our induction-happy minds, most of us are guilty of the same practice in our everyday lives. As soon as we think we are right about something, we narrow our focus, attending only to details that support our belief, or ceasing to listen altogether.

By contrast, when we are aware that we could be wrong, we are far more inclined to hear other people out. We see this in the field of medicine, too, since doctors who *can't* figure out a diagnosis—or who have reason to suspect that the one they settled on is wrong—can become notably patient and acute listeners, taking and retaking a medical history in search of the elusive telling detail. But my favorite illustration of this relationship between learning to listen and learning to accept fallibility comes from a man named John Francis—who, in 1973, took what became a seventeen-year vow of silence.

John Francis isn't a monk, or even particularly monkish. He is a working-class African-American guy from Philadelphia, and his vow of silence came about accidentally, through another, more deliberate pledge. In 1971, after a massive oil spill in the San Francisco Bay, Francis, who was then living in the area, decided to give up driving. (That vow lasted even longer. I know about Francis because I used to edit an online environmental magazine called *Grist*, which ran an interview with him about his twenty-year vacation from the internal combustion engine.) "As I walked along the road," Francis told *Grist*, "people would stop and talk about what I was doing and I would argue with them. And I realized that, you know, maybe I didn't want to do that. So on my birthday"—he had just turned twenty-seven—"I decided I was going to give my community some silence because, man, I just argued all the time."

Francis didn't originally plan to stay quiet for long: "I decided for one day, let's not speak and see what happens." As it turned out, though, the outcome of that experiment was so interesting that he stuck with it. In accordance with Harville Hendrix's point that we must "listen and listen and listen and listen" if we hope to change our relationships for the better, Francis found that ceasing to speak significantly altered the way he viewed other people and their ideas. "When I realized that I hadn't been listening," Francis reflected, "it was as if I had locked away half of my life." Silence, he emphasized, "is *not* just not talking. . . . You hear things you've never heard before, and you hear things in ways you've never heard them before. And what I would disagree with one time, I might now agree with." In his memoir, Francis elaborated on this theme. "Most of my adult life," he wrote, "I have not been listening fully. I only listened long enough to determine whether the speaker's ideas matched my own. If they didn't, I would stop listening, and my mind would race ahead to compose an argument against what I believed the speaker's idea or position to be."

Listening only in order to contradict, argue, and accuse: that reflex will be painfully familiar to many of us. Choosing not to speak might be an extreme countermeasure, but choosing to listen wouldn't hurt. After all, the only way to engage with the possibility that we could be wrong is to stop obsessively defending ourselves for a moment. True, we can sometimes make room for wrongness in the ways we speak—all those maybes and third hands. But we can *always* make room for it in the way we listen. I concede that this is hackneyed advice, but some truisms refuse to die of old age and can't be killed by corniness. In love, as in medicine, as in life more generally, listening is an act of humility. It says that other people's ideas are interesting and important; that our own could be in error; that there is still plenty left for us to learn.

Here, then, are some ways we can try to prevent mistakes. We can foster the ability to listen to each other and the freedom to speak our minds. We can create open and transparent environments instead of cultures of secrecy and concealment. And we can permit and encourage everyone, not just a powerful inner circle, to speak up when they see the potential for error.

These measures might be a prescription for identifying and eliminating mistakes, but they sound like something else: a prescription for democracy. That's not an accident. Although we don't normally think of it in these terms, democratic governance represents another method—this time a political rather than an industrial or personal one—for accepting the existence of error and trying to curtail its more dangerous incarnations.

We can see this relationship to error very clearly when we look at the emergence of the modern democracy. In medieval Europe, the power to govern was widely held to be bestowed by God—a belief that was enshrined in the political and religious doctrine known as the Divine Right of Kings. Explicit in this doctrine was the belief that political leaders weren't subject to any earthly authority; implicit in it was the idea that, as God's elect, they were infallible. (In a sense, these two beliefs are the same. As the French philosopher Joseph-Marie de Maistre pointed out, there is no practical difference between a leader who cannot err and a leader who cannot be accused of erring.) In the fifteenth century, as European politics started to secularize, the power of this doctrine began to wane. Over the next 300 years, the influence of the clergy declined significantly, religious faith was cordoned off into its own sphere instead of defining and absorbing all of public life, and political leaders came to be seen as mere mortals. On the plus side, this meant that corrupt or incompetent rulers could be legitimately deposed. On the downside, it meant that *all* leaders came to seem capable of making mistakes. So Enlightenment thinkers—who, as we've seen, were already obsessed with the problem of error—began to consider what to do about political fallibility.

The answers they came up with gradually converged on the idea of democracy. In his 1762 *Social Contract*, for instance, Jean-Jacques Rousseau famously argued that, although individual rulers were fallible, "the general will cannot err." (Rousseau was greatly influenced by the then-nascent fields of probability and statistics, and the influence shows. His idea that an infallible politics could emerge from the aggregated will of the people owes a great deal to the theory of the distribution of errors.) Meanwhile, on the other side of the Atlantic, Thomas Jefferson averred "that truth is great and will prevail if left to herself, that she is the proper and sufficient antagonist to error, and has nothing to fear from the conflict, unless by human interposition disarmed of her natural weapons, free argument and debate." According to Rousseau, then, error could be combated by letting the people vote for their nation's leaders and policies. According to Jefferson, it could be combated by letting them speak their minds. Direct election and freedom of speech—these are, respectively, the definition and the emblem of democracy.

As one of the founding fathers of the United States, Jefferson was articulating its founding ideal: that political leadership would not come from a single, supposedly infallible ruler, but from an openly fallible body politic, out of whose clamor and error would emerge a path to liberty and justice for all. Young as it was, the nation already had a precedent for tolerating even what were perceived as the gravest of mistakes. As the historian Richard Hofstadter observed in *The Idea of a Party System*, America's political freedom stowed away on the ship of religious freedom. "If [in the colonies] error could be endured where profound matters of faith were concerned," Hofstadter wrote, "a model had been created for the political game, in which also one might learn to endure error in the interest of social peace."

In truth, error was more than endured by Jefferson and other early American statesmen. It was all but embraced, and for reasons that went well beyond a desire to maintain the peace. In keeping with the ethos of the Enlightenment, these thinkers grasped that truth and error are often unrecognizable as such in the moment. As a result, they concluded that all ideas must be permitted to flourish, regardless of their apparent merit. Here is Benjamin Franklin, just before appending his name to the most famous piece of parchment in American history: "I confess there are several parts of this Constitution which I do not at present approve, but I am not sure that I shall never approve them. For having lived long, I have experienced many instances of being obliged by better information, or fuller consideration, to change opinions even on important subjects, which I once thought right, but found to be otherwise." No speech could have been more appropriate for the founding of the United States, a nation established in no small part on the recognition that, for a political system to succeed, a tolerance for error had to be built into its very bones.

And so it was. The often frustrating but ultimately saving American political innovation is this: we are forced to govern in collaboration with people whose political beliefs differ from our own. We see this in federalism (the sharing of power between national and state governments) and we see it in the system of checks and balances (the sharing of power among legislative, executive, and judicial branches). In both cases, the right to govern is distributed across different entities, to protect against the consolidation of power and ensure that no single viewpoint can drown out the rest. We also see this tolerance for error in the very fact that our laws can be changed; we are free to disagree with our own national past. (This idea, so basic to us that we can't imagine life without it, would have been anathema to most forms of government at most times in history.) Most of all, we see this tolerance for error in two of the hallmark ideas of democracy: political parties and freedom of speech.

Acceptance of political parties did not come easily to the United States. In the country's early years, the necessity of embracing disagreement and error was at war with another founding notion: that America would be a political utopia, in which dissent would be unnecessary because perfection would be achieved. Those utopian aspirations prompted powerful anti-party sentiment. Although virtually every politician in the young nation belonged to a party (either Alexander Hamilton's Federalists or Jefferson and James Madison's Democratic-Republicans), all of them decried partisanship as dangerous and hoped to see it end—just as soon as their own party was recognized as the only legitimate one. As Hofstadter pointed out, the United States only stabilized as a nation when it gave up the dream of being a one-party utopia and accepted the existence of political opposition as crucial to maintaining a democracy.

Two and a half centuries later, it's hard to appreciate how radical that shift really was—not just for America, but for the world. Before the emergence of democracy, political opposition was normally regarded as, in Hofstadter's words, "intrinsically subversive and illegitimate," and the usual policy was "to smother or suppress it." This remains the practice in totalitarian regimes, in which dissident opinions are branded as dangerously wrong, and, accordingly, stifled by the apparatus of the state.* By contrast,

---

* In the long run, the suppression of disagreement is likely to be bad for the rulers as well as the ruled over. As the legal scholar Cass Sunstein observed in *Why Societies Need Dissent*, "Dictators, large and small, tend to be error-prone as well as cruel. The reason is that they learn far too little. Those with coercive authority, from presidents to police chiefs, do much better if they encourage diverse views and expose themselves to a range of opinions." This was the lesson of groupthink as well, although power there was consolidated in the hands of a small group instead of in the hands of the individual.

multiparty systems are fundamentally error-tolerant. They do not merely permit but actually *require* competing points of view.

As that suggests, the existence of political parties goes hand-in-hand with the existence of free speech. Governments that refuse to acknowledge their fallibility have no need of (and in fact must destroy) dissent. But those that recognize their potential to err and hope to curtail or correct their mistakes must permit open expression—even if whatever is expressed seems odious, unpatriotic, or simply untrue. "Freedom," Gandhi argued, "is not worth having if it does not include the freedom to make mistakes." I take those words to mean something even stronger: freedom is *not* freedom if it doesn't include the right to make mistakes. A truly open government must recognize that it (like each of us as individuals) can always stumble into error, and that (again like each of us), it will not always know when it has done so. For that, it must rely on its dissidents and whistleblowers, which means it must permit them to speak out without fear of reprisal. Here is our paradox again: the only way to safeguard against error is to embrace it. Democracies, like people, must accept that they will sometimes err; and they must take what comfort they can from remembering that, by those errors, they know themselves to be free.

This is all very well and good—rah rah democracy, et cetera—but what happens when the errors of free and open societies are unconscionable? Back in Chapter Seven, we saw democratic Switzerland decline to extend the vote to women until 1971. Meanwhile, the democratic government of the United States has, in the course of its history, sanctioned the enslavement of human beings, detained its own citizens in internment camps, spied on internal political opposition, tortured suspected enemies of the state, and, in countless other ways, demonstrated the extent and severity of a democratic nation's capacity to err.

One could argue that these ugly episodes represent the breakdown rather than the upshot of democracy, but that is, at best, a partisan's comforting half-truth. If a system makes room for the inevitability of error and, accordingly, permits the expression of any and all beliefs; and if one of those beliefs—say, that debtors should be imprisoned or interracial marriage should be illegal—becomes entrenched policy, who's to say that this is a perversion rather than a product of democracy? Granted, the failures of a democratic society remain preferable to the failures of societies where people cannot speak their minds and cast their votes in freedom. But these failures are still grave—and, what is more, future and equally grave failures are all but inevitable.

In this respect, too, political means for embracing and avoiding error resemble the other methods we saw in the first part of this chapter. Whether in politics, industry, or everyday life, you can implement a system to prevent mistakes, but you can bet your life you won't prevent them all. For instance, many hospitals have some version of a "time-out" protocol, a checklist that surgical teams are supposed to review before beginning any procedure. Beth Israel Deaconess Medical Center had such a time-out system in place before the 2008 wrong-side surgery—but the team didn't use it. Many hospitals now use a magic marker to indicate the correct surgical site on a patient before an operation begins. The correct side of the BIDMC patient was marked—but the doctor didn't notice. For this patient, at least, the existing error-prevention system "wasn't good enough," said Paul Levy. He and his team went back to the drawing board to improve it (generating, among other things, the new time-out checklist on the next page), and, Levy said, "we think it will work better now. But undoubtedly something else will go wrong sometime in the future." And that's pretty much how it goes. You devise a system for preventing error, it works well for a while, and then an error occurs anyway and reveals a flaw in your design. So you modify your system and now it works better—but sooner or later another mistake will slip through and show you still more shortcomings you failed to detect. Error, it would seem, is always one step ahead of us.

So we can't catch all our errors, or catch up to error in general. Nor, however, can we give up the chase, since the price of doing so—in lives, money, and sheer folly—is simply too steep. Our only choice, then, is to keep living with and looking for wrongness, in all its strangely evasive omnipresence. To help us think about how to do so, I want to turn to one final and famous method for embracing (in the interest of curtailing) the

 Beth Israel Deaconess Medical Center

Time-out Script

 A teaching hospital of Harvard Medical School

Time-out occurs after draping unless an explicit exception is documented (i.e. eye)

Scrub person: None of the 4 I's on the Mayo Stand

1.	*Incision:*	No blade mounted on the knife handle. No tip on the ESU pencil
2.	*Infiltration:*	No needle mounted on syringe for local
3.	*Insertion:*	No Speculum or Bronchoscope
4.	*Initiation:*	None of the above apply to start of procedure

ALL MEMBERS OF THE TEAM STOP AND PARTICIPATE

WHO	WHAT TO SAY	WHAT TO DO
CIRCULATOR:	Ready to do Time-out	RN at computer with consent in hand.
ALL:	Yes	Stop activities. Turn radios other devices off.
CIRCULATOR:	Patient's name & MRN	Review name and MRN on computer screen & the consent.
ANESTHESIA PROVIDER:	Jane Doe; MRN# 123456	Review the ID Band *
SURGEON:	Confirms patient's name	
CIRCULATOR:	Allergies	View allergies on PIMS screen.
ANESTHESIA PROVIDER:	Lists allergies or declares none	
SURGEON:	Verbally affirms	
CIRCULATOR:	Antibiotics	
ANESTHESIA PROVIDER:	Name of antibiotic and time completed	Verify documentation in AIMS and time of next dose.
SURGEON:	Verbally affirms	
CIRCULATOR:	DVT prophylaxis Declare name of med given or state not applicable. Declare the pneumatic boots have been applied and are activated or state not applicable.	
CIRCULATOR:	Verification of Procedure	Review consent for accuracy.
SURGEON:	Name of procedure including site and side. (i.e. Right ORIF of the Ankle)	
CIRCULATOR:	Site marking	
SURGEON/DESIGNEE: **	Affirms location of mark or state not applicable.	ALL visualize the mark. Remark site if marking removed during prep process.
CIRCULATOR:	Position	
SURGEON:	Affirms that the patient is in the correct position.	
CIRCULATOR:	Implants and instruments or personnel that have been requested are present or declares the plan to secure them.	Calls out to clinical advisor for assistance in solving the named discrepancy.
SURGEON:	Are all of the requested implants and additional personnel requested in the room or in progress?	
SCRUB:	Names implants, instruments or personnel that have been requested are present or declares the plan to secure them.	
CIRCULATOR:	Please confirm the radiological images.	
SURGEON:	Images present and displayed correctly and patient's name and MRN have been verified.	
CIRCULATOR:	Is there anything else we need to disclose.	Records comments if any.
SCRUB:	Declare one of the 4 I's is ready.	Prepares one of the 4 I's.
ALL:	Respond as needed (may include special precautions).	

* Anesthesia Provider and Circulating Nurse attest that the verification has occurred if ID not accessible during the Time-out.

** Surgeon/Designee = Licensed Individual Provider who marked the site.

Central line insertions are exempt from Universal Protocol in accordance to outpatient central line guideline.
Copyright BIDMC © 2008

The revised "Time-out Script" implemented at Beth Israel Deaconess Medical Center following a wrong-site surgery in the summer of 2008.

likelihood of error. It comes to us from Descartes, who may have had history's most productive obsession with being wrong. In *Meditations on First Philosophy*, Descartes set out to determine how (and if) we can distinguish false beliefs from true knowledge. He began by noting that there is theoretically no limit to how wrong we could be—because, as Descartes pointed out, God could deliberately deceive us about even the most seemingly self-evident matters.

Perhaps because that doesn't seem like very godly behavior, Descartes' conceit has come to be known as the Evil Genius. The Evil Genius might be the most thoroughgoing method ever devised for embracing the possibility that we could be wrong. It led Descartes to doubt everything that could possibly be doubted, including (as I mentioned earlier) his own existence—although, famously, our existence is the one thing he finally conceded that we can bank on. The logic works like this: I might not have arms and legs, although I feel quite convinced that I do; I might not have free will; I might not have a sky overhead or a laptop and a coffee cup in front of me. An all-powerful evil genius could make me believe in all these things, even if none of them exist. But even an evil genius can't trick me into thinking that I'm thinking. If I *think* I am thinking, I am necessarily thinking. Moreover, there must be some kind of "I" hanging around doing this thinking, even if it doesn't happen to have limbs or free will or a caffeine addiction. And there you have it: *cogito, ergo sum*.

It's nice to be reassured that we can think, but we could be forgiven at this point for wondering: To what end? From philosophical treatments of error, we learn that our thoughts exist but that they might not bear much resemblance to the real state of the world. From industrial and political treatments, we learn that even the best efforts to remain alert to error can't always save us and our society from catastrophic mistakes. And recall, too, the Pessimistic Meta-Induction from the History of Everything—the notion that many of our most convincing ideas have proved wrong in the past, and that many of our new ones will therefore prove wrong in the future.

What are we to do with this much pessimism, this much radical uncertainty? Do we need it? Is it useful? The pragmatist Charles Peirce thought not; he scoffed at Descartes, counseling that we should not "doubt in philosophy what we do not doubt in our hearts." Fair enough: as we've seen, all of us hold (and need to hold) some beliefs that are either below the level of conscious awareness or, to our minds, above dispute. I, for one, don't waste time doubting my own existence, or for that matter any of my deepest ethical principles. Still, on the whole, I'm inclined to think that Pierce got it wrong. Doubt is the act of challenging our beliefs. If we have developed formal methods for doing so, it is because, as I have shown, our hearts are bad at it.

And we pay a price for this weakness. I don't just mean we make mistakes we could avoid if we tempered our beliefs with doubt. It's true that those mistakes can be costly, but the price of ignoring our fallibility goes well beyond that. It extends, in fact, to our overall outlook on the world. When Socrates taught his students, he didn't try to stuff them full of knowledge. Instead, he sought to fill them with *aporia:* with a sense of doubt, perplexity, and awe in the face of the complexity and contradictions of the world. If we are unable to embrace our fallibility, we lose out on that kind of doubt. This isn't Hamlet's doubt—that of agony in the face of a difficult decision. Nor is it the doubt of insecurity, apprehension, or indifference. This is an active, investigative doubt: the kind that inspires us to wander onto shaky limbs or out into left field; the kind that doesn't divide the mind so much as multiply it, like a tree in which there are three blackbirds and the entire Bronx Zoo. This is the doubt we stand to sacrifice if we can't embrace error—the doubt of curiosity, possibility, and wonder.

But there's something else, too, that we miss out on if we decline to honor our fallibility. I have written, in this chapter, about the importance of acknowledging our mistakes primarily as a way to prevent them. Sometimes, though, accepting wrongness is not a means to an end, but an end in itself. By way of conclusion, then, I want to turn to a very different reason to embrace error: not for the purpose of eliminating it, but for the pleasure of experiencing it.

15.

The Optimistic Meta-Induction from the History of Everything

> "The secret of life is to appreciate the pleasure
> of being terribly, terribly deceived."
> —OSCAR WILDE, *A WOMAN OF NO IMPORTANCE*

Herewith, a very short story at my own expense: one day in the summer of 2007, I traveled by car from Connecticut to Boston with my sister and her family. The car in question was theirs, and new, but, because I am not much of a car person, I didn't pay it any attention, beyond observing that it was a pleasant shade of blue. In accordance with the principle of Once A Younger Sister, Always A Younger Sister, I was consigned to the backseat with my niece.

A little ways into Massachusetts, we pulled over at a service plaza to grab some food. As we prepared to leave again, the skies, which had been overcast since we left Connecticut, opened up into one of those cats-and-dogs deluges characteristic of summertime in the Northeast. Lacking an umbrella, I returned to the car at a flat run, threw open the door, and flung my sopping self into the backseat—to the visible astonishment and considerable alarm of the total stranger who was sitting there nursing her infant.

It was, you will have surmised, the wrong car. I extricated myself, extremely rapidly and extremely inelegantly; in my final glimpse of the woman, she hadn't yet altered the stunned look on her face, or slackened her protective grip on her baby. When I found my way to the right car, my sister, who had been following my mad dash at a distance (whether it was too much of a distance to warn me of my impending mistake or whether she was simply curious to see what would happen is a point of some contention), was still convulsed with hysterical laughter.

No question about it: being wrong can be funny. And a cruel but indisputable corollary: other people being wrong can be very, very funny. If, at the end of the last chapter, you wondered what I meant by embracing error strictly for the pleasure of experiencing it, this kind of humor is part of it. As we'll see in a moment, wrongness and comedy are entwined at the roots. And not just wrongness and comedy: also wrongness and art, wrongness and learning, wrongness and individuality—even wrongness and survival.

But wrongness and comedy is a good place to start, not least because, whether you know it or not, you are already familiar with this relationship. If you grew up watching sitcoms or comedy routines or Hollywood classics or *Candid Camera*; if you've ever laughed at a joke that starts, "A penguin, a lion, and an ape walked into a bar . . .";* if you have committed or cracked up at linguistic errors (like a friend of mine who famously asked someone with allergies whether he broke out in chives)—if you have done any of this, then you've already experienced error as funny. Such comical mistakes are not rare. Nor are they exceptions to a rule whereby wrongness is normally grim. On the contrary: there is something potentially comedic in the very nature of error. And, conversely, there is something errorlike in the very nature of comedy.

---

* The bartender says, "What is this, some kind of joke?"

For at least two and a half thousand years, writers, philosophers, and critics have been trying to understand the nature of this relationship between humor and error. One longstanding if rather uncharitable claim is that we laugh at situations in which we are able to look down on other people. This is known as the superiority theory of comedy, and its most famous proponent was Thomas Hobbes. According to Hobbes, humor arises "from some sudden conception of some eminency in ourselves, by comparison with the infirmity of others, or with our own formerly." By the logic of the superiority theory, errors make us laugh because they make their perpetrators look foolish, and thereby make us look better. In this model, comedy affirms our default (and desired) relationship to rightness: that we possess it and others do not.

Superiority theory explains why we laugh at, say, *Bill and Ted's Excellent Adventure*, "yo mama" jokes, and people who accidentally walk into unusually clean glass doors. Yet it seems neither necessary to comedy (where is the superiority in an elephant joke?) nor sufficient (what is funny about the infirmity of an aging parent?). And it seems to rob humor of two of its central elements, conviviality and lightness of spirit, replacing them, instead, with a kind of each-man-for-himself vindictiveness.

A more generous view of the relationship between comedy and wrongness suggests that we laugh at the errors of others not out of self-satisfaction but out of self-recognition. Some thinkers have even proposed that the whole point of formal comedy is to show us the error of our ways. This notion—we might call it the self-improvement theory of humor—was summarized by the Elizabethan-era critic Sir Philip Sidney, who argued that comedy should serve as "an imitation of the common errors of our life." Nearly a hundred years later, the great comic playwright Molière echoed that sentiment, observing of his craft that, "the duty of comedy is to correct men by amusing them."

As different as they are in outlook, the self-improvement theory of humor and the superiority theory of humor have something in common. Both concern the substance of error: according to them, we laugh at specific, recognizable mistakes, whether from a feeling of supremacy or from rueful identification. But a different hypothesis dispenses with the substance of errors in favor of their structure. This is the incongruity theory of humor—and, in terms of both staying power and explanatory range, it is by far our strongest account of comedy. Aristotle subscribed to incongruity theory (and possibly invented it), as did the philosophers Schopenhauer, Kierkegaard, and Kant. More recently, Ward Jones (whom we last encountered delineating the 'Cuz It's True Constraint) surveyed the comic domain and concluded that instances of incongruity account for "the vast majority of humor."*

As its name suggests, incongruity theory posits that comedy arises from a mismatch—specifically, a mismatch between expectation and actuality. According to this theory, funny situations begin with attachment to a belief, whether that attachment is conscious or unconscious, fleeting or deep, sincerely held or deliberately planted by a comedian or a prankster. That belief is then violated, producing surprise, confusion, and a replacement belief—and also producing, along the way, enjoyment and laughter. In other words, the structure of humor is—give or take a little pleasure—the structure of error.

We can see this structural resemblance clearly in (what else?) Shakespeare's *Comedy of Errors*. The plot concerns two sets of twins separated at birth—a pair of identical servants bonded to their identical masters—who converge, unbeknownst to all of them, in the city of Ephesus, in modern-day Turkey. Predictably, mayhem ensues. One servant is dispatched to run an errand and the other is beaten for failing to complete it; one twin unwittingly propositions the other twin's sister-in-law, who is appalled at what she takes to be his infidelity; you get the picture.

Why is *The Comedy of Errors* comedic? As the critic Bertrand Evans has

---

* Another traditional explanation of the origins of humor is the relief theory, according to which laughter serves to release pent-up mental, emotional, physical, or sexual tension. The relief theory helps explain why we laugh at dirty jokes and scatological humor, and also why we sometimes get the giggles in the face of stress, gravity, or tragedy. However, since it doesn't bear very much on error, I have left it out of the main discussion. The same goes for more recent theories of humor emerging from evolutionary psychology, most of which are rooted in claims about primordial social hierarchies and/or ancient habits of play.

observed, by many standard metrics, it is not. None of the characters are intrinsically funny (either intentionally, as wags, or accidentally, as buffoons), and almost none of the dialogue packs the one-two punch of wit and raunch characteristic of Shakespeare's later work. *The Comedy of Errors* is exactly what it claims to be: we laugh because (and almost exclusively because) the characters keep getting things wrong. As Evans put it, "the great resource of laughter is the exploitable gulf spread between the participants' understanding and ours."

This "exploitable gulf" that makes *The Comedy of Errors* funny has, in fact, been merrily exploited by other humorists throughout history. False beliefs might be the essence of error, but they are also one of the most popular and effective of comic plot drivers, from *Tartuffe* (possibly the funniest comedy of manners of all time) to *Tootsie* (possibly the funniest romantic comedy of all time).* This gulf in understanding also creates much of the inadvertent comedy of everyday life. Like the misadventures in Ephesus, my misadventure in Massachusetts was funny because of the discrepancy between what I thought I was doing (hurtling into my sister's car) and what I was actually doing (hurtling into a stranger's car). In other words, the very thing that leads us to err—a gap between the world as it is and the world as we think it is—also produces the pleasure of comedy.

We have encountered this pleasure-in-error before, most notably in the form of optical illusions. In fact, comedy and illusion are close kin. In his influential 1900 essay on laughter, Henri Bergson posited that, "A situation

---

* Or possibly the second funniest, which is the ranking it was given by the American Film Institute in a list compiled in 2000. Top honors in that list went to *Some Like It Hot*, which might lead readers familiar with both movies to conclude that the real source of comedy is not confusion and error but rather men in dresses. This cross-dressing theory of comedy receives some support from the rest of AFI's list of all-time funniest movies (*Mrs. Doubtfire* also makes the top 100, as does *Victor Victoria*), not to mention the rest of performance history. (See, for instance, *As You Like It*, *Twelfth Night*, and *The Taming of the Shrew*.) It's true that real or implied gender transgression furnishes its own (complicated) source of humor. But the real comic strength of cross-dressing narratives might be their ability to trigger follies of mistaken identity—much like stories about identical twins separated at birth.

is invariably comic when it belongs simultaneously to two altogether independent series of events and is capable of being interpreted in two entirely different meanings at the same time." When one situation can support two different visual interpretations, you get an optical illusion (such as the vases/faces image, or the young woman and the old maid). When one situation can support two different intellectual interpretations, you get, among other things, *The Comedy of Errors*. You get Abbot and Costello's *Who's on First*. You get puns, where one word or phrase can be interpreted in two different ways. You get misheard song lyrics, where one set of sounds can be parsed to produce two different meanings. You get the children's game of Telephone, whose pleasure derives from the juxtaposition of an original message with the errors introduced into its garbled form. We laugh at all these things for much the same reason that I laughed at my headlong plunge into a stranger's car: because of a gap between what we expect at the beginning (Groucho Marx: "I've had a perfectly wonderful evening") and what actually comes next ("but this wasn't it.")

In saying this, I'm not trying to suggest that incongruity amounts to a Unified Field Theory of humor. After all, I began this book by quoting Bergson's injunction against "imprisoning the comic spirit within a definition." Not every instance of comedy arises from error—from an "exploitable gulf" between expectation and actuality. Conversely, not every error is comedic; we know from painful experience that the violation of belief can disturb or devastate us instead of making us laugh.[†] Still, while humor can sometimes exist apart from error, it couldn't thrive in a world without wrongness. Take error out of the picture and you drain down the well of comedy—not to rock bottom, perhaps, but to drought conditions. If we want to keep laughing as much as we currently do, we must also keep bumbling into the gap between the world as we think it is and the world as it turns out to be; we must keep

---

† Bergson played devil's advocate on this one, arguing that we only fail to find errors funny when we are invested in the beliefs that they destroy. "Look upon life as a disinterested spectator," he proposed, and "many a drama will turn into a comedy." In other words, with sufficient distance and dispassion, all wrongness would be amusing. To the gods, the human spectacle might well constitute one long sitcom.

on getting things wrong. At best, we can learn to laugh at these mistakes—but at the very least, we can take comfort from the fact that, in the broadest sense, we laugh *because* of them.

It is an odd thing, this gap I keep talking about. On the one hand, it forms a moat between us and everything else, giving us both error and (when we look into it too deeply) an unpleasant case of existential vertigo—an awareness of being fundamentally alone. On the other hand, it also gives us comedy, including the kind we deliberately create to leaven one another's lives. Nor is that the only kind of creativity that arises from this gap. The psychologist Rollo May argued that *all* art "issues out of this encounter between a human being . . . and an objective reality." Bergson concurred. "Could reality come into direct contact with sense and consciousness," he wrote, "could we enter into immediate communion with things and with ourselves, probably art would be useless." Like error, art comes about because we cannot grasp things directly as they are.

The fact that art is inherently an inaccurate representation of reality has long been a philosophical objection to the whole enterprise. In one of the most famous passages of *The Republic*, Plato contends that an ideal civilization would banish all artists, on the grounds that they are in the business of distorting the truth. As usual, Plato recruits Socrates as his speaker, and the latter begins his attack on art by asking us to think about (of all things) a bed. A bed, Socrates says, has three forms. The first form is divine. Since God created everything, he must have created the idea of a bed, and so the one truly perfect bed exists only in the mind of God. The second form is the kind you can buy at Ikea. That one is a corruption of the divine ideal, but it still earns a place in the republic, since even a philosopher-king needs somewhere to sleep. The third form, however, is a picture of a bed, and this is where Socrates draws the line. Here, the divine ideal is corrupted for no practical reason whatsoever: you can't sleep on any of the mattresses on which lounge the innumerable nudes of the Uffizi. Pictures, Socrates argued, are nothing more than imitations of imitations, "thrice removed from the truth." And the same goes for the literary arts. "All these poetical individuals, beginning with Homer, are only imitators," Socrates opined. "They copy images of virtue and the like, but the truth they never reach."

Socrates' objection to these imitations wasn't that, like pictures of furniture, they are useless. It was that they are *worse* than useless. Like false fires and superior mirages, art misleads us by presenting representation as reality. He asks: with what part of ourselves do we appreciate art? With our senses, of course—and we already know exactly how trustworthy *those* are. Not only do "[artistic] creations have an inferior degree of truth," Socrates argues, they are "concerned with an inferior part of the soul." For him, that seals the deal: "I have said that painting or drawing, and imitation in general . . . are far removed from truth, and [are] the companions and friends and associates of a principle within us which is equally removed from reason, and therefore we shall be right in refusing to admit [the artist] into a well-ordered State."

Plato's gripe with artists has sent many undergraduates storming out of their introductory philosophy classes in disgust. And with reason: most of us don't care to imagine life without literature and art, and we don't have good associations with the kind of societies that seek to censure, silence, or exile their artists. But the trouble here is not Plato's observation that art is a kind of error. He was right about that. The trouble is that he subscribes to the pessimistic model of wrongness. Having discerned the connection between representation and error, it follows, for him, that art is a mark of our distance from God, the product of an inferior part of our souls, a discredit to our reason, and something we should seek to eliminate. His desire to banish art is part of a long and often sinister tradition (which we glimpsed earlier) of trying to create ideal societies through eradicating error in all its forms.

All of those disgruntled undergraduates, meanwhile, are motivated in part—whether they know it or not—by the optimistic model of wrongness. They recognize, as most of us do, not just the legitimacy but also the potential beauty and power of individual, skewed, inaccurate representations of reality. In this model, the link between error and art is not an indictment of art but a defense of error. Cut off from the absolute essence of things—that ideal form that Plato felt existed only in the mind of God—our separate, subjective consciousnesses look around and see, instead, *Water Lilies*, or *Starry Night*, or *Les Demoiselles d'Avignon*. Likewise, we can make *Beowulf* and *Star Wars* and *Horton Hears a Who!* for the same reason we can make mistakes: because, as I said earlier, we are capable of conjuring the world not just as it is, but also as it is not. Our capacity to err is inseparable from our imagination.

This relationship between art and error can be subtle. When you are reading Dr. Seuss to your six-year-old, you probably aren't thinking about the fundamental fallibility of humanity. In fact, until recently, artists (at least, Western artists) didn't *want* you to think about this relationship. Their goal was to represent the world with as much verisimilitude as possible: to get you to mistake a representation for reality, or admire how nearly indistinguishable the two were—in other words, to paper over the gap between our minds and everything else.

But then modernism came along and changed all that. In dance, music, theater, literature, and the visual arts, the main cultural current shifted from trying to disguise art's connection to error to trying to expose it. Art became interested in exploring its skewed relationship to reality and its status as representation—which is how the great Victorian novels of, say, George Eliot gave way to the modernist funhouses of Gertrude Stein, and the paintings of the realist Gustave Courbet gave way to the works of Picasso. Accompanying this increased interest in error was an increased suspicion of rightness, an ethos succinctly summarized by Tristan Tzara. Tzara was a Romanian poet who helped found Dadaism, a precursor to surrealism that emerged largely in reaction to the carnage of World War I. In one of his manifestos on the nature and obligations of art, Tzara implored his fellow artists, "Let us try for once not to be right."

In an artistic culture where realism had reigned supreme for centuries, trying not to be right was a radical innovation. But if modernism marked a shift in how we think about art (and how we make it), it didn't make any difference whatsoever to the nature of art itself. Whether you are trying to be right, like the realists, or trying not to be right, like the Dadaists, whether your medium is canvas or a urinal or the walls of a cave, the art you make will always be subjective and askew. Plato feared this fact, but no one who makes art can avoid it. If error is a kind of accidental stumbling into the gap between representation and reality, art is an intentional journey to the same place.

It's not surprising, then, that artists often seem unusually aware of this gap, and unusually comfortable with its prevailing weather conditions of uncertainty and error. The most famous formulation of this relationship between art, doubt, and error comes from the Romantic poet John Keats. He had been talking over various matters with a friend, he wrote to his brothers in a letter in 1817, "and at once it struck me,"

> what quality went to form a Man of Achievement especially in literature & which Shakespeare possessed so enormously—I mean Negative Capability, that is when man is capable of being in uncertainties, Mysteries, doubts without any irritable reaching after fact & reason.

Keats's attitude toward uncertainty—and, for that matter, toward "fact & reason"—is not the common one. He embraced unknowability and fallibility, but not for the utilitarian purposes we saw in the last chapter. There, the point of embracing error was to curtail it—a kind of homeopathic remedy for wrongness. But Keats wasn't interested in remedying wrongness. He recognized error and art as conjoined twins, born of the same place and vital to one another's existence. In life as in linguistics, *art* is joined at the root to *artificial*—to the not-true, the un-real—just as a *fiction* is at once a creation and a falsehood.

Keats's observation, while particularly famous, is not particularly unique. If you listen to artists talk about their craft, this concept of "negative capability"—the ability to live comfortably in the presence of mystery and the absence of certainty—comes up with remarkable frequency. "Whatever inspiration is," the Polish poet Wislawa Szymborska said in her 1996 Nobel Prize acceptance speech, "it's born from a continuous 'I don't know.'"* One of her colleagues, the Canadian poet Anne Carson, put it even more plainly in a poem called "Essay on What I Think About Most." (The opening lines are "Error. / And its emotions.") "What we are engaged in when we do poetry," Carson wrote, "is error." I take her to mean by this three things. The first is that poetry is made of words, and, as we've seen, words have error built into them from the get-go. Every syllable is a stepping stone across the gap, an effort to explain something (train tracks, thunder, happiness) by recourse to something it is not (a word). The second is that writing, whether of poetry or anything else, involves a certain inevitable amount of getting it wrong—an awareness that truth is always on the lam, that the instant you think you've got it pinned down on the page, it shimmers, distorts, wiggles away. Last, but possibly most important, I take her to mean that poetry, like error, startles, unsettles, and defies; it urges us toward new theories about old things.

Making mistakes as one might make poems, rejecting certainty, deliberately exploring ambiguity and error: this is the optimistic model of wrongness on Ecstasy. It does not truck with (to borrow Carson's words again) "fear, anxiety, shame, remorse / and all the other silly emotions associated with making mistakes." I don't agree that such emotions are silly, but I do agree that they are not a good place to set down our luggage and settle in. Artists entice us past them, into a world where error is not about fear and shame, but about disruption, reinvention, and pleasure. Art is an invitation to enjoy ourselves in the land of wrongness.

As that suggests, it is not just the makers of art but its beneficiaries—you and me—who get to experience an acute pleasure in error. Think for a moment about "suspension of disbelief," the prerequisite for enjoying fictional narratives of all kinds. As readers, spectators, or listeners, we consent to believe, albeit temporarily, in something we know to be false. What we expect to receive in exchange is pleasure. And we do. But that pleasure often

---

* Szymborska explicitly contrasted the poet's embrace of doubt with its antithesis, the zealot's embrace of certainty. The trouble with "torturers, dictators, fanatics and demagogues," she wrote, is that "they 'know,' and whatever they know is enough for them once and for all. They don't want to find out about anything else, since that might diminish the force of their arguments."

comes to us in forms that—fittingly, since they derive from error—we do not usually enjoy.

Take suspense. Under normal circumstances, we don't relish the anxiety of not knowing, but when it comes to art, we are veritable suspense junkies. I don't just mean that we gravitate toward works that are explicitly created and billed as thrillers, although we certainly love those, too. Virtually all fictional narratives contain some element of strategic withholding, hoodwinking, and revealing, and we simply can't get enough of it. We love to be kept guessing—and, what's more, we are happiest when all of our guesses prove wrong. That's why some of the most satisfying fictional narratives (*The Murder of Roger Ackroyd, Our Mutual Friend, Pride and Prejudice*, and *The Usual Suspects*, to name a few) don't merely resolve their suspense at the end, but do so in a way that comports with the facts yet still contrives to astonish us.†

So one perverse pleasure of art is the pleasure of being lost, in the sense of being confused or in the dark. (Traditionally, this confusion is temporary, and resolves into satisfying clarity at the conclusion. In modern art, with its more acute interest in error, the sense of being lost is often ongoing: see Gertrude Stein.) But a second pleasure is that of being lost in a different sense: of exploring uncharted territory, whether in the world or in the self. We say of a particularly engrossing work of art that we *got lost in it*—as if, through experiencing it, we had wandered into an unfamiliar world. And

---

† I can't resist a footnote on Jane Austen's *Pride and Prejudice*, since it is arguably the best example of pleasure from error in all of literary history—not to mention one of the world's greatest meditations on certainty and wrongness. The book famously opens with the phrase "It is a truth universally acknowledged" ("that a single man, in possession of a good fortune, must be in want of a wife")—but in fact, "truth universally acknowledged" is the plaything of Austin's novel. The more universally or vociferously any "truth" is averred in it, the more you can bet it isn't true at all. This is particularly the case when it comes to ostensible verities about the novel's characters; *Pride and Prejudice* is a book about people who, believing themselves to be astute scholars of human nature, persistently and dramatically misunderstand each other. Unlike in *The Comedy of Errors*, however, we the reader don't stand aside smirking at the sequence of mistakes. On the contrary, we are wholly party to them—with the happy result that we are also party to the pleasurable shock of wrongness when the truth is revealed at the end.

we also say (note the unusual reflexive form) that we *lost ourselves in it*, as if it had caused the confines of a familiar identity to go a little slack. This feeling of being utterly absorbed in something, from cover to cover or curtain to curtain, is the primordial pleasure of art, one that kicks in long before a grasp of tradition or an admiration of technique. It is the kid-happiness of disappearing into another world.

This suggests a curious paradox. If art arises from our fundamental isolation in our own minds—from the way we are denied direct access to the world and all its contents—it also temporarily frees us from that isolation. Art lets us live, for a little while, in other worlds, including in other people's inner worlds; we can hear their thoughts, feel their emotions, even believe their beliefs. (Odd, how able and happy we are to do this with fiction, when we often have so much difficulty doing so in real life.) Put differently, art is an exercise in empathy. Through it, we give the constraints of subjectivity the slip; we achieve, however temporarily, that universal moral aim of seeing the world through someone else's eyes.

If we could contrive to embrace error as we embrace art, we would see that it bestows on us these same gifts. Our mistakes, when we face up to them, show us both the world and the self from previously unseen angles, and remind us to care about perspectives other than our own. And, whether we like it or not, they also serve as real-life plot devices, advancing our own story in directions we can never foresee. Through error—as through the best works of art—we both lose and find ourselves.

The relationship I just described between wrongness and art should seem familiar. Somewhat surprisingly, it looks a lot like the relationship between wrongness and science. Both domains attempt to bridge the gap between our minds and the world, and both rely on their practitioners repeatedly making mistakes. (Scientists, like poets, could fairly claim that, "what we are engaged in . . . is error.") In other words, error is central to both the why and the how of science and art: it gives us a reason as well as a means to pursue them.

Yet if both these fields depend on error, they do so in service of two fundamentally different ideas of truth. Artists take as central what scientists (and the rest of us) usually sideline as much as we can: that reality as we know it is inevitably askew, refracted through an individual and idiosyncratic mind always slightly out of step with the world. Stated in more familiar terms, art is subjective. As Picasso put it, "We all know that Art is not truth. Art is a lie that makes us realize the truth, at least the truth that is given to us to understand."

It's safe to say that no towering figure of scientific genius ever declared, "We all know that Science is not truth." However aware of their limits individual scientists might be, the discipline itself leans heavily on the idea of objectivity. Here some recourse to the dictionary will be helpful, since "objectivity" is more often invoked than defined and can be used to mean different things. According to Merriam-Webster, the first definition of "objective" (after the archaic ones and those pertaining to grammar) is "having reality independent of the mind." In this sense, the objective is what we would see if we could somehow access the world without the involvement of our brain—if we really could figure out how to hold up a mirror, instead of a mind, to reality. This meaning of "objective" is essentially a synonym for "true." The second definition, meanwhile, is essentially a synonym for "impartial": "expressing or dealing with facts or conditions as perceived without distortion by personal feelings, prejudices, or interpretations."

These definitions have two things in common. The first is that they reflect our most entrenched ideas about how our minds work: respectively, the toddler's faith in (and the adult's relapse into) naïve realism, and the more mature if still idealized notion of an unimpeachably rational thinker. The second thing they have in common is what they omit. In one definition, objectivity is characterized by the absence of a mind; in the other, by the absence of feelings, prejudices, and interpretations. In both cases, what's missing is anything like a recognizable human being. Objectivity, in other words, is the absence of the self. Our desire to be right, as ego-driven as it often seems, is essentially a desire to take ourselves out of the picture. We want our beliefs to inhere in the world, not in our mind. The experience of realizing that we were wrong represents the frustration of this desire—the revelation that the self was there all along.

I say "frustration," and that's what we often feel in the face of our mistakes: thwarted, aggravated, disoriented, disturbed. Without dismissing such feelings, one major point of this book has been to urge us to move beyond them—and sometimes forestall them—through the cultivation of a different attitude toward error. In this alternative attitude, wrongness reminds us that the human mind is far more valuable and versatile than it would be if it just passively reflected the precise contours of reality. For those who share this view, the fact that our beliefs inhere in our minds is a given, and a gift—one whose benefits (humor, imagination, intelligence, individuality) are so manifestly worthwhile that we willingly pay for them with our mistakes.

What other entity can lay claim to wrongness, after all? Not God, obviously, since the monotheistic versions, at least, are all-knowing and inerrant. And (as far as we know) not any animals other than ourselves, either. If there's a sense in which a lion errs when it pounces too soon and misses its prey, or a sense in which an owl is somehow mistaken about its notion of the night sky, it is surely nothing like the sense in which we human beings are wrong. It seems safe to say that no lion has ever berated itself for making a mistake, or waxed defensive about it, or turned it into a funny story to recount to the rest of the pride. Nor, presumably, is there any variation between one owl's idea of night and another's, nor any way for them individually or collectively to revise their understanding of the cosmos. These creatures can no more get things wrong than they can make up stories about cowardly lions, or about owls that deliver the mail at Hogwarts School of Witchcraft and Wizardry. In both cases, the limitation is the same: they cannot imagine things that do not exist. We can, and so much the luckier for us.

Machines, too, are incapable of error in the human sense. However much a computer or a BlackBerry or an ATM might excel at revealing our mistakes (as both designers and users), neither they nor any of their electronic kin can make errors on their own. To begin with, error is contingent on belief, and while machines can arguably "know" things—in the sense of possessing accurate information—they can't "believe" things in the way that you and

I can. Granted, certain advanced forms of artificial intelligence have some capacity to generate theories about the world and revise those theories in the face of counterevidence, a capacity that could be said to amount to a crude form of belief. Even the most cutting-edge machines don't do this very well, but that's not the point. The point is that they don't do it with emotion, and emotion is central to both the idea of belief and the idea of wrongness. Surprise, confusion, embarrassment, amusement, anguish, remorse, delight: take away all of that, and whatever process of belief collapse and reconstruction that remains doesn't look anything like error as you and I experience it. In the face of information that violates their (limited) representations of the world, machines do not go into denial or blame their programmer or turn red or laugh out loud. If they are sufficiently sophisticated, they update their representations; otherwise, they freeze, or fail. This is nicely captured by the two stock devices used in science fiction when an android is confronted with input that contradicts its existing database. The first is the freeze response: "does not compute." The second is the fail response: instant and violent self-destruction.

As far as we know, then, error is uniquely ours. "To err is human," "I'm only human": our fallibility is what keeps us suspended between the kingdom of lesser animals and the kingdom of God. The important truth behind these sayings isn't that we must be wrong from time to time; it's that we *can* be wrong. Alone among the creatures of the world, we can hatch crazy ideas, pursue pipe dreams, speculate wildly, keep faith with even the most far-fetched fantasies. Sometimes these notions flourish and bear fruit, and sometimes they collapse. But unlike androids, we humans do not normally self-destruct in the face of our mistakes. On the contrary: we self-create, and self–re-create.

This idea of self-creation suggests something else important about error. Being wrong doesn't just make us human in general; it also helps make each of us the specific person we are. In our inability to get things exactly right, in the idiosyncrasies of our private visions of the world, the outline of selfhood appears. This is what Benjamin Franklin was getting at in the quote I used as an epigraph to this book. Error, he wrote, is "the pure and simple creation of the mind that invents it," a place where "the soul has room enough to expand herself." Mistakes, he meant, are the evidence and expression of an individual identity.

This is an idea with deep and important roots in our intellectual history. It is, in essence, the crucial insight of evolutionary theory. Because of errors in the replication of genetic sequences, we wind up with variation among individual members of a species; and because of that variation, the species as a whole can adapt and survive. Such errors literally keep their hosts alive. A population that is too small or too homogenous to support significant genetic variation is doomed. For every species, then, error is a mechanism of survival and change. For us human organisms, with our richer relationship to wrongness, mistakes enable not only our biological evolution but our social, emotional, and intellectual evolution as well.

And wrongness also allows us to thrive in another way. I began this book by noting that we think of being right as essential to our survival and happiness, but in one key respect, nothing could be further from the truth. Countless studies have shown that people who suffer from depression have more accurate worldviews than nondepressed people. Depressed people do not nurture the cheering illusion that they can control the course of their lives. They rarely possess the conviction, so common in the rest of us, that they are above average in virtually every respect. And they understand, all too acutely, the basic conditions of existence: that their lifespan is just a brief blip in the cold sweep of history, that suffering is real and ongoing, that they and all the people they love are going to die. That outlook is known as depressive realism. Depressed people might be unhappy, but—when it comes to these big-picture, existential matters—they are generally more right than the rest of us.

It scarcely requires saying that this kind of rightness is *not* fun. "To see the world as it really is is devastating and terrifying," wrote the philosopher Ernest Becker. ". . . It makes thoughtless living in the world of men an impossibility. It places a trembling animal at the mercy of the entire cosmos and the problem of the meaning of it." As that indicates, the correlation between accuracy and depression runs both ways: people who are depressed tend to perceive the harsher realities of life more clearly, and people who clearly perceive those harsh realities tend to be (or to get) depressed. In an odd reversal of the usual state of affairs, when it comes to these existential issues, the bigger and more important the belief, the less it pays to be right. That's why, as I've said, the goal of therapy isn't necessarily to make our beliefs more accurate; it is to make them more *functional*. Ronnie Janoff-Bulman, the psychologist, has even argued that "a key to the good life might well be illusions at our deepest, most generalized level of assumptions and accuracy at the most specific, least abstract levels." (Fortunately for us, these two perspectives are compatible: research suggests that people who possess a generally positive outlook are better at acknowledging their everyday errors and changing their minds.)

If excessive accuracy in our self-image and worldview is correlated with depression, the opposite is true, too. Sometimes, being wrong makes us happy. Think of Don Quixote, that exemplary knight errant, who lent his name to the condition of being pleasantly deluded. Ugly, he thinks he is handsome; common, he thinks he is knightly; getting on in age, he thinks he is youthful. A plain farm girl is his lady love, a dimwitted neighbor his loyal squire, a lowly inn his castle, windmills his worthy adversaries. This quixotic version of Quixote is happy. It is only at the conclusion of the novel, when he is stripped of his illusions and forced to confront reality unvarnished, that he falls into melancholy and death.

Michel Foucault once proposed that Quixote represents an extreme version of us all—of "the imaginary relations [man in general] maintains with himself." Like Quixote, most of us think we are a bit younger, better-looking, and more important than strict realism might suggest. Most of us see a little extra loveliness in our loved ones, a little extra grandeur in our homes, a little extra heroism in our contests and quests. And thank God for that. These beliefs might skew the truth, but they stave off depression, give meaning to our lives, and make us and those we love happy.

These kinds of beneficial self-deceptions can be sweeping and existential in nature—as when we ignore or deny the fact that we have only limited control over the course of our lives, and none at all over the inevitability of death. Yet such delusions also get us through life in countless more mundane ways. Here, for instance, is a friend of mine talking about a kind of wrongness that I bet will sound familiar to every reader. Once, this friend told me, back when he was in college, "I said to myself, 'I'm going to read all of *Ulysses* over Christmas break.' And then I read maybe twenty pages of *Ulysses* and ate a lot of chocolate. That's what I did over Christmas break." Nor, he continued, have his powers of accurately forecasting his own actions improved with age: "I still look at a book in the morning and think, *I'm going to finish that book by tonight.* I could just say to myself, 'I'm going to finish the preface by tonight,' and then I might be almost right. But instead I go on letting myself think I'll read the whole thing."

Believing that this time we will succeed where in the past we have failed, or failed to try; believing the best of ourselves even when we are intimately familiar with the worst and the merely average; believing that everything in us that is well-intentioned will triumph over all that is lazy or fickle or indifferent or unkind: this is wrongness as optimism—an endlessly renewable, overextended faith in our own potential. Wrongness as optimism is why my friend thought he would read one of the world's longest and hardest works of literature during a four-week holiday, and why my neighbor swears that he just smoked his last cigarette, and why I thought this book would be done a year and a half ago. As I can tell you from that last example, this kind of wrongness gets us started and keeps us going. Take away our willingness to overestimate ourselves, and we wouldn't dare to undertake half the things we do.

In this sense, *all* wrongness is optimism. We err because we believe, above all, in ourselves: no matter how often we have gotten things wrong in the past, we evince an abiding and touching faith in our own stories and theories. Traditionally, we are anxious to deny that those stories and theories *are* stories and theories—that we must rely on our own imperfect representations to make sense of the world, and are therefore destined to err. But, to risk a bit of blasphemy, stories and theories may be all we have that God does not. They are the hallmark of two of our highest human endeavors, art and science, and through them we can imagine new realities.

That is why error, even though it sometimes feels like despair, is actually much closer in spirit to hope. We get things wrong because we have an enduring confidence in our own minds; and we face up to that wrongness in the faith that, having learned something, we will get it right the next time. In this optimistic vein, embracing our fallibility is simply a way of paying homage to, in the words of the late philosopher Richard Rorty, "the permanent possibility of someone having a better idea." The great advantage of realizing that we have told a story about the world is realizing that we can tell a better one: rich with better ideas, better possibilities—even, perhaps, better people.

ACKNOWLEDGMENTS

Speaking of wrongness: I had no idea, when I began this project, what I was getting into—no idea how challenging it would be, no idea how much I would learn (and would need to learn), and certainly no idea how many intellectual and emotional debts I would accrue along the way. Quite possibly I would never have gotten started if I had known all that. Since I'm glad I did, I should start by thanking those people who *did* know, and wisely kept the information to themselves.

One of these was my agent, Kim Witherspoon, who began by plucking me out of thin air and proceeded to furnish both solid ground and seventh heaven—a nice hat trick if ever there was one. I am immensely grateful to her for her encouragement, dedication, and integrity. Thanks also to all the other kind and helpful people at Inkwell Management. I am likewise grateful to Daniel Halpern and Virginia Smith, my editors at Ecco, whose enthusiasm for this project was matched only by their patience with the time it took me to complete it. Along with the rest of the Ecco/HarperCollins team, they have been a consistent pleasure to work with, and a consistent boon to this book.

The convention, with acknowledgements, is to thank everyone who helped out, then append the courteous caveat that any mistakes in the book are solely the responsibility of the author. In this case, however, many of the people who helped me the most did so precisely by sharing the mistakes that appear in these pages. I would not have been able to write this book if it hadn't been for all those who consented to talk to me about their own experiences of being wrong, and did so with tremendous generosity and insight. In particular, I want to express my gratitude to those people whose stories and reflections appear in the final pages, including Ross Gelbspan, Amy Herzog, Bonnie Scott Jones, Donald Leka, Jonathan Minkoff, Kathy Misak, Elizabeth O'Donovan, Anita Wilson, Mark Zumwalt, and, especially, Penny Beerntsen.

Countless other people helped shape this book in different ways. Among them, I would like to thank Raoul Felder, Stephen Frug, Irna Gadd, Steve Hendricks, Harville Hendrix, William Hirst, Ward Jones, Patricia Kimble, Paul Levy, and Heidi Voskuhl (with gratitude for *The Story of Human Error*). I am indebted to Lee Ann Banaszak and Regina Wecker for helping me understand the history of women's suffrage in Switzerland, and to Peter Neufeld and other members of the Innocence Project for their invaluable assistance on the subject of wrongful convictions. Massive thanks as well to Tod(d) Hymas Samkara, fact checker extraordinaire, who did his best— actually, *the* best—to save me from my own subject matter. In his case, it really is true that whatever errors remain are exclusively my own.

During the earliest stages of this project, I spent several months in Boston, where I was lucky enough to find an ideal intellectual community to help incubate the ideas in this book. Many thanks to Rebecca Saxe, Allan Adams, Peter Godfrey Smith, Josh Tenenbaum, Mira Bernstein, Tom Griffiths, and Tania Lombrozo. I'm especially indebted to Rebecca for pointing me in the direction of William Hirstein and Ward Jones—and, more generally, for her ongoing, unstinting, and immensely helpful interest in and insights about this project. Thanks, too, to MIT's Brain and Cognitive Science Department, which gave me the chance to articulate some of the ideas in this book in public for the first time.

Other friends were generous with their ideas and even more generous with their support, humor, and patience during what proved to be a long and sometimes trying process. I could never thank all of them, or thank any of them enough. But, briefly: deep gratitude to Jill Krauss, Meg Thompson, Robyn Mierzwa, Jen Friedman, Janet Paskin, Jessi Hempel, Lassie Krishnaswami, Cat Hagarty, Amy Cohen, Laura Helton, Chip Giller, Camille Robcis, Yael Kropsky, Kevin Neel, Deborah Schimberg—and, especially, to Leslie Brooks, Emily Siegel, and Liv Gjestvang: always there. Thanks also to James Altucher and Anne Altucher, for the irreplaceable gift of more time at Spy Hill; to Ann and Howard Katz, for their open-armed support of this book and its author (and a much-needed eleventh-hour writing retreat in Vermont); to Denise Bilbao, for the sound files and other amazements; to Yoruba Richen, Noy Thrupkaew, and Stéphanie Giry, for fellowship in the fullest sense; to Amanda Griscom Little, for adventures tropical and lexical; to Jennifer Margulies, my oldest friend, mobile writing retreat, and outstanding last-minute editor; and to my friends in Oregon, for keeping the home fires burning—and especially to Celeste Baskett, without whom I'd be sunk.

A few people deserve special thanks—more, actually, than I know how to express. First among these are my parents, Margot and Isaac Schulz, who nurtured me (and still do) in an atmosphere of stable love and roving curiosity. I have benefited from their unwavering faith in this project more than they can know. My grandmother, Madeline Kann Price, has likewise been steadfast in her love and encouragement. My sister, Laura Schulz, is righter when she is wrong than most of us are when we are right. Her staggeringly large contributions to this book (intellectual and otherwise) are dwarfed only by her place in my heart. I am grateful beyond bounds to her and to the family she has brought into my life: my sister-in-law, Sue Kaufman, who added invaluable insights throughout this book, and who has never once faltered in the provision of support, perspective, sound advice, and a home away from home; my niece and nephew, Martha Jane Philofsky Kaufman and Henry Kaufman Philofsky, long the lights of my life and lately among the best of readers and friends; and their little sister, Adele Rosalie Kaufman Schulz, who brought us all joy when we needed it.

Lastly, I am not sure if this book would have been written (and I'm really not sure *how* it would have been written) without Michael Kavanagh and Amanda Katz. Some of the best ideas and most heartfelt emotions in these pages come, one way or another, from the two of them. Michael was the first person with whom I shared my interest in writing about wrongness, and he has been at my side for every subsequent moment of the process— both when he has known it, and when he has not. I am unaccountably fortunate, and indescribably happy, to have him in my life. Amanda set out to acquire the book and wound up acquiring the author—without question the tougher project. I don't know how to sufficiently express my gratitude for her patience, tenderness, humor, acuity, editorial brilliance, and, above all, her tenacious faith. I do know, though, that she has made this book—and my life—vastly better than it would otherwise be.

Often while working on this project I thought about something the author Philip Gourevitch once said. "One doesn't write what one means to write," he observed. "One writes what one *can* write." This is a variant on the kind of erring I discuss in the final chapter: the gap between the ideal bed (or the ideal book) and the real one—between what we can envision, and what we can pull off. In the end, I finally learned the point of this book by writing it. Aiming and missing, falling short, going astray, getting it wrong: it really did turn out to be both an agonizing lesson and an unparalleled pleasure. I am grateful to have experienced them both.

NOTES

A vast number and variety of sources—comments from friends, conversations with strangers, formal and informal interviews, news items, radio broadcasts, journal articles, websites, books—helped shape this book in ways both subtle and profound. Many of these do not appear in the final text in any explicit way, and it isn't practical to cite them all here. Still, wherever possible I have tried to attribute not just specific facts and quotations but also background sources and influences. More generally, I would like to acknowledge my deep debt to the many thinkers who have grappled with the idea of error, and whose work has made possible my own. Where appropriate, I have prefaced the notes to a given chapter with a brief description of particularly valuable sources. Specific citations then follow. I have sourced my footnotes in the order in which they appear in the book; they are distinguished from the main text by the indication **(FN)**.

A note on Wikipedia: I don't know any writer working today who doesn't regard it as 1) a pretty questionable source; and 2) surpassingly useful. To the second point, I offer my gratitude for the remarkable and largely anonymous collaborative effort it represents. I made use of it regularly to look up passing facts (was Rousseau born before Laplace, or vice versa?) or to get an initial overview of an unfamiliar subject (the proto-Indo-European language). In these cases, either I or my fact checker cross-referenced such information with other, more conventional resources to try to ensure accuracy. To the first point: as grateful as I am for its existence, I have avoided using Wikipedia as the definitive source for any information in this book, let alone for the substantive philosophical, psychological, scientific, and historical ideas I present. Accordingly, I have not cited it.

CHAPTER 1   WRONGOLOGY

5 **"inattention, distraction, lack of interest."** Massimo Piattelli-Palmarini, *Inevitable Illusions: How Mistakes of Reason Rule Our Minds* (Wiley, 1996), 141. In fairness, this quotation is taken somewhat out of context. As a cognitive scientist, Piattelli-Palmarini focuses mainly on the cognitive tendencies that give rise to certain predictable errors; he cites these other reasons largely to sketch the territory he *isn't* exploring.

6 *"fallor ergo sum."* The quotation is from Augustine's *The City of God*, and is rendered in many different ways in English. I have relied on the 2003 Penguin Classics edition, where Henry Bettenson translates the passage in question (it appears on p. 460) as follows: "In respect of those truths"— that I am, that I know that I am, and that I take delight in it—"I have no fear of the arguments of the Academics. They say, 'Suppose you are mistaken?' I reply, 'If I am mistaken, I exist.' A nonexistent being cannot be mistaken; therefore I must exist, if I am mistaken. Then since my being mistaken proves that I exist, how can I be mistaken in thinking that I exist, seeing that my mistake establishes my existence?"

11 **Plato's *Theaetetus*:** The edition of the *Theaetetus* I relied on was translated by Benjamin Jowett and published in 1949 by the Liberal Arts Press. But I first came across this passage as quoted in Leo W. Keeler's *The Problem of Error from Plato to Kant: A Historical and Critical Study* (Apud Aedes Pontificiae Universitatis Gregorianae, 1934), 150: "We proceed wrongly in examining false judgments without first having first determined what knowledge is, for it is impossible to understand the former until the latter has been accurately defined."

12 **"Mistakes may be defined."** James Reason, *Human Error* (Cambridge University Press, 1990), 9. Notwithstanding some dense prose, Reason does a deft and interesting job of ferreting out the practical applications of the insights of cognitive scientists (most famously Amos Tversky and Daniel Kahneman) about predictable failures of human cognition—so-called "cognitive illusions." And he does so while recognizing that, even as such illusions make us err, they also make us swift and often reliable thinkers. See especially Chapter Five, "A Design for a Fallible Machine."

14 **Iris Murdoch.** Murdoch writes: "A portrayal of moral reflection and moral change (degeneration, improvement) is the most important part of any system of ethics." I first came across this passage in the philosopher

Sissela Bok's book *Lying: Moral Choice in Public and Private Life* (Vintage, 1999), xxvi.

16 **rhubarb pie.** First of all, yes, I really don't like rhubarb pie. Sorry. Second, some readers might point out that many aesthetic preferences are inextricably tied to differences that run deeper than mere taste—to culture, to class, to background. That's true, but as I show in Chapter Seven, the same can be said of the vast majority of our "real" beliefs: our ideological convictions, metaphysical assumptions, and interpretation of the facts.

16 **John Updike.** Updike's comment was part of a speech he gave at New York University on May 19, 1987, upon receiving the Elmer Holmes Bobst Award for Fiction. It appears in John Updike, *More Matter: Essays and Criticism* (Ballantine Books, 2000), 810.

17 **Henri Bergson.** The edition I cite here and again in the final chapter appears in *Comedy*, a volume comprised of Bergson's "Laughter" and George Meredith's "Essay on Comedy," Wylie Sypher, ed. (Doubleday and Company, Inc., 1956). The quotation appears on p. 61.

19 **The psychologist Marc Green.** I came across Green's "Mental Act of God" analogy online, at http://www.expertlaw.com/library/malpractice/medical_error.html#6.

19 **an experience recounted by Sigmund Freud.** Sigmund Freud, *The Psychopathology of Everyday Life*, James Strachey, trans. and ed. (W. W. Norton & Co., 1965), 191 (footnote). Somewhat unconvincingly, given the context, Freud says that the patient was "the most remarkable case I had had in recent years, one which taught me a lesson I am not likely ever to forget."

21 **Thomas Aquinas.** For more on accounts of error by Aquinas, Plato, Locke, and many others, see Keeler—whose work is, to my knowledge, the only survey of philosophical treatments of error.

21 **the gates of the Garden of Eden.** For many religious thinkers, the problem of error is simply a subset of the problem of evil. Just as it is notoriously difficult to come up with a morally and theologically satisfying explanation for why an all-knowing, loving God would permit the existence of evil, it is difficult to understand why such a God would permit us to get things wrong, especially when those errors cause harm to us or to others, or lead us away from divine truth. One easy answer is that the fault cannot be God's and therefore must be ours—which is why many religious thinkers have classified error as a form of sin. Augustine, for instance, spends a long time trying to decide whether all error is evil. In the end

he concludes that errors respecting religious matters do count as sins, but that our everyday mistakes do not—or at least, not as serious ones: "to err in these [worldly] matters is not to be considered a sin; or if it is, it is the least and slightest." (See Keeler, pp. 79–82; the quotation is on p. 81.)

CHAPTER 2   TWO MODELS OF WRONGNESS

25 **"Our errors are surely not such awfully solemn things."** This and all the quotations from William James in this chapter are from his "Will To Believe," a lecture he delivered at the Philosophical Clubs of Yale and Brown Universities in 1896. The page citations here and throughout the endnotes are from William James, *The Will to Believe and Other Essays in Popular Philosophy* (Longmans, Green and Company, 1921). The above quotation appears on p. 19.

25 **Ross Gelbspan.** Ross initially shared his story with me via email. The quotations here are from a subsequent phone interview.

28 **"The mind being the faculty of truth."** Keeler, 87.

29 **France's *Larousse* dictionary.** I found both this definition and the one from Diderot's *Encyclopédie* in David Bates's *Enlightenment Aberrations: Error and Revolution in France* (Cornell University Press, 2002), an immensely useful intellectual history of error. The first definition appears on p. 20, the second on p. 25.

29 **James Sully.** James Sully, *Illusions: A Psychological Study* (IndyPublish, undated), 116. Sully goes on to make a much more extensive case that error is on the decline in the human species, an argument he bases in large part on the then-nascent field of evolutionary theory. "All correspondence, [the evolutionist] tells us, means fitness to external conditions and practical efficiency, all want of correspondence practical incompetence. Consequently, those individuals in whom the correspondence was more complete and exact would have an advantage in the struggle for existence and so tend to be preserved. . . . It may be argued, the forces at work in the action of man on man, of society on the individual, in the way of assimilating belief, must tend, in the long run, to bring about a coincidence between representations and facts. Thus, in another way, natural selection would help to adjust our ideas to realities, and to exclude the possibility of anything like a permanent common error." Then there's just the sheer matter of practice: "The exercise of a function tends to the development

of that function. Thus, our acts of perception must become more exact by mere repetition. . . . For external relations which are permanent will, in the long run, stamp themselves on our nervous and mental structure more deeply and indelibly than relations which are variable and accidental." See pp. 192–193.

29 **Joseph Jastrow.** Joseph Jastrow, *The Story of Human Error: False Leads in the Stages of Science* (D. Appelton-Century Company, Inc., 1936), 11. The book is behemoth in scope—Jastrow takes "science" to include anthropology, sociology, psychology, and psychiatry, in addition to the more obvious suspects—but his introduction is both short and charming. He conceives of his work "as a project in errorology," which sounds akin to my own, but he is interested largely in errors that remained unknown to their makers and were revealed only to posterity.

30 **"World of Tomorrow."** Roland Barker, ed., *Official Guide Book: New York World's Fair 1939: The World of Tomorrow* (Exposition Publications, 1939), 2.

31 **error's "grosser forms."** Sully, 186.

31 **Ralph Linton.** Ralph Linton, "Error in Anthropology," in Jastrow, ed., 298.

31 **that era's hallmark development, the scientific method.** Systematic methods for inquiring into the natural world have been around for ages: ancient Greek naturalists practiced a form of empiricism, and medieval Muslim scientists developed a method of inquiry that relied on experimentation to weigh competing hypotheses. But the scientific method as we understand it today was introduced to the world through the work of Francis Bacon in his 1620 *Novum Organum*, and René Descartes in his 1637 *Discourse on the Method.* Whether or not this method has ever been practiced as such (that is, to what extent scientists, especially as individuals, seek to replicate experiments and falsify hypotheses) is an open question, as Thomas Kuhn made abundantly clear in *The Structure of Scientific Revolutions.* But my point here concerns the method as an intellectual ideal more than an actual practice.

33 **"For Satan himself."** *The Bible, New International Version* (HarperTorch, 1993), 2 Corinthians 11:14–15.

33 **errors as *ignes fatui*.** Bates, 46.

34 **Pierre-Simon Laplace.** Bates touches on this development toward the end of *Enlightenment Aberrations* (248), but my primary source here was Steven

M. Stigler's *History of Statistics: The Measurement of Uncertainty Before 1900* (Harvard University Press, 1990), especially 31–38 and 109–148.

34 **"The genius of statistics."** Louis Menand, *The Metaphysical Club: A Story of Ideas in America* (Farrar, Straus and Giroux, 2002), 182.

35 **For more on the potential insidiousness of this innovation (FN).** Many observers have been troubled by the application of the bell curve to the social sciences, since plotting people on a curve like so many data points tends to create an idea of an average or optimal version of a given human characteristic—with correspondingly unwelcome consequences for those who find themselves on the tail end of the curve. In the worst-case scenario, those consequences include stigmatizing variation, equating difference with deviance, and seeking to eradicate anything that diverges from the ideal: in short, all the classic signs of fascism. That's why dystopian literature is full of societies consisting entirely of "average men," clonelike copies of eerily bland, interchangeable people. Nor is this problem limited to literature; history bears tragic witness to the urge to bring these ostensibly ideal societies into being.

This capacity to treat human beings as potentially erroneous data points is why some thinkers blame the intellectual legacy of the Enlightenment for the genocidal horrors of the twentieth century. In more conventional historical accounts, the Enlightenment represents the high-water mark of Western culture, and all subsequent outbreaks of barbarism stem from the abdication of its central values. But other thinkers hold that Enlightenment values are the *source* of that barbarism. They argue that, by elevating cold rationality above all other virtues, esteeming abstract and supposedly universal truths over individual lives, and imposing the values and methods of science on all of human activity, the Enlightenment created the motive, the means, and the justification for systemic violence. This criticism was first articulated during the French Revolution, whose stunning brutality was justified as necessary to the establishment of a perfect government. Since there can be no rational objection to a perfect government (the argument went), all political opposition was dangerously wrong and could—indeed must—be eliminated. This criticism of the Enlightenment was revived (most famously by the German philosopher Theodor Adorno and the associated Frankfurt School of philosophers) in the wake of the twentieth century's spasms of ideologically motivated, mechanically enabled, perfection-minded violence. Incidentally, David Bates, whom I cite above, locates the intellectual roots of such violence later, with the rise of positivism in the nineteenth century.

36 **"baseless chimeras."** Translations of al-Ghazali vary widely, down to the titles of his works and the spelling of his name. I have used two different translations in this book: Abu Hamid Muhammad Al Ghazzali, *The Confessions of Al Ghazzali*, Claud Field, trans. (Cosimo, Inc., 2007) and Abu Hamid Muhammad Al-Ghazali, *Al-Ghazali's Path to Sufism: His Deliverance from Error*, R. J. McCarthy, trans. (Fons Vitae, 2006). This quotation is from the first one and appears on p. 17. For comparison's sake, the same passage in the other translation is rendered as follows: "Don't you see that when you are asleep you believe certain things and imagine certain circumstances and believe that they are fixed and lasting and entertain no doubts about that being their status? Then you wake up and know that all your imaginings and beliefs were groundless and unsubstantial. So . . . what assurance have you that you may not suddenly experience a state which would have the same relation to your waking state as the latter has to your dreaming, and your waking state would be dreaming in relation to that new and further state?" (p. 22)

38 **"in the firm conviction that one is following it."** Both this definition and the quotation from François Boissier de Sauvages in the next paragraph appear in Michel Foucault's *Madness and Civilization: A History of Insanity in the Age of Reason*, Richard Howard, trans. (Vintage Books, 1965), 104. The quotation from Foucault in this same paragraph appears on p. 33.

38 **the medical definition of delusion.** See for instance Caroline Bunker Rosdahl and Mary T. Kowalski, *Textbook of Basic Nursing* (Lippincott Williams & Wilkins; Ninth Edition, 2007), 1469. The italics are mine.

38 **"looking at a gourd."** Desiderius Erasmus, *The Praise of Folly*, in *The Essential Erasmus*, John P. Dolan, trans. (The New American Library, 1964), 128.

39 **"sane and vigorous mental life and dementia."** Sully, 3.

39 **"for wise men are grown foppish."** William Shakespeare, *King Lear*, Russell Fraser, ed. (Signet Classics, 1998). The quotations in this paragraph appear on pp. 30 and 29, respectively.

41 **In ancient Indo-European.** See for instance the entry on "to move" at the Center for Indo-European Language and Culture of the University

of Texas at Austin's Linguistics Research Center (http://www.utexas.edu/cola/centers/lrc/iedocctr/ie-ling/ie-sem/MO/MO_MO.html), and their chart of Proto-Indo-European root words (http://www.utexas.edu/cola/centers/lrc/ielex/PokornyMaster-X.html).

41 **the knight errant and . . . the *juif errant*.** I am indebted to David Bates for this insight. His discussion of the etymology of "error" and of these two wanderers appears on pp. 19–21. The quote appears on p. 21.

CHAPTER 3   OUR SENSES

The story of Captain John Ross's misadventure in the Arctic is drawn from his own account of it, *A Voyage of Discovery: Made Under the Orders of the Admiralty, in his Majesty's Ships Isabella and Alexander, for the Purpose of Exploring Baffin Bay, and Enquiring Into the Probability of a North-West Passage* (Longmans, Hurst, 1819) (the block quote appears on pp. 245–246); from Clive Holland and James M. Savelle, "My Dear Beaufort: A Personal Letter from John Ross's Arctic Expedition of 1829–33," *Arctic*, Vol. 40, No. 1 (March 1987): 66–77; from Earnest S. Dodge, *The Polar Rosses: John and James Clark Ross and Their Explorations* (Faber and Faber, 1973); and from *Antarctica: Exploration, Perception, Metaphor*, Paul Simpson-Housley (Routledge, 1992). The footnote about the Peary expedition comes from a contemporary newspaper account of the MacMillan expedition ("To Seek New Land Peary Saw in Arctic," the *New York Times*, Feb. 14, 1912), and from Peary and MacMillan's own accounts of it, respectively: Robert Edwin Peary, *Nearest the Pole* (Doubleday, Page, and Company, 1907) and Donald Baxter MacMillan, *Four Years in the White North* (Harper and Brothers, 1918).

The information about superior mirages and travelers (other than John Ross) who have been fooled by them is drawn from Simpson-Housley; from *Encyclopedia of Weather and Climate*, Second Revised Edition (Oxford University Press, 1996); and from "The Superior Mirage: Seeing Beyond" (http://www.islandnet.com/~see/weather/history/artmirge.htm) and "The Arctic Mirage: Aid to Discovery" (http://www.islandnet.com/~see/weather/elements/supmrge.htm) both by Keith C. Heidorn, 1999.

Edward Adelson's checkerboard illusion and a complete explanation of how it works can be found on his website at http://web.mit.edu/persci/people/adelson/. The inattentional blindness videos can be found at http://viscog.beckman.illinois.edu/djs_lab/demos.html. The story of the crash of Eastern Airlines #401 comes from Marc Green, the same psychologist who coined

"Mental Act of God," (http://www.visualexpert.com/Resources/inattention-alblindness.html).

48 **Virtually no explorers had sailed to the Arctic from England.** In 1778, James Cook, best known as an Antarctic explorer, took a stab at finding the Northwest Passage from its imagined Western end, but, after his passage was blocked by ice north of the Bering Strait, he gave up and dismissed the existence of the passage as a fantasy.

49 **Ross's reputation was tarnished, and it was soon to tank.** Ironically, Ross's reputation was restored by an expedition that was borderline disastrous. In 1829, he returned to the Canadian Arctic, only to have his ship become trapped in ice to the south of Lancaster Sound. He and his men explored the area while waiting for the ice to break up, but it failed to do so. In 1832, they finally abandoned the ship and walked north across the frozen sea to the site of another, earlier shipwreck. When the ice began to recede around that vessel, they took to its longboats, rowed off, and were eventually rescued—as chance would have it, by the same ship that Ross had captained in 1818. All told, Ross and his crew were stranded for an unprecedented four years. Yet as star-crossed as the expedition was, it redeemed Ross as a man of ability and courage in the eyes of his nation. Parry, meanwhile, garnered (and deserved) a reputation as an outstanding Arctic explorer, but he never achieved the imagined wealth and glory of discovering the Northwest Passage. Nor, for that matter, did anyone else, although the Norwegian explorer Roald Amundsen finally navigated a complete passage in 1906. But that waterway and the others that were eventually discovered in the far north proved too distant and dangerous to rely on as trade routes—and at any rate, by then, the invention of the railroad had yielded an altogether different solution to the problem of transporting goods across North America. (John Ross, *Narrative of a Second Voyage in Search of a North-West Passage, and of a Residence in the Arctic Regions During the Years 1829, 1830, 1831, 1832, 1833* (A. W. Webster, 1835).

55 **stepping outside and looking up.** One of the contributors to Jastrow's *Story of Human Error*, Harlan T. Stetson, makes this point as well in "Error and Astronomy." "Paradoxical as it may seem," Stetson writes on p. 40, "[man's] chief source of error was the tendency to take Nature at her face value, to accept appearances as the warrant of reality. Yet one without as-

tronomical knowledge can readily reenact much of the drama of human error in gaining a knowledge of the universe, by going into the open on any clear night and looking into the vault above him."

55 **the fix favored by Protagoras.** Almost the entirety of Plato's *Theaetetus* is dedicated to dismantling Protagoras's theory of knowledge, but for the issues I'm addressing here, see especially pp. 12–50. Keeler also provides considerable background on what the Sophists, Plato, and other early philosophers thought about the problem of errors of perception. (See especially pp. 1–21.)

59 **Steven Pinker.** Steven Pinker, *How the Mind Works* (W. W. Norton and Company, 1997), 8.

63 **David Brewster.** David Brewster, *Letters on Natural Magic* (Chatto and Windus, Piccadilly, 1883), 91. I tracked down this text after reading about it in Sully's *Illusions*.

64 **Jean Eugène Robert-Houdin.** The story of Robert-Houdin in Algeria can be found in Jim Steinmeyer's *Hiding the Elephant* (De Capo Press, 2004), pp. 145–146.

66 **I've reproduced both illusions in the endnotes (FN).** The two illusions are as follows:

CHAPTER 4   OUR MINDS, PART ONE: KNOWING, NOT KNOWING, AND MAKING IT UP

I'm grateful to Rebecca Saxe for suggesting that I look into confabulation, and specifically for guiding me to William Hirstein's invaluable *Brain Fiction: Self-Deception and the Riddle of Confabulation* (The MIT Press, 2005). Other useful sources on anosognosia and confabulation include George Prigatano and Daniel L. Schacter, eds., *Awareness of Deficit after Brain Injury: Clinical and Theoretical Issues* (Oxford University Press, 1991); Gabriel Anton, "Gabriel Anton and 'Anton's Symptom': On Focal Diseases of the Brain Which Are Not Perceived by the Patient (1898)," with an introduction and translation by Hans Förstl, Adrian M. Owen, and Anthony S. David, *Neuropsychiatry, Neuropsychology, and*

Behavioral Neurology, Vol. 6, No. 1 (1993): 1–8; and from an interview with the neurologist Eric Altschuler of the Mt. Sinai School of Medicine. The story of "Hannah" comes from Georg Goldenberg, Wolf Tollbachert, and Andreas Nowak, "Imagery without Perception: A Case Study of Anosognosia for Cortical Blindness," *Neuropsychologia*, Vol. 33, No. 11 (1995): 1373–1382. Michael Gazzaniga's experiments on split-brain patients appears in Hirstein, pp. 153–154. I first learned about the pantyhose experiment through Hirstein's work as well; see also "Telling More Than We Can Know: Verbal Reports on Mental Processes," Richard E. Nisbitt and Timothy DeCamp Wilson, *Psychological Review*, Vol. 84, No. 3 (May 1977): 231–259.

The following sources helped shape the discussion of memory in this chapter: Daniel Schacter, *The Seven Sins of Memory: How the Mind Forgets and Remembers* (Houghton Mifflin, 2001); Daniel Schacter, ed., *Memory Distortions: How Minds, Brains, and Societies Reconstruct the Past* (Harvard University Press, 1995); Daniel Schacter and Elaine Scarry, eds., *Memory, Brain, and Belief* (Harvard University Press, 2000); and interviews with Daniel Schacter of Harvard, William Hirst of the New School for Social Research, and Elizabeth Phelps of New York University. Hirst was the first person to tell me the story of Ulric Neisser's false flashbulb memory, although it also appears frequently in the memory literature. The *Challenger* study (including the "I know that's my handwriting" quote) was written up by Neisser and Nicole Harsh as "Phantom Flashbulbs: False Recollections of Hearing the News about Challenger," in Eugene Winograd and Ulric Neisser, eds., *Affect and Accuracy in Recall* (Cambridge University Press, 1992), 9–31. The claim that flashbulb memories decline in accuracy at the same rate as more mundane memories was advanced by Jennifer Talarico and David Rubin in their paper "Flashbulb Memories Result from Ordinary Memory Processes and Extraordinary Event Characteristics," in Olivier Luminet and Antonietta Curci, eds., *Flashbulb Memories: New Issues and New Perspectives* (Psychology Press, 2009), 79–98. Information about the 9/11 Memory Consortium can be found online at http://911memory.nyu.edu/.

In addition to the above-mentioned sources, the information on implanted false memories comes from *Trauma and Memory: Reading, Healing, and Making Law*, Austin Sarat, Nadav Davidovitch, and Michal Alberstein, eds. (Stanford University Press, 2008). The story of Chris, the boy who was told that he had been lost in a mall as a child, comes from "The Reality of Illusory Memories," Elizabeth F. Loftus, Julie Feldman, and Richard Dashiell, in Schacter, ed., 62. The study itself was conducted by Loftus and a colleague in 1994.

You can listen to the "Modern Jackass" episode of *This American Life* for free, and you absolutely should. Its real title is "A Little Bit of Knowledge," it was produced by Lisa Pollak and host Ira Glass, it originally aired on July 22, 2005, it is available online at http://www.thisamericanlife.org/Radio_Episode. aspx?sched=1090, and it is very, very funny.

Although I both open and close this chapter with a plea to set aside the category of knowledge, I want to emphasize that my claim, in making that plea, is only that "knowledge" isn't a useful category for thinking about error, not that it isn't a useful category at all. In everyday life, we use phrases like "I know" to indicate that we don't feel any uncertainty and phrases like "I believe" to indicate that we do—distinctions that are extremely helpful, and that we cannot jettison without resorting to the notoriously impractical and unpalatable option of complete capital-S Skepticism. My point here is only that knowledge, as a category, has limitations and assumptions we should come to understand—and that error is predicated on belief, which is, accordingly, a more useful conceptual tool for a book about wrongness.

68 **Justice William Douglas.** Steven Pinker, *The Blank Slate: The Modern Denial of Human Nature* (Penguin, 2003) 265.

69 **the brain mistakes an idea in the mind . . . for a feature of the real world.** Specifically, scientists think that denial of disease arises when a part of the brain called the supplementary motor area remains unaffected by a brain injury. The supplementary motor area is responsible for mental simulations of physical actions; it's what you use when you lie in bed at night picturing yourself raising your hands in triumph as you cross the finish line of the New York marathon. For paralyzed patients who deny their paralysis, this part of the brain works just fine, while damage to other areas (or a conflict between this area and others) prevents them from actually executing the physical activity as well as from distinguishing between the simulated action and a real one. (Sandra Blakeslee, "Discovering that Denial of Paralysis Is Not Just a Problem of the Mind," the *New York Times*, Aug. 2, 2005.)

71 **"Of some things we feel that we are certain."** James, 13.

75 **"a gift of Memory, the mother of the Muses."** Plato, 60. The discussion of memory continues through p. 70.

76 **the real question about this model might simply be whether the non-scientists among us can be brought to believe in it.** Our reluctance

to accept a non-intuitive model of memory (or of anything else) is, itself, somewhat related to the feeling of knowing. Call it the feeling of understanding: we are far more inclined to accept explanations that feel right to us than those that don't. The trouble is that explanations that feel right can be wrong, and explanations that feel confusing or repellant can be right. Nonetheless, even people with a strong grasp of what constitutes good grounds for knowledge can be seduced by this feels-right criterion. The philosopher J. D. Trout cites by way of example Copernicus, that early advocate of heliocentrism, who once said of two other theories about the structure of the galaxy that "the mind shudders at either of these suppositions." Now, famously, Copernicus was right—the earth really does revolve around the sun—but if a shuddering mind had been his only reason for rejecting other hypotheses, his argument would have been profoundly unpersuasive. As Trout notes, "The important question is whether heliocentrism is true, not whether envisioning an alternative is too intellectually painful to bear." (J. D. Trout, "Scientific Explanation and the Sense of Understanding," *Philosophy of Science*, Vol. 6 (June 2002): 212–233.

78 **"plausible-sounding responses."** This quotation and the next one ("One of the characters involved in an inner dialogue . . .") are from Hirstein, 3–4.

82 **"rock-jawed certainty."** Hirstein, 2. The "admitting ignorance in response to a question" passage is on the same page. The "mildly confabulatory personality" and "stubborn, with an emphasis on being right" passages are on p. 4.

86 **"When one admits that nothing is certain."** Bertrand Russell, *The Collected Papers of Bertrand Russell*, Vol. 11, John Slater and Peter Köllner, eds. (Routledge, 1997), 92.

CHAPTER 5   OUR MINDS, PART TWO: BELIEF

To my regret, Alan Greenspan declined (politely) to be interviewed for this book. The complete transcript of the congressional hearings he attended on Oct. 23, 2008 can be found at http://oversight.house.gov/documents/20081024163819. pdf. Unless otherwise noted, all quotes from Greenspan and Waxman are from that transcript. Biographical information on Greenspan comes from his autobiography, *The Age of Turbulence: Adventures in a New World* (Penguin Press, 2008).

I am indebted to Rebecca Saxe for many early, interesting conversations about belief, error, and naïve realism that helped shape this chapter, and for the many related resources she sent my way.

88 **In the words of the *Economist*.** "Alan Greenspan," the *Economist*, Jan. 12, 2006.

88 **$8.5 million dollars.** Motoko Rich, "The Plan to Push That Book Goes Poof," the *New York Times*, Sept. 7, 2007.

88 **In the United States, the stock market had fallen 37 percent since the start of the year. The American economy had lost 1.5 million jobs.** "Job Losses Continue at Accelerated Pace," Heather Boushey, Center for American Progress, Feb. 6, 2009.

88 **a figure that would rise to over 5 million by early 2009.** Peter S. Goodman and Jack Healy, "663,000 Jobs Lost in March; Total Tops 5 Million," the *New York Times*, April 3, 2009.

88 **between 18 and 50 million jobs would vanish.** Carl Mortished, "Global Unemployment Heads Towards 50 Million," the London *Times*, Jan. 29, 2009.

88 **the Blackstone Group.** Megan Davies and Walden Siew, "45 Percent of World's Wealth Destroyed: Blackstone CEO," Reuters, March 10, 2009.

89 **"like being a Scholastic."** This quote comes from "The End," a characteristically remarkable piece by Lewis that appeared in the Dec. 2008 issue of *Portfolio* magazine.

90 **a Cassandra figure.** "The Born Prophecy," Richard B. Schmitt, *ABA Journal*, May 2009; and "Clinton's Belated Advice Should Be Heeded," Liam Halligan, the *Telegraph*, May 23, 2009.

90 **"grave concern about this [proposed regulatory] action."** The press release from which this statement comes is available at http://www.ustreas.gov/press/releases/rr2426.htm.

90 **in Born's word, "absolutist."** "Prophet and Loss," Rick Schmitt, *Stanford Magazine*, March/April 2009.

92 **the everyday concept of belief and the philosophical one differ . . . in how we experience them.** In fact, it is almost impossible to distinguish between implicit assumptions and explicit convictions based on anything *but* personal experience. You might guess that explicit beliefs are more important than implicit ones, since we spend time and energy defending the former while generally remaining oblivious to the latter. But this is

manifestly not the case. Take my implicit belief that my father is, in fact, my father. I am deeply invested in this belief, I make frequent and significant decisions based on the presumption that it is correct, and I would be almost inconceivably shaken if it turned out to be wrong. It's tough to imagine, then, how this belief could be *less* important than my convictions about, say, Reaganomics. Nor are explicit beliefs always hotly contested and implicit ones always broadly accepted, although the examples I used in this chapter (about the regulation of financial markets versus the likely behavior of mattresses) might reasonably suggest as much. Let's say I explicitly believe that I am good at math. My friends and family might share this belief, or they might not trust me to so much as tally the Scrabble score, but either way, my belief is not important enough to merit much controversy. Conversely, I might unconsciously believe that men are better at math than women—needless to say, a deeply controversial stance. This suggests another difficulty with trying to distinguish between implicit and explicit beliefs, which is that they are not mutually exclusive. After all, plenty of people explicitly defend the notion that men are better at math than women. What I believe implicitly and experience not at all, others may believe explicitly and experience as central to their worldview.

93   **beliefs "are really rules for action."** William James, *The Varieties of Religious Experience* (Touchstone, 1997) 347. The words are James's (and he stood by them), but in context, he was paraphrasing his fellow philosopher Charles Sanders Peirce, and describing Pierce's then-new philosophy of pragmatism.

94   **Laser Interferometer Gravitational-Wave Observatory.** The National Science Foundation's fact sheet about LIGO (including the quotation about ripples in the fabric of space-time) is available at http://www.nsf.gov/news/news_summ.jsp?cntn_id=103042.

94   **"a half-billion-dollar machine."** The quote is from Wertheim's contribution to *What We Believe but Cannot Prove: Today's Leading Thinkers on Science in the Age of Certainty*, John Brockman, ed. (Harper Perennial, 2006), 177.

95   **distal beliefs.** I have borrowed the idea of distal beliefs from the philosopher Robert P. Abelson, who glossed the concept in an article called "Beliefs are Like Possessions," *Journal for the Theory of Social Behavior*, Vol. 16, No. 3. (Oct. 1986): 223–250. As Abelson points out, we also face the opposite of the problem of distal beliefs: we have plenty of beliefs we could act

on—say, that it is terrible for impoverished people in our own hometown to go without food and shelter—yet fail to do so.

96 **"the theoretic instinct."** William James, *Talks to Teachers on Psychology: And to Students on Some of Life's Ideals* (Holt, 1906), 47.

98 **there is suggestive evidence that babies as young as seven months are already theorizing.** That suggestive evidence is as follows: researchers have shown that five-month-old babies don't seem to know anything about gravity and other basic physical properties of the world, since they are unfazed when, say, objects float in midair, or when a ball rolled across a table leaps over an obstacle instead of bumping into it. But seven-month-olds *do* seem to possess some basic theories about the laws that govern such situations, which means that they are either born with the ability to generate those theories or acquire that ability in the first few months of life. See for instance Susan Hespos and Renée Baillargeon, "Décalage in Infants' Knowledge About Occlusion and Containment Events: Converging Evidence from Action Tasks." *Cognition*, Vol. 99 (2006): B31–B41; and Yuyan Luo, Lisa Kaufman, and Renée Baillargeon, "Young Infants' Reasoning about Events Involving Inert and Self-propelled Objects," *Cognitive Psychology*, Vol. 58 (2009): 441–486.

98 **Alison Gopnik.** Alison Gopnik, "Explanation as Orgasm and the Drive for Causal Understanding: The Evolution, Function and Phenomenology of the Theory-Formation System," in Frank C. Keil and Robert A. Wilson, eds., *Cognition and Explanation* (The MIT Press, 2000), 299–323.

100 **the false belief test.** The false belief experiment was first proposed by the philosopher Daniel Dennett and later conducted by the Austrian psychologists Heinz Wimmer and Josef Perner, which they then wrote up as "Beliefs about Beliefs: Representation and Constraining Function of Wrong Beliefs in Young Children's Understanding of Deception." *Cognition*, Vol. 13 (1983): 103–128. The candy/pencils variation comes from J. Perner, U. Frith, A. M. Leslie, and S. R. Leekam, "Exploration of the Autistic Child's Theory of Mind: Knowledge, Belief, and Communication," *Child Development*, Vol. 60 (1989): 688–700. For more on the Polaroid version of the task, see Zaitchik, D., "When Representations Conflict with Reality: The Preschooler's Problem with False Beliefs and 'False' Photographs," *Cognition*, Vol. 35 (1990): 41–68.

101 **Recent evidence from infancy experiments (FN).** For the recent challenges to prior beliefs about young children and false beliefs, see Hyun-joo

Song and Renée Baillargeon, "Infants' Reasoning about Others' False Perceptions," *Developmental Psychology*, Vol. 44, No. 6 (Nov. 2008): 1789–1795; Gergely Csibra and Victoria Southgate, "Evidence for Infants' Understanding of False Beliefs Should Not Be Dismissed," *Trends in Cognitive Sciences*, Vol. 10 (2006): 4–5; Kristine H. Onishi and Renée Baillargeon, "Do 15-Month-Old Infants Understand False Beliefs?" *Science*, Vol. 308 (2005): 255–258.

102   **the example of *Romeo and Juliet*.** Rebecca Saxe, "Reading Your Mind: How Our Brains Help Us Understand Other People," *Boston Review*, Vol. 29, No. 1 (Feb./March 2004): 39–41.

104   **the First Person Constraint on Doxastic Explanation.** I am grateful to Rebecca Saxe for pointing me to this concept, and to the philosopher Ward Jones, whose published work and private correspondence with me were invaluable in shaping what I call here the 'Cuz It's True Constraint. The quotes from Jones in this section are from "Explaining Our Own Beliefs: Non-Epistemic Believing and Doxastic Instability," *Philosophical Studies*, Vol. 111, No. 3 (Dec. 2002): 217–249.

106   **"the bias blind spot."** I relied especially on the following four papers about the bias blind spot: Emily Pronin, Thomas Gilovich, and Lee Ross, "Objectivity in the Eye of the Beholder: Divergent Perceptions of Bias in Self versus Other," *Psychological Review*, Vol. 111, No. 3 (2004): 791–799; Joyce Ehrlinger, Thomas Gilovich, and Lee Ross, "Peering into the Bias Blind Spot: People's Assessments of Bias in Themselves and Others," *Personality and Social Psychology Bulletin*, Vol. 31, No. 5 (May 2005): 1–13; Emily Pronin, Daniel Y. Lin, and Lee Ross, "The Bias Blind Spot: Perceptions of Bias in Self versus Other," *Personality and Social Psychology Bulletin*, Vol. 28, No. 3 (March 2002): 369–381; and Emily Pronin, Justin Kruger, Kenneth Savitsky, and Lee Ross, "You Don't Know Me, but I Know You: The Illusion of Asymmetric Insight," *Journal of Personality and Social Psychology*, Vol. 81, No. 4 (2001): 639–656. Pronin's quotation is from "Objectivity in the Eye of the Beholder," 784.

CHAPTER 6   OUR MINDS, PART THREE: EVIDENCE

I am indebted to my sister, Laura Schulz, a cognitive scientist at MIT, whose own work on the double-edged sword of human cognition has been invaluable to me here, and who fundamentally altered and dramatically deepened my understanding of inductive reasoning. I could not have written this chapter without her assistance—or, rather, I could not have written it accurately and well. Among many other things, she supplied me with the idea of the inductive reasoning quiz and pointed me in the direction of Willard Van Orman Quine, whose work on the indeterminacy of translation was originally presented in his *Word and Object* (The MIT Press, 1964). She also supplied the connection between inductive reasoning and Noam Chomsky's "poverty of the stimulus" problem, as well as the example of Neptune and Uranus.

I first learned of Judge William Stoughton upon driving through his name-sake town, Stoughton, Massachusetts. The information about him and about spectral evidence in this chapter comes from biographical information provided by the town (available at http://www.stoughtonhistory.com/williamstoughton.htm), and from Francis Hill, *The Salem Witch Trials Reader* (De Capo Press, 2000), 90. Interestingly, the dispute over the use of spectral evidence was as much theological as judicial, since it centered on the question of whether or not the devil required permission from people to use their image to torment the (ostensible) victims of witchcraft. People who believed that the devil could do whatever he pleased were opposed to the use of spectral evidence, on the theory that the Goody Proctors of the world were not merely blameless but, themselves, victims. By contrast, people who believed that the devil needed permission from mortals in order to use their image supported spectral evidence, since anyone who appeared as an evildoer in dreams or visitations had clearly made a pact with Satan. See David Levin's "Shadows of Doubt: Specter Evidence in Hawthorne's 'In Young Goodman Brown,'" *American Literature*, Vol. 34, No. 3 (1962): 344–352.

Donald Leka and Elizabeth O'Donovan are both strangers who responded to a general request I made for stories about wrongness. The quotations in those passages are from direct communications with the two of them.

113 **"beliefs follow from relatively dispassionate assessment."** "Against Simulation: The Argument From Error," Rebecca Saxe, *Trends in Cognitive Sciences*, Vol. 9, No. 4 (April 2005): 174–179.

113 **Descartes defined error.** See Keeler, 161: "where it is not perfectly evident, there is no true knowledge; and if I assent to something that is really so, without full and firm certitude that it is so, I commit an error. Error does not consist precisely in judging that to be, which is not, but in rashly venturing to pronounce in the absence of evidence." Some readers will

note that this was the position William James argued against in *The Will to Believe*. James, however, took as his intellectual opposition not Descartes but the philosopher William Clifford (James calls him "that delicious *enfant terrible*"), who wrote, "Belief is desecrated when given to unproved and unquestioned statements for the solace and private pleasure of the believer. . . . If [a] belief has been accepted on insufficient evidence . . . [i]t is sinful because it is stolen in defiance of our duty to mankind. That duty is to guard ourselves from such beliefs as from a pestilence which may shortly master our own body and then spread to the rest of the town. . . . It is wrong always, everywhere, and for every one, to believe anything upon insufficient evidence." (James, *The Will to Believe*, 8.)

114 **Augustine, who arrived at Descartes' idea of error.** Keeler, 74–75.

114 **Monotheistic religions have a particularly interesting and troubled relationship to the idea of evidence (FN).** The writer Sam Harris made a similar point in *The End of Faith: Religion, Terror, and the Future of Reason* (W. W. Norton, 2005). See for instance p. 66: "But faith is an imposter. This can be readily seen in the way that all the extraordinary phenomena of the religious life—a statue of the Virgin weeps, a child casts his crutches to the ground—are seized upon by the faithful as *confirmation* of their faith. At these moments, religious believers appear like men and women in the desert of uncertainty given a cool drink of data. There is no way around the fact that we crave justification for our core beliefs and believe them only because we think such justification is, at the very least, in the offing."

118 **David Hume.** Hume lays out the problem of induction in his *Enquiry Concerning Human Understanding* (Oxford University Press, 2006).

119 **"the poverty of the stimulus" (FN).** Chomsky describes this problem in his *Rules and Representations* (Columbia University Press, 2005).

125 **Thomas Kuhn.** Thomas Kuhn, *The Structure of Scientific Revolutions* (The University of Chicago Press, 1996). The anecdote about Chinese and Western astronomers appears on p. 116.

126 **As Alan Greenspan pointed out.** http://oversight.house.gov/documents/20081024163819.pdf

128 **"interpreting increased violence in Iraq."** George Packer, "History Boys," the *New Yorker*, June 11, 2007.

128 **The NASA higher-ups responsible for the . . . *Columbia*.** Henry Petroski, *Success through Failure: The Paradox of Design* (Princeton University Press, 2006), 166.

129 **"The greatest impediment and aberration of the human understanding."** I first stumbled on this quotation in Daniel Gilbert's *Stumbling on Happiness* (Alfred A. Knopf, 2006), 99. The line originally appears in Bacon's *Novum Organum*, Peter Urbach and John Gibson, ed. and trans. (Open Court, 1994), 60.

129 **Vesalius finally showed otherwise.** Jastrow, 15.

129 **Pliny the Elder.** Howard M. Parshley, "Error in Zoology," in Jastrow, 203–204.

130 **(As a European Communist once said).** Whittaker Chambers, *Witness* (Regnery Publishing, Inc., 1952), 79.

131 **Albert Speer.** Albert Speer, *Inside the Third Reich: Memoirs* (Simon and Schuster, 1997), 376.

131 **"I had, during many years, followed a golden rule."** Quoted in Larry R. Squire, "Biological Foundations of Accuracy and Inaccuracy in Memory," in Schacter, ed., 197.

CHAPTER 7 OUR SOCIETY

I have drawn on the following sources for the history of women's suffrage in Switzerland: Lee Ann Banaszak, *Why Movements Succeed or Fail: Opportunity, Culture, and the Struggle for Woman Suffrage* (Princeton University Press, 1996), a comparison of the suffrage movements in the United States and Switzerland; personal communications with Banaszak (who, among other things, supplied the joke about the German, Swiss, and American kids) and with Regina Wecker, a professor of women's history and gender history at the University of Basel in Switzerland; and contemporary news accounts of the Swiss situation, including Michael L. Hoffman, "Swiss Suffrage: The Men Have It, But—Being Swiss— Still Deny It to Their Women," the *New York Times*, Feb. 6. 1955; "Swiss Males Deny Federal Vote to Women, But Yield a Canton," the *New York Times*, Feb. 2, 1959; Edwin Newman, "Can 655,000 Swissmen Be Wrong?" the *New York Times*, Aug. 30, 1959; Thomas J. Hamilton, "Swiss Woman Given the Federal Vote," the *New York Times*, Feb. 8, 1971; and "Eight Women Win in Swiss Election," Thomas J. Hamilton, the *New York Times*, Nov. 2, 1971.

The story of Abdul Rahman comes from the United States Commission on International Religious Freedom, *USCIRF Annual Report 2008—Afghanistan*, May 2008 (available online at http://www.unhcr.org/refworld/docid/4855699 b46.html) and from the following news articles: Kim Barker, "Afghan Man Faces

Death for Being a Christian," *Chicago Tribune*, March 21, 2006; Tim Albone, "Afghan Faces Death Penalty for Christian Faith," the London *Times*, March 20, 2006; Sanjoy Majumder, "Mood Hardens Against Afghan Convert," *BBC News*, March 24, 2006; Abdul Waheed Wafa and David Rohde, "Kabul Judge Rejects Calls to End Trial of Afghan Convert," the *New York Times*, March 24, 2006; "Clerics Call for Christian Convert's Death Despite Western Outrage," Fox News, The Associated Press, March 23, 2006; Rachel Morarjee, "Abdul Rahman's Family Values," *Time*, March 29, 2006; and Syed Saleem Shahzad, "Losing Faith in Afghanistan," *Asia Times*, March 25, 2006.

133 **Women were enfranchised in New Zealand.** For a comprehensive list of when women worldwide gained the right to vote, see the Inter-Parliamentary Union's "World Chronology of the Recognition of Women's Right to Vote and to Stand For Elections," http://www.ipu.org/wmn-e/suffrage.htm.

134 **Switzerland has long been a world leader.** Based on these factors and others, in 2005 the *Economist* magazine ranked Switzerland the second-best country in which to live (after Ireland). According to the World Bank, Switzerland has the sixth-highest per capita income in the world (http://siteresources.worldbank.org/DATASTATISTICS/Resources/GNIPC.pdf).

134 **Carrie Chapman Catt.** Banaszak, 3.

134 **the cantons determine who can vote.** There is a further division of power as well: the cantons decide who can vote for members of the upper house of parliament, while the federal government decides who can elect members of the lower house.

135 **one of the very few large-scale national protests.** It is a measure of the difference between the Swiss suffrage movement and its counterparts in Great Britain and the United States that such public protests were rare. Disinclined to chain themselves to the doors of courtrooms, picket the homes of antisuffrage politicians, or go to jail, Swiss suffragists focused primarily on public education and polite persuasion, and eschewed anything resembling radical activism. As the national Swiss Association for Women's Right to Vote admonished its members in a policy paper on tactics, women who were contemplating public demonstrations "must remain conscious that action going overboard in extent, material contents or even in tone could hurt the cause." (Banaszak, 169)

137 **offendicula.** Jastrow, 16.

138 **the four idols.** Jastrow, 16–17; also, Juergen Klein, "Francis Bacon," *The Stanford Encyclopedia of Philosophy* (Spring 2009 Edition), Edward N. Zalta, ed., (http://plato.stanford.edu/archives/spr2009/entries/francis-bacon); and Francis Bacon, *Bacon's Essays*, Edwin A. Abbott, ed. (Longmans, Green and Co., 1886), lxxii–lxxiii.

138 **Thomas Gilovich.** Thomas Gilovich, *How We Know What Isn't So: The Fallibility of Human Reason in Everyday Life* (The Free Press, 1991), 112.

139 **Cass Sunstein.** Cass Sunstein, *Why Societies Need Dissent* (Harvard University Press, 2005), v.

139 **James Surowiecki.** James Surowiecki, *The Wisdom of Crowds* (Anchor Books, 2005), 43.

139 **John Locke and David Hume.** This rejection of secondhand information as insufficient grounds for knowledge is part of the same epistemological tradition articulated by, among others, Descartes (who cautioned against believing anything based on scanty evidence) and William Clifford (James's foil in "The Will To Believe").

140 **"I began to realize that I believed countless things."** Augustine, *Confessions* (Penguin Classics, 1931), 9.

140 **Leonard Susskind.** Brockman, ed., 89–90.

142 **"a network of witnesses."** Avishai Margalit, *The Ethics of Memory* (Harvard University Press, 2002), 180–181.

142 **people "are swept [into a belief]."** Michel de Montaigne, "Apology for Raymond Sebond," *The Complete Essays of Michel de Montaigne*, Donald M. Frame, trans. (Stanford University Press, 1958), 373.

143 **"Nearly half of all Americans live in 'landslide counties.'"** Shankar Vedantam, "Why the Ideological Melting Pot Is Getting So Lumpy," the *Washington Post*, Jan. 19, 2009. I suspect that this discrepancy between our professed desire for diversity and our actual homogeneity stems in part from the fact that our idea of diversity does not particularly extend to diversity of belief. We like the idea of sharing a community with people who come from different religious, racial, and economic backgrounds— but only if their current beliefs (about, say, that shared community's school system, building codes, tax rates, noise regulations, and marriage laws) dovetail with our own. But of course, different backgrounds often produce different belief systems. If we really want a diverse community, we have

to be prepared to accommodate beliefs that differ from and challenge our own.

144 **Solomon Asch.** Solomon Asch, "Effects of Group Pressure upon the Modification and Distortion of Judgment," in H. Guetzkow (ed.) *Groups, Leadership and Men* (Carnegie Press, 1951) and Solomon Asch, "Opinions and Social Pressure," *Scientific American*, Vol. 193 (1955): 31–35.

145 **modified version of the Asch studies.** Sandra Blakeslee, "What Other People Say May Change What You See," the *New York Times*, June 28, 2005.

146 **"As If Time Had Stood Still."** See the official website of Appenzellerland: http://www.appenzell.ch/en/pages/culture_customs/landsgemeinde.

147 **("there is nothing so unpleasant as a superintellectual woman.")** Edwin Newman, "Can 655,000 Swissmen Be Wrong?" the *New York Times*, Aug. 30, 1959.

147 **("they can influence their men and are happy with their condition.")** Banaszak, 124. The quotation is from "one [prosuffrage] activist in a rural canton."

148 **the right-wing gadfly Ann Coulter (FN).** George Gurley, "Coulter Culture," the *New York Observer*, Oct. 2, 2007.

149 **religious fundamentalists generally don't read Darwin.** Gilovich, 115.

150 **"Try to do and say those things only."** Quoted in Elizabeth Kolbert, "Place Settings: Emily Post, At Home," the *New Yorker*, Oct. 20, 2008. Gilovich also makes the point that Post discouraged confrontational conversations (p. 119), although he quotes different examples. ("The tactful person keeps his prejudices to himself" and "Certain subjects, even though you are very sure of the ground upon which you are standing, had best be shunned; such, for example, as the criticism of a religious creed or disagreement with another's political conviction.")

150 **"shutting up about what you believe."** "Penn Jillette, Telling It Like It Is, with Teller," AskMen.com, undated.

151 **it's impossible to change other people's minds.** One common exception to our reluctance to challenge other people's beliefs concerns children. Most of us are more willing to challenge children's questionable beliefs and share with them our own, different, perspective than we are with adults. This is partly because we feel more moral and intellectual responsibility toward children than we do toward grownups, but it is also

because we feel more optimistic that our intervention will make a difference. With adults, we generally assume that there is nothing we can say that they haven't heard before—whereas, with kids, we can hope that they have not yet been exposed to all the available evidence. In other words, when it comes to children, we stick to the first of the three assumptions I introduced in Chapter Five: we are likely to assume (not without reason) that they are ignorant, but we are usually far more reluctant than we are with adults to conclude that they are idiotic or evil.

151   **an "unwanted reform."** Banaszak, 125. The other quotation in this same paragraph is from p. 211.

152   **groupthink.** Irving Lester Janis, *Victims of Groupthink: A Psychological Study of Foreign-Policy Decisions and Fiascoes* (Houghton Mifflin Company, 1973). The definition appears on p. 9. For his advice on how to avoid groupthink, see especially Chapter Nine.

153   **"vigorous debate inside the White House."** Jake Tapper, "Barack Obama Unveils National Security Team, Taps Former Rival Hillary Clinton for State," ABC News, Dec. 2008.

153   **unanimous guilty verdict in a death penalty case.** See e.g., Ivan L. Tillem, *The Jewish Directory and Almanac*, Vol. 1 (Pacific Press, 1984), 221.

153   **"The laboratory is a latecomer on the human scene."** Jastrow, 12.

154   **"we don't want him in our house."** Morarjee, "Abdul Rahman's Family Values."

154   **"should be killed."** Barker, "Afghan Man Faces Death for Being a Christian."

154   **lysenkoism (FN).** See e.g., Martin Gardner, "Lysenkoism," *Fads and Fallacies in the Name of Science* (Dover Books, 1957), 140–151.

155   **the emperor has no clothes.** Sunstein has made this point as well; see pp. 26–27.

156   **"He will have to be executed."** Shahzad, "Losing Faith in Afghanistan."

CHAPTER 8   THE ALLURE OF CERTAINTY

160   **"an inviolable attachment to liberty."** Both the quotation itself and the history of the zealots more generally comes from Flavius Josephus, *The Works of Josephus: Containing Twenty Books of the Jewish Antiquities, Seven Books of the Jewish War, and the Life of Josephus* (J. Grigg, 1825). The quota-

tion appears on p. 41. The story of Ein-Gedi, including the quotation, appears on p. 354, and the "all sorts of misfortunes" quotation is on p. 40.

163 **"being mistaken at the top of one's voice."** Ambrose Bierce, *The Devil's Dictionary* (NuVision Publications, Feb. 2009), 191.

163 **a more public, action-oriented analogue to knowledge.** This might seem like an imprecise way to define certainty, since presumably we can experience a private, passive version of it as well. For my part, I'm happy to acknowledge that this definition is provisional—convincing in some ways, a bit off in others, but at all events useful for exploring the furthest extreme of "knowing" and its relationship to wrongness. Some recent philosophers, however, including Keith Frankish and Daniel Dennett, argue that this definition isn't provisional at all—that certainty is always a consequence of social interaction, and specifically of communication. In the privacy of our own minds, these philosophers claim, we treat every proposition probabilistically. It is only when we must make pronouncements that we are forced to generate absolutes. That makes fighting with your brother, giving a speech before Congress, and writing a letter to the editor all equally good ways to produce certainty. (I'm grateful to the Harvard philosopher Peter Godfrey Smith for bringing this argument to my attention.)

165 **a man is hiking in the Alps.** James, *The Will to Believe*, 96.

165 **"pathological certainty" (FN).** Hirstein, 22. The reference to obsessive-compulsive disorder and pathological doubt is on pp. 97–98.

166 **"help to *make* the truth which they declare."** "Remarks on Spencer's Definition of Mind as Correspondence," *William James: The Essential Writings*, Bruce W. Wilshire, ed. (State University of New York Press, 1984), 24.

166 **Wittgenstein argued.** Ludwig Wittgenstein, *On Certainty*, G. E. M. Anscombe and G. H. von Wright, eds. (Harper and Row, 1969). The quotation at the end of this paragraph appears on p. 33, as does the first quotation in the next paragraph. The "I should not make sure by looking" quotation appears on pp. 18–19.

166 **"'turtles all the way down'" (FN).** Clifford Geertz, *The Interpretation of Cultures* (Basic Books, 1977), 29.

167 **doubt "a cognitive luxury."** Hirstein, 6.

167 **"Doubt comes *after* belief."** Wittgenstein, 23.

167 **Daniel Gilbert.** Daniel T. Gilbert, Douglas S. Krull, and Patrick S. Ma-

lone, "Unbelieving the Unbelievable: Some Problems in the Rejection of False Information," *Journal of Personality and Social Psychology*, Vol. 59, No. 4 (Oct. 1990): 601–613.

170 **"native hue of resolution."** William Shakespeare, *Hamlet*, Susanne L. Wofford, ed. (St. Martin's Press, 1994), 82.

170 **"vigorous, bold and heroic."** Jenkins is quoted in "A Critical History of Hamlet," Wofford, p. 185. I'm indebted to Wofford's brief history for the point that Prince Hamlet was not always regarded as the embodiment of doubt and indecision.

171 **"Everlasting broodings."** Samuel Taylor Coleridge, *Lectures and Notes on Shakspere* [sic] *and Other English Poets* (George Bell and Sons, 1904), 344.

171 **"Prince Pussyfoot."** John Yoklavich, "Hamlet in Shammy Shoes," *Shakespeare Quarterly*, Vol. 3, No. 3 (July 1952): 217.

171 **"fust in us unus'd."** Shakespeare, 115.

172 **"action comes as naturally as breathing" (FN).** Maynard Mack, "*King Lear* in Our Time," excerpted in William Shakespeare, *King Lear*, Russell Fraser, ed. (Signet Classic, 1998), 227.

174 **both doubt and certainty are as contagious as the common cold.** See for instance Michael A. Hogg et al., "Uncertainty, Entitativity, and Group Identification," *Journal of Experimental Social Psychology*, Vol. 43, No. 1 (January 2007): 135–142; and "Why Do People Join Groups? Three Motivational Accounts from Social Psychology," *Social and Personality Psychology Compass*, Vol. 2, No. 3 (2008): 1269–1280.

174 **"an answer that is possibly (or even probably) wrong."** Hirstein, 5.

174 **article on umpiring (FN).** Joseph Berger, "Calling 'Em as They See 'Em," the *New York Times*, June 7, 2009.

175 **William Safire.** See William Safire, "On Language; Flip-Flop," the *New York Times*, March 28, 2004; and William Safire, "The Waffling of the Wishy-Washy," the *New York Times*, Oct. 25, 2004.

176 **And many of us *are* such people.** For statistics on the changing support for the Iraq War, see the Gallup polls conducted from just before the invasion through to the present day: http://www.gallup.com/poll/1633/Iraq.aspx#4.

176 **"the most repugnant option in government."** Barbara Tuchman, *The March of Folly: From Troy to Vietnam* (Ballantine Books, 1985), 383.

176 **we . . . associate them—inaccurately, but indissolubly—with weakness.** It's a short step from associating doubt with weakness to associating

it with womanliness. Hamlet's problem, says Boswell, is that "he endeavors to stir up his languid mind to a manly boldness, but in vain." John Kerry, too, was charged with insufficient manly boldness—with being effete, effeminate, and, in the immortal phrase of Arnold Schwarzenegger, a "girlyman." Somewhat strangely, this charge of being a girlyman is also linked to the charge of being a thinking man—that is, to excessive intellectualism. (I say "strangely" because of the equally enduring stereotype that women can't hold their own in the intellectual domain.) Coleridge accuses Hamlet of "enormous intellectual activity, and a consequent aversion to real action." And the writer Ariel Dorfman wondered, in an Oct. 22, 2004 editorial for the *Los Angeles Times*, if people saw Kerry's "complexity [of thought] as excessive effeminate suppleness." Nor was it an accident that Kerry's intellectualism was popularly signaled by his fluency in French—among a certain sector of Americans, that most castrated of languages. It would seem that our desire for certainty in our leadership unites the misogynist strain and the anti-intellectual strain of American politics.

177   **the *Daily Show*.** The episode in question, #13127, "The Stupid Vote," aired on Oct. 7, 2008.

177   **"The flight attendant comes down the aisle."** David Sedaris, "Undecided," the *New Yorker*, Oct. 27, 2008.

178   ***"we must be fully committed."*** Rollo May, *The Courage To Create* (W. W. Norton and Co., 1994), 20. The second quotation in this paragraph is from p. 21. In both cases, the italics are his.

179   **cognitive dissonance (FN).** Leon Festinger, Henry W. Riecken, and Stanley Schacter, *When Prophecy Fails* (Torchbooks, 1994).

CHAPTER 9   BEING WRONG

The quotations from Anita Wilson and from the psychoanalyst Irna Gadd are from my interviews with each of them.

185   **Greg Markus.** Marcus, G. B, "Stability and Change in Political Attitudes: Observe, Recall, and 'Explain.'" *Political Behavior*, Vol. 8 (1986): 21–44. The subjects' tendency to conflate their current beliefs with their past beliefs was so strong that an equation set up to predict how people would answer the "what did you use to believe?" question relied almost entirely on

the 1982 answers and almost not at all on the 1973 ones. (See also "Biases of Retrospection," Robyn M. Dawes, *Institute for Psychological Therapies*, Vol. 3. No. 1 (1991)). As a side note, Marcus's study also shed some interesting light on our beliefs about believing. The subjects he chose consisted of 1,669 high school students and at least one of each student's parents. In keeping with the widespread belief that older adults change less than teenagers and young adults, the parent group was more likely than the student group to think that their beliefs in 1972 resembled their beliefs in 1982—but in fact, the beliefs of the older adults had shifted *more* than that of their children.

185 **Philip Tetlock.** Philip Tetlock, *Expert Political Judgment: How Good Is It? How Can We Know?* (Princeton University Press, 2006), 138.

186 **"What scientists never do."** Kuhn, 77.

186 **we almost never find ourselves between theories.** Our reluctance to abandon one belief until we have another one in hand can be demonstrated empirically. In an experiment conducted in 1988, the psychologists David Klahr and Kevin Dunbar introduced subjects to a novel electronic device—a "robot tank" controlled via a keypad mounted on top of it. The subjects were told what every key meant except one labeled "RPT"; they were then asked to figure out for themselves what this key did, and to narrate their thought process as they set about trying to solve the puzzle. Through experimenting with the robot, the subjects frequently disproved their own initial hypotheses. But (as the psychologists Clark Chinn and William Brewer summarized the situation), "subjects who had no alternative hypotheses readily available were less likely to abandon a hypothesis that had been disconfirmed by anomalous data than were subjects who had a readily available alternative. Apparently, a bad theory was better than no theory at all." Clark Chinn and Thomas Brewer, "The Role of Anomalous Data in Knowledge Acquisition: A Theoretical Framework and Implications for Science Instruction," *Review of Educational Research*, Vol. 63, No. 1 (Spring 1993): 22. The original experiment is in David Klahr and Kevin Dunbar, "Dual Space Search during Scientific Reasoning," *Cognitive Science*, Vol. 12 (1988): 1–48.

187 **"All historically significant theories" (FN).** Kuhn, 147

189 **"servile conformism."** Al-Ghazali (2006), 25. The alternative translation offered in the footnote is from Al Ghazzali (2007), 20–21. That one is less acerbic and more sympathetic: "Having once surrendered blind belief, it

is impossible to return to it, for the essence of such belief is to be unconscious of itself. As soon as this unconsciousness ceases it is shattered like a glass whose fragments cannot be again reunited except by being cast again into the furnace and refashioned."

191 **"any great transformation of our environment."** Sully, 160 (footnote #134).

191 **"As trust in oneself and in the outer world develop together."** The quotation is from Helen Merrell Lynd's *On Shame and the Search for Identity* (Routledge, 1999), 46. I came across it in the psychologist Martin Rokeach's *The Three Christs of Ypsilanti: A Psychological Study* (Vintage Books, 1964), 22. Rokeach's book is a fascinating extended meditation on the nature of belief, framed by an account of his work with three men in a psychiatric institution in Ypsilanti, Michigan, all of whom believe themselves to be Jesus. I am grateful to Howard Katz for suggesting that I read it.

193 **Forcing function.** I learned about forcing function (and borrowed the example of the key in the lock) from Donald A. Norman's *The Design of Everyday Things* (Basic Books, 2002), see esp. pp. 131–138.

196 **"The jeering of nonbelievers."** Festinger, 5.

CHAPTER 10   HOW WRONG?

The story of William Miller and the Millerites comes from his own *Apology and Defense* (J. V. Himes, publisher, 1845); from Ronald L. Numbers and Jonathan M. Butler, eds., *The Disappointed: Millerism and Millenarianism in the Nineteenth Century* (The University of Tennessee Press, 1993); and from Everett N. Dick, *William Miller and the Advent Crisis* (Andrews University Press, 1994). All quotes from Miller are from his *Apology*. Luther Boutelle's and Hiram Edson's personal accounts of the Great Disappointment are included in the index to *The Disappointed*. Enoch Jacobs's quotation comes from Lawrence Foster's contribution to *The Disappointed*, "Had Prophecy Failed?", 181. Other, specific citations are below.

Philip Tetlock's work in *Expert Political Judgment* was particularly helpful in shaping my discussion of the "Wrong, Buts."

208 **an explosion of competing hypotheses.** See Kuhn, especially Chapter Eight, "The Response to Crisis," 77–91.

210 **Christ really *had* returned to earth—by entering the hearts of his followers.** See especially Foster, "Had Prophecy Failed?" Here is Enoch Jacobs on the subject (p. 182): "We thought the fault was all without—sad mistake!! It was *within*. This out of doors salvation has always been a precarious thing."

211 **"the error correction [process]."** Norman, 112. The Israeli social scientist Zvi Lanir calls this tendency to minimize our mistakes "the fundamental surprise error." Lanir illustrates the difference between superficial and fundamental surprise with a tale (possibly apocryphal but at any event amusing) from the life of Noah Webster, he of dictionary-writing fame. The story goes that Webster came home one day to find his wife *in flagrante delicto* with his butler. "You surprised me," blurted out the flustered Mrs. Webster. "And you have astonished me," retorted her husband. Mrs. Webster experienced only a superficial surprise; to her, nothing about the situation was unexpected except the sudden appearance of her husband. By contrast, Noah Webster, whose entire married life was turned topsy-turvy, experienced a fundamental surprise. The "error" in the fundamental surprise error is to downgrade a major earthquake into a minor tremor in the interest of protecting our worldview—at the expense, of course, of deriving any deep lessons from the experience. See Reason, 213.

212 **to comfort his fellow Millerites.** For most Millerites, this community-mindedness would not last long. Unsurprisingly, given the close relationship between the communities we live in and the beliefs we hold, the Great Disappointment unraveled not just the theological but also the social underpinnings of Millerism. In the immediate aftermath of their failed prophecy, the Millerites were united in (and by) their shared suffering. But as the initial shock subsided, the once-cohesive community began to splinter—a double blow for those who had lately gotten both their spiritual and social sustenance from Millerism. As one scholar of the period wrote, "Before the disappointment, a common burden to carry the message to the world, and a bond of brotherly love existed in the face of the expected end of all things. Now the divergent opinions and intolerance of another's views broke the body of Adventists into factions and bitter internecine controversies broke out." (Dick, 159.) Or, in the words of Luther Boutelle, "No *Advent Herald*, no meetings as formerly. Everyone felt lonely, with hardly a desire to speak to anyone." (Dick, 156; Numbers and Butler, 211.)

212 **the Seventh-Day Adventists.** See especially Jonathan M. Butler, "The
Making of a New Order: Millerism and the Origins of Seventh-Day Ad-
ventism," in Butler and Numbers, 189–208. Seventh-Day Adventists are
far from alone in their faith that the Judgment Day is close at hand. Although no major religious movement since Millerism has attached a firm
date to the Second Coming, a 2006 poll by the Pew Forum on Religion
and Public Life found that 20 percent of Americans claim to think Jesus
will return to earth during their lifetimes, 33 percent believe that the exact
date of his return is foretold in the Bible, and fully 79 percent believe he
will return to earth someday.

213 **"continued to set times [for the Advent] for the next seven years."**
Butler and Numbers, 199.

214 **"the long march of history."** George W. Bush, "Status of the Nation and
the War: The President's News Conference," Washington, D.C., Dec.
20, 2006. The speech is available at http://www.presidentialrhetoric.com/
speeches/12.20.06.html.

215 **alternative-universe teleportation device.** Tetlock, 146.

217 **"if we were ourselves in the place of the deity" (FN).** James, *The Will
to Believe*, 6.

CHAPTER 11   DENIAL AND ACCEPTANCE

I am grateful to Penny Beerntsen for the generous and detailed interview around
which this chapter is built. Unless otherwise noted, all the specifics of her assault
and the subsequent legal situation come directly from her. Likewise, quotations
from Peter Neufeld are from an interview with him, except where otherwise indicated. That interview and various follow-ups with the Innocence Project helped
tremendously in the writing of this chapter, as did *Actual Innocence: Five Days to
Execution and Other Dispatches from the Wrongly Convicted* (Doubleday, 2000), the
book Neufeld cowrote with Innocence Project cofounder Barry Scheck and with
the journalist Jim Dwyer.

My discussion of denial and self-deception was influenced by the philosopher
Sissela Bok's *Secrecy: On the Ethics of Concealment and Revelation* (Vintage Books,
1989), especially Chapter V, "Secrecy and Self-Deception," and by Alfred R.
Mele, *Self-Deception Unmasked* (Princeton University Press, 2001). Mele actually
argues against the conventional notion that self-deception is paradoxical, but
in doing so, he does an unusually good job of laying out the two prongs of that

paradox: first, that being self-deceived involves knowing something but also not knowing it, a seemingly impossible state of mind; and, second, that it involves intentionally perpetrating a deception without the intentionality of subverting the success of the act, a seemingly impossible process. Mele's own argument is that these apparent paradoxes simply stem from an overcommitment to the analogy between self-deception and interpersonal deception. In fact, he says, we do not necessarily (although we may possibly) believe two things at once when we are self-deceived; nor do we deliberately set out to deceive ourselves. Instead, we might simply engage in actions—such as a faulty assessment of the evidence—that leave us self-deceived. He cites by way of example a teenager who wants to believe that he is a charismatic leader even though he is teased and disliked by his classmates, and who therefore unconsciously begins spending time with younger children, who are more likely to admire him. To some extent I find Mele's argument convincing, but it doesn't seem to account for the kind of situation we are often referring to when we talk about self-deception—the one in which there is a palpable tension between believing one thing and suspecting something else, and a corresponding effort to squelch those suspicions. For that reason, and because it seems more relevant to the experience of being wrong, I have relied on the more traditional understanding of self-deception.

223   **"revelation machine."** Scheck et al., xv.

223   **the science is starting to prevail.** Genetic testing has now been a routine part of the criminal justice system long enough for a sobering statistic to emerge: more than 25 percent of so-called prime suspects are cleared by DNA tests before the prosecution can begin to build a case against them. Needless to say, this has disturbing implications for people who are accused of crimes in which no biological evidence was found, or those who were convicted before DNA testing was standard. "I don't worry for our clients," Peter Neufeld told me, "because our clients are going to get out. They've got the testing. A pig-headed prosecutor can say the earth is flat until the cows come home, but eventually we're going to prevail. What's troubling are all those cases where there's no biological evidence available."

223   **a confident eyewitness.** See e.g., Brian L. Cutler, Steven D. Penrod, and Hedy Red Dexter, "Juror Sensitivity to Eyewitness Identification Evidence," *Law and Human Behavior*, Vol. 14, No. 2 (April 1990): 185–191.

223   **Franz von Liszt.** Sheck et al, 42–43. One of the most telling variants of Liszt's study was conducted in 1973, when the local NBC newscast in

New York City aired a short (acted) clip in which a young man in a hat, sneakers, and leather jacket lurks in a hallway, jumps out at a woman who is walking down it, grabs her handbag, and runs straight toward the camera. After the film, the station showed a lineup of six suspects with a phone number for viewers to call and identify which of the six was the "thief," or to indicate that the suspect was not included in the lineup. The station received 2,145 phone calls before unplugging the phone line. The actual thief received 302 votes, or 14.1 percent of the total. If you assume seven options (the six people in the lineup plus the "not included" choice), the callers were almost exactly at chance (14.3 percent). Most disturbingly: Robert Buckhout, the Brooklyn College professor who organized the experiment, later showed the film to lawyers and judges as well. These legal professionals did just as badly as the general public—and then reacted to their poor performance by complaining that the thief was wearing different clothes in the lineup from those he wore during the film. Needless to say, most real criminals own more than one pair of clothing, too. See Scheck et al., 43–44, and Robert Buckhout, "Nearly 2,000 Witnesses Can Be Wrong," *Social Action and the Law*, Vol. 2, No. 3 (May 1975): 7.

223 **the error rate for DNA testing (FN).** "DNA Evidence," *Encyclopedia of High-Tech Crime and Crime-Fighting*, Michael Newton (Facts On File, 2003).

227 **Glen Woodall.** Woodall's story appears in Scheck et al., 107–114. The story of the victim in the case appears on p. 173. For the official report on Fred Zain, the fraudulent serologist, see "In the Circuit Court of Kanawha County, West Virginia, in the matter of an investigation of the West Virginia State Police Crime Laboratory, Serology Division, Civil Action No 93-MISC-402, James O. Holliday, Senior Judge, Nov. 4, 1993.

228 **compensation for their ordeal.** Only half of all states have laws permitting the wrongfully convicted to seek compensation. Most of those laws come with stringent requirements—such as not having entered a guilty plea, or having been specifically exonerated by the governor—and many of the payments are absurdly small. Suing for fairer compensation isn't likely to get you anywhere either. As Scheck and Neufeld wrote of one of their clients, "if [he] had tripped on a cracked sidewalk and broken his leg, or if he had used a shampoo that made his hair fall out, he would have had a better chance of winning a lawsuit than he would for having been ordered at gunpoint by the state of New Jersey into a prison between the ages nineteen and thirty" for a crime he did not commit. (Scheck et al., 229–230.)

229   **the five stages of grief.** After denial, the other stages are, in order, anger, bargaining, depression, and acceptance. Elisabeth Kübler-Ross, *On Death and Dying* (Scribner, 1997).

229   *forget* **the news within a few days.** Bok, *Secrets*, 70.

230   **"Deny you have ever been in Pittsburgh."** For two variants on this story, see Robert Shogan, *The Fate of the Union: America's Rocky Road to Political Stalemate* (Westview Press, 2004), 10; and Daniel Schorr, "When Presidents Make Mistakes," *NPR Weekend Edition*, Dec. 18, 2005.

230   **"Wooden-headedness" (FN).** Tuchman, 7.

231   **From an outside perspective—yours, say.** Actually, the matter of perspective with regard to self-deception is crucial. As with error more generally, we can't recognize that we ourselves are in denial until we aren't anymore. Thus we can never claim, in the moment, to be self-deceived; we can only impute self-deception to other people. But there are three serious problems with doing so. The first is that it is guaranteed to go badly; few things are more insufferable and insulting than being told that you are in denial. In essence, it is like being told that you are wrong twice: once about a fact (and inevitably an unpleasant one: that your partner is having an affair, that you have a drinking problem, that your finances are in serious jeopardy), and once about the events that are transpiring in your own psyche. The former is bad enough, but the latter is worse: with very few exceptions (e.g., love: see Chapter Twelve), we are deeply unwilling to concede that anyone has a better understanding of what is going on inside us than we do. The second problem with accusing someone of being self-deceived is that it involves assuming that we ourselves are incontestably right and that the putatively deceived person really *is* deceived. That might be the case—but then again, it might not. This leads to the third problem, which is that accusations of self-deception are all but impossible to refute. A person accused of being in denial has no effective way to counter the accusation, since his or her protestations can always be dismissed as the defense mechanism in action. You can be the straightest man on the planet, but the minute you try to dispute the suggestion that you are hiding your secret homosexual desires from yourself, you will start to seem very faggy indeed.

231   **As Sartre wrote.** Quoted in Bok, *Secrets*, 62.

231   **How does the human mind manage this?** My discussion of the conun-

drum of self-deception is heavily indebted to Sissela Bok's work in *Secrets*, 60–64.

232 **South African President Thabo Mbeki.** For more on the consequences of Mbeki's AIDS policy, see Pride Chigwedere et al., "Estimating the Lost Benefits of Antiretroviral Drug Use in South Africa," *Journal of Acquired Immune Deficiency Syndrome*, Vol. 49, No. 4 (Oct. 16, 2008): 410–415.

233 **will simply oppose the . . . request for DNA testing.** Typically, this opposition takes the form of an appeal to finality doctrine. These doctrines, which vary from state to state, are a way of putting an end to judicial proceedings that could otherwise drag on indefinitely. For instance, a finality doctrine might decree that once the appeals process in a criminal case has been exhausted, the verdict will be considered final, virtually regardless of any additional evidence that subsequently surfaces. Having a finality doctrine on the books often makes jurisprudential sense, because the odds of getting closer to the truth of a case typically diminish as you get further from the time of the original trial; memories fade, evidence degrades, witnesses disappear or die. But with the advent of DNA testing, finality doctrine ceased to make sense for certain criminal cases. Biological material (semen, hair, fingernails, skin cells, blood) has been regarded as evidence since time immemorial, but DNA testing of this material has only been standard protocol in the United States since the 1990s. As a result, there are many people serving prison sentences today for crimes in which biological evidence was collected and preserved but never subjected to genetic testing. In cases like these, a finality doctrine is an obstacle rather than an aid to justice. (Scheck et al., 247, and my interview with Neufeld.)

233 **the U.S. Supreme Court ruled in 2009.** Adam Liptak, "Justices Reject Inmate Right to DNA Tests," the *New York Times*, June 18, 2009.

234 **Michael McGrath.** Background information on the Bromgard case comes from my interview with Neufeld; I am grateful to him as well for providing me with a copy of the deposition, from which the direct quotations are taken: "The deposition of Michael McGrath in the United States Judicial District Court for the District of Montana Billings Division, Jimmy Ray Bromgard, plaintiff, v. State of Montana, County of Yellowstone, Chairman Bill Kennedy, Commissioner John Ostlund, Commissioner Jim Reno, Arnold Melnikoff, and Mike Greely, defendants," Sept. 29, 2006.

235 **Chimerism.** Clive Niels Svendsen and Allison D. Ebert, eds., *The Encyclopedia of Stem Cell Research* (Sage Publications, 2008), 96.

235 **When other forensic scientists reviewed his work.** John O. Savino, Brent E. Turvey, and John J. Baeza, *The Rape Investigation Handbook* (Academic Press, 2005), 32.

238 **"'I saw murder in his eyes.'"** This story was told to me by Peter Neufeld. The next story in this paragraph, about Calvin Johnson, was mentioned by Neufeld in our interview and appears as well in Scheck et al., 193–210. The quotation ("He doesn't care about me") appears on p. 209. See also David Firestone, "DNA Test Brings Freedom, 16 Years After Conviction," the *New York Times*, June 16, 1999.

241 **The sheriff's department had failed to follow up.** Penny Beerntsen's story about a police detective visiting the sheriff with a tip about Gregory Allen is corroborated by that detective, Thomas Bergner (later the Manitowoc deputy police chief) in a memo from the Wisconsin Department of Justice: "Correspondence/Memorandum Department of Justice, December 17, 2003, to Mark Rohrer, District Attorney, Manitowoc County, from Peggy A. Lautenschlager, Attorney General, subject: Avery Review." The memo also describes Beerntsen's follow-up phone call to the sheriff's department, and notes that the department's file on her case included information on Allen. However, the memo also indicates that Sheriff Tom Kocourek claimed not to recall either the visit from Bergner or the subsequent conversation with Beerntsen, and denied that he or, to his knowledge, anyone else in the sheriff's department knew of Allen at the time of Beerntsen's assault.

241 **five different hair samples (FN).** Scheck et al., 162–163.

242 **she wrote him a letter.** I am grateful to Penny Beerntsen for sharing her letter to Steven Avery with me.

244 **Teresa Halbach.** For information on the murder and Avery's conviction, see Tom Kertscher, "Avery Found Guilty of Killing Woman," the *Milwaukee Journal Sentinel*, March 19, 2007. As of the time that I finished this book, Steven Avery's attorneys had filed for a new trial (Tom Kertscher, "Attorneys for Avery File for New Trial," the *Milwaukee Journal Sentinel*, June 29, 2009). As I suggest in the chapter, they argue that the evidence against Avery was planted by law enforcement investigators, and base their request for a new trial on the fact that the judge refused to admit evidence that apparently could have implicated other suspects.

CHAPTER 12 HEARTBREAK

Unless otherwise noted, the quotes from Raoul Felder, Irna Gadd, and Harville Hendrix are from my interviews with them.

251 **Pity poor Charles Swann.** Marcel Proust, *Swann's Way*, Lydia Davis, trans., Charles Prendergast, ed. (Viking, 2002).

251 **"always prepared to believe what he hoped for."** Proust, 32.

251 **"To think that I wasted years of my life."** Proust, 396.

252 **"hybrids of plants and of ghosts."** I first came across this quotation in Antonio Damasio's *The Feeling of What Happens: Body and Emotion in the Making of Consciousness* (Harvest Books, 2000), 143.

253 **(as Locke argued).** See Chapter One of this book, p. 22, and Keeler, 214–221.

253 **we can make inferences about other people's internal states based on familiarity with our own.** Taken to an extreme—that is, to the claim that this is the *only* way we make sense of other people's minds—this idea is known as simulation theory. Like theory of mind, simulation theory attempts to explain how we understand each other, but the explanation it proposes is markedly different: rather than claiming that we make use of "naïve psychology"—a theory of how other people's minds work—in order to understand one another, simulation theory claims that we simply draw conclusions about other minds based on the workings of our own. This theory has recently gotten some support from neuroscience, with the discovery of "mirror neurons": nerve cells in the brain that fire both when, say, you perform an action yourself and when you see someone else perform it; or when you either experience a given emotion directly (for example, fear or disgust), or witness someone else experiencing it. In highlighting the utility of extrapolation, I am not trying to make a strong claim for simulation theory, partly because I'm not convinced by it but mainly because I am not qualified to weigh in. For an explanation of simulation theory and an argument against it by someone who *is* qualified to weigh in (and for an argument that is predicated, interestingly, on the kinds of mistakes people make about each other), see Rebecca Saxe, "Against Simulation: The Argument from Error," *Trends in Cognitive Sciences*, Vol. 9, No. 4 (April 2005): 174–179.

253 **"What Is It Like to Be a Bat?"** Thomas Nagel, "What Is It Like to Be

a Bat?" *Philosophy of Mind: Classical and Contemporary Readings*, David J. Chalmers, ed. (Oxford University Press, 2002), 219–226.

254 **"a fundamentally *alien* form of life."** Nagel, 220. The "what it would be like for *me* to behave as a bat behaves" line appears on the same page.

256 **a study conducted by Emily Pronin.** Pronin et al., 2001. The word-completion chart ("Table 2" in the original paper) appears on p. 649.

258 **J. M. Coetzee.** Coetzee's interest in *Robinson Crusoe* is clear; he wrote a short novel called *Foe*, about the fate of a second, female castaway on Crusoe's island and her subsequent relationship with Daniel Defoe (born Daniel Foe), and he spoke about Crusoe in his 2003 Nobel Prize acceptance speech. But I have not been able to verify this particular remark.

259 **hoping to keep the wolves at bay.** Kierkegaard's comment is cited in May, 72.

259 **What happens in Plato's *Symposium*.** Plato, *The Symposium*, Walter Hamilton, trans. (Penguin Classics, 1967).

260 **"desire and pursuit of the whole."** Plato, *The Symposium*, 64.

260 **"whatever our souls are made of."** Emily Brontë, *Wuthering Heights* (Oxford University Press, 2008), 71.

260 **"two hearts living in just one mind."** The song is called "Two Hearts." Written and produced by Collins and Lamont Dozier, it won a Golden Globe for best original song and was the #1 song on the "U.S. Hot 100" list for two weeks. The line quoted a few paragraphs below is from the same song.

261 ***Let me not to the marriage of true minds.*** The sonnet in question is number 116. William Shakespeare, *Complete Sonnets* (Dover Publications, 1991), 51.

261 **"I know we've just met."** Harville Hendrix, *Getting the Love You Want: A Guide For Couples* (HarperPerennial, 1988), 50–51.

262 **"never spoke of the softer passions."** Arthur Conan Doyle, "A Scandal in Bohemia," *Sherlock Holmes: The Complete Novels and Stories*, Vol. I (Bantam Classic, 2003), 239. The "grit in a sensitive instrument" line appears on the same page.

262 **"madness of love."** Plato, *Phaedrus*, Christopher Rowe, trans. (Penguin Classics, 2005). Most of the book is about madness and love.

263 **"The fellow who kisses the mole on his mistress' neck."** Erasmus, 112.

263   **an armada of psychological research.** For a particularly extreme example, see Janine Willis and Alexander Todorov, "First Impressions: Making Up Your Mind After a 100-Ms Exposure to a Face," *Psychological Science*, Vol. 17, Number 7 (July 2006): 592–598.

263   **"Everyone complains about their memory."** I came across this line in Kenneth R. Hammond's *Human Judgment and Social Policy: Irreducible Uncertainty, Inevitable Error, Unavoidable Injustice* (Oxford University Press, 2000), 207.

263   **As Thomas Gilovich has pointed out (FN).** Gilovich, p. 47.

268   **they still end—close to 40 percent of them.** See e.g., "Births, Marriages, Divorces, and Deaths: Provisional Data for June 2008," *National Vital Statistics Reports*, Vol. 57, No. 11; or the data collected at divorcerate.org.

CHAPTER 13   TRANSFORMATION

I couldn't have written this chapter without Osha Gray Davidson's *The Best of Enemies: Race and Redemption in the New South* (Scribner, 1996) and Studs Terkel's interviews of C. P. Ellis and Ann Atwater, "Occurrence in Durham," in *Race: How Blacks and Whites Think and Feel about the American Obsession* (Doubleday, 1992), 271–283. Unless otherwise noted, Atwater and Ellis's direct words come from Terkel, while Davidson provided the in-depth background on their life stories and on the history of race and class conflicts in North Carolina.

My account of the life of Whittaker Chambers is drawn from his autobiography, *Witness* (referenced above).

273   **"We just had a real party at the service station."** Terkel, 278.

273   **112 Klan chapters in the state.** Davidson, 189. For the information about Helms, see pp. 118–119, 149.

274   **"'The Blacks are comin' up tonight.'"** Terkel, 273.

275   **"I don't intend to associate with a bunch of niggers."** Davidson, 251.

275   **"how I just hated that black nigger."** Terkel, 271.

275   **"The problem here today is *niggers*."** Davidson, 253. The Atwater quote that follows is from the same page.

276   **"ain't no way I can work with that gal!"** Davidson, 259.

276   **"help make desegregation less painful for white children."** Davidson, 261.

276   **"You keep working with those niggers and you gonna get yourself shot."** Davidson, 264. The other threat in the same paragraph is from p. 261.

277   **"I began to see, here we are, two people from the far ends of the fence."** Terkel, 275–276. Davidson also recounts the moment in the auditorium—by chance, also on pp. 275–276.

278   **"I'd look at a black person walkin' down the street."** Terkel, 274.

278   **"What . . . had the Klan actually accomplished."** Davidson, 282.

279   **"Something . . . has happened to me."** Davidson, 285–286.

279   **his greatest professional accomplishment.** Davidson, 292.

283   **"Who can plumb its depths?"** Augustine, *Confessions*, 196.

283   *The brain is wider than the sky.* *The Complete Poems of Emily Dickinson*, Thomas H. Johnson, ed. (Back Bay Books, 1976), 312.

284   **Tom Watson (FN).** Davidson, 66–67.

285   **"what remains constant is better."** Augustine, *Confessions*, 133.

286   **"evil, absolute evil."** Chambers, 80.

286   **"I cannot say I changed."** Chambers, 83.

286   **"he had always been a Communist at heart.** Enid Starkie, "André Gide," in Richard H. Crossman, ed., *The God That Failed* (Columbia University Press, 2001), 166.

286   **"for I had placed myself behind my own back."** Augustine, *Confessions*, 169.

287   **Carl Jung.** See e.g., May, 62–63.

287   **"For this I had been a Communist."** Chambers, 533.

289   **"The bud disappears when the blossom breaks through."** G. W. F. Hegel, *The Phenomenology of Mind*, J. B. Baillie, trans. (Dover Philosophical Classics, 2003), 2.

289   **you didn't know much about your own body.** My discussion of what young children do and don't know about themselves and other people is drawn from Susan Carey's *Conceptual Change in Childhood* (The MIT Press, 1987). See especially Chapter Two, "The Human Body." The details of what children know about the contents of their body can be found on pp. 42–43. The quote about lungs being for your hair is on p. 47. The information on gender constancy is on pp. 52–54. A discussion of childhood understandings of sex and reproduction is on pp. 54–59.

290   **Children believe in things like Santa Claus.** This same point was made by Jacqueline Woolley, a psychology professor at the University of Texas

at Austin, in an opinion piece in the *New York Times*, "Do You Believe in Surnits?" Dec. 23, 2006.

290   **"a duck, which then turns into a rabbit" (FN).** Carey, 59. The psychologists she quotes are Anne C. Bernstein and Philip A. Cowan, "Children's Concepts of How People Get Babies," *Child Development*, Vol. 46 (1975), 77–91.

291   **recent work in developmental psychology suggests that error might play the same role in the lives of children as it does in the lives of scientists.** The work in question comes largely from the Early Childhood Cognition Lab at the Massachusetts Institute of Technology, run by the cognitive scientist Laura Schulz—better known to me as my sister.

292   **"attempts to get the client to question and change."** Ronnie Janoff-Bulman, *Shattered Assumptions* (Free Press, 2002), 39.

292   **Heinz Hartmann noted that.** Quoted in Bok, *Secrets*, 61.

294   **"'I hope Jesse Jackson gets AIDS and dies.'"** Terkel, 278.

294   **"The main interest in life and work."** "Truth, Power, Self: An Interview with Michel Foucault, Oct. 25th, 1982," Luther H. Martin et al., eds., *Technologies of the Self: A Seminar with Michel Foucault* (University of Massachusetts Press, 1988), 9.

295   **"Since I changed."** Terkel, 278.

CHAPTER 14   THE PARADOX OF ERROR

The story of the wrong-side surgery at Beth Israel Deaconess Medical Center comes from my interview with Paul Levy, from Levy's postings about the incident on his blog, "Running a Hospital," especially "The Message You Hope Never to Send" (http://runningahospital.blogspot.com/2008/07/message-you-hope-never-to-send.html), and from coverage of the incident in the *Boston Globe*, especially Stephen Smith, "Surgeon Operates on Patient's Wrong Side," July 3, 2008; and Stephen Smith, "Hospital Tells of Surgery on Wrong Side," July 4, 2008. Unless otherwise noted, all quotations from Paul Levy are from my interview with him. Note that there is one inconsistency in the *Globe*'s coverage of the wrong-side surgery; according to the July 3 article, the patient was notified of the mistake by the surgeon. However, Paul Levy told me that the patient informed the doctor of the mistake, not vice versa.

BIDMC's efforts to eliminate medical error are described in Levy's blog in a post entitled "Aspirations for BIDMC and BID-Needham," Jan. 17, 2008 (http://runningahospital.blogspot.com/2008/01/aspirations-for-bidmc-and-bidneedham.html); and in Jeffrey Krasner, "Hospital Aims to Eliminate Mistakes," the *Boston Globe*, Jan. 17, 2008.

The discussion of democracy in this chapter is greatly indebted to Richard Hofstadter's *The Idea of a Party System: The Rise of Legitimate Opposition in the United States, 1780–1840* (University of California Press, 1969), 56. I am grateful to Stephen Frug for suggesting that I read it.

300 **According to the Institute of Medicine.** Linda T. Kohn, Janet M. Corrigan, and Molla S. Donaldson, eds., *To Err Is Human: Building a Safer Health System*, a report by the National Institute of Medicine (National Academies Press, 2000), 26. This is the source for both the number of people killed by medical error every year and for the ranking of medical error among other causes of death in the United States. A third figure, that of the total number of people affected by medical error, is an extrapolation. According to the report, at least a million patients are affected by "adverse events," which include but are not limited to error. (For instance, a case where a patient contracted pneumonia during a postoperative hospital stay would count as an adverse event but not a medical error, unless some specific mistake in treatment or care led to the infection.) The "at least a million" figure comes from two separate studies; in those studies, the subset of people affected specifically by medical error accounted for 57.9 and 68.4 percent of the total adverse events. My claim that "between 690,000 and 748,000 patients are affected by medical errors" is an extrapolation and calculation based on these figures.

300 **"Observing more senior physicians."** Nancy Berlinger, *After Harm: Medical Error and the Ethics of Forgiveness* (The Johns Hopkins University Press, 2005), 41.

300 **a 2002 survey of doctors' attitudes.** Berlinger, 2. The original survey is "Patients' and Physicians' Attitudes Regarding the Disclosure of Medical Errors," *JAMA*, Vol. 289 (2003): 1001–1007.

301 **To excuse their defensiveness and silence (FN).** See Berlinger, especially Chapter Six, "Repentance." The story of the Veterans Affairs Hospital in Lexington appears on pp. 69–70. A discussion of "I'm Sorry" laws appears on pp. 52–58. See also Doug Wojcieszak, John Banja, M.D., Carole Houk, J.D., "The 'Sorry Works!' Coalition: Making the Case for Full Disclosure," *Journal on Quality and Patient Safety*, Vol. 32, No. 6 (June 2006):

344–350; and Kevin Sack, "Doctors Say 'I'm Sorry' Before 'See You in Court,'" the *New York Times*, May 18, 2008.

302 **"all the differing ways patients get hurt."** Krasner, "Hospital Aims to Eliminate Mistakes."

303 **Tenerife.** The Tenerife accident has been widely written about. For a summary of the accident, see the Aviation Safety Network Accident Description at http://aviation-safety.net/database/record.php?id=19770327–0. For a detailed account, see the Netherlands Aviation Safety Board's final report on the accident (one of the two planes involved was a KLM flight; hence the involvement of the Dutch authorities), *Final Report and Comments of the Netherlands Aviation Safety Board of the Investigation into the Accident with the Collision of KLM Flight 4805, Boeing 747–206B, PH-BUF, and Pan-American Flight 1736, Boeing 747–121, N746PA, at Tenerife Airport, Spain, on 27 March 1977* (available online at http://www.project-tenerife.com/nederlands/PDF/finaldutchreport.pdf).

303 **reducing significant commercial aviation accidents.** National Transportation Safety Board Aviation Accident Statistics, Table 2: Accidents and Accident Rates by NTSB Classification, 1988–2007, 14 CFR 121 (available at http://www.ntsb.gov/aviation/Table2.htm). The National Transportation Safety Board divides accidents in commercial scheduled passenger service into "major" and "serious." A major incident is defined as one in which either 1) an aircraft was destroyed, or 2) there were multiple fatalities, or 3) there was one fatality and the aircraft was substantially damaged. A serious incident means that either there was one fatality without substantial damage to the aircraft, or there was at least one serious injury and substantial damage to the aircraft. In addition to the drop in overall accident rates in commercial passenger service between 1998 and 2007, none of the accidents in 2007 were classified as major.

303 **Six Sigma.** Most of the background on Six Sigma is drawn from Peter S. Pande, Robert P. Neuman, Roland R. Cavanagh, *The Six Sigma Way: How GE, Motorola, and Other Top Companies are Honing Their Performance* (McGraw-Hill Professional, 2000). I borrowed (and tweaked) the 300,000 packages example from this book, where it appears on p. 12. My understanding of the "define, measure, analyze, improve, control" process was refined by Forrest W. Breyfogle's *Implementing Six Sigma: Smarter Solutions Using Statistical Methods* (John Wiley and Sons, 2003).

304 **"tolerance for failure"** . . . **"safe failure."** Pande et al., 17–18.

304 **"the enemy" and "evil" (FN).** Pande et al., 23.

305 **crew and ground members are encouraged . . . to report mistakes.** See the Aviation Safety Reporting System Immunity Policy, available on-line at http://asrs.arc.nasa.gov/overview/briefing/br_1.html. The ASRS is run by NASA for the Federal Aviation Administration and dedicated to "confidential, voluntary, nonpunitive" incident reporting.

305 **"opened our culture to ideas from everyone."** See GE's report, "What is Six Sigma? The Roadmap to Customer Impact" (1999), available online at http://www.ge.com/sixsigma/SixSigma.pdf.

305 **"management by fact" . . . "opinions and assumptions."** Pande et al., 15–16.

305 **the open-source movement (FN).** The information here comes from the Open Source Initiative (http://www.opensource.org/), especially Michael Tiemann, "History of the OSI," Sept. 19, 2006 (http://www.opensource. org/history).

305 **"[the surgeon] simply felt that he was on the correct side."** Stephen Smith, "Surgeon Operates on Patient's Wrong Side."

306 **Motorola reported savings of more than $17 billion.** "About Motorola University: The Impact of Six Sigma," http://www.motorola.com/content. jsp?globalObjectId=3081.

306 **annual legal fees dropped from $3 million to $1 million.** Hillary Rodham Clinton and Barack Obama, "Making Patient Safety the Centerpiece of Medical Liability Reform," *The New England Journal of Medicine*, Vol. 354, No. 21 (May 25, 2006): 2205–2008.

306 **medical mistakes cost the United States.** Linda T. Kohn, et al., *To Err is Human*, 1–2.

307 **we learn the word "maybe."** Tetlock, 228

307 **regard the world as a place of absolutes (FN).** See e.g., "Borderline Personality Disorder: Splitting Countertransference," *Psychiatric Times*, Vol. 15, No. 11 (Nov. 1, 1988).

309 **"self-subversive thinking."** Tetlock, 214.

309 **doctors interrupt their patients.** Jerome Groopman, *How Doctors Think* (Houghton Mifflin Company, 2007), 17.

310 **John Francis.** Mark Hertsgaard, "John Francis, a 'Planetwalker' Who Lived Car-Free and Silent for 17 Years, Chats with Grist," *Grist*, May 10, 2005. Francis's book is *Planetwalker: How to Change Your World One Step at a Time* (Elephant Mountain Press, 2005). The quotation appears on p. 44.

312 **Joseph-Marie de Maistre.** Bates, 203.

312 **"the general will cannot err."** Jean-Jacques Rousseau, *The Social Contract and Discourse on the Origin of Inequality,* Lester G. Crocker, ed. (Simon and Schuster, 1973). See especially Chapter III, "Whether the General Will Can Err," 30–32.

312 **"that truth is great."** This widely quoted passage is from the first section of the Virginia Statute for Religious Freedom, which Jefferson wrote in 1779.

313 **"error could be endured."** Hofstadter, 56.

314 **"intrinsically subversive and illegitimate."** Hofstadter, 7.

314 **"Dictators, large and small" (FN).** Sunstein, 68.

315 **"Freedom," Gandhi argued.** The quotation is omnipresent, although I was unable to definitively identify its origin.

318 **the Evil Genius.** Descartes lays out this argument in his *Meditations on First Philosophy,* John Cottingham, ed. and trans. (Cambridge University Press, 1996).

319 **"what we do not doubt in our hearts."** I came across this quotation in Jay F. Rosenberg's *Thinking About Knowing* (Oxford University Press, 2002), 14.

CHAPTER 15 THE OPTIMISTIC META-INDUCTION FROM THE HISTORY
OF EVERYTHING

The discussion of humor in this chapter is especially indebted to Sypher, ed. (see above); and to Ward Jones's "The Function and Content of Amusement," *South African Journal of Philosophy* 25, Vol. 2 (2006): 126–137.

322 **superiority theory of comedy.** See Jones (the Hobbes quotation is on p. 131) and John Morreall, *The Philosophy of Laughter and Humor* (State University of New York Press, 1987) (the Hobbes quotation is on p. 129). Similar ground is covered in Sypher's commentary in *Comedy,* "The Meaning of Comedy"—including, again, the Hobbes quotation, which can be found on p. 203.

322 **"an imitation of the common errors of our life."** I came across this quotation in Harry Levin's introduction to the 1989 Signet Classic edition of Shakespeare's *Comedy of Errors,* p. xxv.

322 **"the duty of comedy."** The line is from a petition Molière sent to Louis

XIV for permission to perform *Tartuffe* ("First Petition Presented to the King Concerning the Comedy *Tartuffe*"), the text of which was included in the third printing of the play.

323 **the incongruity theory of humor.** See "Humor," *The Internet Encyclopedia of Philosophy*, Aaron Smuts, 2009 (http://www.iep.utm.edu/h/humor.htm); Morreall, 172–189; and Jones, 128–130. The "vast majority of humor" line is from Jones, 129.

324 **"the exploitable gulf."** Bertrand Evans, "Shakespeare's Comedies," excerpted in Levin, 164.

324 **"A situation is invariably comic."** Bergson, in Sypher, 123. In the original text, this passage is italicized. Note that Bergson is defining but not subscribing to incongruity theory, which he rejects as descriptive but not explanatory. That is, it tells us *that* we laugh at incongruity, but it doesn't tell us *why*. Bergson locates the source of the comedic instead in that which is essentially automatic and "rigid" instead of "supple."

324 **American Film Institute (FN).** The complete list is available on the Institute's website, http://www.afi.com/tvevents/100years/laughs.aspx.

325 **"a disinterested spectator" (FN).** Bergson, in Sypher, 63. For those of us who aren't divine, Bergson's argument that errors are always funny if viewed from a distance is pretty unsatisfying. Some mistakes really do feel tragic, and trying to make them comic by withdrawing interest or empathy seems cruel. The critic Harry Levin proffered a more palatable theory for why some mistakes are funny and others are not. "Our tragic heroes go astray grandly by committing some single and fatal mistake," he wrote. "Comic figures, on the other hand, run through a whole train of petty errors, and somehow manage to extricate themselves from the final consequences" (Levin, p. xxv). As that suggests, and despite my argument in this chapter, both comedy *and* tragedy depend on error. In fact, false beliefs—which I characterized in this chapter as a classic comic device—are fundamental to the genre of tragedy as well. Romeo killed himself because he misinterpreted the evidence and mistakenly believed that Juliet was dead, and both *King Lear* and *Othello* are about being disastrously wrong about other people. The critic Maynard Mack called the latter "a tragedy of error," a nice counterpoint to the comedy thereof. Mack, in Fraser, 230.

326 **art "issues out of this encounter."** May, 88.

326 **"Could reality come into direct contact."** Bergson, in Sypher, 157.

326 **an ideal civilization would banish all artists.** Plato, *The Republic*, Benjamin Jowett, trans. (Plain Label Books, 1946). The passage in question occurs in Book X. The "thrice removed from the truth" line is on p. 591, "All these poetical individuals" is on p. 586, "inferior degree of truth" is on p. 598, and the "companions and friends and associates" line is on p. 593.

328 **"Let us try for once not to be right."** I came across this Tzara line in Peter Schjeldahl's "Young at Heart: Dada at MOMA," the *New Yorker*, June 26, 2006.

329 **"and at once it struck me."** I first encountered Keats's concept of negative capability in a lovely (and relevant) essay by the poet Jane Hirshfield called "Poetry and Uncertainty" (*The American Poetry Review*, Nov. 1, 2005). The complete quotation used here is taken from *John Keats: His Life and Poetry, His Friends, Critics, and After-Fame*, Sir Sidney Colvin (Macmillan and Co., 1920), 253–254.

329 **Wislawa Szymborska.** The complete text of her speech is available on the Nobel Prize website: http://nobelprize.org/nobel_prizes/literature/laureates/1996/szymborska-lecture.html.

330 **"What we are engaged in when we do poetry."** Anne Carson, "Essay on What I Think About Most," *Men in the Off Hours* (Vintage, 2001), 30–36.

333 **"Art is not truth."** The line appears in Picasso's "Statement to Marius de Zayas," 1923.

335 **instant and violent self-destruction.** For my purposes, the most crystalline example of this might come from the *Star Trek* episode "The Changeling," which concerns a robot that thinks its mission is to eradicate everything that is imperfect and error-prone—a category that includes all organic entities. In the end, the robot learns that it was wrong about its own origins and mandate, and is therefore itself an example of error. Accordingly, it is obliged to destroy itself, and does. Violently.

336 **"To see the world as it really is."** Quoted in Janoff-Bulman, 61.

337 **"a key to the good life."** Janoff-Bulman, 24.

337 **"the imaginary relations."** Foucault, 30.

339 **"the permanent possibility of someone having a better idea."** Richard Rorty, *Philosophy and the Mirror of Nature* (Princeton University Press, 1981), 349.

INDEX